Webster's

21ST CENTURY

Instant Speller

Webster's

21ST CENTURY

Instant Speller

45,000 Words Spelled,
Divided, and Accented

THOMAS NELSON PUBLISHERS
Nashville

Published in Nashville, Tennessee, by Thomas Nelson, Inc., Publishers and distributed in Canada by Lawson Falle, Ltd., Cambridge, Ontario.

Printed in the United States of America.

Library of Congress Cataloging-in-Publication Data

Webster's 21st century instant speller.
    p.   cm.—(21st century desk reference set)
  ISBN 0-8407-4258-4 (HB—Burgundy)
         0-8407-4234-7 (HB—Navy)
         0-8407-3477-8 (PB)
  1. English language—Orthography and spelling. I. Thomas Nelson Publishers. II. Title: Webster's twenty-first century instant speller. III. Series.
PE1143.W38   1992
428.1—dc20   91–46649
                                          CIP

1 2 3 4 5 6 7 8 9 10 — 99 98 97 96 95 94 93 92

Introduction

Webster's 21st Century Instant Speller is a handy tool—smaller and faster to use than a dictionary—for anyone who often needs to check the spelling and division of words. It contains more than 45,000 words, including many geographical names; computer and business terms; common scientific, technical, and medical terms; and colloquialisms. Much effort has also been made to include words that are in general use but which may not yet be included in some dictionaries, such as *colorization, glasnost,* and *homeschooling.*

Each word with more than one syllable is shown with syllable divisions and accent marks to show strong and weak stresses in pronunciation.

Word Order

All words are in strict letter by letter alphabetical order, except for plurals, which are included under the singular form of the word, and some past tense forms, which are included under the present tense form. Occasionally, when the plural is the more commonly used form, it is listed first.

mel″o·dy
  (*pl.* mel″o·dies)
can″o·py
 can″o·pied
 can″o·py·ing

bac·te″ri·a
  (*sing.* bac·te″ri·um)

Words Easily Confused

Some words are easily confused because of similarity in spelling or pronunciation, such as *feet* and *feat; prostrate* and *prostate; emigrant* and *immigrant; band* and *banned*. Each word that could be confused is followed by a very brief definition and a *see* reference to the other word or words with which it might be confused.

dear
  beloved (*see:* deer)

deer
  animal (*see:* dear)

Occasionally, words that are spelled the same are pronounced with the stress on different syllables, depending on the part of speech or the meaning of the word. When this is the case, both words are listed, each followed by the part of speech and a short definition.

di·gest″, *v.*
  absorb

di″gest, *n.*
  summary

Many of the definitions used to distinguish words are taken from Nelson's *Webster's 21st Century Dictionary.*

Compound Words

When two words are used together often as a single unit (e.g. *paper clip, pen name*), they are included in this list. Many hyphenated words are also included (e.g. *red-blooded, round-the-clock*), so that you can check whether a word is spelled as two words, as a hyphenated word, or as one word.

New words in the language often start out as two words, then become hyphenated, and eventually are spelled as one word. *Videotape* was first *video tape,* then *video-tape.* Now it is considered one word. When a discrepancy was found between dictionaries for a particular word, the most compact form was chosen.

Words Not Included

Short words that are commonly used without causing spelling problems for most people, such as *the* or *cat*, are not included. Short words are included when they can be confused with other words, such as *to, too,* and *two*.

Every possible form of a word is not included. Generally, forms that are irregular are included. If a form is not included, it can be easily deduced from the ones that are.

A

aard″vark′
a·back″
ab″a·cus
a·baft″
ab′a·lo″ne
ab·am″pere
a·ban″don
a·ban″doned
a·ban″don·ment
a·base″
a·base″ment
a·bash″
a·bas″ing
a·bat″a·ble
a·bate″
a·bate″ment
a·bat″ing
ab″a·tis
ab″at·toir′
ab·ax″i·al
ab″ba·cy
ab″be
ab″bess
ab″hey
ab″bot
ab·bre″vi·ate′
ab·bre″vi·at′ed
ab·bre″vi·at′ing
ab·bre″vi·a″tion
ab·cou″lomb
ab″di·cate′
ab″di·cat′ed
ab″di·cat′ing
ab″di·ca″tion
ab″do·men
ab·dom″i·nal
ab·dom″i·nous
ab·duct″
ab·duc″tion
ab·duc″tor
a·beam″
a·be′ce·dar″i·an
a·bed″

a·bele′
ab·er″rant
ab′er·ra″tion
a·bet″
a·bet″ted
a·bet″ting
a·bet″ment
a·bet″tor or a·bet″ter
a·bey″ance
ab·far″ad
ab·hen″ry
ab·hor″
ab·horred″
ab·hor″ring
ab·hor″rence
ab·hor″rent
a·bid″ance
a·bide″
ab·i·et″ic
a·bil″i·ty
  (pl. a·bil″i·ties)
a′bi·o·gen″e·sis
a′bi·o″sis
ab″ject
ab·jec″tion
ab·ju·ra″tion
ab·jure″
ab·jured″
ab·jur″ing
ab·la″tion
ab″la·tive
ab″laut
a·blaze″
a″ble
a″ble-bod″ied
a″bler
a″blest
a·bloom″
ab·lu″tion
a″bly
ab″ne·gate′
ab″ne·gat′ed
ab″ne·gat′ing
ab′ne·ga″tion
ab·nor″mal
ab′nor·mal″i·ty

  (pl. ab′nor·mal″i·
  ties)
ab·nor″mal·ly
ab·nor″mi·ty
  (pl. ab·nor″mi·ties)
a·board″
a·bode″
ab·ohm″
a·bol″ish
ab·o·li″tion
ab·o·li″tion·ism′
ab·o·li″tion·ist
ab′o·ma″sum
A″-bomb′
a·bom″i·na·ble
a·bom″i·na·bly
a·bom″i·nate′
a·bom″i·nat′ed
a·bom″i·nat′ing
a·bom′i·na″tion
ab·o·rig″i·nal
ab·o·rig″i·ne
a·born″ing
a·bort″
a·bor″ti·cide′
a·bor″ti·fa″cient
a·bor″tion
a·bor″tion·ist
a·bor″tive
a·bound″
a·bout″
a·bout″-face″
a·bove″
a·bove″board′
a·bove″ground′
ab′ra·ca·dab″ra
a·brade″
a·brad″ed
a·brad″ing
a·bra″sion
a·bra″sive
a·bra″sive·ly
ab′re·act″
a·breast″
a·bri″
  (pl. a·bris″)

a·bridge''
a·bridg''ing
a·bridg''ment
a·broad''
ab''ro·gate
 ab''ro·gat'ed
 ab''ro·gat'ing
ab'ro·ga''tion
a·brupt''
ab''scess
ab·scise''
ab·scis''sa
ab·scond''
ab''sence
ab''sent, *adv.*
 not present
ab·sent'', *v.*
 remove
ab'sen·tee''
ab'sen·tee''ism
ab''sent-mind''ed
ab''so·lute''
ab'so·lute''ly
ab'so·lu''tion
ab'so·lut''ist
ab'so·lu·tis''tic
ab·solve''
 ab·solved''
 ab·solv''ing
ab·sorb''
 ab·sorbed''
 ab·sorb''ing
 take in; soak up
 (*see:* adsorb)
ab·sor'be·fa''cient
ab·sorb''en·cy
ab·sorb''ent
ab·sorp''tion
ab·stain''
ab·ste''mi·ous
ab·sten''tion
ab''sti·nence
ab''sti·nent
ab''stract, *adj., n.*
 reduced; non-
 specific; summary

ab·stract'', *v.*
 ab·stract''ed
 ab·stract''ing
 remove; summarize
ab·strac''tion
ab·strac''tion·ism
ab·struse''
ab·struse''ness
ab·surd''
ab·surd''i·ty
 (*pl.* ab·surd''i·ties)
a·bu''li·a
a·bun''dance
a·bun''dant
a·buse''
a·bus''er
a·bus''ing
a·bu''sive
a·but''
 a·but''ted
 a·but''ting
 a·but''ment
 a·but''tal
ab·volt''
ab·watt''
a·bysm''
a·bys''mal
a·bys''mal·ly
a·byss''
a·ca''ci·a
ac'a·deme''
ac'a·de''mi·a
ac'a·dem''ic
a·cad'e·mi''cian
a·cad''e·my
 (*pl.* a·cad''e·mies)
A·ca''di·an
a·can''thus
 (*pl.* a·can''thus·es)
a' cap·pel''la
A'ca·pul''co
a·car''pous
ac·cede''
 ac·ced''ed
 ac·ced''ing
 consent (*see:* exceed)

ac·ce'le·ran''do
ac·cel''er·ant
ac·cel''er·ate'
 ac·cel''er·at'ed
 ac·cel''er·at'ing
ac·cel'er·a''tion
ac·cel'er·a'tor
ac·cel'er·om''e·ter
ac''cent
ac·cen''tu·al
ac·cen''tu·ate'
 ac·cen''tu·at'ing
ac·cen'tu·a''tion
ac·cept''
 ac·cept''ed
 ac·cept''ing
 receive (*see:* except)
ac·cept'a·bil''i·ty
ac·cept''a·ble
ac·cept''a·bly
ac·cept''ance
ac'cep·ta''tion
ac''cess
 approach (*see:* ex-
 cess)
ac·ces'si·bil''i·ty
ac·ces''si·ble
ac·ces''si·bly
ac·ces''sion
ac·ces''so·ry
 (*pl.* ac·ces''so·ries)
ac·ciac'ca·tu''ra
ac''ci·dent
ac'ci·den''tal
ac'ci·den''tal·ly
ac·claim''
ac'cla·ma''tion
 approval (*see:* accli-
 mation)
ac·cli''mate
 ac·cli·mat''ed
 ac·cli·mat''ing
ac·cli'ma·tion
 adaptation (*see:* ac-
 clamation)
ac·cli''ma·tize'

ac·cli″ma·tized′
ac·cli″ma·tiz′ing
ac·cliv″i·ty
 (*pl.* ac·cliv″i·ties)
ac″co·lade
ac·com″mo·date
 ac·com″mo·dat′ed
 ac·com″mo·dat′ing
ac·com″mo·da″tion
ac·com″pa·ni·ment
ac·com″pa·nist
ac·com″pa·ny
 ac·com″pa·nied
 ac·com″pa·ny·ing
ac·com″plice
ac·com″plished
ac·cord″
ac·cord″ance
ac·cord″ant
ac·cord″ing
ac·cord″ing·ly
ac·cor″di·on
ac·cost″
ac·count″
ac·count″a·ble
ac·count″a·bil″i·ty
ac·count″a·bly
ac·count″ant
ac·cou″ter
ac·cou″ter·ment
ac·cred″it
ac·cred′i·ta″tion
ac·cre″tion
ac·cru″al
ac·crue″
 ac·crued″
 ac·cru″ing
ac·cul″tur·a″tion
ac·cu″mu·late′
 ac·cu″mu·lat′ed
 ac·cu″mu·lat′ing
ac·cu″mu·la″tion
ac·cu″mu·la′tive
ac″cu·ra·cy
 (*pl.* ac″cu·ra·cies)
ac″cu·rate·ly

ac″cu·rate·ness
ac·cursed″
ac·cus″ant
ac·cu·sa″tion
ac·cu″sa·tive
ac·cu″sa·to″ri·al
ac·cu″sa·to′ry
ac·cuse″
 ac·cused″
 ac·cus″ing
ac·cus″tomed
ace
 aced
 ac″ing
a·cerb″
ac″er·bate′
 ac″er·bat′ed
 ac″er·bat′ing
a·cer″bi·ty
ac″er·ose′
a·ce″tic
 vinegary (*see:* ascet-
 ics)
a·cet″i·fy
ac″e·tone′
a·ce″tyl
a·cet″y·lene′
ache
 ached
 ach″ing
a·chieve″
 a·chieved″
 a·chiev″ing
 a·chieve″ment
 a·chiev″er
ach′ro·mat″ic
a·cic″u·lar
ac″id
ac″id head′
a·cid″ic
a·cid′i·fi·ca″tion
a·cid″i·fy′
 a·cid″i·fied′
 a·cid″i·fy′ing
a·cid″i·ty
ac′i·doph″i·lus

ac′i·do″sis
a·cid″u·lous
ac·knowl″edge
ac·knowl″edge·a·ble
ac·knowl″edg·ing
ac·knowl″edg·ment
a·clin″ic
ac″me
ac″ne
ac″o·lyte′
ac″o·nite′
a″corn
a′cot·y·le″don
a·cous″tic
a·cous″ti·cal
a·cous″ti·cal·ly
a·cous″tics
ac·quaint″
 ac·quaint″ed
 ac·quaint″ing
ac·quaint″ance
ac′qui·esce″
 ac′qui·esced″
 ac′qui·esc″ing
ac′qui·es″cence
ac′qui·es″cent
ac·quire″
 ac·quired″
 ac·quir″ing
ac′qui·si″tion
ac·quis″i·tive
ac·quit″
 ac·quit″ted
 ac·quit″ting
ac·quit″tal
a″cre
a″cre·age
ac″rid
a·crid″i·ty
ac′ri·mo″ni·ous
ac″ri·mo′ny
ac″ro·bat′
ac″ro·bat″ic
ac′ro·meg′a·ly
ac″ro·nym
ac′ro·pho″bi·a

a·crop″o·lis
a·cross″
a·cross″-the-board″
a·cros″tic
a·cryl″ic
act″a·ble″
ac″tin
ac·tin″ic
act·ing″
ac″tin·ism
ac·tin″i·um
ac·ti·nom″e·ter
ac·ti·non″
ac″tion
ac″tion·a·ble
ac″ti·vate
 ac″ti·vat″ed
 ac″ti·vat″ing
ac″ti·va″tion
ac″tive
ac″tive·ly
ac″tiv·ism
ac″tiv·ist
ac·tiv″i·ty
 (*pl.* ac·tiv″i·ties)
ac″to·my″o·sin
ac″tor
ac″tress
ac″tu·al
ac″tu·al″i·ty
 (*pl.* ac″tu·al″i·ties)
ac″tu·al·ly
ac′tu·ar″i·al
ac″tu·ar″y
 (*pl.* ac″tu·ar″ies)
ac″tu·ate′
 ac″tu·at″ed
 ac″tu·at″ing
ac″tu·a″tion
ac″tu·a″tor
a·cu″i·ty
a·cu″men
ac″u·pinch
ac″u·punc″ture, *n.*
ac′u·punc″ture, *v.*
 ac′u·punc″tured

ac′u·punc″tur·ing
a·cute″
a·cute″ly
a·cute″ness
ad
 advertisement (*see:*
  add)
A″da
 a computer language
ad ab·sur″dum″
ad″age
a·da″gio
ad″a·mant
ad′a·man″tine
Ad″am′s ap′ple
a·dapt″
 change (*see:* adept
  and adopt)
a·dapt″a·bil″i·ty
a·dapt″a·ble
ad′ap·ta″tion
a·dapt″er
a·dapt″ive
a·dapt″or
add
 total (*see:* ad)
ad″dax
ad″dend
ad·den″dum
 (*pl.* ad·den″da *or*
  ad·den″dums)
add″er
 one who adds
ad″der
 snake
ad·dict″, *v.*
 surrender to habit
ad″dict, *n.*
 addicted person
ad·dic″tion
ad·dic″tive
Ad″dis A″ba·ba
ad·di″tion
 act of adding (*see:*
  edition)
ad·di″tion·al

ad·di″tion·al·ly
ad″di·tive
ad″dle
 ad″dled
 ad″dling
ad″dle·brained
ad·dress″, *v.*
 speak to; apply
ad″dress, *n.*
 speech; location
ad′dress·ee″
ad·dress″er
 or ad·dress″or
Ad·dres″so·graph″™
ad·duce″
ad·duced″
ad·duc″ing
ad·duct″
ad·duc″tion
ad·duc″tive
ad″e·nine′
ad″e·noid′
ad′e·noi″dal
ad′e·noid·ec″to·my
 (*pl.* ad′e·noid·ec″-
  to·mies)
a·den″o·sine′
ad·ept″, *adj.*
 skilled (*see:* adapt
  and adopt)
ad″ept, *n.*
 expert
ad″e·qua·cy
ad″e·quate·ly
ad·here″
 ad·hered″
 ad·her″ing
ad·her″ence
ad·her″ent
ad·he″sion
ad·he″sive
ad hoc″
ad ho″mi·nem′
ad′i·a·bat″ic
a·dieu″
ad in″fi·ni″tum

ad·i·ni″ti·um
ad in″te·rim
a′di·os
ad″i·pose′
Ad′i·ron′dack
ad·ja″cen·cy
ad·ja″cent
ad′jec·ti″val
ad′jec·ti·val·ly
ad″jec·tive
ad·join″
ad·join″ing
ad·journ″
ad·journ″ment
ad·judge″
ad·ju″di·cate′
ad·ju″di·cat′ed
ad·ju″di·cat′ing
ad·ju″di·ca″tion
ad·ju″di·ca′tor
ad″junct
ad′ju·ra″tion
ad·jure″
ad·jur″ing
ad·just″
ad·just″a·ble
ad·just″er
ad·just″ment
ad″ju·tant
ad″ju·tant gen″er·al
  (*pl.* ad″ju·tants
  gen″er·al)
ad-lib″
  ad-libbed″
  ad-lib″bing
ad″man′
  (*pl.* ad″men′)
ad·min″is·ter
ad·min″is·tra·ble
ad·min″is·tra″tion
ad·min″is·tra″tive
ad·min″is·tra′tor
ad·min″is·tra″trix
ad″mi·ra·ble
ad″mi·ra·bly
ad″mi·ral

ad″mi·ral·ty
  (*pl.* ad″mi·ral·ties)
ad′mi·ra″tion
ad·mire″
ad·mir″er
ad·mir″ing
ad·mis″si·bil″i·ty
ad·mis″si·ble
ad·mis″sion
ad·mis″sive
ad·mit″
ad·mit″tance
ad·mit″ted·ly
ad·mit″ting
ad·mix″
ad·mix″ture
ad·mon″ish
ad′mo·ni″tion
ad·mon″i·to′ry
ad″nate
ad nau″se·am
ad″noun
a·do″
a·do″be
ad′o·les″cence
ad′o·les″cent
a·dopt″
  take (*see:* adapt and
  adept)
a·dop″tion
a·dop″tive
a·dor″a·ble
a·dor″a·bly
ad′o·ra″tion
a·dore″
  a·dored″
  a·dor″ing
a·dorn″
a·dorn″ment
ad·re″nal
A·dren″a·lin™
a·dren″a·line
a·dre″no·cor′ti·co·
  trop″ic
a·drift″
ad·sorb″

  take up and hold
  (*see:* absorb)
ad·sorb″ent
ad·sorp″tion
ad″u·late
ad″u·lat″ed
ad″u·lat′ing
ad′u·la″tion
ad″u·la·to′ry
a·dult″
a·dul″ter·ant
a·dul″ter·ate′
  a·dul″ter·at″ed
  a·dul″ter·at″ing
a·dul″ter·er
a·dul″ter·ess
a·dul″ter·ine
a·dul″ter·ous
a·dul″ter·y
  (*pl.* a·dul″ter·ies)
a·dult″hood
ad·um″brate
  ad·um″brat·ed
  ad·um″brat·ing
ad va·lo″rem
ad·vance″
  ad·vanced″
  ad·vanc″ing
ad·vance″ment
ad·van″tage
ad·van″taged
ad·van″tag·ing
ad′van·ta″geous
ad·vec″tion
ad″vent
Ad″vent·ist
ad·ven″ti″tious
ad·ven″ture
ad·ven″tur·er
ad·ven″ture·some
ad·ven″tur·ess
ad·ven″tur·ing
ad·ven″tur·ous
ad″verb
ad·ver″bi·al
ad·ver″bi·al·ly

ad″ver·sar′y
  (*pl.* ad″ver·sar′ies)
ad·verse″
  opposed (*see:* averse)
ad·verse″ly
ad·ver″si·ty
  (*pl.* ad·ver″si·ties)
ad·vert″
ad·vert″ent
ad″ver·tise′
  ad″ver·tised
  ad″ver·tis′ing
ad″ver·tise″ment
ad·vice″
  opinion (*see:* advise)
ad·vis′a·bil″i·ty
ad·vis″a·ble
ad·vise″
  ad·vised
  ad·vis″ing
  recommend (*see:* advice)
ad·vis″ed·ly
ad·vise″ment
ad·vis″er
  or ad·vis″or
ad·vi″so·ry
ad″vo·ca·cy
  (*pl.* ad″vo·ca·cies)
ad″vo·cate
  ad″vo·cat″ed
  ad″vo·cat″ing
adz
ad·zu″ki
ae″gis
ae·o″li·an
ae″on
aer″ate
  aer″at·ed
  aer″at·ing
aer·a″tion
aer·a·tor″
aer″i·al·ist
aer″i·al·ly
aer″ie
  nest (*see:* airy)

aer′o·bat″ics
aer″o″bic
aer′o·bi·o″sis
aer′o·dy·nam″ic
aer′o·dy·nam″i·cal·ly
aer′o·em″bo·lism
aer·om″e·ter
aer″o·naut′
aer′o·nau″tic
aer′o·nau″ti·cal
aer′o·pause′
aer′o·sol′
aer′o·space
aer′o·sphere″
aer″o·stat
aes″thete
aes·thet″ic
  beauty (*see:* ascetic)
aes·thet″i·cal·ly
aes·thet″i·cism′
a·far″
af fa·bil″i·ty
af″fa·ble
af·fair″
af·faire″ d'hon·neur″
af·fect″
  influence (*see:* effect)
af·fec·ta″tion
af·fect″ed
af·fec″tion
af·fec″tion·ate·ly
af″fen·pin′scher
af″fer·ent
  carrying inward
  (*see:* efferent)
af·fi″ance
  af·fi″anced
  af·fi″anc·ing
af″fi·da″vit
af·fil″i·ate, *n.*
af·fil″i·ate′, *v.*
  af·fil″i·a·ted
  af·fil″i·at′ing
af·fil″i·a″tion
af·fin″i·ty

  (*pl.* af·fin″i·ties)
af·fir″ma″tion
af·fir″ma·tive
af·fix″, *v.*
  attach
af·fix″, *n.*
  thing attached
af·flict″
  af·flict″ed
  af·flict″ing
af·flic″tion
af″flu·ence
af″flu·ent
  prosperous (*see:* ef-fluent)
af·ford″
af·ford″a·ble
af·for″est
af·fray″
af″fri·cate
af·fright″
af·front″
Af″ghan′
af·ghan″i
Af·ghan″i·stan″
a·fi·cio′na″do
  (*pl.* a·fi·cio·na·dos)
a·field″
a·fire″
a·flame″
a·float″
a·flut″ter
a·foot″
a·fore″men′tioned
a·fore″said′
a·fore″thought′
a for′ti·o″ri
a·foul″
a·fraid″
A″-frame′
a·fresh″
Af′ri·ca
Af′ri″kaans
Af′ri·kan″der
  cattle
Af′ri·ka″ner

person
Af″ro
  (*pl.* Af″ros)
Af″ro-A·mer″i·can
af″ter·birth′
af″ter·burn′
af″ter·care′
af″ter·damp′
af″ter·deck′
af″ter·ef·fect′
af″ter·glow′
af″ter·growth′
af″ter·im′age
af″ter·life′
af″ter·math′
af″ter·most′
af″ter·noon″
af″ter·taste′
af″ter·tax′
af″ter·thought′
af″ter·ward′
af″ter·word′
af″ter·world′
a·gain″
a·gainst″
a·gam″ic
a·gape″
  wide open
a·ga″pe
  love
a″gar
ag″ate
a·ga″ve
age
  aged
  ag″ing
  old
a″ged
  elderly
age″ism
age″less
a″gen·cy
  (*pl.* a″gen·cies)
a·gen″da
a·gen″dum
  (*pl.* a·gen″da)

a″gent
age″-old
ag·glom″er·ate
  ag·glom″mer·at′ed
  ag·glom″mer·at′ing
  ag·glom er·a″tion
ag·glu″ti·nate′
  ag·glu″ti·nat′ed
  ag·glu″ti·nat′ing
  ag·glu″ti·na″tion
ag·gran″dize
  ag·gran″dized
  ag·gran″diz′ing
  ag·gran″dize·ment
  ag·gran″diz′er
ag″gra·vate
  ag″gra·va″tion
ag″gre·gate
  ag″gre·gat′ed
  ag″gre·gat′ing
  ag gre·ga″tion
ag·gres″sion
ag·gres″sive
  ag·gres″sive·ly
  ag·gres″sive·ness
ag·gres″sor
ag·grieve″
  ag·griev″ing
a·ghast″
ag″ile
a·gil″i·ty
ag″i·o
ag″i·tate′
  ag″i·tat′ed
  ag″i·tat′ing
  ag″i·ta″tion
  ag″i·ta′tor
a·gleam″
ag″let
a·glim″mer
a·glit″ter
a·glow″
ag″nated
ag·nos″ti·cism
Ag″nus De″i
a·go″

a·gog
a·gon″ic
ag″o·nize′
  ag″o·nized
  ag″o·niz′ing
ag″o·ny
  (*pl.* ag″o·nies)
ag″o·ra
  (*pl.* ag″o·rae′)
ag·o·ra·pho″bi·a
a·grar″i·an
a·gree″
  a·greed″
  a·gree″ing
a·gree′a·bil″i·ty
a·gree″a·ble
a·gree″a·bly
a·gree″ment
ag″ri·busi″ness
ag″ri·cul″ture
ag″ri·cul″tur·ist
a·gron″o·mist
a·gron″o·my
a·ground″
a″gue
a·ha″
a·head″
a·hem″
a·hoy″
aid
  help (*see:* aide)
aide
  assistant (*see:* aid)
aide″-de-camp″
AIDS
  acquired im-
    munodeficiency
    syndrome
ai″grette
ai″ki·do
ail
  sicken (*see:* ale)
ai″ler·on′
aim″less
air″ bag′
air″borne′

air″brush′
air″burst′
air″bus
air″-con·di′tion
air″ con·di′tion·er
air″ con·di′tion·ing
air″-cool′
air″craft′
  (*pl.* air″craft′)
air″ cur′tain
air″-dried′
air″drome′
air″drop′
 air″dropped′
 air″drop′ping
air″-dry′
 air″-dried′
 air″-dry′ing
air″ ex·press″
air″field′
air″flow′
air″ force′
air″freight′
air″ gun′
air″head
air″i·er
air″i·ly
air″ lane′
air″less
air″lift′
air″line′
air″lin′er
air″ lock′
air″mail′
air″man
  (*pl.* air″men)
air″plane′
air″ pock′et
air″port′
air″ pres′sure
air″ raid′
air″ ri′fle
air″ship′
air″space
air″speed′
air″strip′

air″tight′
air″waves′
air″way′
air″wor′thy
air″y
 open to air (*see:* ae-
  rie)
aisle
 passageway (*see:*
  isle)
a·jar″
ak″va·vit
a·kim″bo
a·kin″
Ak″ron
Al′a·bam″a
al″a·bas″ter
a′la carte″
a·lack″
a·lac″ri·ty
a′ la king″
Al″a·mo′
a′ la mode″
a″lar
a·larm″ clock′
a·larm″ist
a·las″
A·las″ka
a″late
alb
al″ba·core′
Al·ba″ni·a
Al″ba·ny
al″ba·tross′
al·be″do
al·be″it
Al·ber″ta
al·bi″no
  (*pl.* al·bi″nos)
al″bum
al·bu″men
 egg white (*see:* albu-
  min)
al·bu″min
 protein (*see:* albu-
  men)

Al″bu·quer′que
al·cai″de
al·cal″de
al″che·mist
al″che·my
  (*pl.* al″che·mies)
al″co·hol′
al″co·hol·ic
al″co·hol·ism′
al″cove
al″de·hyde′
al″der·man
  (*pl.* al″der·men)
ale
 drink (*see:* ail)
a·lee″
a·lem″bic
a·lert″
ale″wife′
  (*pl.* ale″wives)
Al′ex·an″dri·a
a·lex″i·a
al·fal″fa
al·fres″co
al″ga
  (*pl.* al″gae)
al″ge·bra
al″ge·bra″ic
al″ge·bra′ist
al″gid
AL″GOL
Al·gon″quin
al″go·rithm
a″li·as
  (*pl.* a″li·as·es)
al″i·bi′
  (*pl.* al″i·bis′)
al″i·dade′
al″ien
al″ien·a·ble
al″ien·ate′
al″ien·at′ed
al″ien·at′ing
al″ien·a″tion
a·lign″
 a·ligned″

a·lign″ing
a·lign″ment
a·like″
al″i·ment
al′i·men′ta·ry
al′i·mo′ny
a·line″
a·lined″
a·lin″ing
a·line″ment
al″i·quant
al″i·quot
a·live″
al″ka·li′
  (*pl.* al″ka·lies)
al′ka·lim″e·ter
al′ka·line′
al″ka·lin″i·ty
al′ka·lin′i·za″tion
al″ka·lin·ize′
  al″ka·lin·ized′
  al″ka·lin·iz′ing
al′ka·li·za″tion
al″ka·lize″
  al″ka·lized′
  al″ka·liz′ing
al″ka·loid′
al″kane
al″kene
al″kyd
al″kyl
al″kyne
all
  whole (*see:* awl)
Al″lah
all′-A·mer″i·can
al·lan″to·is
all′-a·round
al·lay″
  al·layed″
  al·lay″ing
  soothe (*see:* alley
    and ally)
all″ clear
all″-day″
al′le·ga″tion

al·lege″
al·leged″
al·leg″ing
al·leg″ed·ly
al·le″giance
al′le·gor″i·cal
al″le·go′rist
al″le·go′ry
  (*pl.* al″le·go′ries)
al′le·gret″to
al·le″gro
  (*pl.* al·le″gros)
al·lele″
al′le·lu″ia
al″le·munde′
al″ler·gen′
al′ler·gen′ic
al·ler″gic
al″ler·gist
al″ler·gy
  (*pl.* al″ler·gies)
al·le″vi·ate′
  al·le″vi·at′ed
  al·le″vi·at′ing
al·le″vi·a″tion
al″ley
  (*pl.* al″leys)
  street (*see:* ally and
    allay)
al″ley·way′
al·li″ance
al·lied″
al″li·ga′tor
al·lit″er·ate′
  al·lit″er·at′ed
  al·lit″er·at′ing
al·lit′er·a″tion
al·lit″er·a′tive
all″-night″
al″lo·cate′
  al″lo·cat′ed
  al″lo·cat′ing
al′lo·ca″tion
al″lo·morph
al″lo·nym
al″lo·phone

al·lot″
  al·lot″ted
  al·lot″ting
al·lot″ment
al·lo·trope′
al′lo·trop″ic
al·lot″ro·py
all″-out″
all″o′ver
al·low″a·ble
al·low″ance
al·lowed″
  permitted (*see:*
    aloud)
al·loy″, *v.*
  mix; weaken
al″loy, *n.*
  metal
all″-pur′pose
all′ read″y
  prepared (*see:* al-
    ready)
all′ right″
all″-round″
all″spice′
all″-star′
all″-time″
al·lude″
  al·lud″ed
  al·lud″ing
  make reference to
    (*see:* elude)
al·lure″
  al·lured″
  al·lur″ing
al·lure″ment
al·lu″sion
  reference (*see:* illu-
    sion)
al·lu″sive
  suggestive (*see:* elu-
    sive and illusive)
al·lu″vi·al
al″ly, *n.*
  (*pl.* al″lies)
  friend (*see:* alley)

al·ly″, *v.*
al·lied″
al·ly″ing
unite (*see:* allay)
all″-year
al″ma ma″ter
al″ma·nac′
al·might″y
al″mond
al″mond-eyed′
al″most
alms″giv′er
alms″house′
al″oe
(*pl.* al″oes)
a·loft″
a·lo″ha
a·lone″
a·long″
a·long″shore″
a·long″side″
a·loof″
al·o″pe″ci·a
a·loud″
audibly (*see:* al-
lowed)
al·pac″a
al″pen·glow′
al″pen·horn′
al″pen·stock′
al″pha
al″pha·bet′
al′pha·bet″ic
al′pha·bet″i·cal
al′pha·bet″i·cal·ly
al″pha·bet·ize′
al′pha·bet·ized′
al′pha·bet·iz″ing
al′pha·nu·mer″ic
al″pine
al·read″y
so soon (*see:* all
ready)
Al·sace″-Lor·raine″
al″so
al″so-ran′

al″tar
table (*see:* alter)
al″tar boy′
al″tar·piece′
al″ter
change (*see:* altar)
al′ter·a″tion
al′ter·ca″tion
al′ter e″go
al″ter·nate′
al″ter·nat′ed
al″ter·nat′ing
al″ter·nate·ly
al·ter″na·tive
al″ter·na′tor
alt″horn
al·though″
al·tim″e·ter
al″ti·tude′
al′ti·tu″di·nal
al″to
(pl. al″tos)
al′to·cu″mu·lus
al′to·geth″er
al′to·stra″tus
al″tru·ism′
al″tru·ist
al′tru·is″tic
al′tru·is″ti·cal·ly
al″um
a·lu″mi·nize′
a·lu″mi·nized′
a·lu″mi·niz″ing
a·lu″mi·num
a·lum″na
(*pl.* a·lum″nae)
a·lum″nus
(*pl.* a·lum″ni)
al·ve″o·lar
al″ways
a·lys″sum
am
a″mah
a·main″
a·mal″gam
a·mal″ga·mate′

a·mal″ga·mat′ed
a·mal″ga·mat′ing
a·mal′ga·ma″tion
a·man·dine″
a·man·u·en″sis
(*pl.* a·man′u·en″
ses)
am″a·ranth′
am′a·ryl″lis
a·mass″
am″a·teur′
am″a·teur′ish
am″a·to·ry
a·maze″
a·mazed″
a·maz″ing
a·maze″ment
am″a·zon′
am·bas″sa·dor
am·bas′sa·do″ri·al
am·bas″sa·dress
am″ber
am″ber·gris′
am″bi·ance
am·bi·dex·ter″i·ty
am′bi·dex″trous
am″bi·ence
am″bi·ent
am·bi·gu″i·ty
(*pl.* am′bi·gu″i·
ties)
am·big″u·ous
am·bi″tion
am·bi″tious
am·biv″a·lence
am·biv″a·lent
am″ble
am″bled
am″bling
am·bro″sia
am″bu·lance
am″bu·lant
am″bu·late
am″bu·lat·ed
am″bu·lat·ing
am″bu·la·to″ry

am'bus·cade''
am''bush
a·me''lio·rate'
  a·me''lio·rat'ed
  a·me''lio·rat'ing
a·me''lio·ra''tion
a'men''
a·me''na·bil''i·ty
a·me''na·ble
a·me''na·bly
a''men' cor'ner
A·mend''
  alter (see: emend)
a·mends''
a·mend''ment
a·men''i·ty
  (pl. a·men''i·ties)
Am'er·a''sian
A·mer''i·ca
A·mer''i·can
A·mer'i·ca''na
am·er·i''ci·um
Am''er·ind
Am''es·lan
am''e·thyst
a''mi·a·bil''i·ty
a''mi·a·ble
a''mi·a·bly
am'i·ca·bil''i·ty
am''i·ca·ble
am''i·ca·bly
am''ice
a·mi'cus cu''ri·ae'
a·mid''
am''ide
a·mid''ships
a·midst''
a·mi''ga
  (pl. a·mi''gas)
a·mi''go
  (pl. a·mi''gos)
a·mine''
a·mi''no
Am''ish
a·miss''
am''i·ty

Am·man''
am''me'ter
am''mo
am·mo''nia
am·mo''ni·um
am·mu·ni''tion
am·ne''sia
am·ne''si·ac
am''nes·ty
am'ni·o·cen·te''sis
am''ni·on
am''ni·ot''ic
a·moe''ba
a·moe''bic
a·mok''
a·mong''
a·mongst''
a·mon'til·la''do
a·mor''al
a'mo·ral''i·ty
  (pl. a'mo·ral''i·ties)
a·mor''al·ly
am'o·ret''to
am''o·rous
a·mor''phism
a·mor''phous
am·or·ti·za''tion
am''or·tize
a·mount''
a·mour''
am''pere'
am''per·sand'
am·phet''a·mine'
am·phib''i·an
am·phib''i·ous
am·phi·the·a'ter
am''pho·ra
  (pl. am''pho·rae)
am''ple
am''pler
am''plest
am·pi·cil''lin
am'pli·fi·ca''tion
am''pli·fy'
  am''pli·fied'
  am''pli·fy'ing

am''pli·tude'
am''ply
am''pule
am''pu·tate'
  am''pu·tat'ed
  am''pu·tat'ing
am'pu·ta''tion
am'pu·tee''
Am''ster·dam'
Am''trak'
am''u·let
a·muse''
a·muse''ment
am''yl
am''yl·ase'
An'a·bap''tist
a·nab''a·sis
an'a·bol''ic
an'a·bol''ic ster''oid'
a·nach''ro·nism'
a·nach'ro·nis''tic
an'a·con''da
an''a·dem'
a·nae''mi·a
a·nae''mic
an·aer·o''bic
an·aes·the''sia
an·aes·the'si·ol''o·gist
an·aes·the'si·ol''o·gy
an·aes·thet''ic
an·aes''the·tist
an·aes'the·ti·za''tion
an·aes''the·tize'
an''a·gram'
a''nal
an·al·ge''si·a
an·al·ge''sic
an''a·lects'
an'a·log''i·cal
a·nal''o·gous
an''a·logue'
a·nal''o·gy
  (pl. a·nal''o·gies)
a·nal''y·sand'
a·nal''y·sis
  (pl. a·nal''y·ses)

an''a·lyst
  one who analyzes
  (*see:* annalist)
an'a·lyt''ic
an'a·lyt''i·cal
an''a·lyze'
  an''a·lyzed'
  an''a·lyz'ing
an'a·morph''ic
an''a·pest
an·ar''chic
an·ar''chi·cal
an''ar·chism'
an''ar·chist
an''ar·chy
  (*pl.* an''ar·chies)
an''as·tig·mat''ic
a·nath''e·ma
  (*pl.* a·nath''e·mas)
a·nath''e·ma·tize'
  a·nath''e·ma·tiz'ed
  a·nath''e·ma·tiz'ing
an'a·tom''ic
an'a·tom''i·cal
a·nat''o·mist
a·nat''o·mize'
  a·nat''o·mized'
  a·nat''o·miz'ing
a·nat''o·my
  (*pl.* a·nat''o·mies)
an''ces·tor
an·ces''tral
an''ces·try
  (*pl.* an''ces·tries)
an''chor
an''chor·age
an''cho·rite'
an''chor·man'
  (*pl.* an''chor·men')
an''chor·wom'an
  (*pl.* an''chor·wo'
  men)
an''cho·vy
  (*pl.* an''cho·vies)
an''cient
an''cil·lar'y

an·dan''te
  (*pl.* an·dan''tes)
an''dan·ti''no
  (*pl.* an'dan·ti''nos)
and''i'ron
an''dro·gen
an·drog''y·nous
an·drog''y·ny
an''droid
An·drom''e·da
an''ec·do''tal
an''ec·dote'
an'e·cho''ic
a·ne''mi·a
a·ne''mic
an'e·mom''e·ter
a·nem''o·ne'
a·nent''
an''er·oid'
an·es·the''sia
an·es·the''si·ol''o·gist
an·es·the''si·ol''o·gy
an·es·thet''ic
an·es''the·tist
an·es''the·tize'
an''eu·rysm
a·new''
an''gel
  heavenly messenger
  (*see:* angle)
an''gel·dust'
an''gel·fish'
  (*pl.* an''gel·fish')
an·gel''ic
an·gel''i·cal
an·gel''i·cal·ly
an''ger
an·gi''na pec''to·ris
an'gi·o·plas''ty
an'gi·o·sperm
an''gle
an''gled
an''gling
  divergence (*see:* an·
  gel)
an''gler

an''gle·worm'
an''gli·can
An''gli·cize'
an''gling
an''glo-A·mer''i·can
An''glo·phile'
An''glo·phobe'
An''glo-Sax''on
An·go''la
an·go''ra
an''gos·tu''ra
an''gri·er
an''gri·est
an''gri·ly
an''gri·ness
an''gry
angst
ang''strom
an''guish
an''guished
an''gu·lar
an·gu·lar''i·ty
  (*pl.* an'gu·lar''i·
  ties)
an·hy''drous
an''il
an''i·line
an'i·mad·ver''sion
an'i·mad·vert''
an''i·mal
an''i·mate'
  an''i·mat'ed
  an''i·mat'ing
an'i·ma''tion
an''i·ma'tor
an''i·mism'
an''i·mist
an'i·mos''i·ty
  (*pl.* an'i·mos''i·ties)
an''i·mus
an''i'on
an''ise
an''i·seed'
an'i·sette''
ankh
an''kle

an"kle·bone'
an"klet
an"ky·lose'
an"nal·ist
  annals writer (*see:*
   analyst)
an"nals
An·nap"o·lis
an·neal"
an"ne·lid
an·nex", *v.*
an"nex, *n.*
  joined part
an"nex·a"tion
an·ni"hi·late'
  an·ni"hi·lat'ed
  an·ni"hi·lat'ing
  an·ni"hi·la"tion
an·ni·ver"sa·ry
  (*pl.* an·ni·ver"sa·
   ries)
an"no Dom"i·ni'
an"no·tate'
  an"no·tat'ed
  an"no·tat'ing
an·no·ta"tion
an"no·ta·tor
an·nounce"
  an·nounced"
  an·nounc"ing
an·nounce"ment
an·nounc"er
an·noy"
an·noy"ance
an·noy"ing
an"nu·al
an"nu·al·ly
an·nu"i·tant
an·nu"i·ty
  (*pl.* an·nu"i·ties)
an·nul"
  an·nulled"
  an·nul"ling
an"nu·lar
an·nul"ment
an"nu·lus

(*pl.* an"nu·li')
an·nun"ci·ate'
  an·nun"ci·at'ed
  an·nun"ci·at'ing
an·nun"ci·a"tion
an"ode
an"o·dize'
an"o·dyne'
a·noint"
a·nom"a·lous
a·nom"a·ly
  (*pl.* a·nom"a·lies)
an"o·mie'
a·non"
an'o·nym"i·ty
a·non"y·mous
a·noph"e·les'
a"no·rak'
an·o·rex"i·a
an·oth"er
an·ox"i·a
an"swer
an"swer·a·ble
ant
  insect (*see:* aunt)
ant·ac"id
an·tag"o·nism'
an·tag"o·nist
an·tag"o·nize'
ant·arc"tic
Ant·arc"ti·ca
ant" bear'
an"te
  an"teed
  an"te·ing
  stake (*see:* anti)
ant"eat'er
an"te·bel"lum
an"te·ced"ence
an"te·ced"ent
an"te·cham'ber
an"te·date'
  an"te·dat'ed
  an"te·dat'ing
an"te·di·lu"vi·an
an"te·lope'

an"te me·rid"i·em
an·ten"na
  (*pl.* an·ten"nae)
an"te·pe"nult
an"te·pe·nul"ti·mate
an·te"ri·or
an"te·room'
an"them
an"ther
ant"hill'
an·thol"o·gist
an·thol"o·gize'
  an·thol"o·gized'
  an·thol"o·giz'ing
an·thol"o·gy
  (*pl.* an·thol"o·gies)
an"thra·cite'
an"thrax
  (*pl.* an"thra·ces')
an"thro·po·cen"tric
an"thro·poid
an"thro·po·log"i·cal
an·thro·pol"o·gist
an·thro·pol"o·gy
an·thro·pom"e·try
an"thro·po·mor"phic
an"thro·po·mor"phism
an"ti
  (*pl.* an"tis)
  against (*see:* ante)
an"ti·air"craft'
an"ti-A·mer"i·can
an"ti·bac·te"ri·al
an"ti·bal·lis"tic
an"ti·bi·ot"ic
an"ti·bod'y
  (*pl.* an"ti·bod'ies)
an"tic
An"ti·christ'
an·tic"i·pate'
  an·tic"i·pat'ed
  an·tic"i·pat'ing
an·tic"i·pa"tion
an"ti·cler"i·cal
an"ti·cli·mac"tic
an ti·cli"max

an''ti·cline'
an''ti·co·ag''u·lant
an''ti·cy''clone
an''ti·de·pres''sant
an''ti·dote'
an''ti·freeze'
an''ti·fric''tion
an''ti·gen
an''ti·gen''ic
an''ti·he'ro
   (*pl.* an''ti·he'roes)
an''ti·his''ta·mine
an''ti·in·tel·lect''u·al
an''ti·knock''
an''ti·la''bor
an''ti·log''a·rithm'
an''ti·ma·cas''sar
an''ti·mag·net''ic
an''ti·mat''ter
an''ti·mis''sile
an''ti·mo'ny
an''ti·neu·tri''no
an''ti·ox''i·dant
an''ti·neu''tron
an''ti·par''ti·cle
an''ti·pas''to
an''ti·pa·thet''ic
an·tip''a·thy
   (*pl.* an·tip''a·thies)
an''ti·per'son·nel''
an''ti·per''spi·rant
an''ti·phon'
an·tiph''o·nal
an·tiph''o·ny
   (*pl.* an·tiph''o·nies)
an·tip''o·dal
an·tip''o·des
an''ti·pope
an''ti·pov''er·ty
an''ti·pro''ton
an''ti·py·ret''ic
an''ti·py·re''sis
an''ti·quar''i·an
an''ti·quar'y
   (*pl.* an''ti·quar'ies)
an''ti·quate'

an''ti·quat'ed
an''ti·quat'ing
an·tique''
an·tiqued''
an·ti''quing
an·tiq''ui·ty
   (*pl.* an·tiq''ui·ties)
an''ti·re·jec''tion
an''ti-Sem''ite
an''ti-Se·mit''ic
an''ti-Sem''i·tism
an''ti·sep''sis
an''ti·sep''tic
an''ti·slav''er·y
an''ti·so''cial
an·tis''tro·phe'
an''ti·tank''
an·tith''e·sis
   (*pl.* an·tith''e·ses)
an''ti·thet''ic
an''ti·thet''i·cal
an''ti·tox''in
an''ti·trade'
an''ti·trust''
an''ti·un''ion
an''ti·ven''in
an''ti·viv'i·sec''tion
ant''ler
an''to·nym
an·ton''y·mous
an''trum
   (*pl.* an''tra)
Ant''werp
an'u·ret''ic
a''nus
   (*pl.* a''nus·es)
an''vil
anx·i''e·ty
   (*pl.* anx·i''e·ties)
anx''ious
an''y
an''y·bod'y
   (*pl.* an''y·bod'ies)
an''y·how'
an''y·one'
an''y·place'

an''y·thing'
an''y·time'
an''y·way'
an''y·where'
an''y·wise'
A'-O·K'
A'' one
a·or''ta
   (*pl.* a·or''tas)
a''ou·dad'
a·pace''
A·pach''e
   (*pl.* A·pach''es)
a'pa·re''jo
a·part''
a·part''heid
a·part''ment
ap'a·thet''ic
ap'a·thet''i·cal·ly
ap''a·thy
   (*pl.* ap''a·thies)
ape
aped
ap''ing
ape''-man'
a·pe'ri·tif''
ap''er·ture
a''pex
   (*pl.* a''pex·es)
a·pha''sia
a·phe''li·on
a''phid
aph''o·rism
aph'o·ris''tic
aph·ro·dis''i·ac
a''pi·an
a''pi·ar'y
   (*pl.* a''pi·ar'ies)
a·piece''
ap''ish
ap'la·nat''ic
a·plen''ty
a·plomb''
ap·ne''a
a·poc''a·lypse
a·poc''a·lyp'tic

a·poc''o·pe
a·poc''ry·pha
a·poc''ry·phal
ap''o·gee
a·po·lit''i·cal
a·pol·o·get''ic
a·pol·o·get''i·cal·ly
ap'o·lo''gi·a
a·pol''o·gist
a·pol''o·gize
  a·pol''o·gized
  a·pol''o·giz·ing
a·pol''o·gy
  (*pl.* a·pol''o·gies)
ap'o·plec''tic
ap'o·plex''y
a·port''
ap'o·si·o·pe''sis
a·pos''ta·sy
  (*pl.* a·pos''ta·sies)
a·pos''tate
a·pos·te·ri·o''ri
a·pos''tle
a·pos''to·late
ap'os·tol''ic
a·pos''tro·phe
a·poth''e·car·y
  (*pl.* a·poth''e·car·
  ies)
ap''o·thegm'
  saying (*see:* apo-
  them)
ap''o·them'
  geometric line (*see:*
  apothegm)
a·poth'e·o''sis
  (*pl.* a·poth'e·o''ses)
Ap'pa·la''chian
ap·pall''
ap''pa·nage
ap'pa·ra''tus
  (*pl.* ap'pa·ra''tus)
ap·par''el
ap·par''ent
ap'pa·ri''tion
ap·peal''

ap·peal''ing
ap·pear''
ap·pear''ance
ap·pease''
  ap·peased''
  ap·peas''ing
ap·pease''ment
ap·pel''lant
ap·pel''late
ap'pel·la''tion
ap·pend''
ap·pend''age
ap'pen·dec''to·my
  (*pl.* ap'pen·dec''to·
  mies)
ap'pen·di·ci''tis
ap·pen''dix
  (*pl.* ap·pen''dix·es)
ap'per·cep''tion
ap''pe·stat'
ap'per·tain''
ap''pe·tite'
ap''pe·tiz'er
ap·plaud''
ap·plause''
ap''ple·cart'
ap''ple·jack'
ap''ple-pie, *adj.*
  showing American
  values
ap''ple pie', *n.*
  pie
ap''ple-pol'ish
ap''ple·sauce'
ap·pli''ance
ap'pli·ca·bil''i·ty
ap''pli·ca·ble
ap''pli·cant
ap'pli·ca''tion
ap''pli·ca'tor
ap·plied''
ap'pli·qué'
ap·ply''
  ap·plied''
  ap·ply''ing
ap·pog'gia·tu''ra

ap·point''
ap·point''ment
ap·poin''tive
Ap'po·mat''tox
ap·por''tion
ap·por''tion·ment
ap·pose''
  ap·posed''
  ap·pos''ing
ap''po·site
  suitable (*see:* oppo-
  site)
ap'po·si''tion
ap·pos''i·tive
ap·prais''al
ap·praise''
  ap·praised''
  ap·prais''ing
  estimate (*see:* ap-
  prise)
ap·prais''er
ap·pre''ci·a·ble
ap·pre''ci·a·bly
ap·pre''ci·ate'
  ap·pre''ci·at'ed
  ap·pre''ci·at'ing
ap·pre''ci·a''tion
ap·pre''cia·tive
ap'pre·hend''
ap'pre·hen''sion
ap'pre·hen''sive
ap·pren''tice
ap·pren''ticed
ap·pren''tic·ing
ap·pren''tice·ship
ap·prise''
  ap·prised''
  ap·pris''ing
  inform (*see:* ap-
  praise)
ap·proach''
ap·proach'a·bil''ity
ap·proach''a·ble
ap'pro·ba''tion
ap·pro''pri·ate'
  ap·pro''pri·at'ed

ap·pro″pri·at′ing
ap·pro″pri·ate·ly
ap·pro″pri·a″tion
ap·prov″al
ap·prove″
ap·prov″ing
ap·prox″i·mate′
ap·prox″i·mate·ly
ap·prox″i·mat′ing
ap·prox″i·ma″tion
ap·pur″te·nance
a·prax″i·a
a″prés-ski″
ap″ri·cot′
A″pril
a′ pri·o″ri
a″pron
ap″ro·pos″
apse
apt
ap″ti·tude′
apt″ly
apt″ter·ous
A″qa·ba′
aq″ua
Aq″ua-Lung′™
aq′ua·ma·rine″
aq″ua·naut′
aq″ua·plane′
a·quar″i·um
A·quar″i·us
a·quat″ic
aq″ua·tint′
aq″ua vi″tae
aq″ue·duct′
a″que·ous
aq″ui·fer
aq″ui·line′
a·quiv″er
ar′a·besque″
A·ra″bi·a
Ar″a·bic
ar″a·ble
a·rach″nid
Ar′a·ma″ic
A·rap″a·ho′

ar″ba·lest
ar″bi·ter
ar″bi·trage′
ar·bit″ra·ment
ar″bi·trar′i·ly
ar″bi·trar′i·ness
ar″bi·trar′y
 (*pl.* ar″bi·trar′ies)
ar″bi·trate′
ar′bi·trat·ed′
ar′bi·trat′ing
ar′bi·tra″tion
ar″bi·tra′tor
ar″bor
ar·bo″re·al
ar·bo·re″tum
ar″bor vi″tae
 brain structure (*see:*
 arborvitae)
ar″bor·vi″tae
 tree (*see:* arbor vi-
 tae)
ar·bu″tus
arc
 circle segment (*see:*
 ark)
A″R″C″
 AIDS-related com-
 plex
ar·cade″
Ar·ca″di·a
ar·cane″
arced
arch
 (*pl.* arch″es)
ar′chae·o·log″i·cal
ar′chae·ol″o·gy
ar·chae·op″ter·yx
ar·cha″ic
ar″cha·ism′
arch″an′gel
arch″bish″op
arch·bish″op·ric
arch″dea″con
arch′di·oc″e·san
arch″di″o·cese

arch″du″cal
arch″duch″ess
arch″duch″y
arch″duke″
arch″en″e·my
 (*pl.* arch″en″e·
 mies)
arch″er
arch″er·y
ar″che·type
arch″fiend″
ar·chi·e·pis″co·pal
ar″chi·man″drite′
ar′chi·pel″a·go′
ar″chi·tect′
ar′chi·tec·ton″ic
ar′chi·tec·tur·al
ar″chi·tec′ture
ar″chi·trave′
ar″chive
ar″chi·vist
ar″chon
arch″priest″
arch″way
arc″ing
arc″ light′
arc″tic
ar″cu·ate
ar″den·cy
ar″dent
ar″dor
ar″du·ous
ar″e·a
 region (*see:* aria)
ar″e·a code′
ar″e·a·way
ar″e·ca
aren′t
Ar″es
 god of war (*see:*
 Aries)
ar″gent
Ar′gen·ti″na
Ar″gen·tine″
Ar′gen·tin″e·an
ar″gol

ar″gon
Ar″go·naut′
ar″go·sy
ar″got
ar″gu·a·ble
ar″gue
ar″gued
ar″gu·ing
ar″gu·ment
ar′gu·men·ta″tion
ar′gu·men″ta·tive
ar″gyle
a″ri·a
  song (see: area)
Ar″i·an·ism′
ar″id
a·rid″i·ty
Ar″ies
  zodiac sign (see: Ares)
a·right″
ar″il
a·rise″
 a·rose″
 a·ris″en
 a·ris″ing
 a·ris″ta
ar″is·toc″ra·cy
a·ris″to·crat
a·ris″to·crat″ic
Ar′is·to·te″lian
ar·ith″me·tic
ar·ith·met″i·cal
ar·ith·met″i·cal·ly
ar·ith·me·ti″cian
Ar″i·zo″na
ark
  boat (see: arc)
Ar″kan·sas
arm
ar′ma·dil″lo
  (pl. ar′ma·dil″los)
Ar′ma·ged″don
ar″ma·ment
ar″ma·ture
arm″band

arm″chair
Ar·me″ni·a
arm″ful
  (pl. arm″fuls)
arm″hole
arm″i·stice
arm″load
ar·moire″
ar″mor
ar″mored
ar·mor″ri·al
ar″mor·y
  (pl. ar″mor·ies)
arm″pit
arm″rest
ar″my
  (pl. ar″mies)
ar″my·worm′
ar″ni·ca
a·ro″ma
ar′o·mat″ic
ar′o·mat″i·cal·ly
a·rose″
a·round″
a·rous″al
a·rouse″
 a·roused″
 a·rous″ing
ar·peg″gi·o
  (pl. ar·peg″gi·os)
ar·raign″
ar·raign″ment
ar·range″
 ar·ranged″
 ar·rang″ing
 ar·range″ment
 ar·rang″er
ar″rant
ar″ras
ar·ray″
ar·rears″
ar·rest″
 ar·rest″ing
ar·rhyth″mi·a
ar·ri″val
ar·rive″

ar·rived″
ar·riv″ing
ar′ri·ve·der″ci
ar″ro·gance
ar″ro·gant
ar″ro·gate′
 ar″ro·gat′ed
 ar″ro·gat′ing
ar′ro·ga″tion
ar″row·head
ar″row·root′
ar·roy″o
  (pl. ar·roy″os)
ar″se·nal
ar·se″nic, adj.
  containing arsenic
ar″se·nic, n.
  poison
ar″son
art″ de″co
Ar″te·mis
ar·te″ri·al
ar·te″ri·o·scle·ro″sis
ar″ter·y
  (pl. ar″ter·ics)
ar·te″sian
art″ful
art″ful·ly
ar·thrit″ic
ar·thri″tis
ar″thro·pod′
ar″ti·choke′
ar″ti·cle
ar″ti·cled
ar″ti·cling
ar·tic″u·lar
ar·tic″u·late′
 ar·tic″u·lat′ed
 ar·tic″u·lat′ing
 ar·tic′u·la″tion
ar″ti·fact′
ar″ti·fice
ar·tif″i·cer
ar′ti·fi″cial
ar′ti·fi′ci·al″i·ty

(*pl.* ar'ti·fi'ci·al''i·
ties)
ar'ti·fi''cial·ly
ar'til''ler·y
art''i·ness
ar''ti·san
art''ist
ar·tiste''
ar·tis''tic
ar·tis''ti·cal·ly
ar''tist·ry
art''less
art'' nou·veau''
art''work
art''y
A·ru''ba
ar''um
Ar''y·an
ar''yl
as
as'a·fet''i·da
as·bes''tos
as·cend''
as·cend''ance
as·cend''an·cy
as·cend''ant
as·cen''sion
as·cent''
climb (*see:* assent)
as·cer·tain''
as·cet''ic
austere (*see:* aes-
thetic)
as·cet''i·cism
a·scor''bic
as''cot
as·crib''a·ble
as·cribe''
as·cribed''
as·crib''ing
as·crip''tion
a·sep''sis
a·sex''u·al
ash
(*pl.* ash''es)
a·shamed''

ash''can
ash''en
a·shore''
ash''ram
ash''tray
A''sia
a·side''
as''i·nine'
as'i·nin''i·ty
ask
a·skance''
a·skew''
a·slant''
a·sleep''
a·so''cial
asp
as·par''a·gus
as'par·tame''
as''pect
as''pen
as·per''i·ty
as·perse''
as·persed''
as·pers''ing
as·per''sion
as''phalt
as''pho·del'
as·phyx''i·ate'
as·phyx'i·a''tion
asp''ic
as'pi·dis''tra
as''pir·ant
as''pi·rate'
as''pi·rat'ed
as''pi·rat'ing
as'pi·ra''tion
as'pi·ra''tor
as·pire''
as·pired''
as·pir''ing
as''pi·rin
ass
as·sail''
as·sail''a·ble
as·sail''ant
as·sas''sin

as·sas''si·nate
as·sas'si·na''tion
as·sault
as·say
evaluate (*see:* essay)
as''se·gais'
as·sem''blage
as·sem''ble
as·sem''bled
as·sem''bling
(*pl.* as·sem''blies)
as·sem''bler
as·sem''bly line
as·sem''bly·man
(*pl.* as·sem''bly·
men)
as·sent''
agree (*see:* ascent)
as·sert''
as·ser''tion
as·ser''tive
as·sess''
as·sess''a·ble
as·sess''ment
as·sess''sor
as''set
as·sev''e·rate
as·sev''e·ra''tion
as·si·du''i·ty
(*pl.* as·si·du''i·ties)
as·sid''u·ous
as·sign''
as·sign''a·ble
as·sig·na''tion
as·sign·ee''
as·sign''er
as·sign''ment
as·sim''i·la·ble
as·sim''i·late'
as·sim''i·lat'ed
as·sim''i·lat'ing
as·sim'i·la''tion
as·sist''
as·sis''tance
as·sis''tant
as·siz''es

as·so″ci·ate′
  as·so″ci·at′ed
  as·so″ci·at′ing
as·so″ci·a″tion
as·so″ci·at′ive mem″
  o·ry
as″so·nance
as″so·nant
as·sort″
as·sort″ed
as·sort″ment
as·suage″
  as·suaged″
  as·suag″ing
as·sume″
  as·sumed″
  as·sum″ing
as·sump″sit
as·sump″tion
as·sump″tive
as·sur″ance
as·sure″
  as·sured″
  as·sur″ing
As·syr″i·a
a·stat″ic
as″ta·tine′
as″ter
as″ter·isk
a·stern″
as″ter·oid′
as″the″ni·a
asth″ma
asth″mat″ic
as′tig″mat″ic
as′tig″mat″i·cal·ly
a·stig″ma·tism′
a·stir″
As″ti spu·men″te
as″ton″ish
as·tound″
a·strad″dle
as″tra·khan″
as″tral
a·stray″
a·stride″

as·trin″gen·cy
as·trin″gent
as″tro·dome′
as″tro·gate′
as″tro·ga″tion
as″tro·labe′
as·trol″o·ger
as″tro·log″i·cal
as·trol″o·gy
as″tro·naut″
as·tro·nau″tics
as·tron″o·mer
as″tro·nom″i·cal
as·tron″o·my
as″tro·phys″i·cist
as tro·phys″ics
as·tute″
a·sun″der
a·sy″lum
a sym·met″ric
a sym·met″ri·cal
a·sym″me·try
as″ymp·tot″ic
at
at′a·rax″i·a
a·tax″i·a
at′a·vism
at′a·vis″tic
ate
at′el·ier″
a tem″po
a″the·ism
a″the·ist
a″the·is″tic
A·the″na
ath′e·nae″um
Ath″ens
ath′er·o·scle·ro″sis
a·thirst″
ath″lete
ath·let″ic
ath·let″i·cal·ly
a·thwart″
a·tilt″
a·tin″gle
At·lan″ta

At·lan″tic
at″las
at″mos·phere′
at mos·pher″ic
at mos·pher″i·cal·ly
at″oll
at″om
at″om bomb″
a·tom″ic
a·tom″ic bomb″
at″om·ism
at″om·ize
  at″om·ized
  at″om·iz·ing
at″om·iz·er
a·ton″al
a′to·nal″i·ty
a·to″nal·ly
a·tone″
  a·toned″
a·ton″ing
a·tone″ment
at″o·ny
a·top″
a·trip″
a″tri·um
  (pl. a″tri·a)
a·tro″cious
a·troc″i·ty
  (pl. a·troc″i·ties)
at″ro·phy
  at″ro·phied
  at″ro·phy·ing
at·tach″a·ble
at′ta·ché′
at·tach″ment
at·tack″
at·tain″
at·tain″a·ble
at·tain″ment
at·taint″
at″tar
at·tempt″
at·tend″
at·tend″ance
at·tend″ant

at·ten"tion
at·ten"tive
at·ten"tive·ly
at·ten"u·ate'
  at·ten"u·at'ed
  at·ten"u·at'ing
at·ten'u·a"tion
at·test"
at·tes·ta"tion
at"tic
  top floor
At"tic
  Greek
at·tire"
at"ti·tude'
at·ti·tu"di·nal
at·tor"ney
  (pl. at·tor"neys)
at·tor"ney-at-law'
  (pl. at·tor"neys-at-
  law)
at·tor"ney gen"er·al
  (pl. at·tor"neys
  gen"er·al)
at·tract"
at·trac"tion
at·trac"tive
at·trib"ut·a·ble
at·trib"ute, v.
  name as cause
  at·trib"ut·ed
  at·trib"ut·ing
at"trib·ute, n.
  quality
at·tri·bu"tion
at·tri"tion
at·tune"
a·twit"ter
a·typ"i·cal
au·bade"
au"burn
Auck"land
au con·traire"
auc"tion
auc"tion·eer"
auc·to"ri·al

au·da"cious
au·dac"i·ty
  (pl. au·dac"i·ties)
au'di·bil"i·ty
au"di·ble
au"di·bly
au"di·ence
au"di·o
  (pl. au"di·os)
au"di·o fre"quen·cy
au'di·ol"o·gist
au'di·ol"o·gy
au'di·o"me·ter
au"di·o·phile'
au"di·o·tape"
au"di·o·vis"u·al
au"dit
au·di"tion
au"di·tor
au'di·to"ri·um
au'di·to"ry
auf Wie"der·seh'en
au"ger
  drill (see: augur)
aught
  zero (see: ought)
aug·ment"
aug'men·ta"tion
aug·men"ta·tive
au grat"in
Augs"burg
au"gur
  predict (see: auger)
au"gu·ry
  (pl. au"gu·ries)
au·gust"
  majestic (see: Au-
  gust)
Au"gust
  month (see: august)
Au·gus"ta
au jus"
auk
au lait"
auld" lang syne"
au' na·tu·rel"

aunt
  relative (see: ant)
au"ra
au"ral
  related to hearing
  (see: oral)
au"ral·ly
au"re·ate
au"re·ole'
au' re·voir'
au"ri·cle
  outer ear (see: ora-
  cle)
au·ric"u·lar
au·rif"er·ous
au·ro"ra
au·ro"ra aus·tra"lis
au·ro"ra bo·re·al"is
Ausch"witz
aus"cul·tate'
aus'cul·ta"tion
aus"pice
  (pl. aus"pic·es)
aus·pi"cious
aus·tere"
aus·tere"ly
aus·ter"i·ty
  (pl. aus·ter"i·ties)
Aus"tin
aus"tral
Aus'tral·a"sia
Aus'tral"ia
Aus"tria
au"tar·chy
  (pl. au"tar·chies)
au·then"tic
au·then"ti·cal·ly
au·then"ti·cate'
  au·then"ti·cat'ed
  au·then"ti·cat'ing
au·then"ti·ca"tion
au'then·tic"i·ty
au"thor
au"thor·ess
au·thor'i·tar"i·an
au·thor'i·tar"i·an·ism'

au·thor″i·ta′tive
au·thor″i·ty
  (*pl.* au·thor″i·ties)
au″thor·i·za″tion
au″thor·ize
au″thor·ship′
au″tism
au·tis″tic
au″to
  (*pl.* au″tos)
au″to·bahn′
au·to·bi·og″ra·pher
au·to·bi·o·graph″ic
au·to·bi·o·graph″i·cal
au·to·bi·og″ra·phy
  (*pl.* au″to·bi·og″ra·
  phies)
au·toch″tho·nous
au″to·clave′
au·toc″ra·cy
  (*pl.* au·toc″ra·cies)
au″to·crat′
au·to·crat″ic
au″to·crat″i·cal·ly
au·to·er″o·tism′
au″to·fo″cus
au·tog″e·nous
au·to·gi″ro
  (*pl.* au″to·gi″ros)
au″to·graph′
au″to·harp′
au·to·hyp·no″sis
au″to·in·tox′i·ca″tion
au·tol″o·gous
au″to·mat′
au″to·mate′
  au″to·mat·ed
  au″to·mat·ing
au·to·mat″ic
au″to·mat″i·cal·ly
au·to·ma″tion
au·tom″a·tism
au·tom″a·ton′
au″to·mo·bile″
au″to·mo″tive
au″to·nom″ic

au·ton″o·mous
au·ton″o·my
  (*pl.* au·ton″o·mies)
au″to·pi′lot
au″to·plas′ty
au·to·stra″da
au″top·sy
  (*pl.* au″top·sies)
au·to·sug·ges″tion
au″tumn
au·tum″nal
aux·il″ia·ry
  (*pl.* aux·il″ia·ries)
aux″in
a·vail″
a·vail′a·bil″i·ty
  (*pl.* a·vail′a·bil″i·
  ties)
a·vail″a·ble
av″a·lanche
a·vant-garde″
av″a·rice
av·a·ri″cious
a·vast″
av′a·tar″
a″ve Ma·ri″a
a·venge″
a·veng″er
a·veng″ing
av″e·nue
a·ver″
  a·verred″
  a·ver″ring
av″er·age
av″er·ag·ing
a·verse″
  opposed (*see:* ad-
  verse)
a·ver″sion
a·vert″
a″vi·an
a″vi·ar′y
  (*pl.* a″vi·ar′ies)
a·vi·a″tion
a″vi·a·tor
a″vi·a″trix

  (*pl.* a′vi·a″tri·
  ces′)
av″id
a·vid″i·ty
a′vi·on″ics
a·vi·ta·min·o″sis
av·o·ca″do
  (*pl.* av′o·ca″dos)
av·o·ca″tion
av″o·cet′
a·void″
  keep away (*see:*
  ovoid)
a·void″a·ble
a·void″ance
av·oir·du·pois″
a·vouch″
a·vow″
a·vow″al
a·vowed″
a·vun″cu·lar
aw
  exclamation (*see:*
  awe)
a·wait″
a·wake″
a·wak″en
a·wak″ing
a·ward″
a·ware″
a·ware″ness
a·wash″
a·way″
  apart (*see:* aweigh)
awe
  respect (*see:* aw)
a·weigh″
  raised (*see:* away)
awe″some
awe″-strick′en
awe″-struck′
aw″ful
  bad (*see:* offal)
aw″ful·ly
a·while″
a·whirl″

aw″ing
awk″ward
awl
   pointed tool (*see:*
   all)
aw″less
awn
awn″ing
a·woke″
A.W.O.L.
a·wry″
ax
  axed
ax″ing
ax″i·al
ax·il″la
ax″i·om
ax·i·o·mat″ic
ax·i·o·mat″i·cal·ly
ax″is
  (*pl.* ax″es)
ax″le
ax″le·tree′
ax″o·lotl′
ax″on
a′ya·tol″lah
aye
  yes (*see:* eye)
aye″-aye′
a·zal″ea
A·za″ni·an
az″i·muth
az″ure

B

baa
  baaed
  baaing
Ba″al
ba″ba
ba″ba·au·rhum′
Bab″bitt
bab″ble
  bab″bled
  bab″bling

babe
Ba″bel
bab″ka
ba·boon″
ba·bush″ka
ba″by
  ba″bied
  ba″by·ing
  (*pl.* ba″bies)
ba″by's-breath′
ba″by-sit′
ba″by-sat
ba″by-sit′ting
ba″by sit′ter
bac′ca·lau″re·ate
bac″ca·rat′
bac″cha·nal″
bac″cha·na″li·a
bach″e·lor
bach″e·lor's-but′ton
ba·cil″lus
  (*pl.* ba·cil″li)
back
back″ache′
back″beat′
back″bend′
back″bite′
  back″bit′
  back″bit′ing
back″bit′er
back″board′
back″bone′
back″break′ing
back″burn′er
back″court′
back″draft′
back″drop′
back″er
back″field′
back″fill′
back″fire′
  back″fired′
  back″fir′ing
back″for·ma″tion
back″gam′mon
back″ground′

back″hand′
back″hand′ed
back″hoe′
back″ing
back″lash′
back″light′
back″log′
back″pack′
back″rest′
back″saw′
back″side′
back″slap′per
back″slide′
  back″slid′
  back″slid′den
  back″slid′ing
back″slid′er
back″space′
  back″spaced′
  back″spacing
back″spin′
back″stage′
back″stairs′
back″stay′
back″stitch′
back″stop′
back″stretch′
back″stroke′
  back″stroked′
  back″strok′ing
back″swept′
back″swing′
back″talk′
back″track′
back″up′, *n., adj.*
  alternate; support
back′up″, *v.*
  go backwards
back″ward
back″wash′
back″wa′ter
back″wrap′
back″woods″
back′woods″man
  (*pl.* back′woods″
  men″)

ba″con
bac·te″ri·a
  (*sing.* bac·te″ri·um)
bac·te″ri·al
bac·te″ri·cid″al
bac·te″ri·cide″
bac·te″ri·o·log″i·cal
bac·te″ri·ol″o·gist
bac·te″ri·ol″o·gy
bad
  worse
  worst
  not good (*see:* bade)
bade
  did bid (*see:* bad)
badge
  badged
  badg″ing
badg″er
bad′i·nage″
  bad′i·naged″
  bad′i·nag″ing
bad″lands′
bad″ly
bad″man′
  (*pl.* bad″men′)
bad″min·ton
bad″mouth′
bad″-tem′pered
Baf″fin
baf″fle
  baf″fled
  baf″fling
bag
  bagged
  bag″ging
ba·gasse″
bag′a·telle″
ba″gel
bag″ful′
  (*pl.* bag″fuls)
bag″gage
bag″ger
bag″gi·er
bag″gi·est
bag″gy

Bagh″dad
bag″man
  (*pl.* bag″men)
bagn″i·o
bag″pipe
ba·guette″
bag″worm′
Ba·ha′i″
Ba·ha″ma
Bah·rain″
baht
bail
  money; empty of wa-
  ter
bai″ley
bail″iff
bail″i·wick
bail″out
bails″man
  (*pl.* bails″men)
bait
  lure (*see:* bate)
baize
  baized
  baiz″ing
bake
  baked
  bak″ing
Ba″ke·lite™
bak″er
bak″er's doz″en
bak″er·y
  (*pl.* bak″er·ies)
ba″kla·va′
bak″sheesh
bal′a·lai″ka
bal″ance
bal″anc·ing
bal″co·ny
  (*pl.* bal″co·nies)
bald
bal″der·dash
bald″head′ed
bald″pate
bal″dric
bale

baled
bal″ing
  bun″dle (*see:* bail)
ba·leen″
bale″ful
ba″li
balk
Bal″kan
balk″i·er
balk″i·est
balk″line
balk″y
ball
  sphere (*see:* bawl)
bal″lad
bal·lade″
bal″lad·eer″
ball″-and-sock″et
bal″last
ball″bear″ing
bal·le·ri″na
bal·let″
bal·lis″tics
bal·loon″
bal·loon″ist
bal″lot
bal″lot·ing
ball″park
ball″peen″
ball″player
ball″point
ball″room
bal″ly·hoo
  bal″ly·hooed
  bal″ly·hoo′ing
balm
balm″i·er
balm″i·est
balm″y
ba·lo″ney
bal″sa
bal″sam
Bal″ti·more
bal″us·ter
bal″us·trade
bam·boo″

(*pl.* bam·boos″)
bam·boo″zle
  bam·boo″zled
  bam·boo″zling
ban
ba″nal
ba·nal″i·ty
  (*pl.* ba·nal″i·ties)
ba·nan″a
band
  musicians; strip
band″age
Band″-Aid™
ban·dan″na
band″box
ban·deau″
ban·deaux″
ban″de·role
ban″died
ban″dit
band″mas′ter
ban′do·leer″
band″saw′
band″stand′
band″wag′on
ban″dy
  ban″died
  ban″dy·ing
ban″dy-leg′ged
bane″ful
Banff
Bang″kok
Ban′gla·desh‴
ban″gle
bang″-up′
ban″ish
ban″is·ter
ban″jo
bank″a·ble
bank″book′
bank″ card″
bank″er
bank″note′
bank″roll′
bank″rupt
bank″rupt·cy

(*pl.* bank″rupt·cies)
banned
  prohibited (*see:*
  band)
ban″ner
ban″ning
banns
ban″quet
ban″quet·ing
ban·quette″
ban″shee
ban″tam·weight′
ban″ter
ban″yan
ban·zai″
bap″tism
bap″tist
bap″tis·ter·y
bap·tize″
  bap·tized″
  bap·tiz″ing
barb
bar·ba″dos
bar·bar″i·an
bar·bar″ic
bar″ba·rism′
bar·bar″i·ty
bar″ba·rous
bar″be·cue′
bar″be·cu′ing
barbed wire″
bar″bell′
bar″ber
bar″ber·shop′
bar″bi·can
bar′bi·tal″
bar·bi″tu·rate′
barb″wire″
bar′ca·role′
Bar′ce·lo″na
bard
  poet (*see:* barred)
bare
  bared
  bar″ing

uncovered (*see:*
  bear)
bare″back′
bare″faced″
bare″foot′
bare″hand′ed
bare″head′ed
bare″knuck″le
bare″leg′ged
bare″ly
bar″er
bar″est
bar″fly
  (*pl.* bar″flies′)
bar″gain
barge
  barged
  barg″ing
bar″ graph′
bar″ hop′
bar″i·tone′
bar″i·um
bark
bar″keep′er
bar″ken·tine′
bark″er
bar″ley
bar″ley·corn′
bar″maid′
bar″man
  (*pl.* bar″men)
bar mitz″vah
bar″na·cle
barn″dance′
barn″storm′
barn″yard′
bar″o·graph′
ba·rom″e·ter
bar′o·met″ric
bar′o·met″ri·cal
bar″on
  nobleman (*see:* bar-
  ren)
bar″on·ess
bar″on·et
ba·ro″ni·al

ba·roque''
ba·rouche''
bar''racks
bar'ra·cu''da
  (*pl.* bar'ra·cu''da)
bar·rage''
 bar·raged''
 bar·rag''ing
barred
  excluded (*see:* bard
  and bared)
bar''rel
 bar''reled
 bar''rel·ing
bar''rel-chest'ed
bar'ren
  profitless (*see:*
  baron)
bar''ren·ness
bar·rette''
bar''ri·cade'
 bar''ri·cad'ed
 bar''ri·cad'ing
bar''ri·er
bar''ring
  excluding (*see:* bar
  ing)
bar''ri·o
  (*pl.* bar''ri·os)
bar''ris·ter
bar''room'
bar''row
bar''ten'der
bar''ter
ba''sal
ba·salt''
bas''cule
base
 based
 basing
  stand; contemptible
  (*see:* bass)
base''ball'
base''board'
base'' hit''
base''less

base'' line'
base''ly
base''man
  (*pl.* base''men)
base''ment
base''ness
bas''er
bas''est
bash
bash''ful
ba''si·cal·ly
bas''il
ba·sil''i·ca
bas''i·lisk'
ba''sin
ba''sis
  (*pl.* ba''ses)
bas''ket
bas''ket·ball'
bas''ket·ful
  (*pl.* bas''ket·fuls)
bas''ket·ry
bas''ket·work'
has'-re·lief''
bass
  singer (*see:* base)
bass
  fish (*see:* bass)
bass'' clef'
bass'' drum'
bas''set
bas'si·net''
bas''so
  (*pl.* bas''sos)
bas·soon''
bas·soon''ist
bas''so pro·fun''do
bass''wood'
bas''tard
bas''tard·ize
baste
 bast''ed
 bast''ing
bas''tion
bat
 bat''ted

bat''ting
Ba·taan''
batch
bate
 bat''ed
 bat''ing
  lessen (*see:* bait)
ba·teau''
  (*pl.* ba·teaux'')
bath
bathe
 bathed
 bath''ing
bath''er
ba·thet''ic
bath'i·nette''
bath''ing suit
ba''thos
bath''robe
bath''room
bath''tub
bath''y·scape'
bath''y·sphere
ba·tik''
ba·tiste''
ba·ton''
Bat''on Rouge''
bat·tal''ion
bat''ten
bat''ter
bat''ter·ing ram'
bat''ter·y
  (*pl.* bat''ter·ies)
bat''ti·er
bat''ti·est
bat''tle
 bat''tled
 bat''tling
bat''tle-ax'
bat''tle cry'
bat''tle·dore'
bat''tle·field'
bat''tle·front'
bat''tle jack'et
bat''tle line'
bat''tle·ment

bat"tle-scarred'
bat"tle·ship'
bat"ty
bau"ble
baud
baux"ite
Ba·var"i·a
bawd"i·er
bawd"i·est
bawd"i·ness
bawd"y
bawl
  yell (*see:* ball)
bay
bay"ber'ry
  (*pl.* bay"ber'
  ries")
bay" lea'"
bay"o·net
bay"ou
  (*pl.* bay"ous)
bay"rum"
ba·zaar"
  sales place (*see:* bi-
  zarre)
ba·zoo"ka
be
  exist (*see:* bee)
beach
  shore (*see:* beech)
beach"ball'
beach"boy'
beach" bug'gy
beach"comb'er
bea"con
bead
bead"i·er
bead"i·est
bead"ing
bea"dle
bead"work
bead"y
bea"gle
beak
beak"er
beam

bean
  plant (*see:* been)
bean"bag
bean"ball
bean"ie
bean"pole
bean"stalk
bear
  carry; animal (*see:*
  bar)
bear"a·ble
beard"ed
bear"er
bear"hug
bear"ing
bear"ish
bear"skin
beast"li·er
beast"li·est
beast"ly
beat
  beat"en
  hit (*see:* beet)
beat"er
be·a·tif"ic
be·at'i·fi·ca"tion
be·at"i·fy
be·at"i·fied
be·at"i·fy'ing
beat"ing
be·at"i·tude
beat"nik
beat"-up"
beau
  suitor (*pl.* beaus *or*
  beaux) (*see:* bow)
Beau"fort
beau monde"
beau"te·ous
beau·ti"cian
beau'ti·fi·ca"tion
beau"ti·fied
beau"ti·ful
beau"ti·ful·ly
beau"ti·fy
  beau"ti·fied

beau"ti·fy'ing
beau"ty
  (*pl.* beau"ties)
bea"ver
be·calm"
be·came"
be·cause"
be·cha"mel'
beck
beck"on
be·cloud"
be·come"
  be·came"
  be·com"ing
bed
  bed"ded
  bed"ding
be·daub"
be·daz"zle
be·daz"zled
be·daz"zling
bed"board'
bed"bug'
bed"cham'ber
bed"check'
bed"clothes'
be·deck"
be·dev"il
  be·dev"iled
  be·dev"il·ing
bed"fel'low
bed"frame'
be·di"zen
be·dew"
bed"lam
Bed"ou·in
bed"pan'
bed"post'
be·drag"gle
be·drag"gling
bed"rail'
bed"roll'
bed"rid'den
bed"rock'
bed"room'
bed"side'

bed"sore'
bed"spread'
bed"stead'
bed"time'
bee
　insect (*see:* be)
beech
　tree (*see:* beach)
beech"nut'
beef
　(*pl.* beefs)
beef"a·lo
beef"burg'er
beef"eat'er
beef"steak'
bee"hive'
bee"keep'er
bee"line'
been
　exist (*see:* bean)
beep"er
beer
　drink (*see:* bier)
beer" gar'den
Beer·she"ba
bees"wax'
beet
　plant (*see:* beat)
bee"tle
　bee"tled
　bee"tling
be·fall"
　be·fell"
　be·fall"en
　be·fall"ing
be·fit"
　be·fit"ted
　be·fit"ting
be·fog"
　be·fogged"
　be·fog"ging
be·fore"
be·fore"hand'
be·foul"
be·friend"
be·fud"dle

be·fud"dled
be·fud"dling
beg
begged
beg"ging
be·get"
　be·gat"
begot"ten
　be·get"ting
be·get"ter
beg"gar
be·gin"
　be·gan"
　be·gin"ning
　be·gin"ner
be·gone"
be·gon"ia
be·gor"ra
be·grime"
be·grudge"
be·guile"
　be·guiled"
　be·guil"ing
be·guine"
be"gum
be·half"
be·have"
　be·hav"ing
　be·hav"ior
　be·hav"ior·al
　be·hav"ior·ism'
be·head"
be·held"
be·he"moth
be·hest"
be·hind"
be·hind"hand'
be·hold"
　be·held"
　be·hold"en
　be·hold"ing
be·hoove"
　be·hooved"
　be·hoov"ing
beige
be"ing

Bei"jing"
Bei·rut"
be·jew"eled
be·la"bor
be·lat"ed
be·lay"
bel"can"to
belch
be·lea"guer
Bel"fast
bel"fry
　(*pl.* bel"fries)
Bel"gium
Bel"grade'
be·lie"
　be·lied"
　be·ly"ing
　proved as false (*see:* bellied)
be·lief"
bc·liev"a·ble
be·lieve"
be·liev"er
be·liev"ing
be·lit"tle
　be·lit"tled
　be·lit"tling
Be·lize"
bell
　instrument (*see:* belle)
bel'la·don"na
bell"-bot'tom
bell"boy'
bell" buoy
belle
　woman (*see:* bell)
belles-let"tres
bell"hop'
bel"li·cose'
bel'li·cos"i·ty
bel"lied
　bulged (*see:* belied)
bel·lig"er·ence
bel·lig"er·en·cy
bel·lig"er·ent

bell″-ly″ra
bell″man
  (*pl.* bell″men)
bel″low
bel″lows
bell″weth′er
bell″wort
bel″ly
  (*pl.* bel″lies)
bel″ly·ache′
  bel″ly·ached′
  bel″ly·ach″ing
bel″ly·but′ton
bel″ly dance′
bel″ly flop′
bel″ly·ing
bel″ly laugh
be·long″
be·lov″ed
be·low″
belt
  belt″ed
  belt″ing
belt″way
belt″way′ ban″dit
be·lu″ga
bel″ve·dere′
bel″ly·ing
be″ma
  (*pl.* be″ma·ta)
be·mire″
  be·mired″
  be·mir″ing
be·moan″
be·muse″
  be·mused″
  be·mus″ing
Ben″a·dryl™
bench″ war″rant
bend
  bent
  bend″ing
be·neath″
ben″e·dict
ben′e·dic″tine
ben′e·dic″tion

ben″e·fac″tion
ben″e·fac″tor
ben″e·fac″tress
ben″e·fice
ben″e·ficed
be·ne″fi·cence
be·ne″fi·cent
ben′e·fi″cial
ben′e·fi″ci·ar′y
  (*pl.* ben′e·fi″ci·ar′
  ies
ben″e·fic·ing
ben″e·fit
  ben″e·fit·ed
  ben″e·fit·ing
ben″ga·line
be·nev″o·lence
be·nev″o·lent
Ben·gal″
be·night″ed
be·nign″
be·nig″ni·ty
ben″i·son
ben″ny
ben″thic
ben″thos
ben″ton·ite
bent″wood
be·numb″
benz″am·ide
Ben″ze·drine™
ben″zene
ben″zo·caine′
ben″zol
ben″zyl
be·queath″
be·quest″
be·rate″
  be·rat″ed
  be·rat″ing
Ber″ber
ber·ceuse″
be·reave″
be·reave″ment
be·ret″
berg

ben″e·fac″tion
ber″ga·mot
ber″i·ber″i
Ber″ing
berke″li·um
Ber·lin″
berm
Ber·mu″da
Bern
ber″ried
  bearing berries (*see:*
  buried)
ber″ry
  fruit (*pl.* ber″ries)
  (*see:* bury)
ber″ry·ing
  picking berries (*see:*
  burying)
ber·serk″
berth
  bed (*see:* birth)
ber″yl
be·ryl″li·um
be·seech″
be·sought
be·seech″ing
be·seem″
be·set″
  be·set″ting
be·side
be·sides″
be·siege″
  be·sieged″
  be·sieg″ing
be·smear″
be·smirch″
be·som′
be·sot″
  make silly (*see:* be-
  sought)
be·sought″
  requested (*see:* be-
  sot)
be·span″gle
  be·span″gled
  be·span″gling
be·spat″ter

be·speak″
be·spec″ta·cled
be·spread″
be·sprin″kle
best
bes″tial
bes′ti·al″i·ty
  (*pl.* bes ti·al″i·ties)
be·stir″
 be·stirred″
 be·stir″ring
best″ man″
be·stow″
be·strew″
be·stride″
best″ sell″er
best″-sell″ing
bet
be″ta
be·take″
be″ta·tron
be″tel
Be″tel·geuse
bête noir″
beth″el
be·think″
Beth″le·hem
be·tide″
be·times″
be·to″ken
bet″o·ny
be·tray″
be·tray″al
be·troth″
be·troth″al
betted
bet″ter
 greater (*see:* bettor)
bet″ter·ment
bet″ting
bet″tor
 one who bets (*see:* better)
be·tween″
be·twixt″
beurre′ noir″

bev″a·tron
bev″el
 bev″eled
 bev″el·ing
bev″er·age
bev″y
 (*pl.* bev″ies)
be·wail″
be·ware″
be·war″ing
be·whisk″ered
be·wil″der
be·witch
bey
be·yond″
be·zant″
bez″el
bhang
Bhu·tan″
bi·a″ly
bi·an″nu·al
 twice a year (*see:* bi-ennial)
bi·an″nu·al·ly
bi″as
 bi″ascd
 bi″as·ing
bi·ath″lon
bib
bib″cock
bi″be·lot
Bi″ble Belt
bib″li·cal
bib′li·og″ra·pher
bib′li·o·graph″ic
bib′li·og″ra·phy
 (*pl.* bib′li·og‴ra·phies)
bib′li·op″e·gy
bib′li·o·phile
bib″u·lous
bi·cam″er·al
bi·car″bon·ate′
bi·cen·te″na·ry
 (*pl.* bi·cen·te″na·ries)

bi·cen·ten″ni·al
bi″ceps
bi·chlo″ride
bi·cip″i·tal′
bick″er
bi″col′or
bi·con″cave
bi·con″vex
bi·cor″po·ral
bi·cus″pid
bi″cy·cle
 bi″cy·cled
 bi″cy·cling
 bi″cy·clist
bid
 bade *or* bad *or* bid
 bid″den
 bidding
 offer (*see:* bide)
bid″der
bid″dy
 (*pl.* bid″dies)
bide
 wait (*see:* bid)
bi·det″
bi′di′a·lect″tal
bi′dir·ec″tion·al
bield
bi·en″ni·al
 every other year
bi·en″ni·al·ly
bier
 coffin support (*see:* beer)
biff
bi·fi″lar
bi·fo″cal
bi″fur·cate′
 bi″fur·cat′ed
 bi″fur·cat′ing
bi′fur·ca″tion
big
big″a·mist
big″a·mous
big″a·my
 (*pl.* big″a·mies)

big″ger
big″gest
big″gie
big″-heart″ed
big″horn′
bight
  loop (*see:* bite)
big″ot·ed
big″ot·ry
  (*pl.* big″ot·ries)
big″shot′
big″wig″
bike
  biked
  bik″ing
bi·ki″ni
bi·la″bi·al
bi·lat″er·al
bi·lat″er·al·ly
bile
bilge
bilge″ wa′ter
bi·lin″gual
bi·lin″gual·ism
bil″ious
bilk
bill
  billed
  bill″ing
bill″board′
bil″let
bil″let-doux″
bill″fold′
bill″head″
bil″liard
bil″liards
bil″lings·gate′
bil″lion
bil″lion·aire″
bil″lionth
bil″low
bil″low·y
bil″ly goat′
bi″mah
bi·me′tal″lic
bi·met″al·lism′

bi·month″ly
bin
bin·au″ral
bi″na·ry
bind
  bound
  bind″ing
bind″er
bind″er·y
  (*pl.* bind″er·ies)
bind″weed′
binge
bin″go
bin″na·cle
binned
bin·oc″u·lar
bi·no″mi·al
bi′o·as′tro·nau″tics
bi′o·chem″i·cal
bi′o·chem″ist
bi′o·chem″is·try
bi′o·gen″e·sis
bi′o·de·grad″a·ble
bi′o·e·col″o·gy
bi′o·en′gi·neer″ing
bi′o·feed″back′
bi′o·ge·og″ra·phy
bi·og″ra·pher
bi′o·graph″ic
bi·og″ra·phy
  (*pl.* bi·og″ra·phies)
bi′o·log″ic
bi′o·log″i·cal
bi·ol″o·gist
bi·ol″o·gy
bi′o·lu′mi·nes″cence
bi″o-mass′
bi′o·met″rics
bi·on″ic
bi′o·phys″ics
bi″op·sy
  (*pl.* bi″op·sies)
bi′o·re″gion
bi″o·rhythm
bi′o·sci″ence
bi″o·sphere′

bi′o·tech·nol″o·gy
bi′o·te·lem″e·try
bi·ot″ic
bi″o·tin
bi″o·tite′
bi′o·tox″in
bi·par″ti·san
bi·par″tite′
bi·par·ti″tion
bi″ped
bi″plane′
bi″pod′
bi·po″lar
bi·ra″cial
birch
birch″ beer′
bird
bird″bath′
bird″brain′
bird″cage′
bird″call′
bird″ dog′
bird″house′
bird″life′
bird″man′
  (*pl.* bird″men′)
bird″seed′
bird's″-eye′
bi″reme
bi·ret″ta
birl
birr
birth
  being born (*see:*
  berth)
birth″day′
birth″mark′
birth″place′
birth″rate′
birth″right′
birth″stone′
bis″cuit
bise
bi·sect″
bi·sec″tion
bi″sec′tor

bi·sex″u·al
bish″op
bish″op·ric
bis″muth
bi″son
  (*pl.* bi″son)
bisque
bis″ter
bis″tro
bit
  small piece; horse's
  mouthpiece (*see:*
  bite)
bitch
bitch″y
bite
  bit
  bitten
  eat into (*see:* bit)
bit″er
bit″ter
bit″tern
bit″ter·root′
bit″ters
bit″ter·sweet′
bi·tu″men
bi·tu″mi·nous
bi·va″lent
bi″valve′
biv″ou·ac′
  biv″ou·acked′
  biv″ou·ack′ing
bi·week″ly
  (*pl.* bi·week″lies)
bi·year″ly
bi·zarre″
  odd (*see:* bazaar)
blab
  blabbed
  blab″bing
blab″ber
blab″ber·mouth
black
black″-and-blue″
black″ball
black″ bass′

black″ belt
black″ber′ry
  (*pl.* black″ber′ries)
black″bird
black″board
black′bod′y
black″ book
black″damp′
black″en
black″ eye″
black″-eyed
black″face
Black″foot
  (*pl.* Black″feet)
black″ gold
black″guard
black″-heart′ed
black″head
black″ hole″
black″jack
black″leg′
black″ let′ter
black″list
black″mail
black″ mar″ket
black″out
black″ poll
black″smith
black″snake
black″thorn′
black″ tie″
black″top
black″ wid″ow
blad″der
blad″der worm
blad″der·wort′
blade
blah
blain
blam″a·ble
blame
  blamed
  blam″ing
blame″less
blame″wor′thy
blanc′fixe′

blanch
blanc·mange″
bland
blan″dish
blan″dish·ment
bland″ly
blank
blan″ket
blank″e·ty-blank″
blank″ly
blare
  blared
  blar″ing
blar″ney
bla·sé″
blas·pheme″
  blas·phemed″
  blas·phem″ing
blas″phe·mous
blas″phe·my
blast
  blast″ed
  blast″ing
blas·te″ma
blas″tu·la
blast″-off
bla″tan·cy
  (*pl.* bla″tan·cies)
bla″tant
blath″er
blath″er·skite′
blaze
  blazed
  blaz″ing
blaz″er
bla″zon
bla″zon·ry
bleach
bleach″ers
bleak
bleak″ly
blear″i·er
blear″i·est
blear″i·ness
blear″y
bleat

bleed
 bled
 bleed"ing
bleed"er
bleed"ing heart"
blem"ish
blench
blend
 blend"ed
 blend"ing
blend"er
bleph'a·ri"tis
bless
 bless"ed
 blest
 bless"ing
blew
  did blow (*see:* blue)
blight
blimp
blind" date"
blind"fold
blind"man's buff"
blind" spot
blink
blink"er
blintz
blip
bliss"ful
bliss"ful·ly
blis"ter
blithe
blithe"some
blitz"krieg
bliz"zard
bloat
bloat"er
blob
bloc
  group (*see:* block)
block
  thick; short (*see:* bloc)
block·ade"
 block·ad"ed
 block·ad"ing

block·ade"-run'ner
block"age
block"bust'er
block"head'
block" house'
bloke
blond
  or blonde
blood
blood"bank'
blood"bath
blood"cur'dling
blood"ed
blood"hound'
blood"ied
blood"i·er
blood"i·est
blood"less
blood"let'ting
blood"mo·bile'
blood" pres'sure
blood"root'
blood"shed'
blood"shot'
blood"stain'
blood"stone'
blood"stream'
blood"suck'er
blood"thirst'y
blood"worm
blood"y
blood"y·ing
bloom
bloom"ers
bloop"er
blos"som
blot
 blot"ted
 blot"ting
blotch"i·er
blotch"i·est
blotch"y
blot"ter
blot"to
blouse
blou"son'

blow
 blew
 blown
 blowing
blow"fish
blow"gun'
blow"hole'
blow"off'
blow"out'
blow"pipe'
blow"torch'
blow"up'
blow"y
blowz"i·er
blowz"i·est
blowz"y
blub"ber
blu"cher
bludg"eon
blue
  color (*see:* blew)
blue"bell'
blue"bon'net
blue"ber'ry
  (*pl.* blue"ber'ries)
blue"bird'
blue"blood'
blue"book'
blue"bot'tle
blue" chip"
blued
blue"fin'
blue"fish'
blue"grass'
blue"jack'et
blue"jay'
blue"jeans'
blue"nose'
blue"-pen"cil
blue"point'
blue"print'
blu"er
blues
blu"est
blue"stock'ing

blue"stone'
blue"tongue
blu"ets
blu"ey
bluff
bluff"er
blu"ing
blu"ish
blun"der
blun"der·buss'
blunt
blunt"ly
blur
  blurred
  blur"ring
blurb
blur"ry
blurt
blush
blush"er
blus"ter
blus"ter·y
bo"a
boar
  animal (*see:* bore)
board
  wood; meals; go
  onto
board"er
  lodger (*see:* border)
board"ing·house'
board"walk'
boast"ful
boast"ful·ly
boat
boat"el
boat"er
boat" hook
boat"house
boat"load
boat"man
  (*pl.* boat"men)
boat"swain
boat"yard
bob
  bobbed

bob"bing
bob"bin
bob"ble
bob"bled
bob"bling
bob"by
bob"by pin
bob"by·socks'
bob"by·sox'er
bob"cat
bob"o·link
bob"sled
bob"tail
bob"white"
boc"cie
bock"beer'
bode
bo·de"ga
bod"ice
bod"i·less
bod"i·ly
bod"ing
bod"kin
bod"y
  (*pl.* bod"ies)
bod"y·guard'
bof"fo
bog
  bogged
  bog"ging
bo"gey
  golf score (*see:* bogy
  and boggy)
bo"gey·man
  (*pl.* bog"ey·men)
bog"gy
  wet ground (*see:*
  bogy)
Bo·go·ta"
bo"gus
bo"gy
  evil spirit (*pl.* bo"
  gies) (*see:* bogey
  and boggy)
boil
boil"er

boil"er·mak'er
Boi"se
bois"ter·ous
bo"la
bold"er
  more bold (see:
  boulder)
bold"face'
  bold"faced'
  bold"fac'ing
bold"ly
bole
  tree trunk (*see:* boll
  and bowl)
bo·le"ro
Bo"li"var
Bo·liv"i·a
boll
  seed pod (*see:* bole
  and bowl)
bol"lix
bo·lo"gna
Bol"she·vik
bol"ster
bolt
bol"ter'
bo"lus
bomb
bom·bard", *v.*
bom"bard, *n.*
bom'bar·dier"
bom"bast
bom·bas"tic
Bom·bay"
bom'ba·zine"
bom·be"
bomb"er
bomb"load'
bomb"proof'
bomb"shell'
bomb"shel'ter
bomb"sight'
bo"na fide'
bo·nan"za
bon"bon'
bond

bond"age
bond"hold'er
bonds"man
bond" ser"vant
bone
bone" ash'
bone"black'
bone" chi"na
bone"-dry"
bon"er
bone"fish'
bone"head'
bone" meal'
bon"fire'
bon"go
bon'ho·mie"
bo·ni"to
bon" mot'
Bonn
bon"net
bon"ni·er
bon"ni·est
bon"ny
  handsome; pretty
  (*see:* bony)
bon'ny·clab"ber
bon"sai"
bo"nus
  (*pl.* bo"nus·es)
bon vi·vant"
bon' voy·age"
bon"y
  with bones (*see:*
  bonny)
boo
boob
boo"-boo'
  (*pl.* boo"-boos')
boo"by
boo"by prize'
boo"by trap'
boo"dle
boog'ie-woog"ie
boo'hoo"
  boo'hooed
  boo'hoo"ing

book
book"bind'er·y
book"bind'ing
book"case'
book"club'
book"end'
book"ie
book"ing
book"ish
book" jack'et
book"keep'er
book"keep'ing
book"let
book"mak'er
book"mark'
book"mo·bile'
book"plate
book"rack'
book"sell"er
book"shelf'
book"stall'
book"store'
book"worm'
Bool"e·an
boom
boom"er·ang'
boom"let
boom"town"
boon
boon"docks'
boon"dog'gle
  boon"dog'gled
  boon"dog'gling
boor
boor"ish
boost"er
boost"er·ism
boot
boot"black'
boot" camp'
boo"tie
  baby's shoe (see:
  booty)
boot"er·y
booth
boot"jack'

boot"leg'
  boot"legged
  boot"leg'ging
boot"leg'ger
boot"lick"
boo"ty
  plunder (*see:* boo"
  ties)
booze
booz"er
booz"ing
bop
bor"age
bo"rate'
bo"rat'ed
bo"rat'ing
bo"rax
Bor·deaux"
bor·del"lo
  (*pl.* bor·del"los)
bor"der
  edge (*see:* boarder)
bor"der·land'
bor"der·line'
bore
  drill; did bear (see
  boar)
bo"re·al
bored
  uninterested; dug
  (*see:* board)
bore"dom
bo·reen"
bore"hole
bo"ric
bo"ride
bor"ing
born
  brought into life
  (*see:* borne)
born"-a·gain'
borne
  did bear (*see:* born)
Bor"ne·o
bo"ron
bor"ough

town (*see:* burrow
   and burro)
bor''row
borscht
Bor''stal
bor''zoi
bosh
bosk''y
bos''om
bos''om·y
boss
bos''sa no''va
boss''i·er
boss''i·est
boss''i·ness
boss''ism
boss''y
Bos''ton
bo''sun
bo·tan''ic
bo·tan''i·cal
bot''a·nist
bot''a·ny
botch
botch''er
bot''fly'
both
both''er
both''er·some
Bo·tswa''na
bot''tle
bot''tle·neck'
bot''tling
bot''tom
bot''tom·less
bot''tom line''
bot''tom·most'
bot''u·lin'
bot''u·lism'
bou·chee''
bou·cle''
bou''doir
bouf·fant''
bou'gain·vil''laea
bough

limb of tree (*see:*
   bow)
bought
bouil'la·baisse''
bouil''lon
   soup (*see:* bullion)
boule
boul''der
   rock (*see:* bolder)
boul''e·vard'
bou'le·vard·ier''
bounce
bounced
bounc''ing
bounc''er
bound
bound''a·ry
   (*pl.* bound''a·ries)
bound''en
bound''less
boun''te·ous
boun''ti·ful
boun''ti·ful·ly
boun''ty
   (*pl.* boun''ties)
bou·quet''
bour''bon
bour·geois''
bour·geoi·sie''
bourn
bour·ree''
bourse
bour''tree
bou'stro·phe''don
bouse
bout
bou·tique''
bou'ton·niere''
bou·zou''ki
bo''vid
bo''vine
bow
   bend forward;
   weapon (*see:* bough
   and beau)
bowd''ler·ize'

bow''el
bow''er
bow''er·y
bow''head'
bow''ie knife'
bowl
   container (*see:* bole
   and boll)
bow''leg'
bow''leg'ged
bowl''er
bow''line
bowl''ing
bow''man
bow''sprit
bow''string'
bow''tie''
bow''-wow'
box
boxed
box''ing
box''car'
box''el'der
box''er
box'' of'fice
box'' score
box''wood
boy
   young male (*see:*
   buoy)
boy''cott
boy''friend
boy''hood
boy''ish
boy''sen·ber'ry
   (*pl.* boy''sen·ber'
   ries)
bo''zo
brace
braced
brac''ing
brac''er
brace''let
bra·ce''ro
bra''chi·o·pod
brack''en

brack"et
brack"ish
bract
brad
brad"awl'
brae
brag
 bragged
 brag"ging
brag'ga·do'ci·o
brag"gart
brag"ger
Brah"ma
Brah"man
 Hindu priest; kind of
 bovine (see: Brah-
 min)
Brah"min
 cultured person (see:
 Brahman)
braid
 braid"ed
 braid"ing
brail
braille
brain
brain"child
brain"i·er
brain"i·est
brain"less
brain"storm
brain" trust
brain"wash
brain"y
braise
 cook (see: braze)
brake
 braked
 brak"ing
 slow down (see:
 break)
brake"man
 (pl. brake"men)
brake" shoe
bram"ble
bram"bly

bran
branch
branch" wa'ter
brand
bran"died
bran"dish
brand"-new
bran"dy
 (pl. bran"dies)
bran"died
bran"dy·ing
brash"ly
brass
Bra·si"lia
brass" hat"
brass"ie
brass"i·er
bras·siere"
brass"i·est
brass"y
brat
brat"ty'
brat"wurst
braun"schwei'ger
bra·va"do
brave
 braved
 brav"ing
 brave"ly
 brav"er·y
bra·vis"si·mo'
bra"vo
bra·vu"ra
braw
brawl
brawl"er
brawn
brawn"i·er
brawn"i·est
brawn"y
bray
bray"er
braze
 brazed
 braz"ing
 solder (see: braise)

bra"zen
bra"zen·ness
bra"zier
Bra·zil"
Bra·zil" nut
breach
 rift (see: breech)
bread
 food (see: bred)
bread"-and-but"ter
bread"bas'ket
bread"board
bread"fruit
breadth
 width (see: breath)
bread"win'ner
break
 broke
 broken
 break"ing
 fracture (see: brake)
break"a·ble
break"age
break" danc"ing
break"down
break"fast
break"-in'
break"neck'
break"out'
break"point'
break"through'
break"up'
break"wa'ter
bream
breast
breast"bone'
breast"plate
breast"stroke'
breast"work'
breath
 air (see: breadth)
Breath"a·lyzer™
breathe
 breathed
 breath"ing
breath"less

breath''tak'ing
breath''y
bred
  did breed (*see:* bread)
breech
  rear part (*see:* breach)
breech''block'
breech''cloth'
breech''es
breech''load'cr
breed
  bred
  breed''ing
breeze
breeze''way
breez''y
breth''ren
breve
bre·vet''
bre·vi·ar'y
  (*pl.* bre''vi·ar'ies)
brev''i·ty
brew
  brewed
  brew''ing
brew''er
brew''er·y
  (*pl.* brew''er·ies)
brew''house'
bri''ar
bribe
  bribed
  brib''ing
brib''er
brib''er·y
  (*pl.* brib''er·ies)
bric''-a-brac
brick
brick''lay·er
bride
brid''al
  wedding (*see:* bridle)
bride''groom
brides''maid

bridge
  bridged
  bridg''ing
bridge''a·ble
bridge''head
bridge''lamp'
bridge''ta''ble
bridge''town'
bridge''work'
bri''dle
  harness (*see:* bridal)
bri''dle path
brief
  briefed
  brief''ing
brief''case
bri''er
brig
bri·gade''
brig'a·dier''
brig''a·dier gen''er·al
  (*pl.* brig''a·dier gen''er·als)
brig''and
brig''an·tine'
bright''en
bright''ncss
brill
bril''liance
bril''lian·cy
bril''liant
bril''lian·tine'
brim
  brimmed
  brim''ming
brim''ful
brim''stone
brin''dle
brin''dled
brine
bring
  brought
  bring''ing
brin''ing
brink''man·ship
brin''y

bri''o
bri·oche''
bri·quette''
Bris''bane
bris''ket
brisk''ly
bris''ling
bris''tle
bris''tling
brist''ly
Brit''ain
britch''es
Brit''ish
Brit''ish Co·lum''bi·a
Brit''ish Isles''
Brit''ta·ny
brit''tle
broach
  to bring up (*see:* brooch)
broad
broad''ax
broad''band'
broad''cast'
broad''cast'er
broad''cloth'
broad''en
broad''jump'
broad''leaf'
  (*pl.* broad''leaves)
broad''loom'
broad''-mind'ed
broad''side
broad''sword
broad''tail'
Broad''way'
bro·cade''
broc''co·li
bro·chette''
bro·chure''
brock''et
bro''gan
brogue
broil
broil''er
broke

bro″ken
bro″ken·down″
bro″ken·heart″ed
bro″ker
bro″ker·age
bro″mic
bro″mide
bro″me·lain′
bro·me″li·ad
bro·mid″ic
bro″mine
bron″chi·al
bron″chi·ole′
bron·chi″tis
bron″cho·scope′
bron″chus
  (*pl.* bron″chi)
bron″co
bron″co·bust″er
bron″to·saur
Bronx
bronze
  bronzed
  bronz″ing
bronz″er
brooch
  pin (*see:* broach)
brood
brood″y
Brook″lyn
brook″ trout′
broom
broom″corn′
broom″stick′
broth
broth″el
broth″er·hood′
broth″er-in-law′
  (*pl.* broth″ers-in-
  law′)
broth″er·li·ness
brougham
brought
brou″ha·ha
brow
brow″beat′

brow″beat′en
brown
brown″ bear″
brown″ bet′ty
brown″ belt″
brown″ie
brown″out′
brown″stone′
browse
  browsed
  brows″ing
bru′cel·lo″sis
bru″in
bruise
  bruised
  bruis″ing
bruis″er
bruit
  rumor (*see:* brute)
brum″ma·gem
brunch
bru·net″
brunt
brush
brush″ fire′
brush″-off′
brush″up′
brush″wood′
brush″work′
brusque
Brus″sels sprout″
brut
  dry (*see:* brute and
  bruit)
bru″tal
bru·tal″i·ty
  (*pl.* bru·tal″i·ties)
bru″tal·ize
  bru″tal·ized
  bru″tal·iz·ing
brute
  beastlike (*see:* bruit)
brut″ish
bry″o·phyte′
bub″ble
  bub″bled

bub″bling
bub″ble gum′
bub″bly
bu″bo
  (*pl.* bu″boes)
bu·bon″ic
buc″ca·neer″
Bu″cha·rest′
Buch″en·wald′
buck
buck′a·roo″
  (*pl.* buck′a·roos″)
buck″board
buck″et
buck″et·ful
  (*pl.* buck″et·fuls)
buck″et seat
buck″eye
buck″ish
buck″le
  buck″led
  buck″ling
buck″ler
buck″ram
buck″saw′
buck″shot′
buck″skin′
buck″slip′
buck″ thorn″
buck″tooth″
  (*pl.* buck″teeth′)
buck″wheat′
bu·col″ic
bud
bud″ded
bud″ding
Bu″da·pest′
Bud″dha
Bud″dhism
Bud″dhist
bud″dy
  (*pl.* bud″dies)
budge
  budged
  budg″ing
budg″er·i·gar′

budg"et
budg"et·ar'y
budg"ie
Bue"nos Ai"res
buff
buf"fa·lo
  (*pl.* buf"fa·loes')
Buf"fa·lo
buff"er
buf"fet, *v.*
  hit
buf·fet", *n.*
  sideboard
  buf"fet·ed
  buf"fet·ing
buf"fo
buf·foon"
buf·foon"er·y
bug
  bugged
  bug"ging
bug"a·boo
bug"bear'
bug"eyed'
bug"gy
  (*pl.* bug"gies)
bu"gle
bu"gled
bu"gling
bu"gler
bu"gle·weed'
bu"gloss'
buhl
buhr"stone
build
  built
  build"ing
build"-up
built"-in
bul"bul
bulge
  bulged
  bulg"ing
bul"gur
bulg"y
bu·lim"i·a'

bulk"head
bulk" mail"
bulk"y
bul"la
bul"lace
bull"dog'
bull"doze'
bull"doz'er
bul"let
bul"le·tin
bull"let·proof'
bull"fight'
bull"finch'
bull"frog'
bull"head'ed
bull"horn'
bul"lied
bul"lion
  metal (*see:* bouillon)
bull"ish
bull"ock
bull"pen'
bull"ring'
bull"roar'er
bull's"-eye'
bull ter"ri'er
bull"whip'
bul"ly
  (*pl.* bul"lies)
bul"rush
bul"wark
bum
  bummed
  bum"ming
bum"ber·shoot'
bum"ble
bum"ble·bee
bum"boat'
bumf
bum"mer
bump
bump"er
bump"er guard
bump"er stick"er
bump"kin
bump"out'

bump"tious
bump"y
bun
bunch
bunch"ber·ry
bunch"y
bun"co
bun"combe
bun"dle
bung
bun"ga·low
bung"hole
bun"gle
bun"gling
bun"ion
bunk
bun"ker
Bun"ker Hill
bunk"house
bun"ko
bun"kum
bun"ny
  (*pl.* bun"nies)
Bun"sen burn"er
bunt
  bunt"ed
  bun"ting
bunt"line'
bur"bot
bur"den
buoy
  floating marker (*see:* boy)
buoy"an·cy
buoy"ant
bur
  seed capsule (*see:* burr)
bur"ble
bur"bled
bur"bling
bur"den·some
bur"dock
bu"reau
  (*pl.* bu"reaus)
bu·reauc"ra·cy

(*pl.* bu·reauc"ra·
cies)
bu'reau·crat'
bu'reau·crat"ic
bu·rette"
burg"
bur"gee
bur"bess
bur"geon
burg"er
bur'glar"i·ous
bur"glar·ize
bur"glar·iz'ing
bur"gla·ry
(*pl.* bur"gla·ries)
bur"goo
bur"gun·dy
bur"i·al
bur"ied
entombed (*see:* ber-
ried)
bu"rin
burke
burl
bur"lap
bur·lesque"
bur·lesqued"
bur·lesqu"ing
bur"ley
tobacco (*see:* burly)
bur"li·er
bur"li·est
bur"ling·ton
bur"ly
strong (*see:* burley)
Bur"ma
burn
burned
burn"ing
bur"nish
bur·noose"
burn"out'
burn"sides'
burp
burp"gun'
burr

rough edge; sound
(*see:* bur)
bur"ro
donkey (*see:* bor-
ough and burrow)
bur"row
hole (*see:* burro and
borough)
bur"sa
(*pl.* bur"sae)
bur"sar
bur·si"tis
burst
burst"ing
bu·run"di
bur"weed'
bur"y
bur"ied
bur"y·ing
entomb (*see:* berry)
bus
bused
bus"ing
vehicle (*pl.* bus"es)
(*see:* buss)
bus"boy
bus"by
(*pl.* bus"bies)
bush
bush"el
bush"el·ful
Bu"shi·do'
bush"i·er
bush"ing
bush"man
(*pl.* bush"men)
bush"mas'ter
bush"whack'
bush"whack'er
bush"y
bus"ied
bus"i·er
bus"i·est
bus"i·ly
busi"ness
busi"ness·like

busi"ness·man
(*pl.* busi"ness·men')
busi"ness·wom'an
(*pl.* busi"ness·wom'
en)
bus"ker
bus"kin
bus"man
(*pl.* bus"men)
buss
kiss (*see:* bus)
bus"tard
bus"tle
bus"tled
bus"tling
bu·sul"fan
bust
bust"er
bus"y
bus"y·bod'y
bus"y·ing
but
except (*see:* butt)
bu'ta·di"ene
bu"tane
bu"ta·nol'
butch"er
butch"er·y
(*pl.* butch"er·ies)
bu"te·o
but"ler
butt
end; target; join
(*see:* but)
butte
but"ter
but"ter-and-eggs"
but"ter·ball'
but"ter·cup'
but"ter·fat'
but"ter·fin'gered
but"ter·fish'
but"ter·fly'
(*pl.* but"ter·flies)
but"ter·milk'
but"ter·nut'

but"ter·scotch'
but"ter·y
butt"joint'
but"tock
but"ton
but"ton-down'
but"ton·hole'
but"ton·hook'
but"ton·wood'
but"tress
bu"tyl
bux"om
buy
  bought
  buy"ing
    purchase (see: by
      and bye)
buy"er
buzz
buz"zard
buzz"er
buzz"word
bwa"na
by
  close to (pl. byes)
    (see: buy and bye)
by"-and-by"
bye
  sports; something
    secondary (see: buy
    and by)
bye"-bye"
by'-e·lec"tion
by"gone'
by"law'
by"line'
by"path'
by"pass'
by"play'
by"-prod'uct
by"road'
byre
by"stand'er
by"street'
byte
by"way'

by"word'
Byz"an·tine'

C

cab
ca·bal"
ca"ba·la
ca·bal'le·"ro
ca·ban"a
cab'a·ret"
cab"bage
cab"by
cab"driver
cab"in
cab"in boy
cab"i·net
cab"i·net·mak"er
cab"i·net·work'
ca"ble
ca"ble·gram
ca"bling
ca·boo"dle
ca·boose"
cab'o·tage'
cab'ri·o·let'
ca·ca"o
cac'cia·to"re
cache
  hiding place (see:
    cash)
cached
ca·chet"
cach"ing
ca·cique"
cack"le
ca·coph"o·nous
ca·coph"o·ny
  (pl. ca·coph"o·nies)
cac"tus
  (pl. cac"tus·es)
CAD
  computer-aided de-
    sign
ca·dav"er

ca·dav"er·ic
ca·dav"er·ous
cad"die
  golf (see: caddy)
cad"dish
cad"dy
  container (see: cad-
    die)
  (pl. cad"dies)
cad"dy·ing
ca"dence
ca"dent
ca·den"za
ca·det"
cadge
  beg (see: cage)
cadg"ing
  begging (see: cag-
    ing)
cad"mi·um
ca"dre
ca·du"ce·us
  (pl. ca·du"ce·i)
Cae·sar"e·an
cae·su"ra
ca·fe"
ca"fe au lait"
cafe·te"ri·a
caf·feine"
caf"tan
cage
  caged
  cag"ing
    structure (see:
    cadge)
cage"work'
cag"i·er
cag"i·ness
cag"ing
  confining (see: cadg-
    ing)
cairn
Cai"ro
cais"son
cai"tiff
ca·jole"

ca·jol"er·y
ca·jol"ing
cake
  caked
  cak"ing
cake"walk'
cal"a·bar
cal"a·bash
cal"a·boose
ca·la"di·um
cal"a·mine
ca·lam"i·tous
ca·lam"i·ty
  (*pl.* ca·lam"i·ties)
ca·lash"
cal·car"e·ous
cal"ci·fi·ca"tion
cal"ci·fy
  cal"ci·fied
  cal"ci·fy'ing
cal"ci·mine
  cal"ci·mined
  cal"ci·min'ing
cal"cine
cal"cite
cal·cit"ic
cal"ci·pex'y
cal"ci·um
cal"cu·la·ble
cal"cu·late
  cal"cu·la'ted
  cal"cu·la'ting
cal·cu·la"tion
cal"cu·lator
cal"cu·lus
  (*pl.* cal"cu·li)
Cal·cut"ta
cal·de"ra
cal"dron
cal"en·dar
  schedule (*see:* calen-
    der and colander)
ˡ"en·dar'ic
  "en·der
  ʌchine (*see:* calen-
  ʌr and colander)

cal"ends
calf
  (*pl.* calves)
calf"skin
Cal"ga·ry
cal"i·ber
cal"i·brate
  cal"i·bra'ted
  cal"i·bra'ting
cal'i·bra"tion
cal"i·co
  (*pl.* cal"i·coes)
Cal'i·for"nia
cal'i·for"ni·um
cal"i·per
cal"i·pash'
cal"i·pee'
ca"liph
cal"iph·ate
cal·is·then"ics
call
  called
  call"ing
cal"la
call"a·ble
call"back
call" box
call"er
call" girl
cal·lig"ra·pher
cal"li·graph"ic
cal·lig"ra·phy
callʲ" in
cal·li"o·pe
cal'li·pyg"i·an
cal"lous
  insensitive (*see:* cal-
    lus)
cal"low
call"-up
cal"lus
  hard skin (*pl.* cal"
    lus·es) (*see:* cal-
    lous)
calm
calm"a·tive

calm"ly
cal"o·mel'
ca·lor"ic
cal"o·rie
cal'o·rim"e·ter
cal"u·met
ca·lum"ni·ate
  ca·lum"ni·at'ed
  ca·lum"ni·at'ing
ca·lum"ni·ous
cal"um·ny
  (*pl.* cal"um·nies)
cal"va·ri'al
Cal"va·ry
  crucifixion location
  (*see:* cavalry)
calve
  calved
  calv"ing
Cal"vin·ism
Cal"vin·ist
ca·lyp"so
ca"lyx
cal·zo"ne
CAM
  computer-aided man-
    ufacture
ca·ma·ra"de·rie
cam"ber
cam"bi·um
Cam·bo"di·a
Cam"bri·an
cam"bric
Cam"bridge
cam"cord·er
cam"el
ca·mel"lia
cam·el"o·pard'
Cam"e·lot'
Cam"em·bert'
cam"e·o
  (*pl.* cam"e·os)
cam"er·a
cam·er·a·lis"tics
cam"er·a·man'
  (*pl.* cam"er·a·men')

cam″er·a ob·scu″ra
Cam″e·roon′
cam″i·sole′
cam″o·mile′
cam″ou·flage′
  cam″ou·flaged′
  cam″ou·flag′ing
camp
  camped
  camp″ing
cam·paign″
cam·pa·ni″le
  (*pl.* cam·pa·ni″les)
camp″er
camp″fire′
camp″ fol′low·er
camp″ground′
cam″phor
cam″phor·at′ed
cam″phor ball′
cam·phor″ic
camp′o·ree″
camp″site′
camp″stool′
cam″pus
camp″y
çam″shaft′
can, *v.*
  canned
  can″ning
    be able to; preserve
    (*see:* cane)
Ca″naan
Can″a·da
ca·naille″
ca·nal″
ca·nal′i·za″tion
Ca·nal″ Zone′
can″a·pe
  appetizer (*see:* can-
  opy)
ca·nard″
ca·nar″y
  (*pl.* ca·nar″ies)
ca·nas″ta
Can″ber·ra

can″can′
can″cel
  can″celed
  can″cel·ing
can·cel·la″tion
can″cer
Can″cer
  zodiac sign
can″cer·ous
can·de″la
can′de·la″brum
  (*pl.* can·de·la″bra)
can″did
can″di·da·cy
can″di·date
can″died
can″dle
  cand″led
  cand″ling
can″dle·light
can″dle·pin
can″dle·pow′er
can″dle·stick
can″dle·wick
can″dor
can″dy
  (*pl.* can″dies)
can″dy·tuft
cane
  caned
  can″ing
cane″brake
caned
  flogged; made with
  cane (*see:* canned)
cane″ sugar
ca″nine
can″is·ter
can″ker
can″ker sore
can″ker·worm
can″na
can″nel
can″na·bis
can″ner·y
  (*pl.* can″ner·ies)

can″ni·bal
can″ni·bal·ism
can″ni·bal·ize
can″ni·bal·iz′ing
can″ni·er
can″ni·est
can″ni·ly
can″ni·ness
can″non
  gun (*pl.* can″non)
  (*see:* canon)
can″non·ade″
can″non·ad″ing
can″non·ball
can″not
can″ny
ca·noe″
can″on
  law; church official
  (*see:* cannon)
ca·non″i·cal
can·on·ic″i·ty
can″on·ize′
can″o·py
  can″o·pied
  can″o·py·ing
  roof like cover (*pl.*
  can″o·pies) (*see:*
  canape)
cant
  jargon (*see:* can't)
cannot
  (*see:* cant)
can·ta″bi·le′
can·ta·loupe′
can·tan″ker·ous
can·ta″ta
can·teen″
can″ter
  gallop (*see:* cantor)
Can″ter·bur′y
cant″hook
can″ti·cle
can″ti·le′ver
can·ti″na
can″to

(*pl.* can″tos)
can″ton
can·ton″ment
can″tor
  singer (*see:* canter)
can″vas
  cloth (*see:* canvass)
can″vas·back
can″vass
  solicit (*see:* canvas)
can″yon
caou·tchouc′
cap
 capped
 cap″ping
ca·pa·bil″i·ty
  (*pl.* ca′pa·bil″i·ties)
ca″pa·ble
ca″pa·bly
ca·pa″cious
ca·pac″i·tance
ca·pac″i·tate
ca·pac″i·tat′ing
ca·pac″i·tor
ca·pac″i·ty
  (*pl.* ca·pac″i·ties)
ca·par″i·son
cape
ca″per
Ca·per″na·um
Cape′ Horn″
Cape″ Town′
cap″ful
  (*pl.* cap″fuls)
cap″il·lar′y
  (*pl.* cap″il·lar′ies)
cap″i·tal
  city; wealth (*see:*
  capitol)
cap″i·tal·ism′
cap″i·tal·ist
cap″i·tal·is″tic
cap″i·tal·i·za″tion
cap″i·tal·ize′
 cap″i·tal·ized′
 cap″i·tal·iz′ing

cap′i·ta″tion
Cap″i·tol
  US congress building
cap″i·tol
  building (*see:* capi-
  tal)
ca·pit″u·late
 ca·pit″u·la″ted
 ca·pit″u·la″ting
ca·pit′u·la″tion
cap″let
ca″po
ca″pon
ca·pote″
cap″puc·ci″no
Ca·pri″
ca·pric′ci·o
Cap″ri·corn′
  zodiac sign
ca·price
ca·pri″cious
cap″ri·ole
 cap″ri·oled
 cap″ri·ol′ing
cap″si·cum
cap″size
 cap″sized
 cap″siz·ing
cap″stan
cap″stone
cap″su·late
cap″sule
 cap″suled
 cap″sul·ing
cap″tain
cap″tain·cy
cap″tious
cap″ti·vate′
cap ti·va″tion
cap″tive
cap tiv″i·ty
  (*pl.* cap·tiv″i·ties)
cap″tor
cap″ture
 cap″tured
 cap″tur·ing

cap″u·chin
cap′y·ba″ra
ca′ra·ca″ra
Ca·ra″cas
car″a·cole′
car″a·cul
ca·rafe″
car″a·mel
car″a·pace
car″at
  weight (*see:* caret
  and carrot)
car″a·van
car·a·van″sa·ry
  (*pl.* car·a·van″sa·
  ries)
car″a·vel
car″a·way
car″bide
car″bine
car″bo·hy″drate
car·bol″ic
car″bon
car″bon·ate
 car″bon·at′ed
 car″bon·at′ing
 car″bon·a″tion
car·bon″ic
car″bon·if″er·ous
car″bon·ize
car″bun·cle
car·bun″cu·lar
car″bu·re″tion
car″bu·re″tor
car″cass
car·cin″o·gen
car′ci·no″ma
car″coat′
card
car″da·mom
card″board′
car″di·ac
car″di·gan
car″di·nal
car″di·o·gram′
car″di·oid′

car'di·ol''o·gist
car'di·ol''o·gy
car'di·o·pul''mo·
  nar''y
car'di·o·vas''cu·lar
card''sharp'
care
ca·reen''
ca·reer''
ca·reer''ism
care''free
care''ful
care''ful·ly
care''less
ca·ress''
  (*pl.* ca·ress''es)
car'et
  mark (*see:* carat and
  carrot)
care''tak'er
care''worn'
car''fare'
car''go
  (*pl.* car''goes)
car''hop'
Car''ib
  (*pl.* Car''ibs)
Car'ib·be''an
car''i·bou'
  (*pl.* car''i·bou')
car''i·ca·ture'
  car''i·ca·tured
  car''i·ca·tur·ing
car''i·ca·tur'ist
car''il·lon'
ca·ri''na
car''ing
car''load'
car''mine
car''nage
car''nal
car''nal·i·ty
car''nal·ly
car·na''tion
car·nau''ba
car·nel''ian

car''ni·val
car''ni·vore
car·niv''o·rous
car''ob
car''ol, *n.*
  song (*see:* carrel)
car''ol, *v.*
  car''oled
  car''ol·ing
  to sing
Car'o·li''na
car
car''o·tene
ca·rot''id
ca·rous''al
  revelry (*see:* carou-
  sel)
ca·rouse''
  ca·roused
  ca·rous''ing
car'ou·sel''
carp
car''pel
car''pen·ter
car''pen·try
car''pet
car''pet·bag'
car''pet·bag'ger
car''pet·ing
car·pol''o·gy
car'' pool
car''port
car''pus
  (*pl.* car''pi)
car''ra·geen
car''rel
  study space (*see:*
  carol)
car''riage
car''ri·er
car''ri·on
car''rot
  vegetable (*see:* carat
  and caret)
car''ry
  car''ried

car''ry·ing
car''ry·all
car''ry·ing-on
car''ry-on
car''sick
Car''son Cit''y
cart
cart''age
carte'' blanche''
car·tel''
car·te''sian
car''ti·lage
car''ti·lag''inous
car·tog''ra·pher
car·to·graph''ic
car·tog''ra·phy
car''ton
car·toon''
car·toon''ist
car''touche''
car''tridge
cart''wheel
carve
  carved
  carv''ing
car·y·at''id
ca·sa''ba
Ca·sa·blan''ca
Cas'a·nov''a
cas·cade''
  cas·cad''ed
  cas·cad''ing
cas·car''a
case
case''book
case''bound
case''hard'en
ca''sein
case''load
case''mate
case''ment
case''work
cash
  money (*see:* cache)
cash''-and-car''ry
cash''book

cash″box
cash″ew
cash″ flow
cash·ier″
cash″-in
cash″mere
cas″ing
ca·si″no
  (*pl.* ca·si″nos)
  amusement place
  (*see:* cassino)
cask
  barrel (*see:* casque)
cas″ket
Cas″pi·an
casque
  helmet (*see:* cask)
cas·sa″va
cas″se·role
cas·sette″
cas″sia
cas·si″no
  card game (*see:* ca-
  sino)
cas″sock
cas·so·war″y
  (*pl.* cas″so·war″ies)
cast
  throw (*see:* caste)
cas″ta·net″
cast″a·way
caste
  social division (*see:*
  cast)
cas″tel·lan
cas″tel·lat·ed
cast″er
  wheel (*see:* castor)
cas″ti·gate
  cas″ti·ga″ted
  cas″ti·ga″ting
Cas·tile″
cast″ing
cast″ i″ron
cas″tle
  cas″tled

cas″tling
cast″off
cas″tor
  pertaining to beavers
  (*see:* caster)
cas″tor bean″
cas″tor oil″
cas″trate
  cas″trat·ed
  cas″trat·ing
cas·tra″tion
cas″u·al
cas″u·al·ly
cas″u·al·ty
  (*pl.* cas″u·al·ties)
ca″su·ist
ca′su·is″tic
ca″su·ist·ry
cat
cat′a·bol″ic
cat″a·clysm
cat″a·clys″mic
cat″a·combs
cat″a·falque
cat″a·lep·sy
cat′a·lep″tic
cat″a·log
  cat″a·loged
  cat″a·log″ing
cat″a·log′er
ca·tal″pa
ca·tal″y·sis
  (*pl.* ca·tal″y·ses)
cat″a·lyst
cat′a·lyt″ic
cat″a·lyze
cat′a·ma·ran″
cat″a·mount
cat″a·pult
cat″a·ract
ca·tarrh″
ca·tas″tro·phe
cat′a·stroph″ic
cat′a·to″ni·a
cat′a·ton″ic
ca·taw″ba

cat″bird
cat″boat′
cat″call′
catch
  caught
  catch″ing
catch″all′
catch″er
catch″ment
catch″word
catch″y
cat′e·chet″i·cal
cat″e·chism
cat″e·chist
cat″e·chize
cat′e·chu″men
cat′e·gor″i·cal
cat′e·gor″i·cal·ly
cat″e·go·rize
cat″e·go·ry
  (*pl.* cat″e·go′ries)
cat″e·nar′y
  (*pl.* cat″e·nar′ies)
cat″e·nate
  cat″e·na·ted
  cat″e·na·ting
cat′e·na″tion
ca″ter
cat″er-cor″ner
cat″er-cor″nered
ca″ter·er
cat″er·pil′lar
cat″walk′
cat″er·waul′
cat″fish′
cat″gut′
ca·thar″sis
ca·thar″tic
ca·the″dral
cath″e·ter
cath″ode ray
cath″o·lic
  universal
Cath″o·lic
  religion
Ca·thol″i·cism

cath'o·lic''i·ty
cat'i·on''ic
cat''kin
cat''nap'
cat''nap'ping
cat''nip
cat-o-nine''-tails
CAT'' scan'ner
Cats''kill
cat's''-paw
cat''sup
cat''tail
cat''ti·er
cat''ti·est
cat''ti·ly
cat''ti·ness
cat''tle
cat''tle·man
  (*pl.* cat''tle·men)
cat''ty
cat''ty-cor''ner
cat''ty-cor''nered
cat''walk
cau''cus
  (*pl.* cau''cus·es)
cau''dal
cau·dil''lo
caught
caul
caul''dron
cau''li·flow'er
caulk
caus''al
cau·sal''i·ty
  (*pl.* cau·sal''i·ties)
cau·sa''tion
caus''a·tive
cause
 caused
 caus''ing
cause'' ce·le''bre
cau'se·rie''
cause''way
caus''tic
caus''ti·cal·ly
cau''ter·ize

cau''ter·iz·ing
cau''ter·y
  (*pl.* cau''ter·ies)
cau''tion
cau''tion·ar·y
cau''tious
cav''al·cade
cav'a·lier''
cav''al·ry
 fighting force (*pl.*
  cav''al·ries) (*see:*
  calvary)
cav'a·tin''a
cave
ca''ve·at emp''tor
cave''-in
cave''man
cav''en·dish
cav''ern
cav''ern·ous
cav''i·ar
cav''il
 cav''iled
 cav''il·ing
cav''ing
cav'i·ta''tion
cav''i·ty
  (*pl.* cav''i·ties)
ca·vort''
ca''vy
caw
cay
 island (*see:* key and
  quay)
cay·enne''
 pepper
Cay''enne
 city
CD
 compact disc
cease
cease''less
ce''cum
ce''dar
ce''dar chest'
cede

yield (*see:* seed)
ce·dil''la
ceil''ing
cel''a·don'
cel''an·dine
cel''e·brant
cel''e·brate'
 cel''e·brat'ing
 cel'e·bra''tion
ce·leb''ri·ty
  (*pl.* ce·leb''ri·ties)
ce·ler''i·ty
cel''er·y
ce·les''ta
ce·les''tial
ce''li·ac
cel''i·ba·cy
cel''i·bate
cell
 unit of space (*see:*
  sell)
cel''lar
cel'lar·et''
cell''block'
cel''list
cel''lo
  (*pl.* cel''los)
cel''lo·phane'
cel''lu·lar
cel''lu·lar phone''
cel''lu·li''tis
cel''lu·loid'™
cel''lu·lose'
cel''si·us
Celt
Celt''ic
cem''ba·lo'
  (*pl.* cem''ba·los')
ce·ment''
cem''e·ter'y
  (*pl.* cem''e·ter'ies)
cen''a·cle
cen''o·bite'
cen''o·taph'
Ce'no·zo''ic
cen''ser

container (*see:* censor and censure)
cen"sor
    official (*see:* censer and censure)
cen·so"ri·al
cen"sor·ship'
cen"sur·a·ble
cen"sure
  cen"sured
  cen"sur·ing
    rebuke (*see:* censer and censor)
cen"sur·er
cen"sus
cent
    coin (*see:* scent and sent)
cen"taur
cen·ta"vo
cen"te·nar"i·an
cen"te·nar'y
    (*pl.* cen"te·nar ies)
cen·ten"ni·al
cen"ter
cen"ter·board
cen"ter field"
cen"ter·fold
cen"ter·piece
cen"ti·grade
cen"ti·gram
cen"ti·li'ter
cen"time
cen"ti·me'ter
cen"ti·mo
cen"ti·pede
cen"ti·are
cen"tral
cen"tral·ism
cen·tral"i·ty
cen"tral·i·za"tion
cen"tral·ize
cen·trif"u·gal
cen"tri·fuge
cen"tri·ole'
cen·trip"e·tal

cen"trist
cen"tro·some
cen·tu"ri·on
cen"tu·ry
ce·phal"ic
ce"phe·id
ce·ram"ic
ce·ram"i·cist
cer"a·mist
ce"re·al
    grain (*see:* serial)
cer'e·bel"lum
    (*pl.* cer'e·bel"lums)
cer"e·bral
cer'e·bra"tion
cer"e·brum
    (*pl.* cer"e·brums)
cere"cloth
cer'e·mo"ni·al
cer'e·mo"ni·al·ly
cer'e·mo"ni·us
cer"e·mo'ny
    (*pl.* cer"e·mo'nies)
ce·rise"
ce"ri·um
cer"met
cer"tain
cer"tain·ly
cer"tain·ty
    (*pl.* cer"tain·ties)
cer"ti·fi'a·ble
cer·tif"i·cate
cer'ti·fi·ca"tion
cer"ti·fy'
  cer"ti·fied'
  cer"ti·fy'ing
cer'tio·ra·ri
cer"ti·tude'
ce·ru"le·an
ce·ru"men
cer"ve·lat
cer"vi·cal
cer"vix
    (*pl.* cer·vi"ces)
ce"si·um
cess

ces·sa"tion
ces"sion
    yielding (*see:* session)
cess"pool'
ce·ta"cean
Cey·lon"
Cha·blis"
cha'-cha'
cha·conne"
chafe
    rub (*see:* chaff)
chaff
    grain waste (*see:* chafe)
chaf"finch
chaf"ing
chaf"ing dish'
cha·grin"
  cha·grined"
  cha·grin"ing
chain
chain" gang'
chain' saw'
chain" stitch'
chain" store'
chair
chair"man
    (*pl.* chair"men)
chair"per'son
chair"wom'an
    (*pl.* chair"wom'en)
chaise
chaise' longue"
chal·ced"o·ny
    (*pl.* chal·ced"o·nies)
cha·let"
chal"ice
chal"lah
chalk"board'
chalk"i·er
chalk"i·est
chalk"y
chal"lenge
  chal"lenged

chal"leng·ing
chal"leng·er
chal"lis
cham"ber
cham"ber·lain
cham"ber·maid
cham"bray
cha·me"le·on
cham"fer
cham"ois
cham"o·mile
champ
cham·pagne"
  wine (*see:* cham-
  paign)
cham·paign"
  road; plain (*see:*
  champagne)
cham·pi"gnon
cham"pi·on
cham"pi·on·ship
Champs E·ly·see
chance
  chanced
  chanc"ing
chan"ccl
chan"cel·ler·y
  (*pl.* chan"cel·ler·
  ics)
chan"cel·lor
chanc"i·er
chanc"i·est
chanc"y
chan·de·lier"
chan"dler·y
  (*pl.* chan"dler·ies)
change
  changed
  chang"ing
change"a·ble
change"ful
change"less
change"ling
change"o'ver
chan"nel
  chan"neled

chan"nel·ing
chan"son
chant"er
chan"tey
  song (*pl.* chan"teys)
  (*see:* shanty)
chan"ti·cleer
Chan·til"ly
chan"try
  (*pl.* chan"tries)
cha"os
cha·ot"i·cal·ly
chap
chap"ar·ral"
chap"book
cha·peau"
  (*pl.* cha·peaus")
chap"el
chap"er·on *or* chap"
  er·one
chap"lain
chap"let
chap"ping
chaps
chap"ter
char
  charred
  char"ring
  burned (*see:* chard)
char"ac·ter
char"ac·ter·is"tic
char"ac·ter·i·za"tion
char"ac·ter·ize
  char"ac·ter·ized
  char"ac·ter·iz"ing
cha·rades"
char"broil
char"coal
chard
  beet (*see:* charred)
charge
  charged
  charg"ing
charge"a·ble
char·ge" d'af·faires"
charg"er

char"i·est
char"i·ly
char"i·ot
char"i·o·teer"
cha·ris"ma
char"is·mat"ic
char"i·ta·ble
char"i·ty
  (*pl.* char"i·ties)
char"la·tan
Charles"ton
char"ley horse
Char"lotte
Char"lotte·town
charm"er
char"nel house
chart
char"ter
char"tist
Char"tres
char·treuse"
char"wom·an
char"y
  cautious (*see:*
  cherry)
chase
  chased
  chas"ing
  go after (*see:*
  chaste)
chas"er
chasm
chas·se"
  chas·sed"
  chas·se"ing
chas"sis
  (*pl.* chas"sis)
chaste
  pure (*see:* chased)
chas"ten
chas·tise"
chas·tise"ment
chas·tis"ing
chas"ti·ty
chas"u·ble
chat

chat″ted
chat″ting
cha·teau″
  (*pl.* cha·teaus″)
Cha·teau′bri·and″
chat″e·laine
chat″tel
chat″ter
chat″ter·box
chat″ti·er
chat″ti·est
chat″ty
chauf″feur
chau″vin·ist
chau″vin·is″tic
chau″vin·ism
cheap
  low cost (*see:* cheep)
cheap″en
cheap″skate
cheat″er
check
check″a·ble
check″book
check″er·board
check″ered
check″list
check″mark
check″mate
check″off
check″out
check″point
check″rein′
check″room′
check″up
Ched″dar
cheek″bone
cheek″i·er
cheek″i·est
cheek″y
cheep
  chirp (*see:* cheap)
cheer″ful
cheer″ful·ly
cheer″ful·ness
cheer″i·er

cheer″i·est
cheer″i·ly
cheer″i·ness
cheer″i·o
cheer″lead′er
cheer″less
cheer″y
cheese
cheese″burg·er
cheese″cake
cheese″cloth
cheese″par′ing
chees″i·er
chees″i·est
chees″y
chee″tah
chef
  cook (*see:* chief)
chem″i·cal
chem″i·cal·ly
chem″i·ga′tion
che·mise″
chem″i·lum″i·nes″
  cence
che·min′de·fer″
chem″ist
chem″is·try
  (*pl.* chem″is·tries)
chem″o·sphere′
che′mo·sur″ger·y
chem′o·syn″the·sis
che′mo·ther″a·py
chem″ur·gy
che·nille″
cher″ish
Cher″o·kee
  (*pl.* Cher″o·kee)
che·root″
cher″ry
  fruit (*pl.* cher″ries)
  (*see:* chary)
cher″ub
  (*pl.* cher″u·bim′)
che·ru″bic
cher″vil
Ches″a·peake

chess″board
chess″man
  (*pl.* chess″men)
chest
Ches″ter·field
chest″nut
chev′a·lier″
chev″i·ot
chev″ron
chew
chew″i·er
chew″i·est
chew″ing gum
Chey·enne″
  (*pl.* Chey·enne″)
Chi·an″ti
chi·a′ro·scu″ro
chic
  elegance (*see:* sheik
  and chick)
Chi·ca″go
chi·can″er·y
  (*pl.* chi·can″er·ies)
chi·ca″no
  (*pl.* chi·ca″nos)
chi″chi″
chick
  bird (*see:* chic)
chick″a·dee
Chick″a·saw
  (*pl.* Chick″a·saws)
chick″en
chick″en feed
chick″en-heart″ed
chick″en pox
chick″pea
chick″weed
chic″le
chic″o·ry
chide
chid″ed
chid″ing
chief
  principal person
  (*see:* chef)
chif′fo·nier″

chief"ly
chief"tain
chif·fon"
chif"fo·robe
chig"ger
chi"gnon
chig"oe
chi·hua"hua
chil"blain
child
  (*pl*. chil"dren)
child"bear'ing
child"birth
child"hood
child"ish
child"like
child"proof
Chil"e
chil"i
  food (*pl*. chil"ies)
chil"i con car"ne
chill"i·er
chill"i·est
chill"y
  cold (*see:* chili)
chime
chi·me"ra
chi·mer"i·cal
chim"ing
chim"ney
  (*pl*. chim"neys)
chimp
chim'pan·zee"
chin
  chinned
  chin"ning
chi"na
Chi"na
chi"na·town
chi"na·ware
chin·chil"la
chin"cough
Chi·nese"
chi"no
  (*pl*. chi"nos)
chi·nook"

chin"qua·pin
chintz
chintz"i·er
chintz"i·est
chintz"y
chin"-up
chip
  chipped
  chip"ping
chip"board'
chip"munk
Chip"pen·dale
chip"per
chip"py
chi·rop"o·dist
chi·rop"o·dy
chi"ro·prac"tic'
chi"ro·prac"tor
chirp
chir"rup
chis"el
  chis"eled
  chis"el·ing
chis"el·er
chit"chat
chit"lins
chit"ter
chit"ter·lings
chiv·al"ric
chiv"al·rous
chiv"al·ry
chive
chiv"vy
  chiv"vied
  chiv"vy·ing
chlo"ral
chlo"rate
chlor"dane
chlo"ric
chlo"ride
chlo"rin·ate
  chlo"rin·at'ed
  chlo"rin·at'ing
  chlo"rin·a"tion
chlo"rine
chlo"ro·form

chlo"ro·phyll
chock"-a-block
chock"-full"
choc"o·late
Choc"taw
choic"er
choic"est
choir
  chorus (*see:* quire)
choir"boy
choir"girl
choir"mas'ter
choke
  choked
  chok"ing
choke"cher'ry
choke"damp'
chok"er
chol"er·ic
cho·les"ter·ol
chol"la
Chong"qing"
choose
  chose
  choos"ing
choos"i·er
choos"i·est
choos"y
chop
  chopped
  chop"ping
chop"house
chop"per
chop"pi·er
chop"pi·est
chop"pi·ness
chop"stick
chop" su"ey
cho"ral
  sung by choir (*see:* coral)
cho·rale"
  hymn tune; choir (*see:* corral)
cho"ral·ly
chord

tones (*see:* cord)
chor''date
chore
cho·re''a
cho''re·o·graph
cho're·og''ra·pher
cho're·og''ra·phy
cho''rine
cho''ri·on
cho''roid
chor''is·ter
chor''tle
  chor''tled
  chor''tling
cho''rus
chose
cho''sen
chow'' chow'
  dog
chow''chow
  food
chow''der
chow' mein''
chris''ten
  chris''tened
  chris''ten·ing
Chris''tian
Chris ti·an''i·ty
Christ''mas
  (*pl.* Christ''mas·es)
chro''ma
chro''mate
chro·mat''ic
chro''ma·tin
chro'ma·tog''ra·phy
chrome
  chromed
  chrom''ing
chro''mic
chro''mite
chro''mi·um
chro'mo·lith''o·graph'
chro''mo·some
chro''mo·sphere
chron''ic
chron''i·cal·ly

chron''i·cle
chron''i·cler
chron''i·cling
chron''o·graph'
chron'o·log''i·cal
chro·nol''o·gist
chro·nol''o·gy
chro·nom''e·ter
chron'o·ther''a·py
chrys''a·lis
chry·san''the·mum
chub''bi·er
chub''bi·est
chub''bi·ness
chub''by
chuck''hole'
chuck''le
  chuck''led
  chuck''ling
chuck'' wag''on
chug
  chugged
  chug''ging
chuk''ka
  boot (*see:* chukker)
chuk''ker
  polo period (*see:*
    chukka)
chum
chum''mi·er
chum''mi·est
chum''mi·ness
chum''my
chump
chunk
  chunk''i·er
  chunk''i·est
  chunk''y
church
  (*pl.* church''es)
church''go'er
church''man
church''ward'en
church''wom'an
church''yard'
churl

churl''ish
churn
churr
chute
  slide (*see:* shoot)
chut''ing
chut''ney
chutz''pah
chyle
chyme
ciao
ci·ca''da
cic''a·trix
cic'e·ro''ne
ci''der
ci·gar''
cig'a·ril''lo
cig'a·rette''
cil''i·a
cil''i·ar'y
cinch
cin·cho''na
Cin'cin·nat''i
cinc''ture
cinc''tured
cinc''tur·ing
cin''der
cin''der block'
cin''e·ma
cin'e·ma·tog''ra·pher
cin'e·ma·tog''ra·phy
cin'e·ma' ve·ri·te''
cin''na·bar
cin''na·mon
cinque''foil
ci''pher
cir''ca
cir''cle
  cir''cled
  cir''cling
cir''clet
cir''cuit
cir·cu''i·tous
cir''cu·lar
cir'cu·lar·i·za''tion

cir″cu·lar·ize
  cir″cu·lar·ized
  cir″cu·lar·iz′ing
cir″cu·late
  cir″cu·lat′ed
  cir″cu·lat′ing
cir′cu·la″tion
cir″cu·la″tor
cir″cu·la·to′ry
cir″cum·cise
  cir″cum·cised
  cir″cum·cis′ing
cir′cum·ci″sion
cir·cum″fer·ence
cir″cum·flex′
cir′cum·lo·cu″tion
cir″cum·lu″nar
cir′cum·nav″i·gate
  cir″cum·nav″i·gat′ed
  cir″cum·nav″i·gat′
    ing
cir′cum·nav′i·ga″tion
cir′cum·nav″i·ga′tor
cir″cum·po″lar
cir′cum·scribe″
  cir″cum·scribed″
  cir″cum·scrib″ing
cir′cum·scrip″tion
cir″cum·spect
cir′cum·spec″tion
cir″cum·stance
cir′cum·stan″tial
cir′cum·stan″tial·ly
cir′cum·stan″ti·ate
  cir′cum·stan″ti·at′ed
  cir′cum·stan″ti·at′
    ing
cir′cum·vent″
cir″cum·ven″tion
cir″cus
cirque
cir·rho″sis
cir′ro·cu″mu·lus
cir′ro·stra″tus
cir″rus
  plant (*pl.* cir″ri)

cir″rus
  cloud (*pl.* cir″rus)
cis·lu″nar
Cis·ter″cian
cis″tern
cit″a·del
ci·ta″tion
cite
  mention (*see:* sight
    and site)
cit″ing
cit″i·fied
cit″i·zen
cit″i·zen·ry
cit″i·zen's band
cit″i·zen·ship
cit″rate
cit″ric
cit″ron
cit′ro·nel″la
cit″rus
cit″y
  (*pl.* cit″ies)
cit″y·scape
cit″y-state
civ″et
civ″ic
civ″il
ci·vil″ian
ci·vil″i·ty
  (*pl.* ci·vil″i·ties)
civ′i·li·za″tion
civ″i·lize
  civ″i·lized
  civ″i·liz′ing
civ″il·ly
civ″vies
clab″ber
clack
  chatter (*see:* claque)
clad
claim
claim″ant
clair·voy″ance
clair·voy″ant
clam

clam″bake
clam″ber
clam″mi·er
clam″mi·est
clam″mi·ness
clam″ming
clam″my
clam″or
clam″or·ous
clamp
clam″shell
clan
clan·des″tine
clan″gor
clan″nish
clans″man
clans″wom·an
clap
  clapped
  clap″ping
clap″board
clap″per
clap″trap
claque
  applauders (*see:*
    clack)
clar″et
clar′i·fi·ca″tion
clar″i·fy
  clar″i·fied
  clar″i·fy′ing
clar·i·net″
clar·i·net″ist
clar″i·on
clar″i·ty
clash
clasp
clasp″ knife
class
clas″sic
clas″si·cal
clas″si·cal·ly
clas″si·cist
class″i·er
class″i·est
clas′si·fi·ca″tion

clas"si·fy
 clas"si·fied
 clas"si·fy'ing
class"mate
class"room
class"work'
class"y
clat"ter
clau'di·ca"tion
clause
claus'tro·pho"bi·a
clav"i·chord
clav"i·cle
cla·vier"
claw
claw" ham'mer
clay
clay"ey
clay"more
clean"-cut"
clean"er
clean"li·er
clean"li·est
clean"li·ness
clean"ly
clean"ness
cleans"er
clean"-shav"en
cleans"ing
clean"up
clear
clear"a·ble
clear"ance
clear"-cut"
clear"-eyed
clear"head'ed
clear'ing
clear"ing·house
clear"ly
clear"ness
clear"-sight'ed
cleat
cleav"age
cleave
 cleaved
 cleav"ing

adhere
cleave
 cleft, cleaved, *or*
  clove
 cleft, cleaved, *or*
  clov"en
 cleav"ing
 split
cleav"er
clef
 musical symbol (*see:*
  cleft)
cleft
 opening; split (*see:*
  clef)
clem"a·tis
clem"en·cy
clem"ent
clench
clere"sto'ry
 (*pl.* clere"sto'ries)
cler"gy
 (*pl.* cler"gies)
cler"gy·man
 (*pl.* cler"gy·men)
cler"ic
cler"i·cal
Cleve"land
clev"er
clew
cli·che"
click
 noise (*see:* clique)
cli"ent
cli"en·tele"
cliff"-hang'er
cli·mac"ter·ic
cli·mac"tic
 of climax (*see:* cli-
  matic)
cli"mate
cli·mat"ic
 of weather (*see:* cli-
  mactic)
cli·mat"i·cal·ly
cli ma·tol"o·gy

cli"max
climb
climb"a·ble
climb"er
clime
clinch
clinch"er
cling
 clung
 cling"ing
clin"ic
clin"i·cal·ly
cli·ni"cian
clink"er
cli·nom"e·ter clip
clip"-on
clip"per
clip"ping
clique
 group (*see:* click)
cliqu"ish
clit"o·ris
clo·a"ca
 (*pl.* clo·a"cae)
cloak"-and-dag"ger
cloak"room
clob"ber
cloche
clock"wise
clock"work
clod
clod"dish
clod"hop·per
clog
 clogged
 clog"ging
cloi'son·ne"
clois"ter
clone
 cloned
 clon"ing
clop"ping
close
 near; shut (*see:*
  clothes
closed"-cap"tioned

closed''-end
close''fist''ed
close''fit''ting
close''mouthed''
close''out
clos''est
clos''et
close''-up
clos''ing
clo''sure
clo''sur·ing
clot
cloth
clothe
clothed
clothes
   garments (*see:* close)
clothes''line
clothes''pin
clothes''press
cloth''ier
cloth''ing
clot''ting
clo''ture
cloud''burst
cloud''i·er
cloud''i·est
cloud''i·ness
cloud''y
clout
clove
clo''ven-hoofed'
clo''ver
clo''ver·leaf'
   (*pl.* clo''ver·leaves')
clown''ish·ly
cloy''ing·ly
club
club''bi·er
club''bi·est
club''bing
club''by
club''car'
club''foot'
club''foot'ed
club''house'

cluck
clue
  clued
  clu''ing
clump
clum''si·er
clum''si·est
clum''si·ly
clum''si·ness
clum''sy
clung
clus''ter
clutch
clut''ter
Clydes''dale'
clys''ter
coach
coach''man
coach''work'
co·ac''tion
co·ad''ju·tor
co·ag''u·lant
co·ag''u·late'
  co·ag''u·lat'ed
  co·ag''u·lat'ing
  co·ag'u·la''tion
coal
co'a·lesce''
co'a·les''cence
co'a·les''cent
co'a·lesc''ing
co'a·li''tion
coal''tar'
coarse
  rough (*see:* course)
coarse''ly
coars''en
coarse''ness
coars''er
coars''est
coast''al
coast''er
Coast'' Guard
coast''line
coast''ward
coast''wise

co·a''ti
coat''ing
coat'' of arms''
coat'' of mail''
coat''room
coat''tail
co·au''thor
co·ax''er
co·ax''i·al
cob
co''balt
cob''ble
  cob''bled
  cob''bling
cob''bler
cob''ble·stone
CO''BOL
co''bra
cob''web
cob''web'bing
co''ca
co·caine''
coc''cus
  (*pl.* coc''ci)
coc''cyx
  (*pl.* coc·cy''ges)
co·chair''man
co''chin
coch'i·neal''
coch''le·a
cock-a-doo'dle-doo''
cock''a·ma'mie
cock''a·too'
cock''a·trice
cock''boat'
cock''chaf'er
cock''crow
cock''er
cock''er·el
cock''eyed
cock''fight
cock''horse'
cock''i·ly
cock''i·ness
cock''le·bur
cock''le·shell

cock''ney
  (*pl.* cock''neys)
cock''pit
cock''roach
cocks''comb
cock''sure
cock''tail
cock''y
co''co
  coconut (*pl.* co''cos)
    (*see:* cocoa)
co''coa
  drink (*see:* coco)
co''co·nut
co·coon''
co·cotte''
co''da
cod''dle
  cod''dled
  cod''dling
code
  cod''ed
  cod''ing
co''deine
co''dex
  (*pl.* co''di·ces)
cod''fish
codg''er
cod''i·cil
cod'i·fi·ca''tion
cod''i·fy
  cod''i·fied
  cod''i·fy'ing
cod''-liv'er oil''
co''ed'
co·ed''i·tor
co·ed·u·ca''tion
co·ef·fi''cient
coe''la·canth'
coe·len''ter·ate'
co·en''zyme
co·e''qual
co'e·qual''i·ty
co·erce''
  co·erced'
  co·erc''ing

co·er''cion
co·er''cive
co·e·ta''ne·ous
co·e''val
co·ex·is''tence
co·ex·tend''
co·ex·ten''sive
cof''fee
cof''fee·cake
cof''fee klatch
cof''fee·pot
cof''fee shop
cof''fer
cof''fer·dam
cof''fin
cog
co''gen·cy
co''gent
cog''i·tate
  cog''i·tat'ed
  cog''i·tat'ing
cog'i·ta''tion
co''gnac
cog''nate
cog·ni''tion
cog''ni·tive
cog''ni·zance
cog''ni·zant
cog·no''men
co'gno·scen''te
  (*pl.* co'gno·scen''ti)
cog''wheel''
co·hab'i·ta''tion
co''hash
co·heir''
co·here''
co·her''ence
co·her''ent
co·her''ing
co·he''sion
co·he''sive
co''hort
coif·fure''
coil
coin
  money (*see:* quoin)

coin''age
co·in·cide''
co·in''ci·dence
co·in''ci·dent
co·in·ci·den''tal
co·in·cid''ing
co'in·sur''ance
co'in·sure''
  co'in·sured''
  co'in·sur''ing
co·i''tion
co''i·tus
co''la
col''an·der
  strainer (*see:* calen-
  dar and calender)
col''chi·cine'
cold''blood''ed
cold'' cream
cold'' frame
cold''heart''ed
cold'' pack
cold'' sore
cole''slaw
co''le·us
col''ic
col''ick·y
col'i·se''um
  public building (*see:*
  colosseum)
co·li''tis
col·lab''o·rate
  col·lab''o·rat'ed
  col·lab''o·rat'ing
col·lab'o·ra''tion
col·lage''
col''la·gen
col·lapse''
  col·lapsed''
  col·laps''ing
col·laps''i·ble
col''lar
col''lar·bone
col''lard
col·late''
  col·lat''ed

col·lat''ing
col·lat''er·al
col·la''tion
col·la''tor
col''league
col·lect'' v.
 aquire
col''lect, n.
 prayer
col·lect''ed
col·lect''i·ble
col·lec''tion
col·lec''tive
col·lec''tive·ly
col·lec''tiv·ism
col·lec''tiv·ize
 col·lec''tiv·ized
 col·lec''tiv·iz''ing
col·lec''tor
col''leen
col''lege
col·le''gi·al
col·le''ate
col·lide''
 col·lid''ed
 col·lid''ing
col''lie
col''lier
col·lin''e·ar
col''lins
col·li''sion
col·lo·ca''tion
col·lo''di·on
col''loid
col·loi''dal
col·lo''qui·al
col·lo''qui·al·ism
col·lo''qui·um
 (pl. col·lo''qui·a)
col''lo·quy
 (pl. col''lo·quies)
col·lude''
 col·lud''ed
 col·lud''ing
col·lu''sion
col·lu''sive

co·logne''
Co·lom''bi·a
 country (see: Co-
 lumbia)
co''lon
colo''nel
 officer (see; kernel)
co·lo''ni·al
co·lo''ni·al·ism
co·lo''ni·al·ist
col''o·nist
col·o·ni·za''tion
col''o·nize
 col''o·nized
 col''o·niz''ing
 col''o·niz''er
col''on·nade''
col''o·ny
 (pl. col''o·nies)
col''o·phon
col''or
Col'o·ra''do
col·or·a''tion
col·or·a·tu''ra
col''or-blind''
col''or·cast'
col''or·fast'
col''or·ful
col''or·ing
col·or·i·za''tion
col''or·less
co·los''sal
col'os·se''um
 Roman amphitheater
 (see: coliseum)
co·los''sus
 (pl. co·los''si)
co·los''to·my
 (pl. co·los''to·mies)
colt''ish
col'um·bar''i·um
Co·lum''bi·a
 U.S. cities (see: Co-
 lombia)
col''um·bine'

co·lum''bi·um
col''umn
co·lum''nar
col''umn·ist
co''ma
 unconsciousness (pl.
 co''mas) (see:
 comma)
co·bak''er
co·man''age·ment
Co·man''che
 (pl. Co·man''che)
co''ma·tose'
co·mat''ul·a
comb
com·bat'', v.
 fight
com''bat, n.
 battle
com·bat''ant
com·bat''ing
com·bat''ive
comb''er
com·bi·na''tion
com''bi·na''tive
com·bine'', v.
 join together
com''bine, n.
 machine
comb''ings
com·bin''ing
com''bo
com·bus''ti·ble
com·bus''tion
com·bus'tive
come
 came
 com''ing
come''back'
co·me''di·an
co·me'di·enne''
come''down
com''e·dy
 (pl. com''e·dies)
come''ly
come''-on

com″er
co·mes″ti·ble
com″et
come up″pance
com″fort
com″fort·a·ble
com″fort·a·bly
com″fort·er
com″ic
com″i·cal
com″i·ty
  (*pl*. com″i·ties)
com″ma
  punctuation mark
  (*see:* coma)
com·mand″
  com·mand″ed
  com·mand″ing
  order (*see:* com-
  mend)
com·man″dant
com·man·deer″
com·mand″er
com·mand″er in
  chief″
com·mand″ment
com·man″do
com·me″di·a del
  l'ar″te
com·mem″o·rate
  com·mem″o·rat′ed
  com·mem″o·rat′ing
com·mem″o·ra″tion
com·mem″o·ra′tive
com·mence″
com·mence″ment
com·menc′ing
com·mend″
  praise (*see:* com-
  mand)
com·mend″a·ble
com·men·da″tion
com·men″sal
com·men″su·ra·ble
com·men″su·rate
com″ment

com″men·tar′y
  (*pl*. com″men·tar′
  ies)
com″men·ta′tor
com″merce
com·mer″cial
com·mer″cial·ism
com·mer″cial·i·za″
  tion
com·mer″cial·ize
com·mer″cial·ly
com·min″gle
com·min″gling
com·mis″er·ate
  com·mis″er·at′ed
  com·mis″er·at′ing
com·mis″er·a″tion
com″mis·sar′
com″mis·sar′i·at
com″mis·sar′y
  (*pl*. com″mis·sar′
  ies)
com·mis″sion
com·mis″sion·er
com·mit″
  com·mit″ted
  com·mit″ting
com·mit″ment
com·mit″tee
com·mit″tee·man
com·mit″tee·per″son
com·mit″tee·wo″man
com·mix″ture
com·mode″
com·mo″di·ous
com·mod″i·ty
  (*pl*. com·mod″i·
  ties)
com″mo·dore
com″mon·al″ty
  (*pl*. com″mon·al·
  ties)
com″mon·er
com″mon·ly
com″mon·ness
com″mon·place

com″mon sense″
com″mon·weal
com″mon·wealth
com·mo″tion
com·mu″nal
com·mu·nal″i·ty
com·mune″, *v*.
  in intimate commu-
  nication
com″mune, *n*.
  community
com·mu″ni·ca·ble
com·mu″ni·cant
com·mu″ni·cate
com·mu″ni·cat′ing
com·mu″ni·ca″tion
com·mu″ni·ca′tive
com·mun″ing
com·mun″ion
com″mun·ism
com·mu″ni·ty
  (*pl*. com·mu″ni·
  ties)
com·mu·ta″tion
com·mu·ta″tive
com″mu·ta′tor
com·mute″
  com·mut″ed
  com·mut″ing
com·mut″er
com·pact″, *v*.
  occupying minimal
  space
com″pact, *n*.
  small item; agree-
  ment
com″pact disc
com·pac″tor
com·pan″ion
com·pan″ion·a·ble
com·pa·ny
  (*pl*. com″pa·nies)
com″pa·ra·ble
com·par″a·tive·ly
com·pare″
  com·pared″

com·par''ing
com·par''i·son
com·par''o·scope
com·part''ment
com·part·men''tal·ize
  com·part·men''tal·
  ized
  com·part·men''tal·iz'
  ing
com''pass
com·pas''sion
com·pas''sion·ate
com·pat'i·bil''i·ty
com·pat''i·ble
com·pa''tri·ot
com·peer''
com·pel''
  com·pelled''
  com·pel''ling
com·pen''di·ous
com·pen''di·um
com''pen·sate
  com''pen·sat'ed
  com''pen·sat'ing
com''pen·sa''tion
com''pen·sa·to·ry
com·pete''
  com·pet''ed
  com·pet''ing
com''pe·tence
com''pe·tent
com''pe·ti''tion
com·pet''i·tive
com·pet''i·tor
com·pi·la''tion
com·pile''
  com·piled''
  com·pil''ing
com·pil''er
com·pla''cence
  self-satisfaction (*see:*
  complaisance)
com·pla''cen·cy
  (*pl.* com·pla''cen·
  cies)
com·pla''cent

self-satisfied (*see:*
  complaisant)
com·plain''
com·plain''ent
com·plaint''
com·plai''sance
  willingness to please
  (*see:* complacence)
com·plai''sant
  willing to please
  (*see:* complacent)
com''ple·ment
  wholeness (*see:* com-
  pliment)
com''ple·men''ta·ry
  completing (*see:*
  complimentary)
com·plete''
com·plete''ly
com·plete''ness
com·ple''tion
com·plex'', *adj.*
  not simple
com''plex, *n.*
  group of items
com·plex''ion
com·plex''i·ty
  (*pl.* com·plex''i·ties)
com·pli''ance
com·pli''an·cy
com·pli''ant
com''pli·cate'
  com''pli·cat'ed
  com''pli·cat'ing
com''pli·ca''tion
com·plic''i·ty
com·pli''er
com''pli·ment
  praise (*see:* comple-
  ment)
com''pli·men''ta·ry
  praising; free (see
  complementary)
com·ply''
  com·plied''
  com·ply''ing

com·po''nent
com·port''
com·pose''
  com·posed''
  com·pos''ing
com·pos''er
com·pos''ite
com''po·si''tion
com·pos''i·tor
com''post
com·po''sure
com''pote
com·pound'', *v.*
com''pound, *n.*
  complex; mixed ele-
  ments
com''pre·hend''
com''pre·hen''si·ble
com''pre·hen''sion
com''pre·hen''sive
com·press'', *v.*
  press
com''press, *n.*
  pad
com·press''i·ble
com·pres''sion
com·pres''sor
com·pris''al
com·prise''
com·pris''ing
com''pro·mise
  com''pro·mised
  com''pro·mis'ing
  com''pro·mis'er
comp·trol''ler
com·pul''sion
com·pul''so·ry
com·punc''tion
com'pu·ta''tion
com·pute''
  com·put''ed
  com·put''ing
com·put''er
com·put''er·a·cy
com·put'er·i·za''tion
com·pu''ter·ize

com·pu″ter·ized
com·put″er·iz′ing
com″rade
con
  conned
  con″ning
co·nal″
con′ a·mo″re
co·na″tion
con bri″o
con·ca·nav″a·lin
con·cat″e·nate
con·cat′e·na″tion
con·cave″
con·cav″i·ty
  (*pl.* con·cav″i·ties)
con·ceal″
con·ceal″ment
con·cede″
  con·ced″ed
  con·ced″ing
con·ceit″
con·ceit″ed
con·ceiv′a·bil″i·ty
con·ceiv″a·ble
con·ceiv″a·bly
con·ceive″
con·ceiv″ing
con·cel″e·brate
con″cen·trate
con″cen·trat′ing
con′cen·tra″tion
con″cen·tra′tor
con·cen″tric
con″cept
con·cep″tion
con·cep″tu·al
con·cep″tu·al·ize
  con·cep″tu·al·ized
  con·cep″tu·al·iz′ing
con·cep″tu·al·ly
con·cern″
  con·cerned″
  con·cern″ing
con·cert″, *v.*
  devise

con″cert, *n.*
  musical program;
  harmony
con·cert″ed
con′cer·ti″na
con″cert′ize
con″cert·mas′ter
con·cer″to
con·ces″sion
con·ces′sion·aire″
conch
  (*pl.* conchs)
con·chi″form
con·choi″dal
con·chol″o·gy
con·chyl″i·um
con·cierge″
con·cil″i·ate
  con·cil″i·at′ed
  con·cil″i·at′ing
con·cil″i·a·to′ry
con·cise″
con·cise″ly
con·cise″ness
con″clave
con·clude″
  con·clud″ed
  con·clud″ing
con·clu″sion
con·clu″sive
con·coct″
con·coc″tion
con·com″i·tance
con·com″i·tant
con″cord
Con″cord
con·cord″ance
con·cor″dat
Con″corde™
con″course
con″crete
con″cret·ing
con·cre″tion
con·cu″bi·nage
con·cu·bine
con·cu″pis·cence

con·cu″pis·cent
con·cur″
  con·curred″
  con·cur″ring
con·cur″rence
con·cur″rent
con·cus″sion
con·demn″
con′dem·na″tion
con·den·sa″tion
con·dense″
  con·densed″
  con·dens″ing
con·dens″er
con·de·scend″
con·de·scen″sion
con·dign″
con″di·ment
con·di″tion
con·di″tion·al
con·di″tioned
con·di″tion·er
con″do
con·dole″
con·do″lence
con·dol″ing
con·do·lore″
con″dom
con′do·min″i·um
  (*pl.* con′do·min″i·ums)
con′do·na″tion
con·done″
  con·doned″
  con·don″ing
con″dor
con·duce″
  con·duced″
  con·duc″ing
con·du″cive
con·duct″, *v.*
  lead
con″duct, *n.*
  behavior
con·duc″tion

con·duc″tive
con·duc″tor
con″duit
con·du·ran″gin
con″dyle′
cone
 coned
 con″ing
con·fab″u·late
 con·fab″u·lat·ed
 con·fab″u·lat·ing
con·fab′u·la″tion
con·fec″tion
con·fec″tion·er′y
 (*pl.* con·fec″tion·er′
 ies)
con·fed″er·a·cy
 (*pl.* con·fed″er·a·
 cies)
con·fed″er·ate
 con·fed″er·at·ed
 con·fed″er·at·ing
con·fed′er·a″tion
con·fer″
 con·ferred″
 con·fer″ring
con′fer·ee″
con″fer·ence
con·fess″
con·fess″ed·ly
con·fes″sion
con·fes″sion·al
con·fes″sor
con·fet″ti
con·fi·dant″
 friend (*see:* confi-
 dent)
con·fide″
con″fi·dence
con″fi·dence man
con″fi·dent
 sure (*see:* confidant)
con fi den″tial
con fi den″tial·ly
con·fid″ing
con·fig′u·ra″tion

con·fig″u·ra·tive
con·fine″
 con·fined″
 con·fin″ing
con·fine″ment
con·firm″
 con·firmed″
 con·firm″ing
con·fir·ma″tion
con″fis·cate
 con″fis·cated
 con″fis·cat·ing
con·fis·ca″tion
con·fla·gra″tion
con·flict″, *v.*
 be hostile
con″flict, *n.*
 fight
con·flic″tive
con″flu·ence
con″flux
con·form″
con·form″a·ble
con·form″ance
con·for·ma″tion
con·form″ist
con·form″i·ty
 (*pl.* con·form″i·ties)
con·found″
con·fra·ter″ni·ty
con·front″
con·fron·ta″tion
con·fuse″
 con·fused″
 con·fus″ing
con·fu″sion
con·fu·ta″tion
con·fute″
 con·fut″ed
 con·fut″ing
con″ga
con·geal″
con·gen″ial
con·ge·ni·al″i·ty
con·gen″i·tal
con″ger

con·ge″ries
con·gest″
con·ges″tion
con·ges″tive
con·glo″bate
 con·glo″bat·ed
 con·glo″bat·ing
con·glom″er·ate
 con·glom″er·at·ed
 con·glom″er·at·ing
con·glom′er·a″tion
con″go
con″gou
con·grat″u·late
 con·grat″u·lat·ed
 con·grat″u·lat·ing
con·grat′u·la″tion
con·grat″u·la·to′ry
con″gre·gate
 con″gre·gat·ed
 con″gre·gat·ing
con′gre·ga″tion
con′gre·ga″tion·al
con′gre·ga″tion·al·ism
con″gress
con·gres″sion·al
con″gress·man
con″gress·wom′an
con″gru·ence
con″gru·en·cy
con″gru·ent
con·gru″i·ty
 (*pl.* con·gru″i·ties)
con″gru·ous
con″ic
con″i·cal
con″i·cal·ly
co·nid″i·al
co″ni·fer
co·nif″er·ous
con·jec″tur·al
con·jec″ture
 con·jec″tured
 con·jec″tur·ing
con·join″
con·joint″

con''ju·gal
con''ju·gate
  con''ju·gat'ed
  con''ju·gat'ing
con'ju·ga''tion
con·junc''tion
con·junc''ti·val
con·junc''tive
con·junc''ti·vi''tis
con·junc''ture
con'jur·a''tion
con''jure
con''jur·er
con''jur·ing
conk
  strike (*see:* conch)
con'' man
con·nect''
Con·nect''i·cut
con·nec''tion
con·nec''tion·al·ism
con·nec''tive
con''ning
con''ning tow''er
con·nip''tion
con·niv''ance
con·nive''
  con·nived''
  con·niv''ing
con·nois·seur''
con·no·ta''tion
con·no'ta·tive
con·note''
con·not''ing
con·nu''bi·al
co''no·scope
co''noid
con''quer
con''quer·or
con''quest
con·quis''ta·dor
con·san·guin''e·ous
con·san·guin''i·ty
con''science
con·sci·en''tious
con·scio'na·ble

con''scious
con·script''
con·scrip''tion
con''se·crate
  con''se·crat'ed
  con''se·crat'ing
con'se·cra''tion
con'se·cu''tion
con·sec''u·tive
con·sen''su·al
con·sen''sus
con·sent''
con'sen·ta''ne·ous
con''se·quence'
con'se·quen''tial
con·serv''a·ble
con'ser·va''tion
con'ser·va''tion·ist
con·ser''va·tism
con·ser''va·tive
con·ser''va·tor
con·ser''va·to'ry
  (*pl.* con·ser''va·to'
  ries)
con''serve, *n.*
  fruit
con·serve'', *v.*
  save
con·serv''ing
con·sid''er
  con·sid''ered
  con·sid''er·ing
con·sid''er·a·ble
con·sid''er·ate
con·sid'er·a''tion
con·sign''
con'sign·ee''
con·sign''ment
con·sign''or
con·sist''
con·sis''tence
con·sis''ten·cy
  (*pl.* con·sis''ten·
  cies)
con·sis''tent
con·sis·to''ri·al

con·sis''to·ry
  (*pl.* con·sis·to''ries)
con·sol''a·ble
con'so·la''tion
con·sol''a·to'ry
con·sole'', *v.*
  soothe
con'sole, *n.*
  T.V. set
con·sol''i·date
  con·sol''i·dat'ed
  con·sol''i·dat'ing
con·sol'i·da''tion
con·sol''ing
con·som''me''
con''so·nance
con''so·nant
con'so·nan''tal
con·sort'', *v.*
  be in company
con''sort, *n.*
  spouse
con·sor''ti·um
  (*pl.* con·sor''ti·a)
con·spec''tus
con·spic''u·ous
con·spir''a·cy
  (*pl.* con·spir''a·cies)
con·spir''a·tor
con·spire''
con·spir''ing
con''sta·ble
con·stab''u·lar'y
  (*pl.* con·stab''u·lar'
  ies)
con''stan·cy
con''stant
con''stel·late
con'stel·la''tion
con'ster·na''tion
con''sti·pate
  con''sti·pat'ed
  con''sti·pat'ing
con'sti·pa''tion
con·stit''u·en·cy

(*pl.* con·stit"u·en·
cies)
con·stit"u·ent
con"sti·tute
con"sti·tut'ed
con"sti·tut'ing
con·sti·tu"tion
con·sti·tu"tion·al
con·sti·tu"tion·al"i·ty
con·sti·tu"tion·al·ly
con·strain"
con·strained"
con·straint"
con·strict"
con·stric"tion
con·stric"tive
con·struct", *v.*
  build
con"struct, *n.*
  idea; theory
con·struc"tion
con·struc"tive
con·struc"tor
con·strue"
con·stru"ing
con·sub·stan·ti·a"tion
con·sue·tude'
con"sul
  government agent
  (*see:* counsel and
  council)
con"su·lar
con"su·late
con"sul gen"er·al
  (*pl.* con"suls gen"
  er·al)
con·sult", *v.*
con"sult, *n.*
con·sult"ant
con·sul·ta"tion
con·sum"a·ble
con·sume"
con·sum"er
con·sum"er·ism
con·sum"ing
con"sum·mate

con"sum·mat'ed
con"sum·mat'ing
con"sum·ma"tion
con·sump"tion
con·sump"tive
con"tact
con·ta"gion
con·ta"gious
con"tain
con·tain"er
con·tain"ment
con·tam"i·nant
con·tam"i·nate', v.
con·tam"i·nate, *adj.*
con·tam"i·nat'ing
con·tam'i·na"tion
con"te
con·temn"
con·temn"er
  or contem"nor
con·tem"per
con·tem"plate
con"tem·plat'ed
con"tem·plat'ing
con·tem·pla"tion
con·tem"pla·tive
con·tem·po·ra"ne·ous
con·tem"po·rar'y
  (*pl.* con·tem"po·rar'
  ies)
con·tempt"
con·tempt"i·ble
con·temp"tu·ous
con·tend"
con·tend"er
con"tent, *n.*
  something contained
con·tent", *adj.*
  satisfied
con·tent"ed
con·ten"tion
con·ten"tious
con·tent"ment
con"tents
con·ter"mi·nous
con·test", *v.*

dispute
con"test, *n.*
  competition
con·test"a·ble
con·test"ant
con"text
con·tex"tu·al
con·ti·gu"i·ty
con·tig"u·ous
con"ti·nence
con"ti·nent
con·ti·nen"tal
con·tin"gen·cy
  (*pl.* con·tin"gen·
  cies)
con·tin"gent
con·tin"u·al
con·tin"u·al·ly
con·tin"u·ance
con·tin·u·a"tion
con·tin"ue
con·tin"ued
con·tin"u·ing
con·ti·nu"i·ty
  (*pl.* con·ti·nu"i·
  ties)
con·tin"u·ous
con·tin"u·um
  (*pl.* con·tin"u·a)
con"to
con·tort"
con·tor"tion
con·tor"tive
con"tour
con"tra·band
con"tra·bass
con"tra·bas·soon'
con"tra·cep"tion
con"tra·cep"tive
con"tract, *n.*
  agreement
con·tract", *v.*
  acquire; narrow
con·tract"i·ble
con·trac"tile
con·trac"tion

con″trac·tor
con·trac″tu·al
con·trac″tu·al·ly
con′tra·dict″
con·tra·dic″tion
con·tra·dic″to·ry
(*pl.* con′tra·dic″to·ries)
con″tra·dis·tinc″tion
con″trail
con″tra·in′di·ca″tion
con·tral″to
(*pl.* con·tral″tos)
con′tra·po·si″tion
con′tra·pun″tal
con′tra·ri″e·ty
con″trar·i·ly
con″trar·i·ness
con″tra·ri·wise
con″tra·ry
con·trast″, *v.*
show differences
con″trast, *n.*
something different
con·tras″tive
con′tra·vene″
con′tra·ven″ing
con′tra·ven″tion
con″tre·danse
con″tre·temps
(*pl.* con″tre·temps)
con·trib″ute
con·trib″ut·ed
con·trib″ut·ing
con′tri·bu″tion
con·trib″u·tor
con·trib″u·to′ry
con·trite″
con·tri″tion
con·triv″ance
con·trive″
con·trived″
con·triv″ing
con·trol″
con·trol″la·ble
con·trol″ler

con·trol″ling
con·trol″ tow″er
con′tro·ver″sial
con′tro·ver″sy
(*pl.* con′tro·ver′sies)
con″tro·vert′
con′tro·vert″i·ble
con·tu·ma″cious
con″tu·ma·cy
con′tu·me″li·ous
con″tu·me·ly
con·tuse″
con·tus″ing
con·tu″sion
co·nun″drum
con″ur·ba″tion
co″nus
con′va·lesce″
con′va·les″cence
con′va·les″cent
con′va·lesc″ing
con·vect″
con·vec″tion
con·vec″tive
con·vene″
con·ven″ience
con·ven″ient
con·ven″ing
con″vent
con·ven″ti·cle
con·ven″tion
con·ven″tion·al
con·ven′tion·al″i·ty
(*pl.* con·ven′tion·al″i·ties)
con·ven″tion·eer″
con·ven″tu·al
con·verge″
con·verg″ing
con·ver″gence
con·ver″ment
con·vers″a·ble
con·ver″sant
con′ver·sa″tion
con′ver·sa″tion·al

con″verse, *n.*
opposite
con·verse″, *adj.*
talk; reversed
con·verse″ly
con·vers″ing
con·ver″sion
con·ver″sive
con·vert″, *v.*
change
con″vert, *n.*
person
con·vert″er
con·vert″i·ble
con·vert″i·plane′
con″vex, *n.*
con·vex″, *adj.*
con·vex″i·ty
con·vey″
con·vey″ance
con·vey″er (or con·vey″or)
con·vin″ci·ble
con·vict″, *v.*
find guilty
con″vict, *n.*
person
con·vic″tion
con·vince″
con·vinc″ing
con·viv″i·al
con·viv′i·al″i·ty
con′vo·ca″tion
con·voke″
con″vo·lute
con″vo·lut′ing
con′vo·lu″tion
con·vol·vu·la″ceous
con″voy
con·vulse″
con·vuls″ing
con·vul″sion
con·vul″sion·ar′y
con·vul″sive
co″ny
(*pl.* co″nies)

con·y·rine''

coo
  cooed
  coo''ing
cook''book
cook''e·ry
cook''house
cook''ie
  food (*see:* kooky)
cook''out
Cook's'' tour''
cook''stove
cook''top
cool''ant
cool''er
cool''head''ed
coo''lie
  laborer (*see:* coolly
  and coulee)
cool''ly
  calmly (*see:* coolie
  and coulee)
coon
coon'' dog
coon''skin
co''-op
coop
  shelter (*see:* coupe
  and coup)
coop''er·age
co·op''er·ate
co·op''er·a'ting
co·op''er·a''tion
co·op''er·a'tive
co·opt''
co·or''di·nate', *v.*
co·or''di·nate, *n., adj.*
co·or''di·nat'ing
co·or''di·na''tion
co·or''di·na'tor
coot
coot''ie
co-own''
cop, *v.*
  copped
  cop''ping

to catch
cop, *n.*
  policeman
co'pa·cet''ic
co·part''ner
cope
  coped
  cop''ing
Co'pen·ha''gen
Co·per''ni·can
cop''i·er
co''pi'lot
cop''ing saw
co''pi·ous
co·pla''nar
co·pol''y·mer
cop''-out'
cop''per
cop''per·as
cop''per·head
cop''per·plate
cop''per·smith
cop''per·tone
cop''per·y
cop''pice
cop''ra
cop'ro·phil''i·a
co'-pros·per''i·ty
copse
cop''ter
Cop''tic
cop''u·la
cop''u·lar
cop''u·late
cop''u·lat'ing
cop'u·la''tion
cop''y
  cop''ied
  cop''y·ing
  (*pl.* cop''ies)
cop''y·book
cop''y·cat
cop''y-ed'it
cop''y·hold'er
cop''y·ist
cop''y·read'er

cop''y·right
cop''y·writ'er
coq au vin''
co·quet''
co''quet·ry
  (*pl.* co''quet·ries)
co·quette''
co·quet''tish
co·quille''
co·qui''na
cor''a·cle
cor''a·coid
cor''al
  marine skeleton
  (*see:* choral)
co·ri·a''ceous
co''ri·o·lis force
co''ri·um
cor'an·glais'
cor''bel
cord
  string; measure of
  wood (*see:* chord)
cord''age
cor''dial
cor·dial''i·ty
  (*pl.* cor·dial''i·ties)
cor'dil·le''ra
cord''ite
cord''less
cor·do''ba
cor''don
cor·don bleu''
cor·don sa·ni·taire''
cor''do·van
cor''du·roy
cord''wood
core
  center (*see:* corps)
co're·li''gion·ist
co're·spond''ent
  adulterer (*see:* corre-
  spondent)
cor''gi
cor''i·an'der
cor''ing

Cor″inth
Co·rin″thi·an
cork″ade
cork″board
cor″ker
cork″screw
cork″y
cor″co·rant
corm
cor″mo·phyte′
cor″mose
cor·na″ceous
corn″ball
Corn″ Belt
corn″ bread
corn″ cake
corn″cob
corn″crib
cor″ne·a
cor″ne·al
corned
cor″ne·ous
cor″ner
cor″ner·stone
cor·net
  trumpet (see: coro-
  net)
cor·net″ist
corn″fed
corn″flakes
corn″flow′er
corn″husk
corn″husk′er
cor″nice
cor″nic·ing
corn″i·er
corn″i·est
cor·ni·fi·ca″tion
Cor″nish
corn″meal
corn″ oil
corn″ pone
corn″row
corn″ silk
corn″stalk
corn″starch

cor′nu·co″pi·a
cor′nu·co″pi·an
cor·nu″to
corn″y
cor″o·dy
co·rol″la
cor″ol·lar′y
  (pl. cor″ol·lar′ies)
co·ro″na
cor″o·nach
cor″o·nal
cor·o·nene″
cor″o·nar′y
  (pl. cor″o·nar′ies)
cor′o·na″tion
cor″o·ner
cor″o·net
  crown (see: cornet)
cor″po·ral
cor″po·rate
cor″po·ra″tion
cor″po·ra′tive
cor·po″re·al
corps
  group (pl. corps)
  (see: core and
  corpse)
corps de bal·let″
corpse
  dead body (see:
  corps)
corps″man
cor″pu·lence
cor″pu·lent
cor″pus
  (pl. cor″po·ra)
Cor″pus Chris″ti
cor″pus de·lic″ti
cor″pus ju″ris
cor″pus·cle
cor·rade″
  cor·rad″ed
  cor·rad″ing
cor·ral″, v.
  gather together
cor·ral″, n.

  enclosure (see: cho-
  rale)
cor·ra″sion
cor·rect″
cor·rect″a·ble
cor·rec″tion
cor·rec″tive
cor″re·late
cor″re·lat′ing
cor·re·la″tion
cor·rel″a·tive
cor″re·spond″
cor″re·spond″ence
cor″re·spond″ent
  writer (see: core-
  spondent)
cor·ri″da
cor″ri·dor
cor·ri·gen″dum
cor·rob″o·rate
cor·rob″o·rat′ing
cor·rob′o·ra″tion
cor·rob″o·ra′tive
cor·ob″o·ra′tor
cor·rode″
cor·rod″ing
cor·ro″sion
cor·ro″sive
cor″ru·gate
cor″ru·gat′ing
cor·ru·ga″tion
cor·rupt″
cor·rupt″i·ble
cor·rup″tion
cor·rup″tive
cor·sage″
cor″sair
cor″set
cor″set·ing
Cor″si·ca
cor·tege″
cor″tex
  (pl. cor″ti·ces)
cor″ti·cal
cor″ti·cate
cor″ti·sone

co·run″dum
cor″us·cate
cor·us·cat″ing
cor·us·ca″tion
cor·vette″
cor·vee″
cor″y·phee
co·ry″za
Co″sa Nos″tra
co·se″cant
co·sig″na·to·ry
  (*pl.* co·sig″na·to′ries)
co′sign″er
co″sine
cos·met″ic
cos″me·ti″cian
cos″me·tol″o·gy
cos″mic
cos″mi·cal·ly
cos″mic ray″
cos·mog″o·ny
  (*pl.* cos·mog″o·nies)
cos·mog″ra·phy
cos″mo·line
cos·mol″o·gy
cos″mo·naut
cos″mo·pol″i·tan
cos″mos
  (*pl.* cos″mos)
cos″mo·tion′
Cos″sack
cos″set
cost
cos″ta
cos″tal
co″star
cos″tard
Cos″ta Ri″ca
co-star″ring
cost-ef·fec″tive
cos″ter
  street seller
cost″er
  one who finds costs

cos″ter·mong·er
cost″ing
cost″li·er
cost″li·est
cost″li·ness
cost″ly
cost″-plus″
cos″trel
cos·tume″, *v.*
  supply with costume
cos″tume, *n.*
  dress
cos·tum″er
cos·tum″ing
cot
co·tan″gent
co·tan·gen″tial
cote
  shelter (*see:* coat)
co″te·rie
co·thur″nus
co·til″lion
cot″tage
cot″tag·er
cot″ter
cot″ter pin
cot″ton
Cot″ton Belt′
cot″ton can″dy
cot″ton·mouth
cot″ton·pick″in′
cot″ton seed′
cot″ton·tail
cot″ton·wood
cot″ton·y
cot′y·le″don
couch
couch″ant
cou″gar
cough
cough″ drop′
could
cou″lee
  ravine (*see:* coolly
  and coolie)
cou·lisse″

cou″lomb
coul″ter
cou″ma·rin
cou″ma·rone
coun″cil
  assembly (*see:* counsel and consul)
coun″ci·lor
  council member
  (*see:* counselor)
coun″sel
  advice (*see:* council and consul)
coun″seled
coun″sel·ing
coun″se·lor
  adviser (*see:* councilor)
count
count″a·ble
count″down′
coun″te·nance
coun″te·nanc·ing
count″er
coun′ter·act″
coun′ter·ac″tion
coun′ter·at·tack″, *v.*
  to attack
coun′ter·at·tack′, *n.*
  an attack
coun′ter·bal″ance
coun′ter·bal″anc·ing
coun″ter·blow′
coun″ter·charge″, *v.*
  to accuse
coun′ter·charge′, *n.*
  a charge
coun′ter·charg″ing
coun″ter·check
coun″ter·claim″, *v.*
  make a claim
coun″ter·claim′, *n.*
  a claim
coun′ter·clock″wise′
coun′ter·cul″ture
coun′ter·es″pi·o·nage

coun"ter·feit
coun"ter·feit·er
coun"ter·flow
coun"ter·foil
coun'ter·in·sur"gent
coun'ter·in·tel"li·gence
coun'ter·in·tu"i·tive
coun'ter·ir"ri·tant
coun"ter·man'
coun"ter·mand", v.
  cancel
coun"ter·mand', n.
  canceling order
coun"ter·march
coun"ter·meas'ure
coun"ter·mine
coun'ter·of·fen"sive
coun"ter·pane'
coun"ter·part'
coun"ter·point'
coun"ter·poise
coun"ter·pois'ing
coun'ter·pro·pos"al
coun"ter·punch
coun"ter Ref'or·ma"tion
coun"ter·rev'o·lu"tion
coun"ter·sank
coun"ter·shaft
coun"ter·sign
coun'ter·sig"na·ture
coun"ter·sink
  coun"ter·sank
  coun"ter·sunk
  coun"ter·sink'ing
coun"ter·spy
  (*pl.* coun"ter·spies)
coun"ter·state'ment
coun'ter·ten"or
coun"ter·top
coun"ter·thrust
coun"ter·vail
coun'ter·weigh"
coun"ter·weight

count"ess
count"ing·house'
count"less
coun"tri·fied
coun"try
  (*pl.* coun"tries)
coun"try club
coun"try·folk
coun"try·man
coun"try·side
coun"try·wom'an
coun"ty
  (*pl.* coun"ties)
coun'ty seat"
coup
  bold act (*see:* coop
  and coupe)
coup de grace"
  (*pl.* coups de grace")
coup d'e·tat"
  (*pl.* coups d'e·tat")
coupe
  car (*see:* coup and coop)
cou"ple
cou"pler
cou"plet
cou"pling
cou"pon
cour"age
cou·rant"
cou·ra"geous
cou"ri·er
course
  path (*see:* coarse)
cours"er
cours"ing
court
cour"te·ous
cour"te·san
cour"te·sy
  politeness (*see:* curtsy)
cour"te·sy card'
court"house

cour"ti·er
court"li·ness
court"ly
court"-mar'tial
  court"-mar'tialed
  court"-mar'tial·ing
court"room'
court"ship'
court"side"
court"yard'
cous"in
  relative (*see:* cozen)
couth
cou·ture"
cou·tu"ri·er'
co·va"lent
cove
cov"en
cov"e·nant
cov"er
cov"er·age
cov"er·all
cov"er·let
cov"ert
cov"er·ture
cov"er·up'
cov"et
cov"et·ing
cov"et·ous
cov"ey
cov"en
cow"ard
  person lacking courage (*see:* cowered)
cow"ard·ice
cow"ard·ly
cow"bane'
cow"bell'
cow"bird'
cow"boy'
cow"catch·er
cow"er
cow"ered
  did cower (*see:* coward)
cow"girl'

cow"hage'
cow"hand'
cow"herd'
cow"hide'
 cow"hid'ing
cowl
cow"lick'
cowl"ing
co"-work'er
cow"poke'
cow"pox'
cow"rie'
 (*pl.* cow"ries)
cow"slip'
cox"comb'
cox·i"tis
cox"swain
coy"ly
coy"ness
coy·o"te
coz"en
 dupe (*see:* cousin)
coz"i·er
coz"i·est
coz"i·ly
co"zi·ness
co"zy
crab
 crabbed
 crab"bing
crab" ap'ple
crack"back'
crab"by
crab" grass
crack
crack"brain
crack"down
cracked
crack"er
crack"er·bar'rel
crack"er·jack'
Crack"er Jack™
crack"le
crack"le·ware'
crack"ling
crack"nel

crack"pot
crack"up
Crac"ow
cra"dle
cra"dle·song
cra"dling
craft
craft"i·er
craft"i·est
craft"i·ness
crafts"man
craft"y
crag
crag"gi·er
crag"gi·est
crag"gy
cram
cram"ming
cramp
cram"pon
cran"ber'ry
 (*pl.* cran"ber'ries)
crane
cra"ni·al
cra·nid"i·um
cran"ing
cra·ni·om"e·try
cra"ni·um
crank
crank"case
crank"i·est
crank"i·ness
crank"shaft
crank"y
cran"ny
 (*pl.* cran"nies)
crape"hang·er
crap"pie
craps
crap"shoot'er
crash
crash"-land
crash land"ing
cra"sis
crass
crass"ly

cras·su·la"ceous
crate
 crat"ed
 crat"ing
cra"ter
cra·vat"
crave
 craved
 crav"ing
cra"ven
cra"ver
craw
craw"fish
 (*pl.* craw"fish)
crawl
crawl"i·est
crawl"y
cray"fish
 (*pl.* cray"fish)
cray"on
craze
cra"zi·er
cra"zi·est
cra"zi·ly
cra"zi·ness
craz"ing
cra"zy
creak
 squeak (*see:* creek)
creak"y
cream" cheese
cream"-col·ored
cream"er·y
 (*pl.* cream"er·ies)
cream"i·er
cream"i·est
cream"y
crease
creas"ing
cre·ate"
 cre·at"ed
 cre·at"ing
cre·at"i·nine'
cre·a"tion
cre·a"tion"ism
cre·a"tive

cre′a·tiv″i·ty
cre′a″tor
crea″tur·al
crea″ture
creche
cre″dence
cre·den″tial
cre·den″za
cred″it
cred′i·bil″i·ty
cred″i·ble
  believable (*see:* cred-
  itable)
cred″it·a·bil″i·ty
cred″it·a·ble
  deserving of credit
  (*see:* credible)
cred″it·a·bly
cred″it
cred″i·tor
cred″it un′ion
cred″it·wor′thy
cre″do
  (*pl.* cre″dos)
cre·du″li·ty
cred″u·lous
Cree
  (*pl.* Cree)
creed
creek
  stream (*see:* creak
  and crick)
Creek
  (*pl.* Creek)
creel
creep
 crept
 creep″ing
creep″er
creep″i·er
creep″i·est
cre″mate
 cre″mat·ed
 cre″mat·ing
cre·ma″tion
cre′ma·to″ri·um

cre″ma·to″ry
  (*pl.* cre″ma·to′ries)
creme de ca·ca″o
creme de menthe″
cren″el·at·ed
Cre″ole
cre″o·sote
crepe
crepe su·zette″
  (*pl.* crepe su·
  zettes″)
cre·pus″cu·lar
cre·scen″do
cres″cent
cre″sol
cress
cres″set
crest
crest″fall′en
cre·ta″ceous
Crete
cre″tin
cre″tin·ism
cre·tonne″
cre·vasse″
  break (*see:* crevice)
cre·vas″sing
crev″ice
  fissure (*see:* crevass)
crew″ cut
crew″el
crew″neck′
crib
 cribbed
 crib″bing
crib″bage
crick
  cramp (*see:* creek)
crick″et
cried
cri″er
crime
Cri·me″a
crim″i·nal
crim′i·nal″i·ty
crim″i·nal·ly

crim′i·nol″o·gist
crim′i·nol″o·gy
crimp
crim″son
cringe
 cringed
 cring″ing
crin″gle
crin″kle
crin″kli·est
crin″kling
crin″kly
cri″noid
crin″o·line
cri·nos″i·ty
cri″num
cri·o″llo
crip″ple
crip″pling
cri″sis
  (*pl.* cri″ses)
crisp
cris″pate
crisp″er
crisp″i·er
crisp″i·est
crisp″y
criss″cross
cris″ta
cris″tate
cri·te″ri·on
  (*pl.* cri·te″ri·a)
crit″ic
crit″i·cal
crit″i·cal·ly
crit″i·cism
crit″i·cize
crit″i·ciz′ing
cri·tique″
crit″ter
croak
croak″er
Cro·a″tia
cro·chet″
cro·chet″ing
crock″er·y

croc″o·dile
cro·cre″tin
cro″cus
  (*pl.* cro″cus·es)
croft
crois·sant″
Cro-Mag″non
crom″lech
cro″ny
  (*pl.* cro″nies)
crook″ed
croon″er
crop
crop″-dust
crop″-dust′er
crop″per
crop″ping
cro·quet″
  game (*see:* cro-
  quette)
cro·quette″
  food (*see:* croquet)
cro″qui′gnole
cro″sier
cross
cross″arm
cross″bar
cross″beam
cross″bones′
cross″bow′
cross″breed′
  cross″bred′
  cross″breed′ing
cross″-coun″try
cross″cheek′
cross″cur′rent
cross″cut′
crosse
cross″-ex·am′i·na″
  tion
cross″-ex·am′ine
cross″-ex·am″in·ing
cross″-eyed′
cross″-fer′ti·li·za″tion
cross″-fer″ti·lize′
cross″-fer″ti·liz′ing

cross″fire′
cross″-grained″
cross″hair′
cross″hatch′
cross″in″dex
cross″ing
cross″-leg″ged
cross″link
cross″o′ver
cross″patch′
cross″piece
cross″-pol″li·nate′
cross″-pol″li·nat′ing
cross″-pol″li·na″tion
cross″-pur″pose
cross″-ques″tion
cross′-re·fer″
cross′-re·fer′ring
cross′-ref″er·ence
cross″road′
cross″sec′tion
cross″-stitch′
cross″street′
cross″talk′
cross″tie′
cross″-town′
cross″talk′
cross″wind′
cross″wise′
cross″word′ puz′zle
crotch
crotch″et
crotch″et·i·ness
crotch″et·y
crouch
croup
crou″pi·er
crous·tade″
crou″ton′
crow
crow″bar′
crowd
crow″foot′
crown
crown″glass′
crown″piece

crown″saw′
crow's″-foot′
  (*pl.* crow's″-feet′)
crow's″-nest′
C′R′T″
  cathode-ray tube
cruck
cru″cial
cru″ci·ble
cru″ci·fix
cru″ci·fix″ion
cru″ci·form
cru″ci·fy
  cru″ci·fied
  cru″ci·fy′ing
crud
crud″di·est
crude
crude″ly
crude″ness
crude″oil″
cru″di·ty
cru″el
cru″el·ly
cru″el·ty
  (*pl.* cru″el·ties)
cru″et
cruise
  travel (*see:* cruse)
cruise″mis′sile
cruis″er
cruis″ing
crul″ler
crumb
crum″ble
crum″bling
crum″bly
crumb″y
  full of crumbs (*see:*
  crummy)
crum″my
  inferior (*see:*
  crumby)
crump
crum″pet
crum″ple

crum″pling
crunch″i·er
crunch″i·est
crunch″y
crup″per
cru″ral
crus
cru·sade″
cru·sad″ing
cruse
  container (*see:*
  cruise)
crush″a·ble
crust
crus·ta″cean
crus″tal
crust″ed
crust″i·est
crust″y
crutch
  (*pl.* crutch″es)
crux
cru·zei″ro
cry
 cried
 cry″ing
  (*pl.* cries)
cry″ba·by
  (*pl.* cry″ba′bies)
cry′o·bank
cry′o·bi·ol″o·gy
cry′o·gen″ics
cry′o·sur″ger·y
crypt
crypt′a·nal″y·sis
crypt·an″a·lyst
cryp″tic
cryp″to·graph′
cryp·tog″ra·pher
cryp′to·graph″ic
cryp·tog″ra·phy
crys″tal
crys″tal gaz″ing
crys″tal·line
crys′tal·li·za″tion
crys″tal·lize

crys″tal·liz′ing
crys′tal·log″ra·phy
crys′tal·loid″
cub
Cu″ba
cub″a·ture′
cub″by·hole
cube
cu″beb
cubed
cube″ root″
cu″bic
cu″bi·cal
  cube-shaped (*see:*
  cubicle)
cu″bi·cle
  alcove (*see:* cubical)
cub″ing
cub″ism
cu″bit
cu″boid
cuck″old
cuck″oo
cuck″ooed
cu″cum·ber
cu·cur″bit
cud
cud″dle
cud″dling
cudg″el
cudg″el·ing
cue
  signal; stick (*see:*
  queue)
cue″ ball
cuff″ link
cu″ing
  signaling (*see:*
  queuing)
cui·rass″
cui·sine″
cul″-de-sac″
cu″li·na
cull
cul″mi·nate
cul″mi·nat′ing

cul′mi·na″tion
cu·lottes″
cul′pa·bil″i·ty
cul″pa·ble
cul″pa·bly
cul″prit
cultch
cult″ist
cul″ti·va·ble
cul″ti·vate
cul″ti·vat′ing
cul′ti·va″tion
cul″tur·al
cul″tur·al·ly
cul″ture
cul″tured
cul″ture shock
cul″tur·ing
cul″ver·in
cul″vert
cum″ber·some
cum″brance
cum″in
cum lau″de
cum″mer·bund′
cu″mu·la′tive
cu′mu·lo·nim″bus
  (*pl.* cu′mu·lo·nim″
  bi)
cu″mu·lus
  (*pl.* cu″mu·li)
cunc·ta″tion
cu·ne″i·form
cun″ning
cup″board
cup″cake
cup″ful
  (*pl.* cup″fuls)
cu·pid″i·ty
cu″po·la
cupped
cup″ping
cu″pre·ous
cu″pric
cur″a·ble
cu·ra″re

cu″rate
cur″a·tive
cu·ra″tor
curb″stone
curd
cur″dle
cur″dling
cure
cure″-all
cu·ret″tage
cur″few
cur″ing
cu″ri·o
  (*pl.* cu″ri·os)
cu′ri·o″sa
cu·ri·os″i·ty
  (*pl.* cu·ri·os″i·ties)
cu″ri·ous
cu″ri·um
cur″lew
curl″i·cue
curl″i·er
curl″i·est
curl″ing
curl″y
cur·mudg″eon
cur″rant
  berry (*see:* current)
cur″ren·cy
  (*pl.* cur″ren·cies)
cur″rent
  present (*see:* currant)
cur·ric″u·lar
cur·ric″u·lum
cur″ry
  (*pl.* cur″ries)
cur″ry·comb
cur″ry·ing
curse
curs″ing
cur″sive
cur″sor
cur″so·ri·ly
cur″so·ry
cur·tail″
cur″tain

cur″ti·lage
curt″sied
curt″sy·ing
curt″sy
  (*pl.* curt″sies) (*see:*
  courtesy)
cur·va″ceous
cur″va·ture
curve
cur″vet
curv″i·er
curv″i·est
cur′vi·lin″e·ar
curv″ing
curv″y
cush″ion
cusk
cusp
cus″pi·date′
cus″pid
cus″pi·dor
cuss″ed
cus″tard
cus·to″di·al
cus·to″di·an
cus″to·dy
cus″tom
cus″tom·ar″i·ly
cus″tom·ar′y
cus″tom-built″
cus″tom·er
cus″tom·house
cus″tom-made″
cus″toms un′ion
cu·ta″ne·ous
cut″a·way
cut″back
cut″down
cute
cut″ glass″
cu″ti·cle
cut″ie
cut″lass
  (*pl.* cut″lass·es)
cut″ler·y
cut″let

cut″off
cut″out
cut″-rate″
cut″ter
cut″throat
cut″ting
cut″tle·bone′
cut″tle·fish
cut″up
cut″wa′ter
cut″worm
cy″a·nide
cy·an″o·gen
cy′ber·net″ic
cy′ber·net″ics
cy·borg″
cy″cla·mate
cy″cle
cy″cler
cy″clic
cy″cli·cal
cy″cli·cal·ly
cy″cling
cy″clist
cy′clo·hex″ane
cy·clom″e·ter
cy″clone
cy′clo·pe″di·a
cy′clo·ram″a
cy′clo·spor″in
cy″clo·tron
cyg″net
  swan (*see:* signet)
cyl″in·der
cy·lin″dri·cal
cyl″in·droid′
cym″bal
  musical instrument
  (*see:* symbol)
cyme
cyn″ic
cyn″i·cal
cyn″i·cism
cy″no·sure
cy″press

tree (*pl.* cy"press·
es) (*see:* Cyprus)
Cy"prus
nation (*see:* cypress)
cys·tec"to·my
(*pl.* cys·tec"to·
mies)
cyst"ic
cys·ti"tis
cys"to·scope
cys·tos"co·py
(*pl.* cys·tos"co·pies)
cy·tol"o·gist
cy·tol"o·gy
cy"to·plasm'
cy'to·tox"in
czar
czar"e·vitch
cza·ri"na
czar"ist
Czech'o·slo·va"ki·a

D

dab
dabbed
dab"bing
dab"ble
dab"bler
dab"bling
da ca"po
dace
da"cha
Da"chau
dachs"hund'
Da"cron™
dac"tyl
dad"dy
(*pl.* dad"dies)
dad"dy-long"legs'
dade
dae"dal
da"do
(*pl.* da"does)
daf"fo·dil

daf"fy
daft
dag
dag"ger
da·guerre"o·type'
dahl"ia
dai"dle
dai"kon
dai"ly
(*pl.* dai"lies)
dain"ti·er
dain"ti·est
dain"ti·ly
dain"ti·ness
dain"ty
dai·qui·ri
dair"y
(*pl.* dair"ies)
dair"y farm
dair"y·ing
dair"y·maid
dair"y·man
da"is
dai"sy
(*pl.* dai"sies)
Da·ko"ta
dale
Da"lai La"ma
Dal"las
dal"li·ance
dal"ly
Dal·ma"tian
dal se"gno
dalt
dam
dammed"
dam"ming
barrier (*see:* damn)
dam"age
dam"aged
dam"ag·ing
dam"a scene'
Da·mas"cus
dam"ask
dam"mar
dam"ma·ret

damn
damned
damn"ing
condemn (*see:* dam)
dam·na"tion
damp"en
damp"en·er
damp"er
damp"ness
dam"sel
dam"sel fly'
dam"son
dance
danced
danc"ing
danc"er
dan"cer·cise
dan"de·li'on
dan"der
dan'di·fi·ca"tion
dan"di·fy'
dan"di·fied'
dan"di·fy'ing
dan"dle
dan"dling
dan"druff
dan"dy
dan"ger
dan"ger·ous
dan"gle
dan"gling
da"ni·o
dank
dank"ly
dank"ness
danse ma·ca"bre
dan·seur"
Dan"ube
daph"ni·a
daph"ni·oid'
dap"per
dap"ple
dap"pled
dap"pling
darb
Dar·da·nelles"

dare
 dared
 dar"ing
dare"dev'il
dare"say"
dar"i·ole'
Dar·jee"ling
dark"en
dark"ling
dark" horse"
dark" mat"ter
dark"room'
dar"ling
darn
 darned
 darn"ing
dar"nel
darn"ing nee"dle
dart"board'
dart"er
dar"tle
 dar"tled
 dar"tling
Dar·win"i·an
Dar"win·ism'
dash
 dashed
 dash"ing
dash"board'
dash"er
da·shi"ki
dash"pot
das"tard
da"ta
 (*sing.* da"tum)
da"ta·bank'
da"ta·base'
da"ta·flow'
da·ta·ma"tion
da·ta"na'
da"ta proc'ess·ing
da"ta proc'ess·or
date
 dat"ed
 dat"ing
date"less

date"line'
date" palm'
da"tive
da"tum
 (*pl.* da"ta)
da·tu"ra
da·tu"ric
daub"er
dau"dit'
daugh"ter
daugh"ter-in-law'
 (*pl.* daugh"ters-in-
 law')
daun"der
dau'no·my"cin
daunt
daunt"less
dau"phin
dav"en·port'
dav"it
daw
daw"dle
 daw"dled
 daw"dling
daw"dler
dawn
dawn"streak
day"bea'con
day"bed'
day"book'
day"break'
day" camp'
day" care'
day" coach'
day"dream'
day"light'
day"light'-sav'ing
 time'
day" lil'y
day"room'
day"star'
day"time'
daze
 dazed
 daz"ing
daz"zle

daz"zled
daz"zling
D"-day'
dea"con
dea"con·ess
de·ac"ti·vate'
de·ac"'ti·va"tion
dead"beat'
dead"en
dead"-end", *adj.*
 limiting
dead" end", *n.*
 street; impasse
dead"eye'
dead"head'
dead" heat'
dead" let"ter
dead"li·est
dead"line'
dead"li·ness
dead"lock'
dead"ly
dead"ness
dead"pan'
dead"weight'
dead"wood'
deaf
deaf"en
deaf"-mute'
deal
 dealt
 deal"ing
deal"er·ship'
de·am"i·nize"
dean"er·y
 (*pl.* dean"er·ies)
dear
 beloved (*see:* deer)
dearth
de·as"pir·ate'
death
death"bed'
death"blow'
death"knell'
death"less
death"ly

death'' row''
death's''-head'
death''shot'
death'' squad'
death''trap'
death''watch'
de·ba''cle
de·bar''
de·bark''
de·bar·ka''tion
de·bar''ment
de·bar''ring
de·base''
de·based
de·bas''ing
de·bat''a·ble
de·bate''
de·bat''ed
de·bat''ing
de·bat''er
de·bauch''
de·bauch·ee''
de·bauch''er·y
(pl. de·bauch''er·ies)
de·ben''ture
de·bil''i·tate'
de·bil''i·tat'ed
de·bil''i·tat'ing
de·bil''i·ta''tion
de·bil''i·ty
(pl. de·bil''i·ties)
deb''it
deb'o·nair''
de·bouch''
de·bride''ment
de·brief''
de·bris''
debt''or
de·bug''
de·bugged''
de·bug''ging
de·bunk''
de·but''
deb''u·tante'
dec''ade

dec''a·dence
dec''a·dent
de·caf''fein·ate'
de·caf''fein·at'ed
de·caf''fein·at'ing
dec''a·gon'
dec''a·gram'
dec'a·he''dron
(pl. dec'a·he''drons)
de''cal
de·cal'ci·fi·ca''tion
de·cal'ci·fi''er
de·cal''ci·fy'
de·cal'ci·fied'
de·cal'ci·fy'ing
de·cal'co·ma·ni'a
de·ca·les''cence
dec''a·li'ter
Dec''a·logue'
dec''a·me'ter
de·camp''
de·cant''
de·can''ta''tion
de·cant''er
de·cap''i·tate'
de·cap''i·tat'ed
de·cap''i·tat'ing
de·cap'i·ta''tion
de''ca·pod'
dec''are
de·car''bon·ate'
de·car'box''y·lat'ing
de·ca'su·al·i·za''tion
de·cath''lon
de·cay''
de·cease''
de·ceased'
de·ceas''ing
de·ce''dent
de·ceit''ful
de·ceit''ful·ly
de·ceit''ful·ness
de·ceive''
de·ceived''
de·ceiv''ing
de·cel''er·ate'

de·cel''er·at'ed
de·cel''er·at'ing
de·cel'er·a''tion
de·cel'er·a''tor
De·cem''ber
de''cen·cy
(pl. de''cen·cies)
de·cen''ni·al
de·cent''
appropriate (see: de-
scent and dissent)
de·cent·ly
de·cen'tral·i·za''tion
de·cen''tral·ize'
de·cen''tral·ized'
de·cen''tral·iz'ing
de·cep''tion
de·cep''tive
de·cep''tive·ly
de·chlor'i·da''tion
dec''i·are'
dec''i·bel'
de·cide''
de·cid''ed
de·cid''ing
de·cid''u·ate
de·cid''u·ous
dec''i·gram'
dec''i·li'ter
de·cil''lion
dec''i·mal
dec''i·mal·ly
dec''i·mate'
dec''i·mat'ed
dec''i·mat'ing
dec''i·me'ter
de·ci''pher
de·ci''pher·a·ble
de·ci''sion
de·ci''sive
deck'' hand''
deck''house'
deck''le
de·claim''
dec'la·ma''tion
de·clam''a·to'ry

de·clar″a·tive
de·clar″a·to′ry
de·clare″
  de·clared′
  de·clar″ing
de·clas·se″
de·clas″si·fy′
  de·clas″si·fied
  de·clas″si·fy′ing
de·clen″sion
dec′li·na″tion
de·cline″
  de·clined′
  de·clin″ing
de·clin″er
de·cliv″i·ty
  (*pl.* de·cliv″i·ties)
de·coct″
de·cod″a·ble
de·code″
  de·cod″ed
  de·cod″ing
de·cod″er
de·col′le·tage″
de·col′le·te″
de·col′o·ni·za″tion
de·col′o·nize
de·com·mis″sion
de·com·pose″
de·com·po·si″tion
de·com·po″sure
de·com·pres″sion
de·con·gest″ant
de′con·tam″i·nate′
  de′con·tam″i·nat′ed
  de′con·tam″i·nat′ing
de′con·tam′i·na″tion
de·con·trol″
de·con·trol″ling
de·cor″
dec″o·rate′
dec″o·rat′ing
dec″o·ra″tion
dec′o·ra″tion·ist′
dec″o·ra′tive
dec″o·ra′tor

dec″o·rous
de′cor·ti·ca″tion
de·co″rum
de′cou″page′
de·coy″
de·crease″
  de·creased″
  de·creas″ing
de·cree″
  de·creed″
  de·cree″ing
de·cree″ment
de·crep″it
de·crep″i·tude′
de·cre·scen″do
de·cre″tal
de·crim″i·nal·ize′
de·cry″
  de·cried″
  de·cry″ing
de·crypt″
ded″i·cant′
ded″i·cate′
  ded″i·cat′ed
  ded″i·cat′ing
ded′i·ca″tion
ded″i·ca·to′ry
de·duce″
de·duc″i·ble
de·duc″ing
de·duct″
de·duct″i·bil′i·ty
de·duct″i·ble
de·duc″tion
de·duc″tive
deed
deed′hold″er
dee″jay′
deem
de-em″pha·size′
deep
deep″-dish′
deep″en
Deep″freeze™
deep″-fry″
  deep″-fried″

deep″-fry″ing
deep″-root″ed
deep″-sea″
deep″-seat″ed
deep″six
deep″wa′ter·man
deer
  animal (*pl.* deer)
  (*see:* dear)
deer″hound′
deer″skin′
deer″stalk′er′
de·es″ca·late′
de·es″ca·la″tion
de·face″
  de·faced″
  de·fac″ing
de·face″ment
de fac″to
de·fal″cate
de·fal·ca″tion
def′a·ma″tion
de·fam″a·to′ry
de·fame″
  de·famed″
  de·fam″ing
de·fam″ing·ly
de·fault″
de·feas″i·ble
de·feat″
de·feat″ist
def″e·cate′
def′e·ca″tion
de·fect″, *v.*
desert
de″fect, *n.*
  imperfection
de·fec″tion
de·fec″tive
de·fec″tor
de·fen′es·tra″tion
de·fend″
de·fend″ant
de·fense″
de·fense″less
de·fen″si·ble

de·fen″sive
de·fer″
  de·ferred″
  de·fer″ring
def″er·ence
  respect (*see:* differ-
  ence)
def′er·en″tial
  respectful (*see:* dif-
  ferential)
de·fer″ment
de·fer″ral
de·fer″ring
de·fi″ance
de·fi″ant
de·fi″cien·cy
  (*pl.* de·fi″cien·cies)
de·fi″cient
def″i·cit
de·fied″
de·fi″lade″
de·file″
de·fil″ing
de·fin″a·ble
de·fine″
de·fin″ing
def″i·nite
def′i·ni″tion
de·fin″i·tive
de·flate″
de·flat″ing
de·fla″tion
de·fla″tion·ar′y
de·fla″tor
de·flect″
de·flec″tion
de·flec″tor
de·floc″cul·at′ing
de·flow″er
de·fog″
de·fog″ger
de·fo″li·ant
de·fo″li·ate
  de·fo″li·at′ed
  de·fo″li·at′ing
de·fo′li·a′tion

de·for″est
de·for′est·a″tion
de·formed″
de·form″ity
  (*pl.* de·form″i·ties)
de·fraud″
de·fray″
de·fray″al
de·frock″
de·frost″
de·frost″er
deft
de·funct″
de·fuse″
  de·fused″
  de·fus″ing
de·fy″
  de·fied″
  de·fy″ing
de·gauss″
de·gen″er·a·cy
de·gen″er·al·ize′
de·gen″er·ate
de·gen″er·at′ing
de·gen′er·a″tion
de·gen″er·a·tive
de·glaze″
de·glu″ti·nate″
de·grad″a·ble
deg·ra·da″tion
de·grade″
de·grad″ing
de·grad″ed·ly
de·gree″
de·gres″sive
de·hu″man·ize
  de·hu″man·ized
  de·hu″man·iz′ing
de·hu′mid·i·fi·ca″tion
de·hu′mid″i·fi·er
de·hu′mid″i·fy
de·hy″drate
de·hy″drat·ed
de·hy″drat·ing
de·hy″dra″tion
de·hy″dro·gen·ate′

de·hy′dro·gen·a″tion
de·ice″
  de·iced″
  de·ic″ing
de·ic″er
de·i′fi·ca″tion
de·i″fi·er
de″i·fy′
  de″i·fied
  de″i·fy′ing
deign
de″ism
de·is″tic
de″i·ty
  (*pl.* de″i·ties)
de·ja vu″
de·ject″ed
de·jec″tion
de ju″re
Del″a·ware′
del·a·tor″i·an
de·lay″
de·lead″
de·lec″ta·ble
del″e·gate′
  del″e·gat′ed
  del″e·gat′ing
del′e·ga″tion
de·lete″
  de·let″ed
  de·let″ing
del′e·te·ri·ous
de·le″tion
delft
Del″hi
del″i
  (*pl.* del″is)
de·lib″er·ate′
de·lib″er·ate·ness
de·lib′er·a″tion
del″i·ca·cy
  (*pl.* del″i·ca·cies)
del″i·cate
del″i·cate·ly
del′i·ca·tes″sen
de·li″cious

de·lict"u·al
de·light"
de·light"ful
de·light"ful·ly
de·lign'i·fi·ca"tion
de·lin"e·ate
 de·lin"e·at'ed
 de·lin"e·at'ing
de·lin"e·a"tion
de·lin"e·a'tor
de·lin"quen·cy
de·lin"quent
de·lir"i·ous
de·lir"i·um
de·lir"i·um tre'mens
del'i·quesce"
de·liv"er·ance
de·liv"er·er
de·liv"er·y
 (*pl.* de·liv"er·ies)
de·louse"
 de·loused *or* de·lice
 de·lous"ing
del·phin"i·um
del"ta
del"ta ray'
del"ta wave'
del"ta wing"
del"toid
de·lude"
 de·lud"ed
 de·lud"ing
del"uge
 del"uged
 del"ug·ing
de·lu"sion
de·lu"sive
de·luxe"
delve
 delved
 delv"ing
delv"er
de·mag"net·ize
dem'a·gog"ic
dem'a·gog"i·cal·ly
dem"a·gogue

dem"a·gogu'er·y
de·mand
 de·mand"ed
 de·mand"ing
de·mand"-pull'
de·man"toid de·mar"
 cate
de·mar"cat·ed
de·mar"cat·ing
de·mar·ca"tion
de·ma·ter'i·al·i·za"
 tion
de·mean"
de·mean"or
dem"en·cy
de·ment"ed
de·men"tia
de·mer"it
de·mes"mer·ize'
de·mesne"
dem"i·god'
dem"i·john'
de·mil"i·ta·rize'
de·min"er·al·ized"
dem'i·prem"ise
dem"i·qua'ver
de·mise
dem'i·sem"i·quav'er
dem'i·tasse'
de·mit"ting
dem"o
de·mo"bi·li·za"tion
de·mo"bi·lize'
 de·mo"bi·lized'
 de·mo"bi·liz'ing
de·moc"ra·cy
 (*pl.* de·moc"ra·cies)
dem"o·crat'
dem'o·crat"ic
dem'o·crat"i·cal·ly
de·moc"ra·tize'
de·moc"ra·tiz'ing
de·mog"ra·pher
de·mo·graph"ic
de·mo·graph"i·cal·ly
de·mog"ra·phy

de·mol"ish
dem'o·li"tion
de"mon
de·mon"e·tize'
 de·mon"e·tized'
 de·mon"e·tiz'ing
de·mon"i·cal·ly
de·mon"stra·ble
de·mon"strant
dem"on·strate'
 dcm"on·strat'ed
 dem"on·strat'ing
dem'on·stra"tion
de·mon"stra·tive
dem"on·stra'tor
de·mor"al·ize
 de·mor"al·ized
 de·mor"al·izing
de·mote"
 de·mot"ed
 de·mot"ing
de·mot"ic
de·mo"tion
de·mount"
de·mount"a·ble
de·mul"cent
de·mur"
 object (*see:* demure)
 de·murred"
 de·mur"ring
de·mure"
 modest (*see:* demur)
de·mur"ra·ble
de·mur"rage
de·mur"rer
den
de·na'tion·al·i·za"tion
de·na"tion·al·ize'
de·na"tion·al·iz'ing
de·nat"u·ral·ize'
de·na"ture
de·na"tur·ing
den"drite
den'dro·chro·nol"o·gy
den'drol"o·gist
den·drol"o·gy

dene
den"gue
de·ni"a·ble
de·ni"al
de·ni"er
de·nier"
de·nier"age
den"i·grate
den"i·gra"tion
den"im
de·ni"tri·fy'
den"i·zen
Den"mark
de·nom"i·nate'
de·nom"i·na"tion
de·nom"i·na"tion·al
de·nom"i·na"tor
de·no·ta"tion
de"no·ta'tive
de"no·ta'tive·ness'
de·note"
de·not"ed
de·not"ing
de·noue·ment"
de·nounce"
de·nounced"
de·nounc"ing
dense
dense"ly
dens"er
dens"est
den"si·ty
(pl. den"si·ties)
den"tal
den"tal·ly
den"tate'
den·tic"u·lar
den"ti·frice
den"tin
den"ti·na"sal
den"tist
den"tist·ry
den"ti"tion
de·nu"cle·ar·ize'
de·nude"
de·nud"ed

de·nud"ing
de·num"er·ant'
de·nun"ci·a"tion
Den"ver
de·ny"
de·nied"
de·ny"ing
de·o"dor·ant
de·o"dor·ize'
de·o"dor·ized'
de·o"dor·iz'ing
de·o"dor·iz"er
de·ox'i·di·za"tion
de·ox'i·dize'
de·ox'i·dized'
de·ox'i·diz"ing
de·ox"i·diz"er
de·ox"y·gen·ate
de·part"
de·part"ment
de·part·men"tal
de·part·men"tal·ize
de·part·men"tal·iz'ing
de·par"ture
de·pend'a·bil"i·ty
de·pend'a·ble
de·pend"ence
de·pend"en·cy
(pl. de·pend"en·cies)
de·pend"ent
de·per"son·al·ize'
de·phos"phor·y·la"tion
de·pict"
de·pic"tion
dep"i·lat"ed
de·pil"a·to·ry
(pl. de·pil"a·to'ries)
de·plane"
de·plete"
de·plet"ed
de·plet"ing
de·ple"tion
de·ple"tive
de·plor'a·ble

de·plore"
de·plored"
de·plor"ing
de·ploy"
de·ploy"ment
de·po'lar·i·za"tion
de·po"lar·ize'
de·po·ly"mer·ize'
de·po"nent
de·pop"u·late'
de·pop'u·la"tion
de·por·ta"tion
de·por·tee"
de·port"ment
de·pos"a·ble
de·pose"
de·pos"it
dep'o·si"tion
de·pos"i·to·ry
(pl. de·pos"i·to'
ries)
de"pot
dep'ra·va"tion
corruption (see: dep-
rivation)
de·prave"
de·prav"ing
de·prav"i·ty
(pl. de·prav"i·ties)
dep're·cate'
dep're·cat'ed
dep're·cat'ing
dep're·ca"tion
dep're·ca·to·ry
de·pre"ci·ate'
de·pre"ci·at'ed
de·pre"ci·at'ing
de·pre"ci·a"tion
dep're·date
dep're·dat'ed
dep're·dat'ing
dep're·da"tion
de·press"
de·pressed"
de·pres"sing
de·pres"sion

de·pres"sive
dep'ri·va"tion
 withholding (*see:*
  depravation)
de·prive"
 de·prived"
 de·priv"ing
de·pro"gram
de·pro"gram·mer
depth
dep'u·ta"tion
dep"u·tize'
 dep'u·tized'
 dep"u·tiz'ing
dep"u·ty
 (*pl.* dep"u·ties)
de·rac'i·na"tion
de·rail"
de·range"
 de·ranged"
 de·rang"ing
de·range"ment
de·rat"ed
de·reg"is·ter'
der"e·lict
der'e·lic"tion
de·ride"
 de·rid"ed
 de·rid"ing
de ri·gueur"
de·ri"sion
de·ri"sive
der'i·va"tion
de·riv"a·tive
de·rive"
 de·rived"
 de·riv"ing
der'ma·bra"sion
der'ma·tine"
der'ma·ti"tis
der'ma·tol"o·gist
der'ma·tol"o·gy
der'mat"o·mere'
der"mis
der"o·gate'
 der"o·gat'ed

der"o·gat'ing
der'o·ga"tion
de·rog'a·tive
de·rog'a·to"ri·ly
de·rog'a·to"ry
der"rick
der·ri·ere"
der"ring-do"
der"rin·ger
der"ris
de·sal'i·na"tion
de·sal'i·ni·za"tion
des"cant
de·scend"
de·scend"ance
de·scend"ant, *n.*
 offspring
de·scend"ent, *adj.*
 descending
de·scent"
 downward movement
 (*see:* decent and
 dissent)
de·scrib"a·ble
de·scribe"
 de·scribed"
 de·scrib"ing
de·scrip"tion
de·scrip"tor·y
de·scrip"tive
de·scry"
 de·scried"
 de·scry"ing
des"e·crate
 des"e·crat'ed
 des"e·crat'ing
des'e·cra"tion
de·seg"re·gate'
 de·seg"re·gat'ed
 de·seg"re·gat'ing
de·seg're·ga"tion
de·sen'si·ti·za"tion
de·sen"si·tize'
des"ert
 wasteland (*see:* des-
 sert)

de·sert"
 abandon; reward
 (*see:* dessert)
de·ser"tion
de·sert"less'ly
de·serve"
 de·served"
 de·serv"ing
 de·serv"ed·ly
de·sex"
des"ic·cant
des"ic·cate'
 des"ic·cat'ed
 des"ic·cat'ing
des'ic·ca"tion
de·sid'er·a"tum
 (*pl.* de·sid'er·a"ta)
des"ig·nate'
 des"ig·nat'ed
 des"ig·nat'ing
des'ig·na"tion
de·sign"er
de·sign"er drug
de·sign"ing
de·sir'a·bil"i·ty
de·sir"a·ble
de·sire"
 de·sired"
 de·sir"ing
de·sir"ous
de·sist"
Des Moines
des"o·late'
 des"o·lat'ed
 des"o·lat'ing
 des"o·late'ness
des'o·la"tion
des·ox·y'ri"bo·nu·cle'
 ic
de·spair"
des'per·a"do
 (*pl.* des'per·a"does)
des"per·ate
 reckless (*see:* dispar-
 ate)
des"per·ate'ness

des'per·a"tion
des"pi·ca·ble
des"pi·ca·bly
de·spise"
 de·spised"
 de·spis"ing
de·spite"
de·spite"ful·ly
de·spoil"
de·spo'li·a"tion
de·spond"
de·spond"en·cy
de·spond"ent
des"pot
des·pot"ic
des·pot"i·cal·ly
des"pot·ism
des·sert"
 food (see: desert)
des·sert"spoon'
des"ti·na"tion
des"tine
 des"tined
 des"tin·ing
des"ti·ny
 (pl. des"ti·nies)
des"ti·tute'
des"ti·tu"tion
de·stroy"er
de·struct"
de·struc'ti·bil"i·ty
de·struc"ti·ble
de·struc"tion
de·struc"tive
de·sub·stan"ti·al·ize'
des"ue·tude
de·sul'phur·at"ed
des"ul·to·ry
de·tach"
de·tach"a·ble
de·tach"ment
de·tail"
de·tain"
de·tect"
de·tect"a·ble
de·tec"tion

de·tec"tive
de·tec"tor
de·tente"
de·ten"tion
de·ter"
de·ter"gent
de·te"ri·o·rate'
 de·te"ri·o·rat"ed
 de·te"ri·o·rat"ing
de·te"ri·o·ra"tion
de·ter"mi·na·ble
de·ter"mi·nate
de·ter"mi·na·tion
de·ter"mine
 de·ter"mined
 de·ter"min·ing
de·ter"mined·ly
de·ter"min·ism
de·ter"rence
de·ter"rent
de·ter"ring
de·test"
de·test"a·ble
de·test"a·bly
de·tes·ta"tion
de·throne"
de·thron"ing
det"o·nate'
 det"o·nat"ed
 det"o·nat"ing
det"o·na"tion
det"o·na"tor
de"tour"
de·tract"
de·trac"tion
de·trac"ter
de·train"
det"ri·ment
det'ri·men"tal
det'ri·men"tal·ness'
de·tri"tus
De·troit"
de trop"
de·tum'es"cence
deuce
deu·te"ri·um

deu"ter·on'
Deut"sche mark'
de·val"u·ate'
de·val'u·at"ing
de·val'u·a"tion
de·val"ue
 de·val"ued
 de·val"u·ing
de·vast"
dev"as·tate'
dev"as·tat"ed
dev"as·tat"ing
dev'as·ta"tion
de·vel"op
de·vel"oped
de·vel"op·ing
de·vel"op·er
de·vel"op·ment
de·vel'op·men"tal
de·vel'op·men"tal·ly
de·vi"ance
de·vi"ant
de·vi·ate', v.
 turn aside
de·vi·ate, adj., n.
 deviant person
de·vi·at"ing
de·vi·a"tion
de·vice"
 tool (see: devise)
dev"il
dev"il·ing
dev"il·ish
dev"il-may-care"
dev"il's ad"vo·cate
dev"il·try
 (pl. dev"il·tries)
de·vi"ous
de·vis"a·ble
de·vise"
 contrive (see: device)
de·vised"
de·vis"ing
de·vi"tal·ize'
de·vit"ri·fy'
de·void"

de·vol′a·til·ized″
dev′o·lu″tion
de·volve″
  de·volved″
  de·volv″ing
de·vote″
dev′o·tee″
de·vot″ing
de·vo″tion
de·vo″tion·al
de·vour″
de·vout″
dew″ber′ry
  (*pl.* dew″ber′ries)
dew″cap′
dew″drop′
dew″lap′
dew″lapped′
dew″y
dew″y-eyed′
dex·ter″i·ty
dex″ter·ous
dex″ter·ous′ly
dex″trin
dex″trose
dhar″ma
dho″bi
dho″ti
dhow
di′a·be″tes
di′a·be″tes mel·li″tus
di′a·bet″ic
di″a·ble
di′a·bol″ic
di′a·bol″i·cal·ly
di·ac″o·nal
di·ac″o·nate
di′a·crit″i·cal
di″a·dem′
di″a·doche
di″a·glyph
di″ag·nose′
di″ag·nos′ing
di″ag·no″sis
  (*pl.* di″ag·no″ses)
di″ag·nos″tic

di′ag·nos″ti·cal·ly
di′ag·nos·ti″cian
di·ag″o·nal
di·ag″o·nal·ly
di″a·gram′
  di″a·grammed′
  di″a·gram′ming
di″a·gram·mat″i·cal·ly
di′a·he·li·o·trop″i·
  cal·ly
di″al
  di″aled
  di″al·ing
di″a·lect′
di′a·lec″tal
di′a·lec″ti·cal
di″a·logue′
di·al″y·sis
  (*pl.* di·al″y·ses′)
di′a·lyz″ate
di·am″e·ter
di′a·met″ri·cal
di′a·met″ri·cal·ly
di″a″mond
di·a′mond″ize
di·a·pa″son
di′a·pause″
dia″per
di·aph″a·nous
di·aph″a·nous·ness
di″a·phragm′
di″a·rist
di″ar·rhe″a
di″a·ry
  (*pl.* di″a·ries)
Di·as″po·ra
di·as″tas·es
di·as″tol″ic
di′a·stroph″ic
di·a·syn″the·sis
di″a·ther′my
di″a·tom″ic
di″a·ton″ic
di′a·trop″ism
di″a·tribe′
di·az″e·pam′

di·a·zo·al″kane
dib
dib″hole′
di·bu″tyr′in
di·chot″o·mous
di·chot″o·my
  (*pl.* di·chot″o·mies)
dic″i·er
dic″i·est
dic″ing
dick″ens
dick″ey
di·cot′y·le″don
dic″to·graph
Dic″ta·phone™
dic″tate
  dic″tat·ed
  dic″tat·ing
dic·ta″tion
dic″ta·tor
dic·ta·to″ri·al
dic·ta″tor·ship′
dic″tion
dic″tion·ar·y
  (*pl.* dic″tion·ar·ies)
dic″tum
dict′y·o·stele′
di·dac″tic
di·dac″ti·cal·ly
di·da·scal″ic
did″dle
di·dy″mo·lite′
die
  cease living (*see:*
    dye)
die
  stamp; cube (*pl.* dies
    or dice) (*see:* dye)
died
  ceased living;
    stamped (*see:* dyed)
die″-hard
die″ing
  stamping (*see:* dye-
    ing and dying)
di′en·ceph″a·lon

di·er″e·sis
  (*pl.* di·er″e·ses′)
die″sel
di″et
di″e·tar′y
di″e·tet″ic
di″et·ing
di′e·ti″tian
di′e·zeug′me″non
dif″fer·ence
  unlikeness (*see:* def-
  erence)
dif″fer·ent
dif″fer·en″tial
  distinctive (*see:* def-
  erential)
dif″fer·en″ti·ate
  dif″fer·en″ti·at′ed
  dif″fer·en″ti·at′ing
dif″fer·en″ti·a″tion
dif″fi·cult
dif″fi·cul′ty
  (*pl.* dif″fi·cul′ties)
dif″fi·dence
dif″fi·dent
dif·fract″
dif·frac″tion
dif·fuse″
  dif·fused″
  dif·fus″ing
dif·fus″i·ble
dif·fu″sion
dif·fu″sive
dig″al·late
dig″a·my
di·gest″, *v.*
  absorb
di″gest, *n.*
  summary
di·gest″ant
di·gest″i·ble
di·ges″tive
dig″ger
dig″ging
dig″gings
dight″ed

dig″it
dig″it·al
dig″it·al disk
dig′i·tal″is
dig′i·tal·ly
dig′i·ti·nerved′
dig′i·tox″in
di·glos″si·a
dig″ni·fy′
  dig″ni·fied′
  dig″ni·fy′ing
dig″ni·tar′y
  (*pl.* dig″ni·tar′ies)
dig″ni·ty
di·gress″
di·gres″sion
di·he″dral
di·hy″dric
dike
di·lap″i·dat′ed
di·lap′i·da″tion
di·lat″ing·ly
dil′a·ta″tion
di·late″
di·lat″ed
di·lat″ing
dil′a·to·ry
di·lem″ma
dil″et·tante′
  (*pl.* dil″et·tantes′)
dil″i·gence
dil″i·gent
dil″ly·dal′ly
  dil″ly·dal′lied
  dil″ly·dal′ly·ing
dil″u·ent
di·lute″
di·lut″ed
di·lut″ing
di·lu″tion
di·lu″vi·al
dim
  dimmed
  dim″ming
di·men″sion
di·mer′ized″

di·met″ro·don′
di·min″ish
di·min·u·en″do
dim′i·nu″tion
di·min″u·tive
di·min″u·tiv′al
dim″i·ty
dim″mer
dim″mest
dim″met
dim″-out
dim″ple
dim″pling
dim″wit
din
  noise (*see:* dine)
dine
  eat (*see:* din)
din″er
  eater (*see:* dinner)
di·ner″o
di·nette″
di·neu″tron
ding″bat
ding″-dong
din″ghy
  boat (*see:* dingy)
din″gi·er
din″gi·est
din″gi·ness
din″gle
din″gy
  dark (*see:* dinghy)
din″ing
  eating (*see:* dinning)
din″ing room
din″ky
din″ner
  meal (*see:* diner)
din″ner jack′et
din″ner·ware
din″ning
  beset with noise
  (*see:* dining)
di″no·saur′
di·oc″e·san

di″o·cese′
di″ode
di″o·ram″a
di·ox″ide
dip
di·pet″al·ous
di″phase′
di·phos″phid
diph·the″ri·a
diph″thong
di·pleur″u·la
dip″loid
dip″lois
di·plo″ma
di·plo″ma·cy
dip″lo·mat
  official (*see:* diplo-
  mate)
dip″lo·mate
  specialist (*see:* dip-
  lomat)
dip′lo·mat″ic
dip′lo·mat″i·cal·ly
di″plont
di·po″did
di″pole
dip″ping
dip″py
di·prop″ar·gyl′
dip′so·ma″ni·a
dip″stick′
dip″sy
dip″tych
dire
  dreadful (*see:* dyer)
di·rec″tion
di·rec″tion·al
di·rec″tive
di·rect″ly
di·rect″ mail″
di·rec″tor
di·rec″to·ry
  (*pl.* di·rec″to·ries)
dire″ful
dir″er
dir″est

dirge
dir″i·gi·ble
dirn″dl
dirt″-cheap″
dirt″i·er
dirt″i·est
dirt″i·ness
dirt″y
dis′a·bil″i·ty
  (*pl.* dis′a·bil″i·ties)
dis·a″ble
  dis·a″bled
  dis·a″bling
dis′a·buse″
  dis′a·bused″
  dis′a·bus″ing
dis′ac·quaint″
dis′ad·van″tage
dis·ad′van·ta″geous
dis′af·fect″
dis′af·fec″tion
dis′a·gree″
dis′a·gree″a·ble
dis′a·gree″a·bly
dis′a·gree″ing
dis′a·gree″ment
dis′al·low″
dis′ap·pear″ance
dis′ap·point″ed
dis′ap·point″ment
dis′ap·pro·ba″tion
dis′ap·prov″al
dis′ap·prove″
dis·arm″
dis·ar″ma·ment
dis′ar·range″
dis′ar·ray″
dis′ar·tic″u·la′tion
dis·as·sem″ble
dis·as·so″ci·ate
dis·as·so′ci·a″tion
dis·as″trous
dis′at·taint″
dis′a·vow″
dis′a·vow″al
dis·band″

dis·bar″
dis·bar″ment
dis′be·lief″
dis′be·lieve″
dis′be·liev″er
dis·burse″
  pay out (*see:* dis-
  perse)
dis·burse″ment
dis·burs″ing
  paying out (*see:* dis-
  persing)
dis·bur″then
disc
dis·card″, *v.*
  throw away
dis·card″, *n.*
  thing thrown away
dis·car·na″tion
dis·cern″
dis·cern″i·ble
dis·cern″ing
dis·cern″ment
dis·cern′i·bil″i·ty
dis·charge″, *v.*
  emit; release
dis″charge, *n.*
  act *or* thing dis-
  charged
dis·charge″a·ble
dis·ci″ple
dis′ci·pli·nar″i·an
dis″ci·pli·nar″y
dis″ci·pline
  dis″ci·plined
  dis″ci·plin·ing
dis·claim″
dis·claim″er
dis·close″
dis·clos″er
dis·clo″sure
dis″co
  (*pl.* dis″cos)
dis·cog″ra·pher
dis·cog″ra·phy
dis″coid

dis·col″or
dis·col′or·a″tion
dis·com·bob″u·late
dis·com″fit
dis·com″fi·ture
dis·com″fort
dis·com·pose″
dis·com·pos″ing
dis·com·po″sure
dis·con·cert″
dis·con·nect″
dis·con·nec″tion
dis·con″so·late
dis·con·tent″
dis·con·tin″u·ance
dis·con·tin″ue
dis·con·ti·nu″i·ty
dis·con·tin″u·ous
dis″co·phile
dis″co″phor·ous′
dis″cord
dis·cord″ant
dis″co·theque″
dis″count
dis″count house″
dis·cour″age
  dis·cour″aged
  dis·cour″ag·ing
dis·cour″age·ment
dis·course″, v.
  converse
dis″course, n.
  conversation
dis·cour″te·ous
dis·cour″te·sy
dis·cov″er
dis·cov″er·er
dis·cov″er·y
  (pl. dis·cov″er·ies)
dis·cred″it
dis·creet″
  prudent (see: dis-
  crete)
dis·crep″an·cy
  (pl. dis·crep″an·
  cies)

dis·crete″
  separate (see: dis-
  creet)
dis·cre″tion
dis·cre″tion·ar′y
dis·crim″i·nate
dis·crim″i·nat′ing
dis·crim′i·na″tion
dis·crim′i·na′tive
dis·crim′i·na·to′ry
dis·cur″sive
dis″cus
  round throwing ob-
  ject (pl. dis″cus·
  es) (see: discuss)
dis·cuss″
  talk about (see: dis-
  cus)
dis·cuss″sion
dis·dain″ful
dis·dain″ful·ly
dis·ease″
dis′em·bark″
dis·em′bar·ka″tion
dis′em·bod″i·ment
dis′em·bod″y
dis′em·bow″el
dis′em·bow″el·ing
dis′em·broil″
dis′en·chant″ment
dis′en·cum″ber
dis′en·gage″
dis′en·roll″
dis′en·tan″gle
dis′es·tab″lish
dis′es·teem″
dis′en·ti″tle·ment
dis′es·tab″lish′er
dis·fa″vor
dis·fea″ture
dis·fig″ure
dis·fran″chise
  dis·fran″chised
  dis·fran″chis·ing
dis·gorge″
  dis·gorged″

dis·gorg″ing
dis·grace″
  dis·graced″
  dis·grac″ing
dis·grace″ful
dis·gre″ga″ting
dis·grun″tle
  dis·grun″tled
  dis·grun″tling
dis·guise″
  dis·guised″
  dis·guis″ing
dis·gust″
  dis·gust″ed
  dis·gust″ing
dis·ha·bille″
dis·har″mo·ny
dish″cloth
dis·heart″en
dis·her″ent
di·shev″el
  di·shev″eled
  di·shev″el·ing
dis·hon″est
dis·hon″es·ty
dis·hon″or
dis·hon″or·a·ble
dish″pan
dish″rag
dish″tow′el
dish″wash′er
dish″wa′ter
dis·il·lu″sion
  dis·il·lu″sioned
  dis·il·lu″sion·ing
dis·in·car″cer·a″tion
dis·in·cen″tive
dis·in·cli·na″tion
dis·in·fect″
dis·in·fect″ant
dis·in·fest″
dis·in·gen″u·ous
dis·in·her″it
dis·in″te·grant
dis·in″te·grate′
  dis·in″te·grat′ed

dis·in″te·grat′ing
dis·in″te·gra″tion
dis′in″ter″
 dis′in·terred″
 dis′in·ter″ring
dis·in″ter·est′ed
dis·in″tri·cate′
dis·join″
dis·joint″
 dis·joint″ed
 dis·joint″ing
disk drive
dis·like″
dis·lik″ing
dis″lo·cate
dis′lo·ca″tion
dis·lodge″
dis·loy″al
dis·loy″al·ty
dis·lus″ter
dis″mal
dis″mal·ly
dis·man″tle
dis·mar″ket·ed
dis·may″
dis·mem″ber
dis·mem″bra′tor
dis·miss″
dis·miss″al
dis·mount
dis′o·be″di·ence
dis′o·be″di·ent
dis′o·bey″
dis·ob″li·ga″tion
dis′or·dained″
dis·or″der
dis·or″gan·ize
dis·o″ri·ent
dis·o″ri·en·ta″ted
dis·own″
dis·par″age
dis·par″age·ment
dis·par″ag·ing
dis″pa·rate
 distinct (*see:* desperate)

dis·par″i·ty
dis·pas″sion·ate
dis·patch″
dis·patch″er
dis·pel″
 dis·pelled″
 dis·pel″ling
dis·pen″sa·bil″i·ty
dis·pen″sa·ble
dis·pen″sa·ry
 (*pl.* dis·pen″sa·ries)
dis′pen·sat″ing
dis′pen·sa″tion
dis·pense″
dis·pens″er
dis·pens″ing
dis·per″sal
dis·perse″
 dis·persed″
 dis·pers″ing
 scatter (*see:* dis-burse)
dis·per″sion
dis·pir″it·ed
dis·pi″te·ous″ness
dis·place″
dis·place″ment
dis·play″
dis·please″
dis·pleas″ure
dis·pleas″ur·a′bly
dis·port
dis·pos″a·ble
dis·pos″al
dis·pose″
 dis·posed″
 dis·pos″ing
dis·pos·sess″
dis·pos·es″sion
dis·prize″
dis·proof″
dis′pro·por″tion
dis′pro·por″tion·ate
dis·prove″
dis·put″a·ble
dis·pu″tant

dis′pu·ta″tion
dis′pu·ta″tious
dis·pute″
 dis·put″ed
 dis·put″ing
dis·qual′i·fi·ca″tion
dis·qual′i·fy
dis·qui″et
dis·qui″e·tude
dis·qui·par″an·cy
dis·qui·si″tion
dis·re·gard″
dis·re·gard″ful
dis·re·pair″
dis·rep″u·ta·ble
dis·rep″u·ta·bly
dis·re·pute″
dis·re·spect″ful
dis·robe″
dis·rupt″
dis·rup″tion
dis·rup″tive
dis·sat·is·fac″tion
dis·sat″is·fy′
 dis·sat″is·fied′
 dis·sat″is·fy′ing
dis·scep″tre
dis·scet″
dis·sec″tion
dis·seiz″or
dis·sem″ble
dis·sem″bler
dis·sem″bling
dis·sem″i·nate
dis·sem′i·na″tion
dis·sen″sion
dis·sent″
 disagree (*see:* decent and descent)
dis·ser″ta·tion
dis·serv″ice
dis·sev″er
dis″si·dence
dis″si·dent
dis·sim″i·lar
dis·sim″i·lar″i·ty

dis·sim″u·late′
  dis·sim″u·lat′ed
  dis·sim″u·lat′ing
dis·sim″u·la″tion
dis″si·pate′
dis″si·pat′ing
dis″si·pa″tion
dis·so″ci·ate
  dis·so″ci·at′ed
  dis·so″ci·at′ing
dis·so″ci·a″tion
dis·so″ci·a″tive
dis·sol″u·ble
dis″so·lute
dis″so·lu″tion
dis·solve″
  dis·solved″
  dis·solv″ing
dis″so·nance
dis″so·nant
dis·suade″
  dis·suad″ed
  dis·suad″ing
dis·sua″sion
dis·suit″ed
dis·sym″me·try
dis″taff
dis″tal
dis·tal″i·a′
dis″tance
dis″tant
dis·taste″ful
dis·tem″per
dis·tend″
dis·ten″si·ble
dis·ten″tion
dis·till″
dis″til·late
dis·til·la″tion
dis·till″er
dis·till″er·y
  (*pl.* dis·till″er·ies)
dis·tinct″
dis·tinc″tion
dis·tinc″tive
dis·tin″guish

dis·tin″guish·a·ble
dis·tin″guish·a·bly
dis·tort″
dis·tort″ed
dis·tor″tion
dis·tract″
dis·trac″tion
dis·trait″
dis·traught″
dis·tress″
dis·trib″ute
  dis·trib″ut·ed
  dis·trib″ut·ing
dis·tri·bu″tion
dis·tri·bu″tion·al
dis·trib″u·tive
dis·trib″u·tor
dis·trib″u·tor·ship
dis″trict
dis·trust″ful
dis·turb″
dis·turb″ance
di′sul·fide″
dis·un″ion
dis·u·nite″
dis·u·ni·ty
dis·use″
dis·us″ing
ditch
  (*pl.* ditch″es)
ditch″wa′ter
dith″er
dith″y·ramb′
dit′sy
dit″to
  (*pl.* dit″tos)
dit″ty
  (*pl.* dit″ties)
di′u·re″sis
di′u·ret″ic
di·ur″nal
di″va
di·van″
di·var″i·cat′ed
dive
  dived *or* dove

div″ing
div″er
di·verge″
di·ver″gence
di·ver″genc·y
di·ver″gent
di·verg″ing
di·verse″
di·ver″si·fi·ca″tion
di·ver″si·fy
di·ver″sion
di·ver″sion·ar′y
di·ver″si·ty
di·vert″
di·vert″ing·ly
di·ver″tisse·ment
di·vest″
di·vid″a·ble
di·vide″
  di·vid″ed
  di·vid″ing
div″i·dend
div″i·na″tion
di·vine″
di·vined″
di·vin″ing rod
di·vin″i·ty
  (*pl.* di·vin″i·ties)
di·vin″yl
di·vis′i·bil″i·ty
di·vis″i·ble
di·vi″sion
di·vi″sion·al
di·vi″sive
di·vi″sor
di·vorce″
di·vor″ce″
di·vor·cee″
di·vorc″ing
div″ot
di·vulge″
  di·vulged″
  di·vulg″ing
div″vy
div″vy·ing
dix″ie

dix"ie·land
diz"zi·er
diz"zi·ly
diz"zi·ness
djinn
djer"sa
dob"bin
do"cent
doc"ile
do·cil"i·ty
dock"age
dock"et
dock"hand'
dock'i·za"tion
dock"yard'
doc"tor
doc"tor·al
doc"tor·ate
doc'tri·naire"
doc"tri·nal
doc"trine
doc"u·ment
doc'u·men"ta·ry
  (*pl.* doc'u·men"ta·
  ries)
doc'u·men·ta"tion
dod"der
do·dec"a·gon'
do·dec'a·he"dron
do·dec'a·sem"ic
dodge
dodg"er
dodg"ing
do"do
doe
  animal (*pl.* does)
  (*see:* dough)
do"er
does
doe"skin'
does"n't
dog"bane'
dog"bush'
dog"catch'er
dog" col'lar
dog"-ear'

dog"-eared'
dog"fight'
dog"ged
dog"ger·el
dog"ger·el·er
dog"gie bag'
dog"ging
dog"gone"
dog"gon·est
dog"house'
do"gie
dog"leg'
dog"ma
  (*pl.* dog"mas)
dog·mat"ic
dog·mat"i·cal·ly
dog·ma·tism'
do"-good"er
dog" tag'
dog"-tired'
dog"wood'
do"gy
doi"ly
  (*pl.* doi"lies)
do"-it-your·self"
do·lab"rate
Dol"by™
dol"ce vi"ta
dol"drums
dole
dole"ful
do·le·rit"ic
dol"i·o·form
doll
dol"lar
doll"house'
doll"y
  (*pl.* doll"ies)
do"lo·mite'
dol"or·ous
dol"phin
dolt"ish
do·main"
do·ma"ti·um
dome
do·mes"tic

do·mes"ti·cal·ly
do·mes"ti·cate'
do·mes"ti·cat'ing
do·mes·tic"i·ty
  (*pl.* do·mes·tic"i·
  ties)
dom"i·cile
dom"i·nance
dom"i·nant
dom"i·nate
dom"i·nat'ed
dom"i·nat'ing
dom'·na"tion
dom'i·neer"
dom"ing
dom"i·nie
do·min"ion
dom"i·no
  (pl. dom"i·noes)
don
do"nar·y
do"nate
do"nat·ed
do"nat·ing
do·na"tion
do·na"tor·y
done
  finished (*see:* dun)
do·nee"
Don Juan"
don"key
  (*pl.* don"keys)
don"ning
don"ny·brook
do"nor
do"nor card
do"-noth'ing
don't
do"nut
don"zel
doo"dad
doo"dle
doo"dle·bug
doo"dling
doo"hick'ey
dooms"day

doon
door"bell'
door"jamb'
door"keep'er
door"knob'
door"man'
door"mat'
door"nail'
door"plate'
door"prize'
door"step'
door"stop'
do"pa
dope
dop"ing
Dop"pler
Dor"ic
dor"man·cy
dor"mant
dor"mer
dor"mie
dor"mi·to'ry
  (*pl.* dor"mi·to'ries)
dor"mouse'
  (*pl.* dor"mice')
dor"sal
dor·si'ven·tral"i·ty
dor"so·pleur"al
do"ry
  (*pl.* do"ries)
dos'-a-dos"
dos"age
dose
  amount (*see:* doze)
dos"si·er'
dot
  round mark (*see:*
  dote)
dot"age
do"tard
dote
  dot"ed
  dot"ing
  show fondness (*see:*
  dot)
dot" ma"trix'

dot"ting
  marking (*see:* dot-
  ing)
dot"ty
dou"ble
dou"ble-bar"reled
dou"ble bass"
dou"ble bas·soon"
dou"ble bed'
dou"ble-breasted
dou"ble-check"
dou"ble-cross", *v.*
  deceive
dou"ble cross", *n.*
  act of betrayal
dou"ble-deal"er
dou"ble-deal"ing
dou"ble-deck"er
dou"ble-dig"it
dou"ble-dip"per
dou"ble-edged"
dou"ble en·ten"dre
dou"ble head"er
dou"ble-hung"
dou"ble-joint"ed
dou"ble-knit
dou"ble-park"
dou"ble play
dou"ble-quick"
dou"ble-space"
dou"ble star"
dou"blet
dou"ble take
dou"ble-talk
dou"ble·think"
dou"ble-time
dou"ble-tongue
dou"bling
dou·bloon"
dou"bly
doubt
doubt"er
doubt"ful
doubt"ful·ly
doubt"less
douche

douch"ing
dough
  pastry (*see:* doe)
dough"bird'
dough"boy'
dough"nut
dough"ty
dough"y
dour
douse
dous"ing
dove"cote'
dove"tail'
dow"a·ger
dow"di·er
dowd"i·ly
dowd"i·ness
dow"dy
dow"el
dow"er
down"beat'
down"cast'
down"court
down"er
down"fall'
down"feed'
down"grade'
down"heart"ed
down"hill"
down"i·er
down"play'
down"pour'
down"range"
down"right'
down"rush'
down"scale'
down"shift'
down"size'
down"stage"
down"stairs"
down"stream"
down"swing
down"take'
down"time
down"-to-earth"
down"town"

down"trod'den
down"turn'
down" un"der
down"ward
down"weight'
down"wind"
down"y
dow"ry
  (*pl.* dow"ries)
dox·ol"o·gy
  (*pl.* dox·ol"o·gies)
doy·enne"
doylt
doze
  sleep (*see:* dose)
doz"en
drab
drab"best
drach"ma
Dra·co"ni·an
draft
  version (*see:*
  draught)
draft·ee"
drafter
draft"i·est
drafts"man
draft"y
drag
drag"bolt'
drag"ging
drag"gle
  drag"gled
  drag"gling
drag"net'
drag"o·man
drag"on
drag"on·fly'
  (*pl.* drag"on·flies)
drag"on·nade'
dra·goon"
drag" race'
drag" strip'
drail
drain"age
drain"pipe'

dram
dra"ma
dra·mat"ic
dra·mat"i·cal·ly
dra·mat"ics
dram"a·tis per·so"nae
dram"a·tist
dram'a·ti·za"tion
dram"a·tize'
  dram"a·tized'
  dram"a·tiz'ing
dram"a·tur'gy
dram"mock
drank
drap"ing
dra"per·y
  (*pl.* dra"per·ies)
dras"sid
dras"tic
dras"ti·cal·ly
draught
  drink (*see:* draft)
draw"back'
draw"bor'ing
draw"bridge'
draw"ee
draw"er
draw"ing
draw"ing board'
draw"ing room'
draw"knife'
  (*pl.* draw"knives')
drawl
drawn
draw"string'
dray"age
dread"ful
dread"ful·ly
dread"nought'
dreamed
dream"i·ly
dream"ing
dream"land'
dream'y
drear"i·ly
drear"i·ness

drear"i·est
drear"y
dredge
  dredged
  dredg"ing
dreg"gi·ly
dregs
drench
Dres"den
dres·sage"
dress"er
dress"ers
dress"i·est
dress"ing
dress"ing-down"
dress"ing gown'
dress"mak'er
dress"mak" ing
dress"up
dress"y
drew
drib"ble
  drib"bled
  drib"bling
drib"let
dried
dri"er
dri"est
drift"age
drift"er
drift"wood'
drill"mas'ter
drill" press'
dri"ly
drink
drink"a·ble
drink"ing
dripped
drip"-dry
drip"ping
drip"pings
drive
  drove
  driv"en
  driv"ing
drive"bolt

drive''-in
driv''el
driv''el·ing
drive'' shaft
drive''way
driz''zle
driz''zling
droll''er·y
   (*pl.* droll''er·ies)
drol''ly
drom''e·dar'y
   (*pl.* drom''e·dar'ies)
drone
drone''pipe''
dron''ing
droop
droop''y
drop''cloth'
drop''-forge'
drop''let
drop''out'
dropped
drop''per
drop''ping
drop''sy
dross
dross''ing
drought
drouth
dro''ver
drown
drowse
drow''si·est
drow''si·ly
drow''si·ness
drows''ing
drow''sy
drub
 drubbed
 drub''bing
drudge
drudg''er·y
drudg''ing
drug
drug''ging
drug''gist

drug''store'
drum''beat'
drum'' corps
drum''fire
drum''head
drum''mer
drum''ming
drum''stick'
drum''wood
drunk''ard
drunk''en
drunk''en·ness
dru''pel
drux''y
dry
dry''ad
dry'' cell'
dry-clean'ing
dry'' dock'
dry''er
dry''ing
dry''ly
dry''ness
dry'' rot''
dry'' run''
dry''wall'
du''al
   twofold (*see:* duel)
du''al·ism
du·al''i·ty
du''al-pur''pose
dub
 dubbed
 dub''bing
du·bi''e·ty
du''bi·ous
Dub''lin
Du·buque
du''cal
duc''at
du''ce
duch''ess
duch''y
   (*pl.* duch''ies)
duck''bill'
duck''board'

duck''house
duck''ling
duck''pin'
duck''weed'
duc''tile
duct''less
dude
dudg''eon
due
du''el
   combat (*see:* dual)
du''eled
du''el·ing
du''el·ist
du·en''na
dues
du·et''
duf''fa·dar'
duf''fel
duf''fel bag'
dug''dug
du''gong
dug''out
duke''dom
dul''cet
dul''ci·mer
dull''ard
dull''ness
dul''ly
   not sharply (*see:* duly)
Du·luth''
du''ly
   due manner (*see:* dully)
dumb''bell'
dumb·found''
dumb''ly
dumb''ness
dumb''struck'
dumb''wait'er
dum''dum''
dum''my
   (*pl.* dum''mies)
dump''age
dump''i·est

dump"ling
dump" truck'
dump"y
dun
  recover debt (*see:* done)
dunc'i·fy"ing
dune" bug'gy
dung
dung·an"no·nite'
dun'ga·ree"
dun"geon
dung"hill'
dunk"er
dun"ning
du"o
  (*pl.* du"os)
du'o·dec"i·mal
du'o·de"nal
du'o·de"num
du"o·tone
dupe
 duped
 dup"ing
du"ple
du"plex
du"pli·cate
 du"pli·cat'ed
 du"pli·cat'ing
du'pli·ca"tion
du'plic"a·ture
du·plic"i·ty
du·ra·bil"i·ty
du"ra·ble
du·ra"tion
du·ress"
dur"ing
dur"ra
du"rum
Dur'za"da
dusk"i·er
dusk"i·ness
dusk"ly
dusk"y
dust" bowl'
dust" cov'er

dust"er
dust"i·er
dust"i·est
dust"i·ness
dust"pan
dust" storm
dust"y
du"stuk
Dutch
Dutch" ov'en
dutch" treat
du"te·ous
du"ti·a·ble
du"ti·ful
du"ti·ful·ly
du"ty
  (*pl.* du"ties)
dwarf
dwarf"ish
dwell
 dwelt
 dwell"ing
dwin"dle
 dwin"dled
 dwin"dling
dy"ad
dyb"buk
dye
  stain (*pl.* dyes) (*see:* die)
dyed
  stained (*see:* died)
dyed"-in-the-wool"
dy"er
  one who stains (*see:* dire)
dye"ing
  staining (*see:* dieing and dying)
dye"stuff
dy"ing
  ceasing to live (*see:* dieing and dyeing)
dyke
dy·nam"ic
dy·nam"i·cal·ly

dy·nam"ics
dy·na"mis
dy"na·mism'
dy"na·mite'
dy"na·mit'ing
dy"na·mo
  (*pl.* dy"na·mos)
dy'na·mog'e·nous·ly
dy'na·mom"e·ter
dy"nas·ty
  (*pl.* dy"nas·ties)
dys'a·cous"ma
dys'cras"i·a
dys·en"ter·y
dys·func"tion
dys·gen"ics
dys·lex"i·a
dys·lex"ic
dys·men·or·rhe"a
dys·mer"o·morph
dys·pep"sia
dys·pep"tic
dys·pha"gic
dys·pno·ic
dys"to·mous
dys·troph"ic
dys"tro·phy

E

each
ea"ger
ea"gle
ea"gle-eyed'
ea"gle scout'
ea"glet
ear
ear"ache'
ear"drum'
ear"flap'
ear"ful
earl
earl"dom
ear"li·er
ear"li·est

ear''li·ness
ear''ly
ear''ly bird'
ear''mark'
ear''muff'
earn
  gain (*see:* urn)
ear''nest
earn''ing
ear''phone'
ear''piece'
ear''plug'
ear''ring'
ear''shot'
ear''split'ting
earth''bound'
earth''drake'
earth''en
earth''en·ware'
earth''i·ness
earth''light'
earth''ling
earth''ly
earth''nut'
earth''quake'
earth''shak'ing
earth''shine'
earth''wards
earth''work'
earth''worm'
earth''y
ear''wax'
ear''wig'
ease
ea''sel
ease''ment
eas''i·er
eas''i·est
eas''i·ness
eas''ing
east''bound'
east''er
east''ern
east''ern·er
east''wards
eas''y

eas''y chair'
eas''y·go''ing
eas''y street'
eat
eat''en
eat''ing
eau'' de co·logne''
eaves''drop'
eaves''drop'per
eaves''drop'ping
ebb
eb''on·y
e·bul''lience
e·bul''lient
eb'ul·li''tion
e·burn'i·fi·ca''tion
ec''bole'
ec'ce ho''mo
ec·cen''tric
ec·cen''tri·cal·ly
ec'cen·tric''i·ty
  (*pl.* ec'cen·tric''i·
  ties)
ec·cle'si·as''ti·cal
ec·cle'si·as''ti·cism
ec·cri·nol''o·gy
ech''e·lon'
ech''i·nid'
e·chi''no·derm'
e·chi''no·derm'ic
e·chi''no·sto·mi·a'sis
ech''o
  (*pl.* ech''oes)
ech''o·ing
ech''o·car'di·o·gram
ech·om''e·ter
e·clair''
e·clat''
ec·lec''tic
ec·lec''ti·cism
ec''legm
ec''logue
e·clipse''
e·clips''ing
e·clip''tic
ec'o·log''i·cal

ec'o·log''i·cal·ly
e·col''o·gist
e·col''o·gy
e·con'o·met''rics
e·con'o·met''ri·cal
e'co·nom''ic
e'co·nom''i·cal
e'co·nom''i·cal·ly
e'co·nom''ics
e·con''o·mist
e·con''o·mize'
  e·con''o·mized'
  e·con''o·miz'ing
e·con''o·my
  (*pl.* e·con''o·mies)
ec''o·sys''tem
ec''o·tone'
ec'o·ton''al
e'co·to''pi·an
ec''o·type'
ec''re·visse'
ec''ru
ec''sta·sy
  (*pl.* ec''sta·sies)
ec·stat''ic
ec·stat''i·cal·ly
ec''to·blas''tic
ec''to·cun'i·form
ec''to·pic'
ec''to·plasm'
ec''to·som'al
Ec''ua·dor'
ec'u·men''i·cal
ec'u·men''i·cal·ly
ec'u·men''ics
ec''ze·ma
e·dac''i·ty
ed''dy
  (*pl.* ed''dies)
e'del·weiss'
e·de''ma
edge
edge''ways
edge''wise'
edg''i·er
edg''i·est

edg″i·ness
edg″ing
edg″y
ed′i·bil″i·ty
ed″i·ble
e″dict
ed′i·fi·ca″tion
ed′i·fi″ca·tor·y
ed″i·fice
ed″i·fied
ed″i·fy
ed″i·fy′ing
Ed″in·burgh
ed″ing·ton′ite
ed″it
ed″it·ing
e·di″tion
  printing (*see:* addi-
  tion)
ed″i·tor
ed″i·to″ri·al
ed″i·to″ri·al·ize
ed″i·to″ri·al·iz′ing
ed″i·to″ri·al·iz′er
ed″i·tor in chief″
  (*pl.* ed″i·tors in
  chief″)
Ed″mon·ton
ed·u·ca·bil″i·ty
ed″u·ca·ble
ed″u·cate
 ed″u·cat′ed
 ed″u·cat′ing
ed″u·ca″tion
ed″u·ca″tion·al·ly
ed″u·ca′tor
e·duce″
 e·duced″
 e·duc″ing
e·duc″i·ble
eel″fare
ee″rie
ee″ri·er
ee″ri·est
ee″ri·ly
ee″ri·ness

ee″ri·some
ef·face″
ef·fac″er
ef·face″a·ble
ef·face″ment
ef·fac″ing
ef·fect″
  result (*see:* affect)
ef·fec″tive
ef·fec″tive·ness
ef·fec″tu·al
ef·fec″tu·al·ly
ef·fec″tu·al′i·ty
ef·fec″tu·ate′
ef·fec″tu·at″ing
ef·fem″i·na·cy
ef·fem″i·nate
ef·fem″i″nize′
ef·fen″di
ef″fer·ent
ef′fer·vesce″
ef′fer·ves″cence
ef′fer·ves″cent
ef′fer·vesc″ing
ef′fer·vesc″ing·ly
ef·fete″
ef′fi·ca″cious
ef″fi·ca·cy
ef·fi·cien·cy
  (*pl.* ef·fi″cien·cies)
ef·fi″cient
ef″fi·gy
  (*pl.* ef″fi·gies)
ef·flo·resce″
ef′flo·res″cence
ef′flo·res″cing
ef″flu·ence
ef″flu·ent
  flowing out (*see:* af-
  fluent)
ef·flu″vi·um
  (*pl.* ef·flu″vi·a)
ef′for·ma″tion
ef″fort·less
ef·fron″ter·y
  (*pl.* ef·fron″ter·ies)

ef·fulge″
ef·ful″gence
ef·fu″sion
ef·fu″sive
e·gal′i·tar″i·an
egg
egg″beat′er
egg″ber·ry
egg″drop
egg″head′
egg″nog′
egg″plant′
egg″roll′
egg″shell′
e·gla″tere
e″go
e′go·cen″tric
e′go·cen·tric″i·ty
e″go·ism′
e″go·ist
e′go·is″tic
e′go·is″ti·cal
e′go·is″ti·cal·ly
e″go·tism′
e″go·tist
e′go·tis″tic
e′go·tis″ti·cal
e′go·tis″ti·cal·ly
e″go trip′
e·gre″gious
e″gress
e″gret
e′gro·man″cy
E″gypt
E′gyp·tol″o·gy
ehl″ite
ei″der·down′
ei″der duck′
ei″do·lon′
eight″ball′
eight″een″
eight″eenth″
eighth
eight″i·eth
eight″-track′
eight″y

(*pl.* eight″ies)
Eir″e
ei′se·ge″sis
ei′stedd″fod
ei″ther
e·jac″u·late′
  e·jac″u·lat′ed
  e·jac″u·lat′ing
e·jac′u·la″tion
e·ject″
e·jec″ta·ble
e·jec″tion
e·jur·a″tion
eke
ek″ing
e·lab″o·rate′
e·lab″o·rate·ly
e·lab″o·rate·ness
e·lab″o·rat′ing
e·lab′o·ra″tion
e·lan″
e·lan′vi·tal″
e·lap″id
e·lapse″
e·laps″ing
e·las″tic
e·las·tic″i·ty
e·las·to·mer″ic
e·late″
e·lat″ing
e·la″tion
El″be
el″bow grease′
el″bow·piece′
el″bow·room′
eld″er
el″der·ber′ry
eld″er·ly
eld″er·wood′
eld″rich
e·lec″tion
e·lec′tion·eer″
e·lec″tive
e·lec″tiv·ism
e·lec″tor
e·lec″tor·al

e·lec″tor·ate
e·lec″tric
e·lec″tri·cal
e·lec″tri·cal·ly
e·lec″tri·cian
e·lec·tric″i·ty
e·lec′tri·fi·ca″tion
e·lec″tri·fy′
e·lec″tri·fy′ing
e·lec″tri·on
e·lec′tro·bal·lis″tic
e·lec′tro·car″di·o·
  gram
e·lec′tro·car″di·o·
  graph
e·lec′tro·chem″i·cal
e·lec′tro·col·loi″dal
e·lec′tro·cute′
  e·lec′tro·cut·ed
  e·lec′tro·cut·ing
e·lec′tro·cu″tion
e·lec″trode
e·lec′tro·dy·nam″ics
e·lec′tro·dy″na·mism
e·lec′tro·en·ceph″a·
  lo·gram
e·lec′tro·en·ceph″a·
  lo·graph
e·lec′tro·form″ing
e·lec′tro·lum·i·nes″
  cence
e·lec·trol″y·sis
e·lec″tro·lyte′
e·lec′tro·lyt″ic
e·lec″tro·lyze′
e·lec″tro·lyz′ing
e·lec′tro·mag″net
e·lec′tro·mag·net″ic
e·lec·trom″e·ter
e·lec′tro·met″ric
e·lec′tro·mo″tive
e·lec″tron
e·lec′tro·nar″co·sis
e·lec·tron″ic
e·lec·tron″i·cal·ly

e·lec′tro·pho·to·
  graph″ic
e·lec″tro·plate′
  e·lec″tro·plat′ed
  e·lec″tro·plat′ing
e·lec″tro·re·fin″ing
e·lec″tro·scope′
e·lec″tro·shock′
e·lec′tro·stat″ic
e·lec′tro·stat″ics
e·lec′tro·stric″tion
e·lec′tro·tel′e·ther·
  mom″e·ter
e·lec″tro·ther″a·py
e·lec″tro·type′
e·lec′tro·val″ent·ly
el′ee·mos″y·nar·y
el″e·gance
el″e·gant
el′e·gi″ac
el″e·gist
el′e·gize′
  el″e·gized
  el″e·giz′ing
el″e·gy
  (*pl.* el″e·gies)
el″e·ment
el′e·men″tal
el′e·men″tar·ist
el′e·men″ta·ry
el″e·phant
el′e·phan·ti″a·sis
el′e·phan″tine
el″e·vate′
  el″e·vat′ed
  el″e·vat′ing
e′le·va″tion
el″e·va′tor
e·lev″en
e·lev″enth
elf
  (*pl.* elves)
elf″in
elf″ish
elf″lock
e·lic″it

draw forth (*see:* il-
licit)
e·lic'i·ta"tion
e·lic"it·ing
e·lic"i·to'ry
e·lide"
e·lid"ing
el'i·gi·bil"i·ty
el"i·gi·ble
suitable (*see:* illeg-
ible)
e·lim"i·nate'
e·lim"i·nat'ed
e·lim"i·nat'ing
e·lim"i·na"tion
e·li"sion
e·lite"
e·lit"ism
e·lit"ist
e·lix'a"tion
e·lix"ir
E·liz'a·be"than
elk"hound
el·lipse"
el·lip"sis
(*pl.* el·lip"scs)
el·lip·soi"dal
el·lip"ti·cal
el'o·cute"
el'o·cu"tion
el'o·cu"tion·ist
E'lo·him"
e·lon"gate
e·lon"gat·ing
e·lon·ga"tion
e·lope"
e·loped"
e·lop"ing
e·lope"ment
el"o·quence
el"o·quent
el'pi·dite"
El Pas"o
El Sal"va·dor'
else"when
else"where'

e·lu"ci·date'
e·lu"ci·dat'ing
e·lu'ci·da"tion
e·lude"
e·lud"ed
e·lud"ing
avoid (*see:* allude)
e·lu"sive
evasive (*see:* allusive
and illusive)
e·lu"sive·ly
e·ma"ci·ate'
e·ma"ci·at'ed
e·ma"ci·at'ing
e·ma"ci·a"tion
em"a·nate'
em"a·nat'ed
em"a·nat'ing
em'a·na"tion
e·man"ci·pate'
e·man"ci·pat'ed
e·man"ci·pat'ing
e·man"ci·pa"tion
e·man"ci·pa'tor
e·man"i·um"
e·mas"cu·late'
e·mas"cu·lat'ed
e·mas"cu·lat'ing
e·mas"cu·la"tion
em·balm"
em·bank"ment
em·bar"go
(*pl.* em·bar"goes)
em·bar"go·ing
em·bark"
em·bar·ka"tion
em·bar"rass
em·bar"rass·es
em·bar"rass·ment
em"bas·sy
(*pl.* em"bas·sies)
em·bat"tle
em·bat"tling
em·bay"
em·bed"
em·bel"ish

em·bel"lish·ing
em"ber
em·bez"zle
em·bez"zle·ment
em·bez"zling
em·bind"
em·bit"ter
em·blaze"
em·bla"zon
em·bla"zoned
em"blem
em"blem·at"ic
em"blem·at·i·cal·ly
em"ble·ment
em·bod"i·ment
em·bod"y
em·bod"y·ing
em·bold"en
em·boi"te
em"bo·lism
em"bo·lite'
em"bo·lus
(*pl.* em"bo·li)
em·boss"
em'bou·chure"
em·bowed"
em·brace"
em·brace"a·ble
em·brac"ing
em·brace"ment
em·brang"ling
em·bra"sure
em·bro·ca"ted
em·broi"der
em·broi"der·y
(*pl.* em·broi"der·
ies)
em·broil"
em·brue"
em"bry·o
(*pl.* em"bry·os)
em'bry·ol"o·gy
em'bry·o"graph·er
em'bry·o·nat"ed
em'bry·on"ic
em'bry·ot"o·mies

em·bussed''
em''cee''
em''cee''ing
e·mend''
  correct (*see:* amend)
e'men·da''tion
em''er·ald
em''er·al·dine'
e·merge''
e·mer''gence
e·mer''gen·cy
  (*pl.* e·mer''gen·cies)
e·mer''gi·cen·ter
e·merg''ing
e·mer''i·ted'
e·mer''i·tus
e·mer''sion
  coming out (*see:* im-
  mersion)
em''er·y
em''er·y board
e·met''ic
em''i·grant
  one leaving (*see:* im-
  migrant)
em''i·grate'
  leave (*see:* immi-
  grate)
em''i·grat'ing
em''i·gra''tion
e''mi·gre'
em''i·gree'
em''i·nence
em''i·nent
  high ranking (*see:*
  immanent and im-
  minent)
em''i·nent'ly
e·mir''
e·mir''ate
em''is·sar'y
  (*pl.* em''is·sar'ies)
e·mis''sion
e·mit''
  e·mit''ted
  e·mit''ting

em''mar''bled
e·mol''lient
e·mol''u·ment
e·mote''
e·mo''tion
e·mo''tion·al
e·mo''tion·al·ism
e·mo''tion·al''ist'
e·mo''tion·al·ly
e·mo''tive
e·mo·tiv''i·ty
em·pan''o·ply
em·path''ic
em''pa·thize'
em''pa·thiz''ing
em''pa·thy
em''pen·nage''
em''per·or
em''pha·sis
  (*pl.* em''pha·ses')
em''pha·size'
em''pha·siz''ing
em·phat''ic
em·phy·se''ma
em·phy·se·ma''tous
em''pire
em·pir''i·cal
em·pir''i·cal·ly
em·pir''i·cism
em·pir''i·cist
em·place''ment
em·plas''trum
em·ploy''
em·ploy''a·ble
em·ploy''ee
em·ploy''er
em·ploy''ment
em·po''di·a
em·po''ri·um
em·pov''er·ish
em·pow''er
em''press
emp''ti·ness
emp''ty
  (*pl.* emp''ties)
emp''ty-hand''ed

emp''ty·ing
em''py·re''an
em''raud
em''u·late
em''u·lat'ing
em·u·la''tion
em''u·la·tor''y
em''u·lous
e·mul'si·fi·ca''tion
e·mul''si·fy'
e·mul''si·fy'ing
e·mul''sin
e·mul''sion
en·a''ble
en·a''bling
en·act''ment
en·act''or
e''nam
e·nam''el
e·nam''eled
e·nam''el·ing
e·nam''el·ware'
en·am''or
e·nam''o·ra''to
en·an''ti·om''er·ide
en·arched''
en·cag''ing
en·camp''ment
en·cap''su·late
  en·cap''su·lat'ed
  en·cap''su·lat'ing
en·cap''su·la''tion
en·car·di''tis
en·case''
en·cas''ing
en·cas''se·role
en·caus''tic
en·ceph'a·li''tis
en·ceph'a·lo''lo·gy
en·ceph'a·lo·my'e·li''
  tis
en·ceph'a·lo·path''ic
en·chained''
en·chant''
en·chant''ment
en·chant''ress

en·charge"
en'chi·la"da
en'chir·id"i·ons
en·ci"pher
en·cir"cle
 en·cir"cled
 en·cir"cling
en·cir"cle·ment
en"clave
en·cli"sis
en·close"
en·clos"ing
en·clo"sure
en·code"
 en·cod"ed
 en·cod"ing
en·co"mi·ast'
en·com'i·as"tic
en·co"mi·um
en·com"pass
en"core
en"cor·ing
en·coun"ter
en·cour"age
en·cour"age·ment
en·cour"ag·ing
en·crin"ic
en·croach"ment
en·crown"ment
en·crust"
en·crus·ta"tion
en·cum"ber
en·cum"ber·ing·ly
en·cum"brance
en·cyc"li·cal
en·cy·clo·pe·di·a
en·cy·clo·ped"i·cal
en·cyr"tid
en·dam"e·bic
en·dan"ger
en·darch"
en·dear"
en·deared"
en·dear"ment
en·deav"or
en·dem"ic

en'der·ma"tic
end"ing
en'dive
end"less
end"most
en'do·blast"
en'do·crine
en'do·cri·nol"o·gy
en'do·cri·no·ther"a·py
en'do·derm'
en'do·dy·nam'o·
  morph"ic
en·dog"a·my
en·dog"e·nous
en'do·lymph"ic
en'do·morph'
en'do·phas"i·a
en'do·plas"tule
en·dorse"
en·dors·ee"
en·dorse"ment
en·dors"er
en·dors"ing
en'do·scope'
en'do·skel"e·ton
en'do·thel"i·a
en·dow"
en·dow"ment
end'pa'per
end"prod"uct'
end"run'
end"ta'ble
en·due"
en·dur"a·ble
en·dur"ance
en·dur"ant
en·dure"
en·dur"ing
end"ways'
end"wise'
end"zone'
en"e·ma
 (*pl.* en"e·mas)
en"e·my
 (*pl.* en"e·mies)
en'er·get"ic

en'er·get"i·cal·ly
en"er·gize'
 en"er·gized'
 en"er·giz'ing
en"er·giz'er
en·er"gu·men
en"er·gy
 (*pl.* en"er·gies)
en"er·vate'
 en"er·vat'ed
 en"er·vat'ing
en"er·va"tion
en·fac"ing
en·fant ter·ri"ble
en·fee"ble
en·fee"ble·ment
en·fee"bling
en·fes"ter
en"fi·lade'
en"fi·lad'ing
en·fleur"age
en·fold"
en·force"
en·force"a·ble
en·forced"ly
en·forc"ing
en·fram"ing
en·fran"chise
 en·fran"chised
 en·fran"chis·ing
 en·fran"chise·ment
en·gage"
en·gage"ment
en·gag"ing
en garde"
en·gen"der
en·ger"mi·nate'
en"gine
en"gi·neer"
en"gi·neer"ing
En"gland
En"glish·man
En"glish·wom'an
en·graft"
en·gram·ma"tic
en·grave"

en·grav″ing
en·grav″ings
en·gross″
en·gulf″
en·gulf″ment
en·hance″
en·hanc″ing
en·hard″en
e·nig″ma
en·ig·mat″ic
en·ig·mat″i·cal
en·ig·mat″i·cal·ly
en·jambed″
en·join″
en·joyed″
en·joy″a·ble
en·joy″a·bly
en·joy″ment
en·large″
en·large″ing
en·large″ment
en·leaf″
en·light″en
en·light″en·ment
en·linked″
en·list″
en·list·ee″
en·list″ment
en·liv″en
en·lodge″
en masse″
en·mesh″
en″mi·ty
  (pl. en″mi·ties)
en·no″ble
en·no″ble·ment
en·no″bling
en·no″ic
en·nui″
en·o·da″tion
e·nor″mi·ty
e·nor″mous
e·nough″
e·nounce″
en·plane″
en·plan″ing

en·quir″y
  (pl. en·quir″ies)
en·race″
en·rage″
en·rag″ing
en·rap″ture
en·rav″ished
en·rich″
en·rich″ing
en·rich″ment
en·rock″ment
en·roll″
en·roll″ee
  en·rol″ling
  en·rolled″
en·roll″ment
en·root″
en route″
en·scroll″
en·sconce″
en·sconc″ing
en·sem″ble
en·sep″ul·chered
en·shrine″
  en·shrined″
  en·shrin″ing
en·sign
en·slave″
en·slave″ment
en·slav″ing
en·slumb″er
en·snare″
en·snare″ment
en·sphere″
en·su″a·ble
en·sue″
en·su″ing
en·sure″
en·sur″ing
en·tab″la·ture
en·tab″la·tured
en·tail″
en·tan″gle
en·tan″gle·ment
en·tente″
en·ter″ic

en″ter·ing
en″ter·i″tis
en″ter·o·my·co″sis
en″ter·or″rhe·a
en″ter·o′zoon″
en″ter·prise′
en″ter·pris′ing
en″ter·tain″
en″ter·tain″ing
en″ter·tain″er
en″ter·tain″ment
en·thrall″
en·thrall″dom
en·throne″
en·thron·ized″
en·thuse″
en·thu″si·asm′
en·thu″si·as″tic
en·thu″si·as″ti·cal·ly
en·thus″ing
en·tice″
en·tice″a·ble
en·tice″ment
en·tic″ing
en·tire″
en·tire″ly
en·tire″ty
  (pl. en·tire″ties)
en·ti″tle
en″ti·ty
  (pl. en″ti·ties)
en″to·gen″ous
en·tomb″
en·tomb″ment
en·tom″i·on
en″to·mol″o·gist
en″to·mol″o·gy
en″to·moph″a·gan
en·tou·rage″
en″tr′acte′
en″trail
en″trails
en″train″
en·trance″, v.
  fill with wonder
en″trance, n.

way in
en·tranc"ing
en"trant
en·trap"
  en·trapped"
  en·trap"ping
en·trap"ment
en·trap"per
en·treat"
en·treat"y
  (*pl.* en·treat"ies)
en"tree
en·trench"ment
en·tre·pre·neur"
en·tre·pre·neur"i·al
en·tro"pi·um
en"tro·py
en·trust"
en"try
  (*pl.* en"tries)
en"try·way
en·twine"
en·twine"ment
e·nu"mer·ate'
  e·nu"mer·at'ed
  e·nu"mer·at'ing
e·nu"mer·a'tion
e·nu"mer·a'tor
e·nun"ci·ate'
e·nun"ci·at'ing
e·nun"ci·a"tion
e·nured"
en·u·re"sis
en·vel"op
en·ve·lope
en·vel"op·ing
en·vel"op·ment
en·ven"om
en"vi·a·ble
en"vi·a·bly
en"vied
en"vi·ous
en"vi·ous·ly
en·vi"ron·ment
en·vi"ron·men"tal
en·vi"rons

en·vis"age
en·vis"ag·ing
en·vi"sion
en·vi"sioned
en"voy
en"vy
en"vy·ing
en·wind"
en·wrapt"
en·wrap"
  en·wrapped"
  en·wrap"ping
en"zyme
e"o·cene
e"on
ep"au·let
e·pee"
e·pend"y·mal
e·pergne"
e·perv"a
e·phem"er·a
e·phem"er·al
e·phem"er·al"i·ty
ep"ic
ep'i·can"thus
ep'i·card"i·a
ep"i·cene
ep"i·cen·ism
ep'i·cen"tcr
ep'i·chon·dro"tic
ep·ic·nem"i·al
ep'i·cor"mic
ep"i·cure
ep'i·cu·re"an
ep'i·cyte"
ep'i·dem"ic
ep'i·de'mi·ol"o·gy
ep'i·dem"y
ep'i·der"mis
ep'i·der·mol"y·sis
ep'i·ge·net"i·cal·ly
ep'i·glot"tis
ep"i·gone
ep'i·gram
ep'i·gram·mat"ic
ep'i·gram·ma"tist

ep"i·graph
ep'i·hy"al
ep'i·lat"or
ep'i·lep"sy
ep'i·lep"tic
ep'i·limn"i·on
ep"i·logue
ep'i·log"uing
ep'i·mer"i·tic
E·piph"a·ny
ep'i·phe·nom"e·non
ep'i·phys"i·al
e·pis"co·pa·cy
  (*pl.* e·pis"co·pa·cies)
e·pis"co·pal
e·pis"co·pate'
e·pi·plec"tic
e·pi"pol·ism
e·pir·rhe·ma"tic
ep"i·sode'
ep'i·sod"ic
ep'i·sta"sis
e·pis"te·mol"o·gy
ep'i·ster·nal"i·a
e·pis"tle
e·pis"to·lar'y
e·pis"to·lised'
e·pis"tro·phe'
ep'i·taph"
ep'i·taph"i·cal
ep·i·the"li·al
ep·i·the"li·um
ep"i·thet'
ep'i·them'
e·pit"o·me
e·pit"o·mize'
e·pit"o·miz'ing
ep'i·tu·ber"cu·lous
e' plu"ri·bus' u"num
ep"och
  period (*see:* epic)
ep"och·al
e·pol"li·cate'
ep"o·nym
ep·on"y·mous

ep·ox″y
ep″si·lon′
ept
eq·ua·bil″i·ty
eq′ua·ble
eq′ua·bly
e″qual
e″qual·ing
e″qual·i·tar″i·an
e·qual″ity
  (*pl.* e·qual″i·ties)
e″qual·i·za″tion
e″qual·ize′
  e″qual·ized′
  e″qual·iz″ing
e″qual·ly
e″qua·nim″i·ty
e·quate″
e·quat″ing
e·qua″tion
e·qua″tor
e·qua·to″ri·al
eq″uer·ry
  (*pl.* eq″uer·ries)
e·ques″tri·an
e·ques′tri·enne″
e·qui·an″gu·lar
e·qui·dense″
e·qui·dis″tant
e·qui·gla″cial
e·qui·lat″er·al
e·qui·lib″ri·um
e·qui·lib″rist
e·qui·nate″
e″quine
e·qui·noc″tial
e′qui·nox′
e·quip″
eq″ui·page
e·quip″ment
e·qui·poise′
e·qui·pol″lent
e·quip″ping
e·qui·pro·por″tion·al
e·qui·sized″
eq″ui·ta·ble

eq″ui·ta·bly
eq″ui·ty
  (*pl.* eq″ui·ties)
e·quiv″a·lence
e·quiv″a·lent
e·quiv″o·ca′cy
e·quiv″o·cal
e·quiv″o·cal·ly
e·quiv″o·cate
e·quiv″o·cat″ing
e·quiv″o·ca″tion
e·quiv″o·ca·tor
e″ra
e·rad″i·ca·ble
e·rad″i·cate
  e·rad″i·cat″ed
  e·rad″i·cat″ing
e·rad″i·ca″tion
e·ras″a·ble
  able to erase (*see:* ir-
  ascible)
e·rase″
  e·rased″
  e·ras″ing
e·ras″er
e·ras″ure
e·rect″
e·rect″ing
e·rec″tile
e·rec″tion
er′e·mit″i·cal
erg
er·ga″to·morph
er″go
er·gon″
er′go·nom″ics
er·gos″ter·ol
er″got
er·got″in
Er″ie
erl″king
er″mine
e·rode″
e·rod″ing
e·ro″gate
e·rog″e·nous

e·ro″sion
e·ro″sive
e·ro″strate
e·rot″ic
e·rot″i·ca
e·rot″i·cism
e·rot″o·gen″ic
err
er″ra·ble·ness
er″rand
er″rant
er·rat″ic
er·rat″i·cal·ly
er·ra″tum
  (*pl.* er·ra″ta)
er·ro″ne·ous
er″ror
er″ror·less
er″satz
erst″while′
e·ru″be·scite′
e·ruct″
er″u·dite′
er″u·dite′ness
er·u·di″tion
e·rupt″
  break forth (*see:* ir-
  rupt)
e·rup″tion
  bursting forth (*see:*
  irruption)
e·rup″tive·ly
er′y·the″ma
e·ryth″re·an
e·ryth′ro·carp″ous
e·ryth″ro·cyte
e·ryth″ro·der″ma
e·ryth″ro·my″cin
e·ryth″ro·scope
es′ca·drille″
es″ca·late′
es″ca·lat′ing
es″ca·la″tion
es″ca·la″tor
es·cal″lop
es″ca·pade″

es·cape″
es·cap·ee″
es·cape″ment
es·cap″ing
es·cap″ism
es·cap″ists
es·car·got″
es″ca·role
es·carp″ment
es·cha″to·col
es·cha·tol″o·gy
es·chew
es′cri·toire″
es′cri·tor″i·al
es·cort″, v.
  accompany
es″cort, n.
  one who escorts
es·crow
es′cu·lent
es·cutch″eon
es·guard
Es″ki·mo
  (pl. Es″ki·mos′)
es·mer·al″dite
e·soph′a·ge″al
e·soph′a·gal″gi·a
e·soph′a·gus
  (pl. e·soph″a·gi)
es′o·ter″ic
es′o·ter″i·cal·ly
es′o·ter″i·cism
es″pa·drille
es·pal″ier
es·pe″cial
es·pe″cial·ly
Es″pe·ran′to
es·pied″
es·pi″gle
es″pi·o·nage
es′pla·nade″
es·pous″al
es·pouse″
es·pous″ing
es·pres″so
es·prit″ de corps″

es·py″
es·py″ing
es″quire
es·say″, v.
  attempt (see: assay)
es″say, n.
  writing
es″say·ist
es·sede″
es″sence
es·sen″tial
es·sen″tial·ly
es·sen″ti·al″i·ty
es·tab″lish
es·tab″lish·ment
es·ta″fette
es·tan″cia
es·tate″
es·tat″ed
es·teem″
es·the·si·ol″o·gy
es·thete″
es·thet″ic
es″ti·ma·ble
es″ti·mate
es″ti·mat″ing
es″ti·ma″tion
es″ti·ma″tor
es″ti·val
es″ti·vate
es″ti·vat″ing
Es·to″ni·a
es·trange″
es·trange″ment
es·trang″ing
es·trayed″
es″tro·gen
es″trus
es·tu·ar″y
  (pl. es″tu·ar′ies)
es″tu·ous
et cet″er·a
etch″er
etch″ing
e·ter″nal
e·ter′nal·ize″

e·ter″nal·ly
e·ter″ni·ty
  (pl. e·ter″ni·ties)
eth″a·nol′
e″ther
e·the″re·al
e·the″ri·on
e″ther·ize′
e″ther·iz′ing
eth″i·cal
eth″i·cal·ly
eth″ics
E′thi·o″pi·a
eth″nic
eth″ni·cal·ly
eth·nic″i·ty
eth′no·bi·o·log″i·cal
eth′no·cen″tric
eth′no·cen″trism
eth′no·ge·o·graph″ic
eth′no·lin·guis″tics
eth′no·log″ic
eth·nol″o·gist
eth·nol″o·gy
eth′no·zo·ol″o·gy
e″thos
eth″yl
e·ti·ol″in
e·ti·ol″o·gy
et″i·quette
e″tude
e·tui″
et′y·mo·log″i·cal
et′y·mol″o·gy
  (pl. et′y·mol″o·
  gies)
et″y·mon′
eu·ca·lyp″tus
  (pl. eu·ca·lyp″tus·
  es)
Eu″cha·rist
Eu·clid″e·an
eu·de·mon″ist
eu·gen·es″ic
eu·gen″ic
eu·gen″i·cal·ly

eu·gen''ics
eu·he''dral
eu·la·chon''
eu·log''ic
eu''lo·gize'
  eu''lo·gized'
  eu''lo·giz'ing
eu''lo·gy
  (*pl.* eu''lo·gies)
eu''nuch
eu'nuch·i''zing
eu''phe·mism'
eu''phe·mis''tic
eu''phe·mis''ti·cal·ly
eu·phon''ic
eu·pho''ni·ous
eu·pho''ni·um
eu''pho·ny
  (*pl.* eu''pho·nies)
eu·pho''ri·a
eu·phor''ic
eu''phu·ism'
eu''phu·ist''ic
eu·plo''tid
eu·pyr''i·on
Eur·a''sian
eu·re''ka
eu·rhyth''my
Eu'ro·dol''lars
Eu'ro·par''lia·ment
Eu''rope
Eu'ro·pe''an
eu·sta''chi·an tube''
eu''style
eu·tex''i·a
eu'tha·na''sia
eu·toc''i·a
eu·xen''ite
e·vac''u·ate'
  e·vac''u·at'ed
  e·vac''u·at'ing
e·vac'u·a''tion
e·vac'u·ee'
e·vade''
e·vad''ing
e·vad''er

e·val''u·ate'
e·val''u·at'ing
e·val'u·a''tion
ev'a·nes''cence
e'van·gel''i·cal
e'van·gel''i·cal·ly
e·van''ge·lism'
e·van''ge·list
e·van'ge·lis''tic
e·van''ge·lize'
e·van''ge·liz'ing
e·van'gel·i·za''tion
Ev''an·ston
e·vap''o·rate'
e·vap''o·rat'ing
e·vap'o·ra''tion
e·vap''o·ra'tor
e·vap'o·rom'e·ter
e·va''sion
e·va''sive
e·vec''tion
ev''en·blush
e'ven·hand''ed
eve''ning
ev'en·mind''ed
e''ven·ness
e·vent''
e·vent''ful
e·ven·tra''tion
e·ven''tu·al
e·ven'tu·al''i·ty
  (*pl.* e·ven'tu·al''i·ties)
e·ven''tu·al·ly
e·ven''tu·ate'
e·ven''tu·at'ing
ev'er·bear''er
Ev''er·est
ev''er·glades'
ev'er·green''
ev'er·last''ing
ev'er·more''
e·vers''ive
e·vert''
eve''ry·bod'y
eve''ry·day'

eve''ry·how'
eve''ry·one'
eve''ry·place'
eve''ry·thing'
eve''ry·where'
e·vict''
e·vic''tion
ev''i·dence
ev''i·denc'ing
ev''i·dent
ev'i·den''tial
e''vil·do'er
e''vil·ly
e'vil·mind''ed
e·vince''
e·vin''ci·ble
e·vinc''ing
e·vis''cer·ate'
  e·vis''cer·at'ed
  e·vis''cer·at'ing
e·vis'cer·a''tion
ev'o·ca''tion
e·vok''ing
e·voc''a'tive
e·voke''
ev'o·lu''tion
ev'o·lu''tion·ar'y
ev'o·lu''tion·ist
ev'o·lu''tion·ism
e·volve''
e·volv''ing
ev''zone'
ewe
  sheep (*see:* you and
  yew)
ew''er
ex·ac''er·bate'
ex·ac''er·bat'ing
ex·ac'er·ba''tion
ex·act''
ex·ac''tion
ex·act''i·tude'
ex'' ad·vers''o
ex·ag''ger·ate'
ex·ag''ger·at'ing
ex·ag'ger·a''tion

ex·al´bu·min´´ous
ex·alt´´
  praise (*see:* exult)
ex´al·ta´´tion
ex·am´i·na´´tion
ex·am´´ine
ex·am´´in·er
ex·am´´in·ing
ex·am´´ple
ex·as´´per·ate
ex·as´´per·at´ing
ex·as´per·a´´tion
ex´´camb
ex´´ca·vate´
ex´´ca·vat´ing
ex´ca·va´´tion
ex´´ca·va´tor
ex·ceed´´
  surpass (*see:* accede)
ex·ceed´´ing·ly
ex·cel´´
ex´´cel·lence
ex´´cel·len·cy
  (*pl.* ex´´cel·len·cies)
ex´´cel·lent
ex·cel´´ling
ex·cel´´si·or
ex·cept´´
  excluding (*see:* ac-
  cept)
ex·cept´´ant
ex·cept´´ing
ex·cep´´tion
ex·cep´´tion·a·ble
ex·cep´´tion·al
ex·cep´´tion·al·ly
ex·cep´´tive
ex·cerpt´´, *v.*
  select
ex´´cerpt, *n.*
  quotation
ex·cess´´, *n.*
  surplus (*see:* access)
ex´´cess, *adj.*
  surplus
ex·ces´´sive

ex·ces´´sive·ly
ex·change´´
ex·change´´a·ble
ex·chang´´ing
ex·cheq´´uer
ex·cide´´
ex·cise´´, *v.*
  cut out
ex´´cise, *n.*
  tax
ex·cis´´ing
ex·ci´´sion
ex·cit´a·bil´´i·ty
ex·cit´´a·ble
ex·ci·ta´´tion
ex·cite´´
ex·cite´´ment
ex·cit´´ing
ex·claim´´
ex·cla·ma´´tion
ex·clam´´a·to´ry
ex´´clave
ex·clude´´
ex·clud´´ed
ex·clud´´ing
ex·clu´´sion
ex·clu´´sive
ex·clu·siv´´i·ty
ex·clu´´so·ry
ex´com·mu´´ni·cate´
ex´com·mu´´ni·cat´ing
ex´com·mu·ni·ca´´tion
ex·co´´ri·ate´
ex·co´´ri·at´ing
ex·co´ri·a´´tion
ex´´cre·ment
ex´cre·men·ti´´tious
ex·cres´´cence
ex·cre´´tal
ex·crete´´
ex·cret´´ing
ex·cre´´tion
ex·cru´´ci·at´ing
ex·cub´it·tor´´i·a
ex´´cul·pate
ex´´cul·pat´ing

ex´cul·pa´´tion
ex·cul´´pa·to·ry
ex·cur´´sion
ex·cur´´sion·ist
ex·cur´´sion·a·ry
ex·cus´´a·ble
ex·cus´´a·bly
ex·cuse´´
ex·cus´´ing
ex´´e·cra·ble
ex´´e·crate
ex´e·crat´ing
ex´e·cra´´tion
ex´´e·cute´
ex´´e·cut´ing
ex´e·cu´´tion
ex´e·cu´´tion·er
ex·ec´´u·tive
ex·ec´´u·tor
ex·ec´´u·trix
  (*pl.* ex·ec´´u·trix·es)
ex´e·ge´´sis
ex·em´´plar
ex·em´´pla·ry
ex·em´´pli·fy
ex·em´´pli·fy´ing
ex·em´´pli·fi´a·ble
ex·empt´´
ex·emp´´tion
ex´´er·cise´
  activity (*see:* exor-
  cise)
ex´´er·cis´ing
  doing exercise (*see:*
  exorcising)
ex·ert´´
  put into action (*see:*
  exsert)
ex·er´´tion
ex´´e·unt
ex·fol´´i·a·tor´y
ex·ha·la´´tion
ex·hale´´
ex·hal´´ing
ex·haust´´
ex·haust´´i·ble

ex·haus″tion
ex·haus″tive
ex·hib″it
ex·hi·bi″tion
ex·hi·bi″tion·ism
ex·hib″i·tor *or* exhib-
 iter
ex·hil″a″rant
ex·hil″a·rate′
ex·hil″a·rat′ing
ex·hil′a·ra″tion
ex·hort″
ex′hor·ta″tion
ex′hu·ma″tion
ex·hume″
ex·hum″ing
ex″i·gen·cy
 (*pl.* ex″i·gen·cies)
ex″i·gent
ex·ig″u·ous
ex″ile
ex″il·ing
ex·ist″
ex·ist″ence
ex·ist″ent
ex·is·ten″tial
ex·is·ten″tial·ism′
ex″it poll′
ex li″bris
ex·o·can″ni·bal·ism
ex·o·co·li″tis
ex·od″i·um
ex″o·dus
ex of·fi″ci·o
ex·og″a·my
ex·o·gas″tri·cal·ly
ex·on″er·ate′
ex·on″er·at′ing
ex·on′er·a″tion
ex·or″bi·tance
ex·or″bi·tant
ex·or·cise
 expel (*see:* exercise)
ex″or·cised′
ex″or·cis′ing

expelling (*see:* exer-
 cising)
ex″or·cism
ex″or·cist
ex′o·skel″e·ton
ex″o·sphere
ex′o·ter″ics
ex·ot″i·cal·ly
ex·pand″
ex·pand″ing·ly
ex·panse″
ex·pan″si·ble
ex·pan″sion
ex·pan″sion·ist
ex·pan″sive
ex par″te
ex·pa″ti·ate′
ex·pa″ti·a″tion
ex·pa″tri·ate′
ex·pa″tri·at′ing
ex·pa″tri·a″tion
ex·pect″
ex·pect″an·cy
ex·pect″ant
ex·pec·ta″tion
ex·pec″to·rant
ex·pec″to·rate′
ex·pec″to·rat′ing
ex·pec″to·ra″tion
ex·pe″di·ence
ex·pe″di·en·cy
 (*pl.* ex·pe″di·en·
 cies)
ex·pe″di·ent
ex·pe·di″tate
ex·pe·dite″
ex·pe·dit″er
ex·pe·dit″ing
ex·pe·di″tion
ex·pe·di″tion·ar′y
ex·pe·di″tious
ex·pel″
ex·pel″ling
ex·pend″
ex·pend″a·ble
ex·pend″i·ture

ex·pense″
ex·pen″sive
ex·pen″sive·ly
ex·pe″ri·ence
ex·pe″ri·enc·ing
ex·per′i·en″tial
ex·per″i·ment
ex·per′i·men·tal
ex·per′i·men·ta″tion
ex″pert
ex″per·tise″
ex·pi·a·ble
ex″pi·ate′
ex″pi·at′ing
ex·pi·a″tion
ex·pi·a·to′ry
ex·pi·la″tion
ex·pi·ra″tion
ex·pire″
ex·pir″ing
ex·plain″
ex′pla·na″tion
ex·plan″a·to′ry
ex″ple·tive
ex·pli·ca·ble
ex″pli·cate
ex″pli·cat′ing
ex′pli·ca″tion
ex·plic″it
ex·plode″
ex·plod″er
ex·plod″ing
ex·ploit″, *v.*
 take advantage of
ex″ploit, *n.*
 daring deed
ex′ploi·ta″tion
ex·ploit″a·tive
ex·plo″ra″tion
ex·plor″a·to′ry
ex·plore″
ex·plor″er
ex·plor″ing
ex·plo″sion
ex·plo″sive
ex·po″nent

ex·po·nen″tial
ex·port″, *v.*
  ship out
ex′port, *n.*
  thing exported
ex·por″ta·ble
ex·por·ta″tion
ex·port″er
ex·pose″
ex′po·se″
ex·pos″ing
ex·po·si″tion
ex·pos″i·tor
ex·pos″i·to·ry
ex″ post′ fac″to
ex·pos″tu·late′
ex·pos″tu·lat′ing
ex·pos″tu·la″tion
ex·po″sure
ex·pound″
ex·press″
ex·press″agc
ex·press″i·ble
ex·pres″sion
ex·pres″sion·ism
ex·pres″sion·ist
ex·pres″sion·is′tic
ex·pres″sive
ex·press″way
ex·pro″pri·a′ble
ex·pro″pri·ate′
ex·pro″pri·at′ing
ex·pro″pri·a″tion
ex·pul″sion
ex·punge″
ex·pung″ing
ex″pur·gate′
ex″pur·gat′ing
ex″pur·ga″tion
ex″qui·site
ex·scind″ed
ex·sert″
  protrude (*see:* exert)
ex″tant
  alive (*see:* extent)
ex·tem′po·ra″ne·ous

ex·tem″po·re
ex·tem″po·rize′
ex·tem″po·riz′ing
ex·tend″
ex·tend″i·ble
ex·ten″si·ble
ex·ten″sion
ex·ten″sive
ex·tent″
  amount (*see:* extant)
ex·ten″u·ate
ex·ten″u·at′ing
ex·ten″u·a″tion
ex·te″ri·or
ex·te″ri·or·ized″
ex·ter″mi·nate
ex·ter″mi·nat′ing
ex·ter′mi·na″tion
ex·ter″mi·na′tor
ex·ter″nal
ex·ter″nal·ly
ex·tinct″
ex·tinc″tion
ex·tin″guish
ex·tin″guish·er
ex″tir·pate′
ex″tir·pat′ing
ex″tir·pa″tion
ex·tol″
ex·tolled″
ex·tol″ling
ex·tort″
ex·tor″tion
ex·tor″tion·er
ex·tor″tion·ist
ex″tra
ex′tra·cell″u·lar
ex′tra·cost″al
ex·tract″, *v.*
  draw out
ex″tract, *n.*
  thing extracted
ex·trac″tion
ex′tra·cur·ric″u·lar
ex′tra·dit′a·ble
ex″tra·dite′

ex″tra·dit′ing
ex′tra·di″tion
ex·tra·dot″al
ex′tra·haz″ar·dous
ex′tra·le″gal
ex′tra·mar″i·tal
ex′tra·mu″ral
ex″tra″ne·ous
ex′tra·norm″al
ex·traor′di·nar″i·ly
ex·traor″di·nar′y
ex·trap″o·late′
ex·trap″o·lat′ing
ex·trap″o·la″tion
ex′tra·sen″so·ry
ex′tra·ter·ri·tor″i·al
ex′tra·u″ter·ine
ex·trav″a·gance
ex·trav″a·gant
ex·trav′a·gan″za
ex′tra·ve·hic″u·lar
ex′tra·vers″ive
ex·treme″
ex·treme″ly
ex·trem″ism
ex·trem″ist
ex·trem″i·ty
  (*pl.* ex·trem″i·ties)
ex″tri·ca·ble
ex″tri·cate′
ex″tri·cat′ing
ex″tri·ca″tion
ex·trin″sic
ex″tro·ver″sion
ex″tro·vert″
ex·trude″
ex·trud″ing
ex·tru″sion
ex·tund″
ex·u″ber·ance
ex·u″ber·ant
ex′u·da″tion
ex·ude″
ex·ud″ing
ex·ult
  rejoice (*see:* exalt)

ex·ult"ant
ex'ul·ta"tion
ex"urb
ex·ur"ban·ite'
ex·ur"bi·a
ex·uv"i·al
eye
  sight organ (*pl.* eyes)
  (*see:* aye)
eye"ball'
eye"balm'
eye"brow'
eye" con"tact'
eye"cup'
eyed
eye"drop'per
eye" drops'
eye"ful'
eye"glass'
eye"ing
eye"lash'
eye"let
  hole (*see:* islet)
eye"lid'
eye"-o'pen·er
eye"sight'
eye"sore'
eye"strain'
eye"tooth'
  (*pl.* eye"teeth')
eye"wash'
eye"wit'ness
ey"rie

F

fa"ble
fa"bled
fa"ble·mon"ger·ing
fab"ric
fab"ri·cate'
  fab"ri·cat·ed
  fab"ri·cat'ing
fab'ri·ca"tion
fab"u·list

fab"u·lize'
fab"u·lous
fa·cade"
face
face"less
face"-lift'
face"-sav'ing
fac"et
  gem; aspect (*see:* faucet)
fac"et·ed
fa·ce"tious
face" val"ue
fa"cial
fac"ile
fac"ile·ness
fa·cil"i·tate
fa·cil"i·tat'ing
fa·cil"i·ta"tion
fa·cil"i·ty
  (*pl.* fa·cil"i·ties)
fac"ing
fac·sim"i·le
fact"-find'ing
fac"tion
fac"tion·al
fac"tion·al·ism'
fac"tious
fac·ti"tial
fac·ti"tious
  artificial (*see:* ficti-tious)
fac"tor
fac·to"ri·al
fac"to·ry
  (*pl.* fac"to·ries)
fac·to"tum
fac"tu·al
fac"tu·al·ly
fac"u·lar
fac"ul·ty
  (*pl.* fac"ul·ties)
fad"dish
fad"dist
fade
fade"-in'

fade"-out'
fad"ing
faf"fle
fag
fag" end"
fag"ging
fag"ot
fag"ot·ing
Fahr"en·heit
fai"ence
fail"ing
fail"-safe"
fail"ure
faint
  weak (*see:* feint)
faint"heart"ed
fair
  just; sales place (*see:* fare)
fair"ground'
fair"-haired'
fair"ly
fair"mind"ed
fair"spo"ken
fair"-trade"
fair"way
fair"-weath'er
fair"y
  creature (*pl.* fair" ies) (*see:* ferry)
fair"y·land'
fair"y tale
fait ac·com·pli"
faith"ful
faith"ful·ly
faith" heal'er
faith"less
fake
fak"er
  deceiver (*see:* fakir)
fak"ing
fa·kir"
  beggar (*see:* faker)
fal·ca"tion
fal"con
fal'con·elle"

fal''con·ry
fall
fal·la''cious
fal''la·cy
  (*pl.* fal''la·cies)
fal·la''tion
fal'li·bil''i·ty
fal''li·ble
fal''li·bly
fall''ing-out''
fall''off'
fal·lo''pi·an
fall''out'
fal''low
false
false'' a·larm''
false''-heart''ed
false''hood
fals''er
fal·set''to
fal'si·fi·ca''tion
fal''si·fied'
fal''si·fi'er
fal''si·fy
fal''si·fy'ing
fal''si·ty
  (*pl.* fal''si·ties)
fal''ter
fame
fa·mel''ic
fa·mil''ial
fa·mil''iar
fa·mil'i·ar''i·ty
  (*pl.* fa·mil'i·ar''i·
  ties)
fa·mil'iar·i·za''tion
fa·mil''iar·ize
fa·mil''iar·iz'ing
fam''i·ly
  (*pl.* fam''i·lies)
fam''ine
fam''ished
fa''mous
fan
fa·nat''ic
fa·nat''i·cal

fa·nat''i·cal·ly
fa·nat''i·cism
fan''cied
fan''ci·er
fan''ci·ful
fan''ci·ful·ly
fan''cy
  (*pl.* fan''cies)
fan''cy-free''
fan''cy·ing
fan''cy·work'
fan·dan''go
fan''dom
fan''fare
fang
fan''jet'
fan''light'
fan'' mail'
fan''ning
fan''ny
fan''tail'
fan·ta''sia
fan''ta·size'
fan''ta·siz'ing
fan·tas''mal
fan·tas''tic
fan·tas''ti·cal·ly
fan''ta·sy
  (*pl.* fan''ta·sies)
far''ad
far'a·dized''
far''a·way''
farce
far''ci·cal
fare
  money; food; result
  (*see:* fair)
Far'' East''
fared
fare''-thee-well'
fare'well''
far''-fetched''
far''-fetched''ness
far''-flung''
fa·ri''na
far'i·na''ceous

far''ing
far''kle·ber'ries
farm''a·ble
farm'er·ship''
farm''hand'
farm''house'
farm''land'
farm''out'
farm''stead'
farm''yard'
far''o
far''-off''
far''-out''
far''rage
far·ra''go
far''-reach''ing
far''rel .
far''row
far''see''ing
far''sight''ed
far''ther
far''thing
fas''ci·cle
fas''ci·nate'
fas''ci·nat'ed
fas''ci·nat'ing
fas'ci·na''tion
fas''cism
fas''cist
fas'cis·ti·za''tion
fash''ion
fash''ion·a·ble
fash''ion·a·bly
fass
fast''back'
fas''ten
fas''ten·er
fas''ten·ing
fast''-food'
fas·tid''i·ous
fas·tig''i·at'ed
fa''tal
fa''tal·ism'
fa''tal·ist
fa'tal·is''tic
fa'tal·is''ti·cal·ly

fa·tal″i·ty
  (pl. fa·tal″i·ties)
fa′tal·ize″
fa″tal·ly
fate
  destiny (*see:* fete)
fat″ed
  destined (*see:* fatted)
fate″ful
fat″farm′
fat″head′
fa″ther·hood′
fa″ther-in-law′
  (*pl.* fa″thers-in-
  law′)
fa″ther·land′
fa″ther·less
fa″ther·ly
Fa″ther's Day
fath″om
fath″om·a·ble
fath″om·less
fath·om″e·ter′
fat·i·gate′
fa·tigue″
fa·tigu″ing
fat″-sol′u·ble
fat″ted
  made fat (*see:* fated)
fat″ten
fat″ter
fat″ti·er
fat″ty
fa·tu″i·ty
  (*pl.* fa·tu″i·ties)
fat″u·ous
fau″cet
  valve (*see:* facet)
fault″find′er
fault″i·er
fault″i·ly
fault″less
fault″y
faun
  Roman deity (*see:*
  fawn)

fau″na
fau·na″ted
fau·vette″
faux pas″
  (*pl.* faux pas″)
fa″vor·a·ble
fa″vor·a·bly
fa″vor·ite
fa″vor·it·ism′
fawn
  deer; show servility
  (*see:* faun)
fay
  fairy (*see:* fey)
faze
  daunt (*see:* phase)
faz″ing
  daunting (*see:* phas-
  ing)
feak
fe″al·ty
fear″ful
fear″ful·ly
fear″less
fear″some
fea·si·bil″i·ty
fea″si·ble
fea″si·bly
feat
  act (*see:* feet)
feath″er·bed″
feath″er·bed″ding
feath″er·brain′
feath″er·pate′
feath″er·weight′
feath″er·y
fea″ture
fea″ture·less
fea″tur·ing
feb″ri·fuge′
fe″brile
Feb″ru·ar′y
fe″cal
fe″ces
fe″cu·lent′
feck″less

fe″cund
fe″cun·date′
fe″cun·dat′ing
fe·cun″di·ty
fe·da·yeen″
fed″er·al
fed″er·al·ism
fed″er·al·ize
fem″i·cide′
fem″i·nine
fem·i·nin″i·ty
fem″i·nism′
fem″i·nist
femme′ fa·tale″
fem″o·ral
fe″mur
fence
fenc″er
fenc″ing
fend
fend″er
fen″el
fen″ter
fe·rac″i·ty
fe″ral
fer-de-lance″
fer·ment″, *v.*
  cause fermentation;
  agitate
fer″ment, *n.*
  agitation
fer·men″ta·ble
fer′men·ta″tion
fern
fe·ro″cious
fe·roc″i·ty
  (*pl.* fe·roc″i·ties)
fer″ret
fer″ret·ing
fer″ric
fer″ried
fer″rite
fer″ri·tin′
fer′ro·mag·net″ic
fer′ro·mag″ne·tism′

fer″ro·type′
fer″rous
fer″rule
  metal ring (*see:* ferule)
fer″ry
  boat (*pl.* fer″ries)
  (*see:* fairy)
fer″ry·boat′
fer″ry·ing
fer″tile
fer·til″i·ty
fer″til·i·za″tion
fer″til·ize′
fer″til·iz′er
fer″til·iz′ing
fer″ule
  stick (*see:* ferrule)
fer″vent
fer·vent″ness
fer″vid
fer″vor
fes″cue
fes″tal
fes″ter
fes″ti·val
fes″tive
fes·tiv″i·ty
  (*pl.* fes·tiv″i·ties)
fes·toon″
Fest″schrift′
  (*pl.* Fest″schrif′ten)
fe″tal
fetch″ing
fete
  entertainment; honor
  (*see:* fate)
fe″ti·cide′
fe″ti·cid″al
fet″ing
fet″ish
fet″lock′
fet″ter
fet″tle
fet′tu·ci″ni
fe″tus

(*pl.* fe″tus·es)
feu″dal
feu″dal·ism′
feu″dal·ist′
feu″dal·is″tic
fe″ver·ish
few
fey
  strange (*see:* fay)
fez
  (*pl.* fez″zes)
fi′an·ce″, *mas.*
fi′an·cee″, *fem.*
fi·as″co
  (*pl.* fi·as″coes)
fi″at
fi″at mon′ey
fib
fib″ber
  liar (*see:* fiber)
fib″bing
fi″ber
  material (*see:* fibber)
fi″ber·board′
Fi″ber·glas′™
fi″ber·glass′
fi″ber·ize″
fi″ber op″tics
fi′bri·form″
fib″ril·late
fib″ril·lat·ing
fi′bril·la″tion
fi′bro·cys″tic
fi″broid
fi″brous
fi′bro·vas″cu·lar
fib″u·la
  (*pl.* fib″u·lae)
fice
fiche
fick″le
fic″tion
fic″tion·al
fic′tion·al·i·za″tion
fic·ti″tious

not true (*see:* facti-
  tious)
fid″dle
fid″dler crab′
fid″dle·faced′
fid″dle-fad″dle
fid″dle·sticks′
fid″dling
fi·del″i·ty
  (*pl.* fi·del″i·ties)
fidg″et
fidg″et·ing
fidg″et·y
fi·du″ci·ar′y
fief″dom
field″ day′
field″er
field″ glass′es
field″ goal′
field″ hock′ey
field″ house′
field″ mouse′
field″ trip′
fiend
fiend″ish
fierce
fierce″ly
fierce″ness
fierc″er
fier″i·er
fier″i·est
fier″y
fi·es″ta
fife
fif″teen″
fif″teenth″
fifth
fif″ti·eth
fif″ty
  (*pl.* fif″ties)
fif″ty-fif″ty
fight
fight″er
fight″ing
fig″ment
fig″u·late′

fig″ur·a·tive
fig″ure
fig″ure·head′
fig′u·rine″
Fi″ji
fil″a·ment
fil″bert
file
fi′let mi·gnon″
fil″i·al
fil″i·bus′ter
fil″i·gree′
fil″ing
   putting into file (*see:* filling)
Fil′i·pi″no
fill″er
fil″let
fill″-in
fill″-ing
   making full (*see:* fil-ing)
fill″ing sta′tion
fil″lip
fil″ly
   (*pl.* fil″lies)
film″dom
film″strip′
film″y
film″i·er
fil″ter
   screening out (*see:* philter)
fil″ter tip′
filth″i·er
filth″i·ness
filth″y
fil″trate
fil″trat·ing
fil·tra″tion
fi·na″gle
fi·na″gler
fi·na″gling
fi″nal
fi·na″le
fi″nal·ist

fi·nal″i·ty
fi″nal·ize′
fi″nal·iz′ing
fi·nance″
fi·nan″cial
fi·nan″cial·ly
fin′an·cier″
fi·nanc″ing
find
find″ing
fine″-drawn
fine″ly
fine″ness
fin″er·y
   (*pl.* fin″er·ies)
fine″spun″
fi·nesse″
fi·ness″ing
fin″ger bowl′
fin″ger·ing
fin″ger·nail′
fin″ger paint′ing
fin″ger·print′
fin″ger·tip′
fin″i·al
fin″ick·i·ness
fin″ick·y
fin″ing
fi″nis
fin″ish
fin″ished
fi″nite
fink
Fin″land
fin″less
fin″nan had″die
fin″ny
fiord
fir
   tree (*see:* fur)
fire″ alarm″
fire″arm′
fire″ball′
fire″bolt·ed′
fire″brand′
fire″break′

fire″bug′
fire″crack′er
fire″ drill′
fire″-eat′er
fire″ en′gine
fire″ es·cape′
fire″ fight″er
fire″fly′
   (*pl.* fire″flies′)
fire″flow·er′
fire″house′
fire″light′
fire″man
   (*pl.* fire″men)
fire″place′
fire″plug′
fire″pow′er
fire″proof′
fire″-re·sist′ant
fire″side′
fire″stop′
fire″ wall′
fire″wa′ter
fire″wood′
fire″works′
fir″ing line′
fir″ma·ment
firm″ly
first″ aid″
first″born″
first″-class″
first″hand″
first″ly
first′-night″er
first″-rate″
first″-string″
fish″back′
fish″bowl′
fish″er
   fisherman (*see:* fis-sure)
fish″er·man
fish″er·y
   (*pl.* fish″er·ies)
fish″hook′
fish″i·er

fish"ing rod'
fish"mong'er
fish"net'
fish"plate'
fish"tail'
fish"wife'
fish"y
fis"sion
fis"sion·a·ble
fis"sure
   crack (see: fisher)
fis"sur·ing
fist"ful'
   (pl. fist"fuls')
fist"i·cuff'
fis"tu·la
fit"ful
fit"ful·ly
fit"ted
fit"ter
fit"ting
five"-and-ten"
five"-star"
fix
fix·a"tion
fix"a·tive
fix·a"tor
fixed
fix"ings
fix"i·ty
fix"ture
fizz"ing
fiz"zle
fiz"zling
fjord
flab
flab"ber·gast'
flab"bi·er
flab"bi·ness
flab"by
flac"cid
flag
flag"el·lant
flag"el·late'
flag"el·la"tion
fla·gel"lum

(pl. fla·gel"la)
flag'eo·let"
flag"fish'
flag"ging
flag"man
flag"on
flag"pole'
fla"grance
fla"grant
fla·gran'te de·lic"to
flag"ship'
flag"staff'
flag"stone'
flag"-wav'ing
flail
flair
   talent (see: flare)
flake
flak"i·er
flak"i·ness
flak"ing
flak"y
flam
flam·be"
flam"beau
   (pl. flam"beaux)
flam·boy"ance
flam·boy"ant
flame
fla·men"co
   (pl. fla·men"cos)
flame"out'
flame"proof'
flame"throw'er
flam"ing
fla·min"go
   (pl. fla·min"gos)
flam"ma·bil"i·ty
flam"ma·ble
flange
flank
flank"er
flan"nel
flan"nel·et"
flan"nel·ing
flap

flap"jack'
flap"per
flap"ping
flare
   blaze (see: flair)
flared
flare"-up'
flar"ing
flash"back'
flash"bulb'
flash"card'
flash"cube'
flash"i·er
flash"i·ly
flash"i·ness
flash"light'
flash"y
flat"bed'
flat"boat'
flat"car'
flat"fish'
flat"foot'
flat"foot"ed
flat"head'
flat"i'ron
flat"land"ers
flat"ten
flat"ter
flat"ter·y
flat"top'
flat"u·lence
flat"u·lent
flat"ware'
flat"work'
flat"worm'
flaugh"ter
flaunt
flaunt"y
flau"tist
fla"vic
fla"vor
fla"vor·ful
fla"vor·ing
fla"vor·y
flaw"less
flax"en

flax"seed'

flea
  insect (*see:* flee)
flea"bag'
flea"bite'
flea"bit'ten
flea" mar"ket
fleck
fledg"ling
flee
  escape (*see:* flea)
fleece
fleec"i·er
fleec"ing
fleec"y
flee"ing
fleet
fleet"ing
flesh"i·er
flesh"i·ness
flesh"ly
flesh"li·ness
flesh"pot'
flesh"y
fletch"er
fleur'-de-lis"
  (*pl.* fleurs'-de-lis")
fleur"ette
flew
  did fly (*see:* flu and
  flue)
flex'i·bil"i·ty
flex"i·ble
flex"i·bly
flex"i·place'
flex'o·graph"ic
flex"time'
flib"ber·ti·gib'bet
flick"er
fli"er
flight" deck'
flight"i·er
flight"i·ness
flight'-test'
flight"wor'thy
flight"y

flim"flam'
flim"flam'ming
flim"si·er
flim"si·ly
flim"si·ness
flim"sy
fling
fling"ing
flint"i·er
flint" glass'
flint"lock'
flint"work·er
flint"y
flip" chart'
floo"zies
flop
flop"house'
flop"ping
flop"py
flop"py disk"
flop"wing'
flo"ra
flo"ral
flor"ate
Flor"ence
flo·res"cence
  blooming (*see:* fluo-
  rescence)
flo·res"cent
flor'i·cul"tur·al·ly
flor"id
Flor"i·da
flor"i·leg'i·um
flor"in
flo"rist
floss"i·er
floss"y
flo·ta"tion
flo·til"la
flot"sam
flounce
flounc"ing
floun"der
flour
  grain (*see:* flower)

flour"ish
flout
flow
  liquid movement
  (*see:* floe)
flow"chart'
flow"er
  blossom (*see:* flour)
flow"ered
flow"er·i·ness
flow"er·pot'
flow"er·y
flown
flu
  influenza (*see:* flue
  and flew)
flub
flubbed
fluc"tu·ate'
fluc"tu·at'ing
fluc"tu·a"tion
flue
  passage (*see:* flu and
  flew)
flu"en·cy
flu"ent
flue"work'
fluff
fluff"i·er
fluff"i·ness
fluff"y
flu"id
flu·id"i·ty
flu'id·i·fy"ing
flu"id ounce"
fluke
fluke"worm'
fluk"y
flume
flum"ing
flung
flun"ky
  (*see:* flun"kies)
flu'o·resce"
flu'o·res"cence

lighted (*see:* flores-
cence)
flu'o·res''cent
fluor''i·date'
fluor''i·dat'ing
fluor''i·da''tion
flu'o·car''bo·nate
flu''o·ride'
fluor''i·nate'
fluor''i·nat'ing
fluor''i·na''tion
flu''o·rine'
fluor''o·scope'
fluor·os''co·py
flur''ried
flur''ry
flur''ry·ing
flush
flus''ter
flute
flut''ing
flut''ist
flut''ter
flu''vi·al
flux
fly
(*pl.* flies)
fly'' ball'
fly''blown'
fly''-by-night'
fly''brush'
fly''cast'er
fly''catch'er
fly''ing fish'
fly''ing sau''cer
fly''leaf'
(*pl.* fly''leaves')
fly''pa'per
fly''speck'
fly''swat'ter
fly''trap'
fly''weight'
fly''wheel'
foal
foam''i·er
foam''i·ness

foam''y
fob
fob''bing
fo''cal
fo''cal·ized'
fo''cal·ly
fo''cus
fo''cused''
fo''cus·ing
fod''der
foe
foehn
fog
fog''bound'
fog''gi·er
fog''gi·ness
fog''ging
fog''gy
obscured (*see:* fogy)
fog''horn'
fo''gy
reactionary (*pl.* fo''
gies) (*see:* foggy)
foi''ble
foie gras''
foist
fold''a·ble
fold''a·way'
fold''er
fol''de·rol'
fo''li·age
fo''li·age'ous
fo li·a''tion
fo''lic
fo''li·o'
(*pl.* fo''li·os')
fo''li·oed'
fo''li·o'ing
folk'' dance'
folk''lore'
folk·lor''ic
folk''-rock'
folks''i·est
folk'' sing''er
folk'' song'
folk''sy

folk'' tale'
folk''way'
fol''let·age'
fol''li·cle
fol''low·er
fol''low·ing
fol''low·through
fol''low-up'
fol''ly
(*pl.* fol''lies)
fo·ment''
fo'men·ta''tion
fon''dant
fon''dle
fon''dling
fond''ness
fon·due''
fon·ti''na
food'' proc'ess·or
food'' stamp'
food''stuff'
fool''er·y
fool''har'di·ly
fool''har'di·ness
fool''har'dy
fool''ish
fool''proof'
fools''cap'
fool's'' gold''
foot
(*pl.* feet)
foot''age
foot''ball'
foot''bridge'
foot''-can''dle
foot''fall'
foot''hill'
foot''hold'
foot''ing
foot''lights'
foot''lock'er
foot''loose'
foot''note'
foot''path'
foot''-pound''
foot''print'

foot"race'
foot"rest'
foot"sie
foot"sore'
foot"step'
foot"stool'
foot"-ton"
foot"wear'
foot"work'
fop"doo·dle
fop"pish
for"age
for"ag·er
for"ag·ing
for·am'i·na"tion
for"as·much"
for"ay
for·bade"
for·bear"
  refrain (*see:* fore-
  bear)
for·bear"ance
for·bear"ing
for·bid"
for·bid"den
for·bid"ding
for·bore"
for·borne"
force
force"ful
force"ful·ness
for"ceps
for"ci·ble
for"ci·bly
forc"ing
for·cip"u·late'
ford
fore'ac·count"ing
fore"-and-aft"
fore·arm", *v.*
  prepare for fight
fore"arm, *n.*
  part of arm
fore"bear
  ancestor (*see:* for-
  bear)

fore·bode"
fore·bod"ing
fore"cast
fore"cast'er
fore"cast'ing
fore"cas"tle
fore·close"
fore·clos"ure
fore"court
fore·doom"
fore"face'
fore"fa'ther
fore"fin'ger
fore"foot'
  (*pl.* fore"feet')
fore"front'
fore·go"
  go before (*see:*
  forgo)
fore·go"ing
  preceding (*see:* for-
  going)
fore·gone"
  previous (*see:* for-
  gone)
fore"ground'
fore"hand'ed
fore"head'
for"eign
for"eign-born"
for"eign·er
fore"knowl'edge
fore"leg'
fore"limb'
fore"lock'
fore"man
fore"mast'
fore"men·tion
fore"most'
fore"name'
fore"noon"
fore"note
fo·ren"sic
fo·ren"si·cal·ly
fore'or·dain"
fore"pay·ment

fore"play'
fore"quar'ter
fore"run'ner
fore"sail'
fore·saw"
fore·see"
fore·see"a·ble
fore·see"ing
fore·seen"
fore·shad"ow
fore·short"en
fore"sight'ed
fore"skin
fore·stall"
for·es·ta"tion
for"est·er
for·es·tol"o·gy
for"est·ry
fore"taste'
fore·tell"
fore·tell"ing
fore"thought
fore·to'ken, *v.*
  foreshadow
fore"to'ken, *n.*
  omen
fore·told"
fore"top'
for·ev"er
for·ev'er·more"
fore·warn"
fore·went"
  went before (*see:*
  forwent)
fore"word
  book introduction
  (*see:* forward)
for"feit
for"fei·ture
for·gave"
forge
forg"er
for"ger·y
  (*pl.* for"ger·ies)
for·get"
for·get"-me-not'

for·get"ta·ble
for·get"ful
forg"ing
for·giv"a·ble
for·give"
for·giv"en
for·give"ness
for·giv"ing
for·go"
  do without (see:
    forego)
for·go"ing
  doing without (see:
    foregoing)
for·gone"
  gave up (see: fore-
    gone)
for·got"
for·got"ten
forked
fork"lift'
for·lorn"
for"mal
form·al"de·hyde'
for"mal·ist
for·mal"i·ty
  (pl. for·mal"i·ties)
for"mal·i·za"tion
for"mal·ize'
for"mal·iz'ing
for"mal·ly
for"mat
for·ma"tion
form"a·tive
form"a·ture
for"mer
form"fit'ting
For·mi"ca™
for"mi·da·ble
for"mi·da·bly
form"less·ly
form" let'ter
For·mo"sa
for"mu·la
for'mu·la"ic

for"mu·lar'ist
for"mu·late'
for"mu·lat'ing
for"mu·la"tion
for"mu·la'tor
for"mu·liz"ing
for"ni·cate'
for"ni·cat'ing
for"ni·ca"tion
for·sake"
for·sak"en
for·sak"ing
for·sook"
for·sooth"
for·sung"
for·swear"
for·swear"ing
for·swore"
for·sworn"
for·syth"i·a
fort
  fortified place (see:
    forte)
forte
  ability (see: fort)
for"te
  music (see: fourth)
forth
  forward (see: fourth)
forth"bring"ing
forth"com"ing
forth"right'
forth"with"
for"ti·eth
for"ti·fi·ca"tion
for"ti·fied'
for"ti·fy'
for"ti·fy'ing
for"ti·tude'
fort"night'ly
FOR"TRAN
for"tress
for·tu"i·tous
for·tu"i·ty
  (pl. for·tu"i·ties)
for"tu·nate

for"tu·nate'ly
for"tune
for"tune·tell'er
Fort' Worth"
for"ty
  (pl. for"ties)
fo"rum
for"ward
  to the front (see:
    foreword)
for·went"
  did without (see:
    forewent)
fos"sage
fos'si·la"ted
fos"sil fu"el
fos"si·li·za"tion
fos"sil·ize'
fos"ter·a'ble
fos"ter child'
fos"ter home'
fos"ter par"ent
fought
foul
  dirty (see: fowl)
fou·lard"
foul" ball"
foul" mouthed"
foul" play'
foul"-up'
found
foun·da"tion
foun·da"tion·al·ly
found"er
found"ling
found"ry
  (pl. found"ries)
foun"tain
foun"tain·head'
four"flush'er
four"fold'
four"-foot"ed
four"-in-hand'
four" post'er
four"score"
four"some

four"square"
four"teen"
four"teenth"
fourth
  number (*see:* forth)
four"-wheel'
fowl
  bird (*see:* foul)
fox"fire'
fox"glove'
fox"hole'
fox"hound'
fox"i·er
fox"i·ly
fox"i·ness
fox"y
foy"er
fra"cas
frac"tal
frac"tion
frac"tion·al
frac"tious
frac"tu·os'i·ty
frac"ture
frac"tur·ing
frag"ile
fra·gil"i·ty
frag"ment
frag"men·tar y
fra"grance
fra"grant
frail
frail"ty
  (*pl.* frail"ties)
frame
frame" house"
frame"-up'
frame"work'
fram"ing
franc
  coin (*see:* frank)
France
franc"o·phile
fran"chise
fran'chi·see"
fran"chis·er

fran"chis·ing
fran"gi·ble
frank
  not deceitful (*see:*
  franc)
Frank"fort
frank"furt·er
frank"in·cense'
fran"tic
fran"ti·cal·ly
frap·pe"
fratch
fra·ter"nal
fra·ter"nal·ly
fra·ter"ni·ty
  (*pl.* fra·ter"ni·ties)
frat'er·ni·za"tion
frat"er·nize'
frat"er·niz'ing
frat"ri·cide
fraud"less
fraud"u·lence
fraud"u·lent
fraught
fraz"zle
fraz"zling
freak"ish
freck"le
freck"ling
free" base'
free" bas'ing
free"bie
free"born'
freed
freed"man
free"dom
freed"wom'an
free"fall"
free"-for-all'
free"hand"
free"hand'ed
free"ing
free"-lance"
free"load'
free"man
free"ma'son

fre"er
free"-spo"ken
free"stand"ing
free"stone'
free"style'
free"think"er
free"way'
free"wheel"ing
freeze
  harden from cold
  (*see:* frieze)
freeze"-dried"
freeze"-dry"
freez"er
freez"ing
freight"age
freight" car'
freight"er
French
fre·net"ic
fre·net"i·cal·ly
fren"u·la
fren"zied
fren"zy
Fre"on™
fre"quen·cy
  (*pl.* fre"quen·cies)
fre"quent
fres"co
  (*pl.* fres"coes)
fresh"en
fresh"et
fresh"man
fresh"wa'ter
fret
fret"ful
fret"ful·ly
fret"ful·ness
fret"less
fret"ting
fret"work'
Freud"i·an
fri"a·ble
fri"ar
  monk (*see:* fryer)
fric'as·see"

fric'as·seed"
fric'as·see"ing
fric"a·tive
fric"tion
Fri"day
fried
friend"less
friend"li·er
friend"li·ness
friend"ly
friend"ship
frieze
  decoration (*see:* freeze)
frig"ate
fright"en
fright"ful
frig"id
fri·gid"i·ty
fri"jol
  (*pl.* fri·jo"les)
frill"y
fringe
fring"ing
frip"per·y
  (*pl.* frip"per·ies)
fris"bee™
frisk"i·er
frisk"i·ness
frisk"y
frit"ter
fri·vol"i·ty
  (*pl.* fri·vol"i·ties)
friv"o·lous
friz"zi·ness
friz"zle
friz"zy
frock" coat'
frog"man'
frol"ic
frol"ick·er
frol"ick·ing
fruc"tes'cence
fruc'tip"a·rous
fruc"tose
frug

fru"gal
fru·gal"i·ty
fru"gal·ly
fruit"cake'
fruit" fly'
fruit"ful
fruit"i·er
fru·i"tion
fruit"less
fruit"y
frump"i·er
frump"ish
frump"y
frus"trate
frus"trat·ing
frus·tra"tion
frus"tum
fry
  (*pl.* fries)
fry"er
  one who fries (*see:* friar)
fry"ing pan'
fry"pan'
fuch"sia
fud"dy·dud'dy
fudge
fudg"ing
fu"el
fu"el cell'
fu"eled
fu"el·ing
fu"gi·tive
fugue
ful"crum
ful·fill"
ful·fill"ing
ful·fill"ment
full"back'
full"-blood"ed
full"-blown"
full"-bod"ied
full"-dress"
full"-fledged"
full"-length"
full" moon"

full"ness
full"-scale"
full"-time"
ful"ly
ful"mi·nate'
ful"mi·nat'ing
ful'mi·na"tion
ful"mi'nous
ful"some
ful·ves"cent
fum"a·gine
fum"ble
fum"bling
fume
fumed
fum"ing
fu"mi·gant
fu"mi·gate'
fu"mi·gat'ing
fu'mi·ga"tion
func"tion·al
func"tion·al·ly
func"tion·ar'y
  (*pl.* func"tion·ar' ies)
func"tion·less
fund"a·ble
fun'da·men"tal
fun'da·men"tal·ism
fun'da·men"tal·ist
fund"hold'er
fu"ner·al
fu·ne"re·al
fun'gi·cid"al
fun"gi·cide
fun"gous
fun"gus
  (*pl.* fun"gi)
fu·nic"u·lar
funk
funk"i·er
funk"y
fun"nel
fun"neled
fun"nel·ing
fun"ni·est

fun″ni·ness
fun″ning
fun″ny
  (*pl.* fun″nies)
fur
  animal hair (*see:* fir)
fur″be·low′
fur″bish
fu″ri·ous
furl
fur″long
fur″lough
fur″nace
fur″nish·ings
fur″ni·ture
fu″ror
furred
fur″ri·er
fur″ring
fur″row
fur″ry
  having fur (*see:*
  fury)
fur″ther
fur″ther·ance
fur″ther·more′
fur″ther·most′
fur″thest
fur″tive
fu″ry
  rage (*pl.* fu″ries)
  (*see:* furry)
furze
fuse
  electrical device;
  melt (*see:* fuze)
fu·see″
fu″se·lage
fu·si·bil″i·ty
fu″si·ble
fu″sil·ier
fu″sil·lade′
fus″ing
fu″sion
fuss″budg′et
fuss″i·er

fuss″i·ly
fuss″i·ness
fuss″y
fus″tian
fus″tic
fus″tle
fus″ty
fu″tile
fu·til″i·ty
  (*pl.* fu·til″i·ties)
fu″ture
fu″tur·ist
fu·tur·is″tic
fu·tu″ri·ty
fuze
  detonating device
  (*see:* fuse)
fuzz
fuzz″i·er
fuzz″i·ness
fuzz″y

G

gab
gab″ar·dine′
gab″bard′
gab″bi·er
gab″bing
gab″ble
  gab″bled
  gab″bling
  babble (*see:* gable)
gab″by
gab″en·dum′
gab″fest′
ga″ble
  roof (*see:* gabble)
Ga·bon″
gad″a·bout′
gad″ding
gade
gad″fly′
  (*pl.* gad″flies′)
gadg″et

gadg″et·ry
gad″i·nine′
gaff
  hook (*see:* gaffe)
gaffe
  blunder (*see:* gaff)
gaf″fer
gag
gage
  challenge (*see:*
  gauge)
gag″er·ship
gag″ging
gag″gle
gai″e·ty
gai″ly
gain″age
gain″er
gain″ful
gain″ful·ly
gain″giv·ing
gain″said′
gain″say′
gain″say′ing
gait
  walk (*see:* gate)
gait″er
ga″la′
ga·lac″tic
gal·act″ose
gal″ax·y
  (*pl.* gal″ax·ies)
gale
ga·lem″pong
ga·le″na
Gal″i·lee′
gal″lant
gal″lant·ize
gal″lant·ry
  (*pl.* gal″lant·ries)
gall″blad′der
gall″bush
gall″le·on
gal″ler·y
  (*pl.* gal″ler·ies)
gal″ley

(pl. gal"leys)
gall"fly
gal"li·cize'
gal"li·vant'
gal"line
gal"lo·flav'in
gal"lon
gal"lop
gal"loped
gal"lop·ing
gal"low·glass'
gal"lows
gall"stone'
gal"lus
ga"loot
ga·lore"
gal·van"ic
gal"va·nism'
gal'va·ni·za"tion
gal"va·nize'
gal'va·nized'
gal"va·niz'ing
gal'va·nol"o·gy
gal'va·nom"e·ter
gal"va·no·psych"ic
gam
Gam"bi·a
gam"bit
gam"ble
　risk (see: gambol)
gam"bler
gam"ble·some'
gam"bling
gam"bol
　romp (see: gamble)
gam"bol·ing
gam"brel'
game"cock'
game"keep'er
game"craft'
gam"er
game"ly
game"ness
game" room'
gam"ete
gam"in

gam"i·ness
gam"in·ish'
gam"ing
gam"ma
gam'o·pha"gi·a
gam"ut
gam"y
gan"der
gang"bus'ter
gang"land'
gan"gling
gan"gli·on
　(pl. gan"gli·a)
gang"ly
gang"plank'
gan"grene
gan"gre·nous
gang"ster
gang"way'
gan'o·blast"
ga·nom"a·lite'
gant"let
　railroad tracks; pun-
　ishment (see: gaunt-
　let)
gan"try
　(pl. gan"tries)
gaol
gap
gape
gap"ing
　staring (see: gap-
　ping)
gap"ping
　opening (see: gap-
　ing)
gar
ga·rage"
ga·rag"ing
gar"bel
gar"bage
gar·ban"zo
gar"ble
gar"bling
gar"boil'
gar·con"

gar"den·er
gar·de"nia
gar·gan"tu·an
gar"gle
gar"gling
gar"goyle
gar"ish
gar"land
gar"lic
gar"lick·y
gar"ment
gar"ner
gar"nered
gar"ner·ing
gar"net
gar"net·work'
gar"nish
　(pl. gar"nish·es)
gar'nish·ee"
gar'nish·ee"ing
gar"nish·ment
gar"ret
gar"ri·son
gar·rote"
gar·rot"ed
gar·rot"ing
gar·rot"ing
gar·ru"li·ty
gar"ru·lous
gar"ter
gar"ter snake'
gar"vie
gas"e·ous
gas"e·ous'ness
gas"i·fied"
gas"ket
gas"light'
gas" mask'
gas"o·hol'
gas"o·line"
gas"si·er
gas"sing
gas"sy
gas" tank'
gas"tral
gas"tric

gas″tri·lo′qui·al
gas′tro·a·tro″phi·a
gas′tro·co·los″to·my
gas′tro·en·ter·i″tis
gas′tro·in·tes″ti·nal
gas′tro·nom″ic
gas·tron″o·my
gas′trop″a·thy
gas′tro·pneu·mon″ic
gas″tro·scope′
gas′tro·vas″cu·lar
gas″works′
gatch
gate
  door (*see:* gait)
gate″-crash′er
gate″house′
gate″keep′er
gate″post′
gate″way′
gath″er·ing
gauche
  awkward (*see:*
  gouache)
gau′che·rie″
gau″cho
gau″cy
gaud″i·er
gaud″i·ly
gaud″i·ness
gaud″ish
gaud″y
gauge
  measure (*see:* gage)
gaug″ing
gaunt
gaunt″let
  glove; challenge
  (*see:* gantlet)
gauze
gauz″y
gav″el
ga·votte″
gawk″y
gay″ness
Ga″za

gaze
ga·ze″bo
ga·zelle″
ga·zette″
gaz′et·teer″
gaz′et·teer″age
gaz″ing
gaz′pach″o
gear″box′
gear″shift′
gear″wheel′
geck″o
  (*pl.* geckoes)
gee″zer
ge·fil″te fish″
Gei″ger
gei″sha
  (*pl.* gei″sha)
gei′so·therm″al
gei′to·nog″a·my
gel
  jellylike substance
  (*see:* jell)
gel″a·tin
ge·la·ti·na″tion
ge·la·ti·ni·za″tion
ge·lat″i·nous
geld
geld″ing
gel″id
ge·lid″i·ty
gelled
gell″ing
gel′o·ther″a·py
gelt
gem″el
gem″i·nal
Gem″i·ni
  zodiac sign
gem″stone′
gen″darme
gen″der gap′
ge′ne·a·log″i·cal
ge′ne·a·log″i·cal·ly
ge′ne·al″o·gist
ge′ne·al″o·gy

  (*pl.* ge′ne·al″o·gies)
gen″er·al
gen′er·al·is″tic
gen′er·al″i·ty
  (*pl.* gen′er·al″i·ties)
gen′er·al·i·za″tion
gen″er·al·ize′
gen″er·al·iz′ing
gen″er·al·ly
gen″er·al·ness
gen″er·ate
gen″er·at′ing
gen′er·a″tion
gen′er·a″tive·ness
gen″er·a″tor
ge·ner″ic
ge·ner″i·cal·ly
gen′er·os″i·ty
  (*pl.* gen′er·os″i·
  ties)
gen″er·ous
gen″er·ous·ness
gen″e·sis
  (*pl.* gen″e·ses)
ge·net″ic
ge·net″i·cal·ly
ge·net″i·cal
Ge·ne″va
gen″ial
ge·ni·al″i·ty
gen″ial·ly″
gen″ial·ness
ge″nie
gen′i·ta″lia
gen″i·tals
gen′i·to·u″ri·nar′y
gen″ius
ge·nom″ic
Gen″o·a
gen″o·cide′
gen″o·gram′
gen″o·type′
gen″re
  (*pl.* gen″res)
gen·teel″
gen·teel″ism

gen"tial
gen"tian·ose'
gen"tile
gen·til"i·tial
gen·til"i·ty
gen"tle
gen"tled
gen"tle·folk'
gen"tle·man
gen"tle·man·ly
gen"tle·wom"an
gen"tler
gen"try
gen"u·flect'
gen"u·ine
gen"u·ine·ly
ge"nus
   (*pl.* gen"er·a *or* ge-
   nuses)
ge'o·bo·tan"i·cal
ge'o·cen"tric
ge'o·chem"i·cal
ge'o·chron·ol·o"gist
ge·ode"
ge'o·des"ic
ge'o·des"i·cal
ge'o·det"ic
ge'o·dy·nam"i·cal
ge'o·gen"ic
ge·og"o·ny
ge·og"ra·pher
ge'o·graph"ic
ge'o·graph"i·cal
ge·og"ra·phy
   (*pl.* ge·og"ra·phies)
ge·oid"al
ge'o·log"ic
ge'o·log"i·cal
ge'o·log"i·cal·ly
ge·ol"o·gis'ing
ge·ol"o·gist
ge·ol"o·gy
   (*pl.* ge·ol"o·gies)
ge·om"a·ly
ge'o·met"ric
ge'o·met"ri·cal·ly

ge·om"e·try
ge'o·me·tri"cian
ge·om'e·tri"zing
ge'o·mor"phic
ge'o·mor·phol"o·gy
ge'o·my"id
ge'o·pha"gist
ge'o·phys"i·cal
ge'o·phys"i·cist
gc'o·phys"ics
ge'o·phyte"
ge'o·pol"i·tics
ge'o·pon"ics
George"town'
Geor"gia
ge'o·sphere"
ge'o·ther"mal
ge'o·ton"ic
ge·ra"ni·um
ger"bil
ger'i·at"rics
ger·mane"
ger·ma"ni·um
Ger"ma·ny
ger"mi·cid"al
ger"mi·cide'
ger"mi·fuge'
ger"mi·nate'
ger"mi·nat'ing
ger"mi·na"tion
ger·mon"
ger'o·don·tol"o·gy
ger'on·to·cra"tic
ger'on·tol"o·gist
ger'on·tol"o·gy
ger"ry·man'der
ger"und
ge·stalt"
ges"tate
ges"tat·ing
ges·ta"tion
ges"tic
ges·tic"u·late'
ges·tic"u·lat'ing
ges·tic'u·la"tion
ges"ti·o

ges"ture
ges"tur·ing
ge·sund"heit
get"a·way'
Geth·sem"a·ne
get"ting
get"-to·geth'er
Get"tys·burg
get"-up'
gew"gaw
gew"gawed
gey"ser
gey"ser·ish
gha"ist
Gha"na
ghast"ful
ghast"li·ness
ghast"ly
ghaut
ghee
gher"kin
ghet"to
   (*pl.* ghet"toes)
ghost"i·fied'
ghost"li·ness
ghost"ly
ghost"mon·ger
ghost"town'
ghost"write'
ghost"writ'er
ghost"writ"ten
ghoul"ish
ghoul"ish·ly
gi"ant
gi"ant·ism
gi"ant·size'
giaour
gib"ber
gib"ber·ish
gib"bet
gib"bet·ed
gib"bon
gib"bose·ly
gib"bous
gibe

jeer (*see:* jibe and
jib)
gib"ing
jeering (*see:* jibing
and jibbing)
gib"let
Gi·bral"tar
gid"di·er
gid"di·ly
gid"di·ness
gid"dy
gift"ed
gift" wrap'
gift" wrap'ping
gig
gi·gan"tic
gi·gan"ti·cal·ly
gi·gan"ti·cide
gi·gan"tism
gig"ging
gig"gle
gig"gling
gig"gly
gig"o·lo'
(pl. gig"o·los')
gild
cover with gold (*see:*
guild)
Gil"e·ad
gil"gul
gill"bird
gil"lo·tage'
gil"pey
gilt
gilded; pig (*see:*
guilt)
gilt"-edged"
gim"bals
gim"crack'
gim"crack·er'y
gim"let
gim"mick
gim"mick·ry
gim"mick·y
gim"mor
gin"ete

gin"ger
gin"ger·ale"
gin"ger·bread'
gin"ger·snap'
gin"ger·y
ging"ham
gin"gi·vi"tis
gin"house'
gink"go
gin"ner·y
gin"seng
gi·raffe"
gird
gird"er
gird"er·age
gird"ing
gir"dle
gir"dling
girl"hood'
girl"ie
girl" scout'
girth
gis"mo
gist
basic meaning (*see:*
jest)
give"-and-take"
give"a·way'
giv"ing
giz"zard
gla·ce"
gla·ceed"
gla·ce"ing
gla"cial
gla·ci·a"tion
gla"cier'
ice mass (*see:* gla-
zier)
gla·ci·om"e·ter
glad"den
glad"der
glad"dest
glad"ful·ness
glad"i·a'tor
glad'i·o"lus
glad"some

glam"or·i·za"tion
glam"or·ize'
glam"or·ized'
glam"or·iz'ing
glam"or·ous
glam"our
glance
glanc"ing
gland
glan"ders
glan"du·lar
glan"du·lous
glare
glar"ing
glar"e·ous
Glas"gow
glas·nost"
glass"ful'
glass"i·er
glass"ine
glass"i·ness
glass"ware'
glass"work'
glass"y
glau·co"ma
glau'co·nite"
glaze
glaz"er
gla"zier
glass worker (*see:*
glacier)
glaz"ing
gleam
glean
gleanings
glean"er
glee"ful
glee"ful·ly
gleit
glent
glib
glib"ber
glide
glid"er
glid"er·port'
glid"ing

glid"er
glimps"ing
glint
glist
glis"ten
glitch
glit"ter
gloat"ing
gloat
glob
glob"al
globe"let
globe"-trot'ter
glob"in
glob"u·lar
glob"ule
glob'u·li"tic
glo'chi"di·um
glock"en·spiel'
glome
gloom"i·er
gloom"i·ly
gloom"i·ness
gloom"ing·ly
gloom"y
glo"ried
glo'ri·fi·ca"tion
glo"ri·fied
glo"ri·fy'
glo"ri·ty'ing
glo"ri·ous
glo"ry
glo"ry·ing
glos"sa·ry
    (*pl:* glos"sa·ries)
gloss"i·er
gloss"i·est
gloss'o·la"li·a
gloss'o·scop"ia
gloss"y
    (*pl.* gloss"ies)
glot"tal
glot'tal·iz"ing
glot·tol"o·gist
Glouces"ter
glove

glov"er
glov"ing
glow"er
glow"ing
glow"worm'
glox·in"i·a
glu"cose
glu"co·sine'
glue
glu"i·er
glu"ing
glut
glu"ta·mate'
glu"ten
glu"te·nous
    of gluten (*see:* gluti-
    nous and glutton-
    ous)
glu"ti·nous
    sticky (*see:* glutenous
    and gluttonous)
glu·toid"
glut"ting
glut"ton
glut"ton·ous
    overeating (*see:* glu-
    tinous and gluten-
    ous)
glut"ton·y
gly·ce·ral"de·hyde
glyc"er·in
gly"cide
gly"co·gen
gly'co·gen"ic
gly'co·lip"ide
gly·con"ic
glyph·og"raph·er
glypt"o·lith
G"-man'
    (*pl.* G"-men')
gnarled
gnarr
gnash
gnat
gnath·id"i·um
gnat"like

gnaw
gnaw"ing
gneiss
    rock (*see:* nice)
gnome
gnom"ish
gnom'o·log"i·cal
gnos"tic
gnu
    animal (*see:* knew
    and new)
goad
go"-a·head'
goal"ie
goal"keep'er
goal" line'
goal" post'
goat·ee"
goat"herd'
goat"skin'
gob
go"ban
gob"ble
gob"ble·dy·gook'
gob"bler
gob"bling
go"-be·tween'
gob"let
gob"lin
gob"stick'
go"-cart'
god
god"child'
god"daugh'ter
god"dess
god"fa'ther
god"for·sak'en
God"head'
god"less
god"li·er
god"like'
god"li·ness
god"ling
god"ly
god"moth'er
god"par'ent

god''send'
god''son'
god''speed'
go''er
go·et''i·cal
go''fer'
  menial employee
  (*see:* gopher)
go''-get''ter
gog''gle
gog''gling
go''-go'
go''ings-on''
goi''ter
gold'' dig'ger
gold''en
gold''en·rod'
gold''field·er
gold''-filled''
gold''finch'
gold''fish'
gold'' mine'
gold'' rush'
gold''smith'
gold''weed'
golf'' ball'
golf'' club'
golf''er
Gol''go·tha
go''nad
go·nad''al
gon''do·la
gon'do·lier''
gon''er
gong
go·nio·met''ri·cal
gon'nard·ite''
gon''o·coc'ci
gon''o·phore'
gon'or·rhe''a
gon''o·some'
goo''ber
good·bye''
good''-for-noth''ing
good''-heart''ed
good''-hu''mored

good''-look''ing
good''ly
good''-na''tured
good''ness
good''-sided''
good'' will''
good''y-good''y
goo''ey
goof''i·ness
goof''y
goo''gol
goo''i·er
gook
goon
goop
goose
  (*pl.* geese)
goose''ber'ry
  (*pl.* goose''ber ries)
goose'' egg'
goose''fish'
goose''neck'
goose''necked'
goose''-step'
goos''ish
go''pher
  animal (*see:* gofer)
gore
gorge
gor''geous
gorg''ing
gor''i·est
go·ril''la
  animal (*see:* gue-
  rilla)
gor''ing
gos''hawk'
Go''shen
gos''ling
gos''pel
gos''sa·mer
gos''sip
gos''sip·ing
gos''sip·y
Goth''ic
got''ten

Got'ter·dam''mer·ung'
gouache
  painting (*see:*
  gauche)
Gou''da
gouge
goug''ing
gou''lash
gou''ra·mi
gourd
gour''mand
gour''met
gour''met·ism
gout
gout''i·ly
gout''y
gov''ern·a·bil'i·ty
gov''ern·a·ble
gov''ern·ess
gov''ern·ment
gov''ern·ment'al
gov''er·nor
gown
grab
grab''ber
grab''bing'
grab''bler
grace
grace''ful
grace''ful·ly
grace''ful·ness
grace''less
grace'' note'
grac''ile·ness
grac''ing
gra''cious'
grack''le
gra·da''tion
gra''da·tor·y
grade
gra''di·ent
grad''ing
grad''u·al
grad''u·al·ly
grad''u·ate'
grad·u·at''i·cal

grad″u·at′ing
grad′u·a″tion
graf·fi″ti
  (*sing.* graf·fi″to)
graft″er
gra″ham
grained
grain″field′
grain″sick′
grain″y
gram′i·na″ceous
gram″mar
gram·mar″i·an
gram·mat″i·cal
gram·mat″i·cal·ly
gram·mat″i·cize′
Gra·na″da
  Spain (*see:* Grenada)
gran″a·ry
  (*pl.* gran″a·ries)
grand″aunt′
grand″child′
  (*pl.* grand″chil′
  dren)
grand″dad′
grand″daugh′ter
gran″deur
grand·ev″i·ty
grand″fa′ther
gran·dil″o·quence
gran·dil″o·quent
gran·dil″o·quent′ly
gran″di·ose′
gran′di·os″i·ty
grand″moth′er
grand″neph′ew
grand″niece′
grand″par′ent
grand″son′
grand″stand′
grand″stand′ing
grand″un′cle
grange
gran″ite
gra·no″la
grant·ee″

grant″-in-aid″
  (*pl.* grants″-in-aid)
gran″u·lar
gran″u·late′
gran″u·lat′ing
gran·u·la″tion
gran·u·la″ter
gran″ule
gran·u·li·za″tion
gran″u·lous
grape
grape″fruit′
grape″shot′
grape″vine′
graph″ic
graph″i·cal·ly
graph″ite
gra·phit″ic
graph″i·toi′dal
graph·ol″o·gy
graph″o·mo′tor
grap·nel
grap″ple
grap″pling
grap″soid
grasp″ing
grass″cut·ter
grass″hop′per
grass″i·er
grass″roots′
grass″y
gra″ta
grate
  metal bars; grind
  (*see:* great)
grate″ful
grat′i·fi·ca″tion
grat′i·fi″er
grat″i·fy′
  grat″i·fied′
  grat″i·fy′ing
grat″ing
grat″is
grat″i·tude′
gra·tu″i·tous
gra·tu″i·tous·ly

gra·tu″i·ty
  (*pl.* gra·tu″i·ties)
grave
grave″dig′ger
grav″el
  grav″eled
  grav″el·ing
grave″ly
grav″el·ly
grav″er
grave″stone′
grave″yard′
gra·vim″e·ter
grav′i·met″ric
grav″i·tate′
grav″i·tat′ing
grav′i·ta″tion
grav″i·ty
  (*pl.* grav″i·ties)
gra″vy
  (*pl.* gra″vies)
gray″beard′
gray″mat′ter
graze
graz″ers
graz″ing
grease
grease″ball′
grease″paint′
greas″i·er
greas″i·ness
greas″ing
greas″y
great
  large (*see:* grate)
great″-aunt′
great″coat′
great′-grand″child′
  (*pl.* great′-grand″
  chil′dren)
great′-grand″daugh″
  ter
great′-grand″fa′ther
great′-grand″moth′er
great′-grand″par′ent
great′-grand″son′

great"ly
great"mouthed'
great"-neph'ew
great"ness
great"-niece'
great"-un'cle
Gre'co-Ro"man
Greece
greed"i·er
greed"i·ly
greed"i·ness
greed"y
green"back'
green"belt'
green"bone'
green"er·y
green"-eyed'
green"gage'
green"gro'cer
green"head'ed
green"horn'
green"house'
green"ish·ness
Green"land
green"let
green"ness
green"room'
green"sward'
greet"er
greet"ing
gre·gar"i·ous'
greg"gle
grem"i·o
grem"lin
gre·nade"
Gre·na"da
island (see: Gra-
nada)
gren'a·dier"
gren'a·dine
grey"flies'
grey"hound'
grid"dle
grid"dle·cake'
grid"dler
grid"dling

grid"i'ron
grid"lock'
grief"ful·ly
grief"-strick'en
griev"ance'
grieve
griev"ing
griev"ous
grif"fin
grill
gridiron; broil; ques-
tion (see: grille)
grille
grating (see: grill)
grill"work'
grim
grim"ace
grim"ac·ing
grime
grim"i·er
grim"i·ness
grim"mer
grim"y
grin
grind
grin·del"i·a
grind"er
grind"ing
grind"stone'
grin"go
(pl. grin"gos)
grin"gole
grinned
grin"ning
grin"ter
grip
grasp (see: gripe and
grippe)
gripe
pain; complain (see:
grip and grippe)
grip"ing
complaining (see:
gripping)
grippe

influenza (see: grip
and gripe)
grip"pers
grip"ping
grasping (see: grip-
ing)
gris"li·ness
gris"ly
horrible (see: gristly
and grizzly)
grisp"ing
gris"tle
gris"tli·ness
gris"tly
of cartilage (see:
grisly and grizzly)
grist"mill'
grit
grits
grit"ti·er
grit"ti·ness
grit"ting
grit"ty
griz"zled
griz"zling
griz"zly
grayish; bear (see:
grisly and gristly)
groan
utterance (see:
grown)
groats
gro"cer
gro"cer·y
(pl. gro"cer·ies)
gro"dy
grog"gi·er
grog"gi·ly
grog"gi·ness
grog"gy
groin
grom"met
groom
groom"er
groove

shallow depression
 (*see:* grove)
groov"i·er
groov"ing
groov"y
grope
grop"ing
gros"grain'
gross
gross"er
gro·tesque"
gro·tesque"ly
gro·tesque"ness
grot"to
 (*pl.* grot"toes)
grouch"i·er
grouch"i·ly
grouch"i·ness
grouch"y
ground"er
ground" floor"
ground"hog'
ground"ing
ground"less'
ground" rule'
grounds
ground"swell'
ground"work'
ground"y
group
group"ie
group"think"
grouse
 (*pl.* grouse)
grous"ing
grout
grove
 trees (*see:* groove)
grov"el
 grov"eled
 grov"el·ing
grov"el·er
grow"ing
growl"er
growl"ing
grown

mature (*see:* groan)
grown"up'
growth
grub
grub"bi·er
grub"bing
grub"by
grub"stake'
 grub"staked'
 grub"stak'ing
grudge
grudg"er·y
grudg"ing
grudg"ing·ly
gru"el
gru"el·ing
grue"some
gruff"ly
gruff"ness
grum"ble
grum"bler
grum"bling
grump"i·er
grump"i·ly
grump"i·ness
grump"y
grun"gy
grun"ion
grunt
grun"tle
G"-string'
gua'ca·mo"le
Guam
guan
Guang"zhou
gua"no
guar'an·tee"
guar'an·tee"ing
guar"an·teed'
guar"an·tee'ship
guar"an·tor'
guar"an·ty'
 (*pl.* guar"an·ties')
guar"an·ty'ing
guard"ed
guard"house'

guard"i·an'
guard"rail'
guard"room'
guards"man
Gua'te·ma"la
gua"va'
gu'ber·na·to"ri·al'
gudg"eon
Guern"sey
 (*pl.* Guern"seys)
guer·ril"la
 soldier (*see:* gorilla)
guess"ti·mate
guess"work'
guest"house'
guest" room'
guest"ship'
guf·faw"
gu"gal
guid"a·ble'
guid"ance
guide"book'
guide"line'
guide"post'
guide"way'
guid"ing
guild
 organization (*see:*
 gild)
guild"ship
guile"ful
guile"ful·ly
guile"less
guil·lo·tine", *v.*
 to behead
guil"lo·tine', *n.*
 beheading instru-
 ment
guil"lo·tin"ing
guilt
 shame (*see:* gilt)
guilt"i·er
guilt"i·ly
guilt"i·ness
guilt"less
guilt"y

Guin″ea
guin″ea pig′
guise
guis″ing
gui·tar″
gui·tar″ist
gui·tar″fish
gulch
gulf″y
gul″let
gull″er
gul′li·bil″i·ty
gul″li·ble
gul″li·bly
gul″ly
  (*pl.* gul″lies)
gulp″er
gum″bo
gum″drop′
gum″mi·er
gum″mi·ness
gum″ming
gum″mose
gum″my
gump″tion
gum″shoe′
gum″shoe′ing
gun·a″tion
gun″boat′
gun″cot′ton
gun″dog
gun″fight′
gun″fight′ing
gun″fire′
gung″ho″
gun″ite
gun″lock′
gun″man′
gun″ner·y
gun″ning
gun″ny·sack′
gun″point′
gun″pow′der
gun″run′ning
gun″ship
gun″shot′

gun″shy′
gun″smith′
gun″wale
gup″py
  (*pl.* gup″pies)
gur″gle
gur″gling
gur·gu·la″tion
gu″ru
gur″let
gush″er
gush″y
gush″i·est
gus″set
gus″ta·to′ry
gust″i·er
gust″i·ly
gus″to
gust″y′
gut″less
guts″i·er
guts″y
gut″ta-per″cha
gut″ter·snipe′
gut″ter·ing
gut″ti·fer′al
gut″ting
gut″tul·ous
gut″tur·al
gut″tur·ize′
guy
Guy·a″na
guy″ing
guz″zle
guz″zling
gybe
gym·nas″tic
gym·na″si·um
gym″nast
gym·nas″tics
gym·no·car″pous
gym″no·sperm′
gy′ne·col″o·gist
gy′ne·col″o·gy
gy′ne·co·path″ic
gyn′i·at″rics

gy·noe″ci·um
gyn·o·steg″i·um
gyp
gypped
gyp″ping
gyp·sol″o·gy
gyp″sum
Gyp″sy
  (*pl.* Gyp″sies)
gy″rate
gy″rat·ed
gy″rat·ing
gy·ra″tion
gy″ro
  (*pl.* gy″ros)
gy″ro·com″pass
gy″ro·scope
gy″ro·sta″bi·liz′er
gy″rus

H

ha·be·as cor″pus
hab″er·dash′er
hab″er·dash′er·y
  (*pl.* hab″er·dash′er·
  ies)
ha″ber·dine′
ha·bil′i·ta″tor
hab″it·a·ble
hab″it·a·bly
hab″i·tat
hab′i·ta″tal
hab′i·ta″tion
hab″it-form′ing
ha·bit″u·al
ha·bit″u·al·ly
ha·bit″u·ate′
ha·bit″u·at′ing
ha·bit″u·e′
ha·chure′
ha·ci·en″da
hack″a·more
hack″bush′
hack″er

hack″ing
hack″le
hack″ling
hack″ney
  (*pl.* hack″neys)
hack″neyed
hack″saw′
hack″work′
had″dock
  (*pl.* had″dock)
Ha″des
ha′dro·saur″us
haft
hag″bush′
Hag·ga″dah
  (*pl.* Hag·ga″doth)
hag″gard
hag″gis
hag″gle
hag″gler
hag″gling
hag′i·og″ra·pha
hag′i·og″ra·phal
hag′i·og″ra·pher
hag′i·og″ra·phy
hag″like
Hague
hai″ku
hail
  ice; shout (*see:* hale)
hail″stone′
hail″storm′
hain
hair
  growth from skin
  (*see:* hare)
hair″breadth′
hair″brush′
hair″cut′
hair″do′
  (*pl.* hair″dos′)
hair″dress′er
hair″dress′ing
hair″i·er
hair″i·ness
hair″less

hair″like
hair″line′
hair″net′
hair″piece′
hair″pin′
hair-rais′ing
hair's′-breadth″
hair″spray′
hair″spring′
hair″style″
hair″tail′
hair″trig′ger
hair″y
  covered with hair
  (*see:* harry)
Hai″ti
hajj
haj″ji
ha·la″tion
hal″berd
hal″cy·on
hale
  summon; healthy
  (*see:* hail)
haled
hale″day′
half
  (*pl.* halves)
half″-and-half″
half″back′
half″-baked″
half″broth′er
half″-caste″
half″-cocked″
half″dol″lar
half″heart″ed
half″-hour″
half″life′
half″-mast″
half″-moon″
half″note′
half″sis″ter
half″-slip′
half″step′
half″time′
half″tone′

half″-track′
half″-truth′
half″way″
half″wise
half″-wit″ted
hal″i·but
  (*pl.* hal″i·but)
Hal″i·fax′
hal″ing
hal′i·to″sis
hall
  room (*see:* haul)
hal′le·lu″jah
hall″mark′
hal·loo″
  shout (*see:* halo and
  hallow)
hal″low
  sanctify (*see:* hallow
  and halo)
Hal″low·een″
hal·lu″ci·nate′
hal·lu″ci·nat′ing
hal·lu″ci·na″tion
hal·lu″ci·na·to′ry
hal·lu″cin·o·gen
hall″way′
hal″ma·lille″
ha″lo
  ring (*pl.* ha″los)
  (*see:* halloo and
  hallow)
hal′o·gen
hal′o·ge·na″tion
hal′o·phyt″ism
hal″sen
hal″ter
halt″ing
halve
halv″ers
halv″ing
  making halves (*see:*
  having)
hal″yard
ham
ham″at·ed

Ham"burg
ham"burg'er
ham"let
ham"mer
ham"mer·head'
ham"ming
ham"mock
ham"per
ham"ster
ham"string"
hand"bag'
hand"ball'
hand"bill'
hand"book'
hand"cart'
hand"clasp'
hand"cuff'
hand"ful'
hand"gun'
hand"hole'
hand"i·cap'
hand"i·cap'ping
hand"i·craft'
hand"i·er
hand"i·ly
hand"i·ness
hand"i·stroke'
hand"i·work'
hand"ker·chief
han"dle
han"dle·bar'
hand"line'
han"dling
hand"made"
  made by hand (*see:*
  handmaid)
hand"maid
  attendant (*see:* hand-
  made)
hand"-me-down'
hand"off
hand"out'
hand"pick"
hand"rail'
hand"saw'
hand"set'

hand"shake'
hand"some
  good-looking (*see:*
  hansom)
hands"-on"
hand"spike'
hand"spring'
hand"-to-hand"
hand"-to-mouth"
hand"work'
hand"wo"ven
hand"writ'ing
hand"y
han"dy·man
hang
hang"ar
  aircraft shelter (*see:*
  hanger)
hang"dog'
hang"er
  thing that hangs
  (*see:* hangar)
hang"er-on"
hang" glid"er
hang" glid"ing
hang"ing
hang"man
hang"nail'
hang"out
hang"o'ver
hang"-up
han"ker
han"ky-pan"ky
Ha·noi"
han"som
  carriage (*see:* hand-
  some)
Ha"nuk·kah
hap·haz"ard
hap"less
hap"less·ness
hap"pen
hap"pen·ing
hap"pen·stance'
hap"pi·est
hap"pi·ly

hap"pi·ness
hap"py
hap"py-go-luck"y
hap"ter·on
ha"ra-ki"ri
ha·rangue"
ha·rangu"ing
har·ass"
har·ass"ment
har"bin·ger
har"bin·ger'ship
har"bor
hard"-and-fast"
hard"back'
hard"ball
hard"-bit"ten
hard"-boiled"
hard"bound'
hard"-core"
hard"cov"er
har"dened
hard" hat"
hard" head"ed
hard" heart"ed
har"di·er
har·di·hood'
har"di·ly
har"di·ness
hard"-lin"er
hard"ly
hard"mouthed'
hard"-of-hear"ing
hard"-pressed"
hard"scrab'ble
hard"-shell'
hard"ship
hard"tack'
hard"top'
hard"ware'
hard"-wired"
hard"wood'
hard"work'ing
har"dy
hare
  animal (*see:* hair)
hare"brained'

Ha″re Krish″na
hare″lip′
hare″lipped′
har″em
hark″en
Har″lem
har″le·quin
har″lot
harm″ful
harm″less
har·mon″ic
har·mon″i·ca
har·mon″ics
har·mo″ni·ous
har′mo·ni·za″tion
har″mo·nize′
har″mo·niz′ing
har″mo·ny
har″most′
har″ness
har″ness·like
harp″ist
harp″less
har·poon″
harp″si·chord′
harp″way·tun′ing
har″rid
har″ri·dan
har″ri·er
Har″ris·burg′
har″row
har″ry
  harass (*see:* hairy)
har″ry·ing
harsh″en
harsh″ly
hart
  deer (*see:* heart)
hart″all
har″te·beest′
Hart″ford
har″um-scar″um
har′us·pi·ca″tion
har″ves·ter
has″-been′
ha″sen·pfef′fer

hash″ing
hash″ish
hask″ness
hasp
has″sle
has″sling
has″sock
haste
haste″ful
has″ten
hast″i·er
hast″i·ly
hast″i·ness
hast″ing
hast″y
hat″box′
hatch′a·bil″i·ty
hatch″back′
hatch″er·y
  (*pl.* hatch″er·ies)
hatch″et
hatch″et·fish′es
hatch″ing
hatch″way′
hate
hate″ful
hat″ing
ha″tred
hat″ter
haugh″ti·er
haugh″ti·ly
haugh″ti·ness
haugh″ty
haul
  pull (*see:* hall)
haul″age
haulm
haunch
haunt″ed
haunt″ing
haup″i·a
hausse
haut″boy′
haute cou·ture″
haute cui·sine″
hau·teur″

Ha·van″a
have″-not′
hav″er·sack′
hav″il·dar′
hav″ing
  possessing (*see:*
  halving)
hav″oc
Ha·wai″i
hawk
hawk″eye·
hawk″ish
hawk″weed′
haw″ser
haw″thorn′
hay″cock′
hay″fe′ver
hay″fork′
hay″loft′
hay″mar·ket
hay″mow′
hay″rack′
hay″shock
hay″stack′
hay″wire′
haz″ard·ous
haze
haz″el
ha″zel·nut′
ha″zi·er
ha″zi·ly
ha″zi·ness
haz″ing
haz″le
ha″zy
H″-bomb
head″ache′
head″band′
head″board′
head″box
head″cheese′
head″dress′
head″er
head″first″
head″gear′
head″hunt′er

head″i·er
head″i·ly
head″i·ness
head″land
head″less
head″light′
head″like′
head″line′
head″lin′er
head″lin′ing
head″long′
head″mas″ter
head″mis″tress
head″-on″
head″phone′
head″piece′
head″quar′ters
head″race′
head″rest′
head″set′
head″ shop″
head″shrink·er
heads″man
head″start″
head″strong′
head″wall′
head″wait″er
head″wa′ters
head″way′
head″wind′
head″y
heal
  make well (*see:* heel)
heal″er
health″ful·ly
health″i·er
health″i·ness
health″y
heap
hear
  listen (*see:* here)
hear″a·ble
heard
  did hear (*see:* herd)
hear″ing

hark″en
hear″say′
hearse
heart
  blood pump (*see:* hart)
heart″ache′
heart″at·tack′
heart″beat′
heart″break′
heart″bro′ken
heart″burn′
heart″ed·ly
heart″en
heart″felt′
hearth″stone′
hearth″ward
heart″i·er
heart″i·ly
heart″i·ness
heart″less
heart″rend′ing
heart″sick′
heart″strings′
heart″-to-heart″
heart″warm′ing
heart″y
heat″ed·ly
heat″er
heath
hea″then
heath″er
heat″stroke′
heat″ wave′
heave
heave″-ho″
heav″en·ly
heav″en·ward
heav″i·er-than-air″
heav″i·ly
heav″i·ness
heav″ing
heav″y
  (*pl.* heav″ies)
heav″y-du″ty
heav″y-hand″ed

heav″y-heart″ed
heav″y met″al
heav″y·weight′
heb″e·tate
He·bra″ic
He″brew
heb″ron·ite
hec′a·toph″yl·lous
heck″le
heck″ler
heck″ling
hec″tic
hec″ti·cal·ly
hec·tog″ra·phy
hec″to·gram′
hec″to·graph′
hec″to·li′ter
hec″to·me′ter
hed′e·rif″er·ous
hedge
hedge″hog′
hedge″hop′
hedg″ing
hedge″less
he″don·ism′
he″don·ist
hee″bie-jee″bies
heed″ful
heed″ful·ly
heed″less
hee″haw′
heel
  foot; lean (*see:* heal)
heel″plate
heel″-and-toe″
heft″i·er
heft″y
he·gem″o·ny
he·gi″ra
heif″er
height
height″en
Heim″lich
hei″nous
heir
heir″ess

heir″loom′
heist
Hel″e·na
hel″i·cal
he″li·o·chrome′
hel″i·cop′ter
he″li·o·cen″tric
he″li·o·graph′
he″li·o·gra·vure′
he″li·o·phil′i·a
he″li·o·scope
he″li·o·trope′
hel″i·port′
he″li·um
he″lix
· (*pl.* he″lix·es)
hell″bent′
hell″cat′
Hel·len″ic
hel″len·ist
hell″gram·mite
hcll″hole′
hel″lion
hell″ish
hel″lo
hel″met
hel″minth·o·log″i·cal
helms″man
he″lo·der·ma″tous
hel″ot
help″er
help″ful
help″ful·ly
help″less
help″mate′
Hel″sin·ki
hel″ter-skel″ter
hem
he″ma·drom″e·ter
he″-man
hem″ase
hem″a·tin
he″ma·to·ge·net″ic
he″ma·tol″o·gist
he″ma·tol″o·gy
he″ma·to·ma″ta

he″ma·tox″y·lin
hem″i·cir′cle
hem″i·dome′
hem″i·glos′sal
hem″i·me·tab″o·ly
hem″i·ol″ic
hem″i·pin′ate
hem″i·sphere′
hem i·spher″ic
hem″line′
hem″lock′
hem″mel
hem″ming
he″mo·con′i·a
he″mo·drom″e·ter
he″mo·glo′bin
he″mo·lym·phat″ic
he″mo·phil″i·a
he″mo·phil″i·ac′
hem″or·rhage
hem″or·rhag″ing
hem″or·rhoid′
he″mo·spas′i·a
he″mo·stat′
hemp″bush
hem″stitch′
he″nad
hence″forth″
hench″man
hen″na
hen″o·the′ist
hen″peck′
hen″roost′
hen″ry
(*pl.* hen″rys)
hep″a·rin
he″pa·tect″o·my
he·pat″ic
hep·a·ti″tis
he″pa·to·gas″tric
he″pa·top″a·thy
Hep″ple·white
hep″ta·gon′
hep·tam″e·ter
hep·ta·met″ri·cal
hep·tar″chist

hep″tine
her″ald
he·ral″dic
her″ald·ry
(*pl.* her″ald·ries)
her·ba″ceous
herb″age
herb″al
herb″al·ist
her·bar″i·um
her″bi·cide′
her″bish
her″biv·ore′
her·biv″o·rous
her·cu·le″an
herd
group (*see:* heard)
herd″er
here
in this place (*see:* hear)
here″a·bouts′
here·af″ter
here·by″
he·red″i·tar′y
he·red″i·ty
(*pl.* he·red″i·ties)
here·in″
here′in·a″bove
here′in·af″ter
her″e·sy
(*pl.* her″e·sies)
her″e·tic
he·ret″i·cal
here′to·fore″
here′un·to″
here′up·on″
here·with″
her″it·a·ble
her″it·age
her·maph″ro·dite′
her·met″ic
her·met″i·cal·ly
her″mit
her″mit·age
her″ni·a

he''ro
  (*pl.* he''roes)
he·ro''ic
her''o·in
  narcotic (*see:* hero-
  ine)
her''o·ine
  courageous woman
  (*see:* heroin)
her''o·ism'
he''ro·like
he''ro·wor'ship
her''on
her''pes
her'pe·tol''o·gist
her'pe·tol''o·gy
her'pe·to·phob''i·a
her''ring
her''ring·bone'
her·self''
hertz
  (*pl.* hertz)
hes''i·tance
hes''i·tan·cy
hes''i·tant
hes''i·tate'
hes''i·tat'ing
hes'i·ta''tion
het'er·o·blas''tic
het'er·o·chrom''a·tism
het'er·o·clite''
het'er·o·don''tism
het'er·o·dox'
het''er·o·dox'y
  (*pl.* het''er·o·dox'
  ies)
het'er·o·dyne'
het'er·o·ge·ne''i·ty
het'er·o·ge''ne·ous
het'er·o·kin·et'ic
het'er·o·phile'
het'er·o·sex''u·al
het'er·o·trop''al
hew
  chop (*see:* hue)
hewed

hew''ing
hex''a·chlo''ro·phene'
hex''ade
hex''a·gon'
hex·ag''o·nal
hex''a·gram'
hex'a·he''dron
hex'a·hy''dride
hex·am''e·ter
hex'a·pod''an
hey''day'
hi·a''tus
  (*pl.* hi·a''tus·es)
hi·ba''chi
hi''ber·nate'
hi''ber·nat'ing
hi'ber·na''tion
hi·bis''cus
hic''cup
hic''cuped
hic''cup·ing
hick''ey
hick''ish
hick''o·ry
  (pl. hick''o·ries)
hid''al·go'ism
hid''den
hide'-and-seek''
hide''a·way'
hide''bound'
hide''land
hid''e·ous
hide''out'
hid''ing
hi·dro·sis''
hi'er·ar''chic
hi''er·ar''chi·cal
hi''er·ar''chy
  (*pl.* hi''er·ar''chies)
hi'er·o·glyph''ic
hi'er·ol''a·try
hi'er·o·phan''ti·cal·ly
hi''-fi''
hig''gle·dy-pig''gle·dy
high''ball'
high''born'

high''boy'
high''bred'
high''brow'
high''chair'
high''-class''
high''er-up''
high'fa·lu''tin
high'' fi·del''i·ty
high''fly·er
high''-flown''
high''-fly''ing
high''-grade''
high''-hand''ed
high'' jump'
high''-lev''el
high''land'
high''light'
high''light'ing
high''ly
High'' Mass''
high''mind''ed
high''-oc''tane
high''-pitched''
high''-pres''sure
high'' priest''
high''-rise''
high'' school'
high''-sound''ing
high''-speed''
high spir''it·ed
high-strung''
high''tail'
high'' tech·nol''o·gy
high''-ten''sion
high''-test''
high''-toned''
high''-wa''ter mark'
high''way'
hi''jack'er
hike
hik''er
hik''ing
hi·lar''i·ous
hi·lar''i·ty
hill''bil'ly
  (*pl.* hill''bil'lies)

hill″i·er
hill″ock
hill″side′
hill″top′
hill″y
Him′a·la″yas
him·self″
hind″cast′
hin″der
Hin″di
hind″most′
hind″quar′ter
hin″drance
hind″sight′
Hin″du
hinge
hing″ing
hin″ny
hin″ter·land′
hip′bone
hip′pi·at″rics
hip″pie
hip″po
  (*pl.* hip″pos)
hip′pol″lite
hip′po·pot″a·mus
hip″ster
hire
hire″ling
hir″ing
Hi′ro·shi″ma
hir″sute
His·pan″ic
his″ta·mine′
his″to·cyte′
his′to·log″i·cal
his·tol″o·gist
his·tol″o·gy
his·tol″y·sis
his′to·phys·i·o·log″i·
  cal
his·to″ri·an
his·tor″ic
his·tor″i·cal·ly
his·to·ric″i·ty
his·to·ri·og″ra·phy

his″to·ry
  (*pl.* his″to·ries)
his′to·trop″ic
his·tri·on″ic
his·tri·on″ics
hit″-and-run″
hitch″er
hitch″hike′
hitch″ hik′er
hitch″ hik′ing
hith″er·to′
hit″-or-miss″
hit″ting
hive
hives
hoa″gie
hoar
  white (*see:* whore)
hoard
  accumulate (*see:*
   hord)
hoard″ing
  accumulating (*see:*
   hording)
hoar″frost′
hoar″ness
hoarse
  harsh sound (*see:*
   horse)
hoarse″ly
hoar″i·ness
hoar″y
hoax
  (*pl.* hoax″es)
hob″ble
hob″bling
hob″by
  (*pl.* hob″bies)
hob″by horse′
hob″gob′lin
hob″nail′
hob″nob′
hob″nob′bing
ho″bo
  (*pl.* ho″bos)
hock″ey

ho″cus-po″cus
hodge″podge′
hoe
hoe″down′
hoe″ing
ho″gan
hog″back′
hog″cote′
hog″ging
hog″gish
hog″nut′
hogs″head′
hog″tie′
hog″ty′ing
hog″wash′
hog″-wild″
hog″wort′
hoi″ pol·loi″
hoised
hoi″ty-toi″ty
ho″key
ho″kum
hold″er
hold″er·ship′
hold″ing
hold″out′
hold″o′ver
hold″up′
hole
  opening (*see:* whole)
holed
hol″ey
  with holes (*see:* holy
   and wholly)
hol″i·day′
ho″li·er-than-thou″
ho″li·ness
hol″ing
ho·lis″tic
Hol″land
hol″lan·daise′
hol″ler
hol″low
hol″ly
  (*pl.* hol″lies)
hol″ly·hock′

Hol''ly·wood'
hol''o·caine'
hol''o·caust'
hol''o·gram'
hol''o·graph'
ho·log''ra·phy
ho·lo·met'a·bol''ic
ho''lo·phase'
Hol''stein
hol''ster
holt
ho''ly
   sacred (*see:* wholly
   and holey)
Ho''ly Fa''ther
Ho''ly Ghost'
Ho''ly Spir''it
hom''age
hom''a·rine'
hom''bre
hom''burg
home
home''bod'y
home''bred''
home''-brew''
home''build
home''com'ing
home''grown''
home''land'
home''less
home''li·er
home''li·ness
home''ly
home''made''
home''mak'er
ho'me·o·morph''ous
ho'me·o·path''ic
ho'me·o·therm''
ho'me·op''a·thy
ho'me·o·some''
ho'me·o·sta''sis
home''own'er
home'' plate''
hom''er
home''room'
home'' run'

home''school'ing
home''sick'
home''spun'
home''stead'
home''stretch''
home''town''
home''ward
home''work'
home''y
home''y·ness
hom'i·ci''dal
hom''i·cide
hom''i·er
hom·i·let''ics
hom''i·ly
   (*pl.* hom''i·lies)
hom''ing
hom''i·nid
hom''i·noid'
hom''i·ny
ho·mo·ge·ne''i·ty
ho·mo·ge''ne·ous
ho·mog''e·nize'
ho·mog''e·niz'ing
ho·mog''o·ny
hom''o·graph'
ho·mo·le·gal''is
ho·mol''o·gous
ho'mo·morph''ous
hom''o·nym
ho'mo·pla''sis
ho''mo sa''pi·ens
ho'mo·sex''u·al
ho'mo·sex'u·al''i·ty
ho'mo·tax''eous
ho·mot''o·ny
ho'mo·zy''gous
hon''cho'
Hon·du''ras
hone
hon''est
hon''es·ty
hon''ey
   (*pl.* hon''eys)
hon''ey·bee'
hon''ey·comb'

hon''ey·dew'
hon''eyed
hon''ey·ing
hon''ey·moon'
hon''ey·mouth'
hon''ey·suck'le
Hong'' Kong''
hon''ing
hon''ky-tonk'
Hon'o·lu''lu
hon''or·a·ble
hon'o·rar''i·um
hon''or·ar'y
hon'or·if''ic
hon''or roll'
hood''ed
hood''lum
hoo''doo
hood''wink'
hood''y
hoo''ey
hoof
hook''ah
hook''er
hook''up'
hook''worm'
hook''y
hoo''li·gan
hoop''la
hoot''en·an'ny
   (*pl.* hoot''en·an'
   nies)
hootch
hop
hope'' chest'
hoped
   wanted (*see:*
   hopped)
hope''ful
hope''ful·ly
hope''less
Ho''pi
   (*pl.* Ho''pis)
hop''ing
   wanting (*see:* hop-
   ping)

hop
  hopped
  hop″ping
  jump (*see:* hope)
hop″sack·ing
hop″scotch′
ho″ra
ho·ra″ti·an
horde
  multitude (*see:* hoard)
hord″ing
  gathering (*see:* hoarding)
hore″hound′
ho·ri″zon
hor′i·zon′tal
hor·mo″nal
hor″mone
horned
horn″fish′
hor″net
horn″i·er
horn″like
horn″pipe′
horn″-reed″
horn″swog′gle
horn″weed′
horn″y
hor′o·log″ic
ho·rol″o·gy
hor″o·scope′
hor·ren″dous
hor″ri·ble
hor″ri·bly
hor″rid
hor″ri·fied′
hor″ri·fy′
hor″ri·fy′ing
hor″ror·ful
horse
  animal (*see:* hoarse)
horse″back′
horse″cloth′
horse″flesh′
horse″fly′

  (*pl.* horse″flies′)
horse″hair
horse″head′
horse″hide
horse″laugh′
horse″lock′
horse″man
horse″play
horse″pow′er
horse″rad′ish
horse″sense′
horse″shoe′
horse″shoe′ing
horse″whip′
horse″wom′an
hors″y
hor″ta·to′ry
hor″ti·cul″tur·al
hor″ti·cul″tur·ist
ho·san″na
hose
hosed
ho″sier·y
hos″ing
hos″pice
hos″pi·ta·ble
hos″pi·ta·bly
hos″pi·tal
hos′pi·tal″i·ty
  (*pl.* hos′pi·tal″i·ties)
hos′pi·tal·i·za″tion
hos″pi·tal·ize′
hos″pi·tal·iz′ing
hos″tage
hos″tag·ing
hos″tel
  inn (*see:* hostile)
hos″tel·ry
host″ess
hos″tile
  unfriendly (*see:* hostel)
hos·til″i·ty
  (*pl.* hos·til″i·ties)
hos″tler

hot″bed′
hot″blood″ed
hot″box′
hot″cake′
hot″cross′buns″
hot″dog′
ho·tel″
hot″foot′
  (*pl.* hot″foots′)
hot″head″ed
hot″house′
hot″line′
hot″plate′
hot″rod′der
hot″shot′
hot″ter
hound
hound″fish
hour″glass′
hour″less
hour″ly
house″boat′
house″boy′
house″break′er
house″bro′ken
house″clean′
house″clean′ing
house″coat′
house″fly′
  (*pl.* house″flies′)
house″ful′
house″hold′
house″hold′er
house″keep′er
house″let
house″lights′
house″maid′
house″man
house″moth′er
house″slip′per
house″top′
house″warm′ing
house″wife′
  (*pl.* house″wives′)
house″work′
hous″ing

Hous"ton
hout"ing
hov"el
hov"el·ing
hov"er
Hov"er·craft'™
how·be"it
how"-do-you-do"
how·ev"er
how"itz·er
howl"ing
how'so·ev"er
hoy"den
hua·ra"che
hub"bub
hub"cap"
hu"bris
huck"le·ber'ry
  (*pl.* huck"le·ber'
  ries)
huck"ster
huck"ster·ize'
hud"dle
hud"dling
Hud"son
hue
  color (*see:* hew)
hue"less
huff"i·er
huff"ish
huff"y
hug
huge
huge"ly
hug"er
  more huge (*see:* hug-
  ger)
hug"ger
  one who hugs (*see:*
  huger)
hug"ging
Hu"gue·not
hu"la hoop'
hu"la skirt'
hulk"ing
hull

hul"la·ba·loo'
  (*pl.* hul"la·ba·loos')
hum
hu"man
hu·mane"
hu"man·ism'
hu"man·is"tic
hu·man'i·tar"i·an
hu·man'i·tar"i·an·
  ism'
hu·man"i·ty
  (*pl.* hu·man"i·ties)
hu"man·ize'
hu"man·iz'ing
hu"man·like'
hu"man·kind'
hu"man·ly
hu"man·ness
hu"man·oid'
hu"man-pow'ered
hum"ble
hum"ble·ness
hum"bling
hum"bug'
hum"ding"er
hum"drum'
hu·mec"tant
hu"mer·us
  bone (*pl.* hu"
  mer·i') (*see:* hu-
  morous)
hu"mid
hu·mid'i·fi·ca"tion
hu·mid"i·fied'
hu·mid"i·fi'er
hu·mid"i·fy'
hu·mid"i·fy'ing
hu·mid"i·ty
hu"mi·dor'
hu·mil"i·ate'
hu·mil"i·at'ing
hu·mil'i·a"tion
hu·mil"i·ty
hummed
hum"ming·bird'
hum"mock

hu"mor
hu"mored
hu"mor·esque"
hu"mor·ist
hu"mor·ous
  comical (*see:* hu-
  merus)
hu"mor·some
hump"back'
hu"mus
hun
hunch"back'
hun"dred·man
hun"dredth
hun"dred·weight'
hung
Hun"ga·ry
hun"ger
hun"ger·ing
hun"gri·er
hun"gri·ly
hun"gri·ness
hun"gry
hun'ky-do"ry
hunt"er
hunt"ing
hunt"ress
hunts"man
hur"dle
  barrier (*see:* hurtle)
hur"dling
hur"dy-gur"dy
hurl"bar·row'
hurl"er
hurl"y-burl"y
Hu"ron
hur·rah"
hur"ri·cane'
hur"ried·ly
hur"ry
hur"ry·ing
hurt"ful
hurt"ful·ly
hurt"ing
hur"tle

move fast (*see:* hur-
dle)
hur"tling
hus"band
hus"band·ry
hush"-hush'
hush" pup'py
husk"i·er
husk"i·ly
husk"i·ness
husk"y
  hoarse; robust
hus"ky
  dog (*pl.* hus"kies)
hus"sy
  (*pl.* hus"sies)
hus"tle
hus"tler
hus"tling
hutch
  (pl. hutch"es)
hy"a·cinth
hy"brid
hy"brid·ize'
hy"brid·iz'ing
hy·dran"gea
hy"drant
hy"drar·gy"ric
hy"drate
hy"drat·ing
hy"dra·tor
hy·drau"lics
hy·dra"zo
hy·dride
hy'dro·car"bon
hy'dro·ce·phal"ic
hy'dro·ceph"a·lus
hy'dro·chlo"ric
hy'dro·cor"ti·sone'
hy·dro·e·lec"tric
hy·dro·fer'ro·cy"an·ic
hy"dro·foil'
hy"dro·gen
hy"dro·gen·ate'
hy"dro·gen·at'ing
hy"dro·gen·a"tion

hy'dro·ge"o·log"ic
hy·dro·id"e·an
hy·drol"o·gy
hy·drol"y·sis
hy·dro·man"cy
hy'dro·met'al·lur"gi·
  cal
hy·drom"e·ter
hy'dro·pho"bi·a
hy"dro·phone'
hy'dro·phor"i·a
hy"dro·plane'
hy"dro·plan'ing
hy'dro·pon"ics
hy'dror·rhe"a
hy'dro·som"a
hy"dro·sphere'
hy'dro·stat"ics
hy·dro·sul"phate
hy·dro·ther"a·py
hy"dro·type'
hy"drous
hy·drox"ide
hy·e"na
hy"giene
hy'gi·en"ic
hy'gi·en"i·cal·ly
hy·gien"ist
hy·grom"e·ter
hy"gro·scope'
hy·lo·zo"ism
hy"men
hy'me·ne"al
hymn
hym"nal
hym"nar·i·a
hym"no·dy
hym·nol"o·gy
hy'o·styl"ic
hy·pal"gic
hype
hy'per·a·cid"i·ty
hy'per·ac"tive
hy·per"bo·la
  curve (*see:* hyper-
  bole)

hy·per"bo·le
  exaggeration (*see:*
  hyperbola)
hy'per·bol"ic
hy'per·crit"i·cal
  over-critical (*see:*
  hypocritical)
hy'per·fas·ti"di·ous
hy'per·gly·ce"mi·a
  high blood sugar
  (*see:* hypoglyce-
  mia)
hy'per·ki·ne"sis
hy'per·son"ic
hy'per·ten"sion
hy'per·ten"sive
hy'per·thy"roid
hy'per·thy"roid'ism
  nervousness (*see:* hy-
  pothyroidism)
hy'per·troph"ic
hy'per·vas·cu·lar"i·ty
hy'per·ven'ti·la"tion
hy"phen
hy"phen·ate'
hy"phen·at'ing
hy'phen·a"tion
hyp"ing
hyp·no"sis
  (*pl.* hyp·no"ses)
hyp·not"ic
hyp·not"i·cal·ly
hyp"no·tism
hyp"no·tist
hyp"no·tize'
hyp"no·tiz'ing
hy'po·chlor"ic
hy'po·chon"dri·a
hy'po·chon"dri·ac'
hy·poc"ri·sy
hyp"o·crite
hyp'o·crit"i·cal
  false pretension (*see:*
  hypercritical)
hy'po·der"mic
hy'po·gly·ce"mi·a

low blood sugar
(*see:* hyperglyce-
mia)
hy'po·stase''
hy·pot''e·nuse
hy·poth''e·cate'
hy·po·ther''mi·a
hy·poth''e·sis
(*pl.* hy·poth''e·ses')
hy·poth''e·size'
hy·poth''e·siz'ing
hy'po·thet''i·cal
hy'po·thy''roid·ism''
sluggishness (*see:*
hyperthyroidism)
hy'po·tox''ic
hyr''a·cid
hys''sop
hys'ter·ec''to·my
(*pl.* hys'ter·ec''to·
mies)
hys'ter·el·co''sis
hys·te''ri·a
hys·ter''ic
hys·ter''i·cal

I

i·am''bic
i·at'ro·gen''ic
I·be''ri·a
i''bex
(*pl.* i''bex·es)
i''bis
(*pl.* i''bis·es)
ice''berg
ice''boat'
ice''bound'
ice''box'
ice''break'er
ice''cap'
ice''-cold''
ice''craft'
ice''cream'
ice''cube'

ice''land
ice''like
ice''man'
ice''pack'
ice''skat'ing
ich''no·graph''i·cal
ich''thy·o·ceph'a·lous
ich''thy·oid'al
ich'thy·o·log''i·cal
ich'thy·ol''o·gist
ich'thy·ol''o·gy
ich''thy·o·morph'ic
ich''thy·op'o·list
ich''thy·o·saur'
i''ci·cle
i''ci·er
i''ci·ly
i''ci·ness
ic''ing
i''con
i·con''o·clast'
i·con''o·clas''tic
i·con''o·graph
i'co·nog''ra·phy
i·con''o·man'i·a
i'co·nos'ta·sis
ic''ter·o·ge·net'ic
i''cy
id
I''da·ho'
id''dat
i·de''a
i·de''al
i·de''al·ism'
i·de''al·ist
i·de''al·is''ti·cal·ly
i·de'al·i·za''tion
i·de''al·ize'
i·de''al·iz'ing
i·de''al·ly
i''de·ate'
i'de·a''tion
i·den''ti·cal
i·den'ti·cal·ly
i·den'ti·fi''ca·ble
i·den'ti·fi·ca''tion

i·den''ti·fied'
i·den''ti·fy'
i·den''ti·fy'ing
i·den''ti·ty
(*pl.* i·den''ti·ties)
id'e·o·gram'
i'de·o·log''i·cal
i'de·ol''o·gist
i'de·o·glyph'
i'de·ol''o·gy
(*pl.* i'de·ol''o·gies)
i'de·o·type
id''i·o·cy
id''i·o·cra'sy
id''i·o·glot'tic
id''i·om
id'i·o·mat''ic
id'i·o·mat''i·cal·ly
id'i·oph''a·nous
id''i·o·spasm'
id'i·o·syn''cra·sy
(*pl.* id'i·o·syn''cra·
sies)
id'i·o·syn·crat''ic
id''i·ot
id''i·ot''ic
id''i·ot''i·cal·ly
i''dle
inactive (*see:* idol
and idyll)
i''dle·ness
i''dler
i''dling
i''dly
i''dol
worshiped object
(*see:* idle and idyl)
i·dol''a·ter
i·dol''a·trous
i·dol''a·try
i·dol''a·tri'zer
i·dol''i·za''tion
i''dol·ize'
i''dol·iz'ing
i·dol''ous
i''dyll

poem (*see:* idle and idol)
i·dyl″lic
if ″fy
ig″loo
  (*pl.* ig″loos)
ig″ne·ous
ig·nit″a·ble
ig·nite″
ig·nit″ing
ig·ni″tion
ig·no″ble
ig″no·min″i·ous
ig″no·min′y
  (*pl.* ig″no·min″ies)
ig″no·ra″mus
  (*pl.* ig″no·ra″mus·es)
ig″no·rance
ig″no·rant
ig·nore″
ig·nor″ing
i·gua″na
il′e·i″tis
il′e·o·co·lot″o·my
il″e·um
  intestine (*see:* ilium)
il″i·a
il″i·um
  bone (*see:* ileum)
ilk
ill″-ad·vised″
ill″-bred″
ill″-con·ceived″
ill″-dis·posed″
il·le″gal
il′le·gal″i·ty
  (*pl.* il′le·gal″i·ties)
il·le″gal·ly
il·leg′i·bil″i·ty
il·leg″i·ble
  unreadable (*see:* eligible)
il·leg″i·bly
il′le·git″i·ma·cy

  (*pl.* il′le·git″i·ma·cies)
il′le·git″i·mate
il′le·git″i·mate·ly
ill′e·quipped″
ill″-fat″ed
ill″-fa″vored
ill″-got″ten
ill″-hu″mored
il·lib″er·al
il·lic″it
  not allowed (*see:* elicit)
il·lim″it·a·ble
il·lim″it·a·bly
il·lim″it·ed
Il′li·nois″
il·li″sion
il·lit″er·a·cy
il·lit″er·ate
il·lit″er·ate·ly
ill″-man″nered
ill″-na″tured
ill″ness
il·lo″cal·ly
il·log″i·cal
il·log″i·cal·ly
ill″-starred″
ill″-tem″pered
ill″-timed″
ill″-treat″ment
il·lu″mi·nate′
 il·lu″mi·nat″ed
 il·lu″mi·nat′ing
il·lu″mi·na″tion
il·lu″mine
il·lu″min·ing
ill″-us″age
ill″-use″
il·lu″sion
  false idea (*see:* allusion)
il·lu″sion·ist
il·lu″sive
  deceptive (*see:* allusive and elusive)

il·lu″so·ry
il″lus·trate′
il″lus·trat′ing
il″lus·tra″tion
il·lus″tra·tive
il·lus″tra·tor
il·lus″tri·ous
ill″ will″
im″age
im″age·a·ble
im″age·ry
  (*pl.* im″age·rics)
i·mag″i·na·ble
i·mag″i·na·bly
i·mag″i·nar′y
i·mag′i·na″tion
i·mag″i·na·tive
i·mag″ine
im″ag·ing
i·mag″in·ing
im″ag·ism′
i·mam″
i·mam″ic
im·bal″ance
im·ban″nered
im″be·cile
im′be·cil″i·ty
im·bed″
im·bibe″
im·bit″ter·ment
im·bib″ing
im·bra″cer·y
im·bro″glio
im·brue″
im·bru″ing
im·bue″
im·bu″ing
im·bue″ment
im″i·ta·ble
im″i·tate′
im″i·tat′ing
im″i·ta″tion
im″i·ta′tive
im·mac″u·late
im″ma·nent

inherent (*see:* immi-
nent and eminent)
im'ma·te''ri·al
im'ma·te''ri·al·ized
im'ma·ture''
im'ma·tu''ri·ty
im·meas''ur·a·ble
im·me''di·a·cy
im·me''di·ate
im·me''di·ate·ly
im·mem''or·a·ble
im'me·mo''ri·al
im·mense''
im·mense''ly
im·men''si·ty
im·merged''
im·merse''
im·mers''ing
im·mer''sion
dipping; absorption
(*see:* emersion)
im'mi·grant
one entering (*see:*
emigrant)
im'mi·grate'
enter (*see:* emigrate)
im'mi·grat'ing
im'mi·gra''tion
im'mi·nence
im'mi·nent
soon to happen (*see:*
immanent and emi-
nent)
im·min''gle
im·mis''ci·ble
im·mo''bile
im·mo·bil''i·ty
im·mo'bi·li·za''tion
im·mo''bi·lize'
im·mo''bi·liz'ing
im·mod''er·ate
im·mod''est
im·mod''es·ty
im''mo·late'
im''mo·lat'ing
im·mor''al

im'mo·ral''i·ty
im·mor''al·ize
im·mor''al·ly
im·mor·tal''i·ty
im·mor''tal·ize'
im·mor''tal·iz'ing
im·mor''tal·ly
im·mov'a·bil''i·ty
im·mov''a·ble
im·mune''
im·mu''ni·ty
(*pl.* im·mu''ni·ties)
im''mu·nize'
im''mu·niz'ing
im·mun'o·gen''i·cal·ly
im·mu'nol''o·gist
im·mu'no·mod''u·la'
tor
im·mu'no·stim''u·lant
im·mure''
im·mur''ing
im·mus''i·cal
im·mu'ta·bil''i·ty
im·mu''ta·ble
im·mu''ta·bly
im·pact'', *v.*
force together
im''pact, *n.*
collision
im·pac''tion
im·pac''tual
im·pair''ment
im·pa''la
im·pale''
im·pal''ing
im·pall''
im·pal'pa·bil''i·ty
im·pal''pa·ble
im·pal''pa·bly
im·pan''el
im·pan''el·ing
im·part''
im·part''a·ble
im·par''tial
im·par'ti·al''i·ty
im·pass''a·ble

not passable (*see:*
impassible)
im''passe
im·pas''si·ble
unfeeling (*see:* im-
passable)
im·pas''sioned
im·pas''sive
im·pas·siv''i·ty
im·pa''tience
im·pa''tiens'
(*pl.* im·pa''tiens')
im·pa''tient
im·peach''
im·peach''ment
im·pec'ca·bil''i·ty
im·pec''ca·ble
im·pec''ca·bly
im·pe·cu''ni·ous
im·pede''
im·ped''i·ment
im·ped'i·men''ta
im·ped''ing
im·pel''
im·pel''ling
im·pend''en·cy
im·pend''ing
im·pen'e·tra·bil''i·ty
im·pen''e·tra·ble
im·pen''i·tence
im·pen''i·tent
im·per''a·tive
im·per·cep'ti·bil''i·ty
im·per·cep''ti·ble
im·per·cep''ti·bly
im·per·cep''tive
im·per''fect
im·per·fec''tion
im·per''fo·rate
im·pe''ri·al
im·pe''ri·al·ism'
im·pe'ri·al·is''tic
im·pe''ri·al·ly
im·per''il
im·per''iled
im·per''il·ing

im·pe″ri·ous
im·per′ish·a·ble
im·per·ma·nence
im·per·ma·nent
im·per′me·a·bil″i·ty
im·per″me·a·ble
im·per″son·a·ble
im·per″son·al·ly
im·per″son·al″i·ty
im·per″son·ate′
im·per″son·at′ing
im·per″son·a″tion
im·per″son·a′tor
im·per·suas″i·ble
im·per″ti·nence
im·per″ti·nent
im·per′turb′a·bil″i·ty
im·per·turb″a·ble
im·per″turbed″
im·per″vi·ous
im·pe·ti″go
im·pe·ti″tion
im·pet′u·os″i·ty
im·pet″u·ous
im″pe·tus
im·pi″e·ty
  (*pl.* im·pi·pi″e·ties)
im·pinge″
im·pinge″ment
im·ping″ing
im″pi·ous
imp″ing
imp″ish
im·pi″ti·a·ble
im·pla″ca·ble
im·pla″ca·bly
im·plant″, *v.*
  plant firmly
im″plant, *n.*
  planted thing
im′plan·ta″tion
im·plau″si·ble
im·plau″si·bil′i·ty
im″ple·ment
im′ple·men·ta″tion
im″pli·cate′

im″pli·cat′ed
im″pli·cat′ing
im′pli·ca″tion
im·plic″it
im·plied″
im·plode″
im·plod″ing
im·plore″
im·plor″ing
im·plo″sion
im·plo″sive
im·ply″
im·ply″ing
im′po·lite″
im·pol″i·tic
im·pon″der·a·ble
im·poned″
im·port″, *v.*
  bring in
im″port, *n.*
  something imported
im·port′a·bil″i·ty
im·port″a·ble
im·por″tance
im·por″tant
im·por·ta″tion
im·port″cr
im·por″tu·nate
im·por·tune″
im′por·tun″ing
im′por·tu″ni·ty
  (*pl.* im′por·tu″ni·
  ties)
im·pose″
im·pos″ing
im·po·si″tion
im·pos·si·bil″i·ty
  (*pl.* im·pos·si·bil″i·
  ties)
im·pos″si·ble
im″post
im·pos″tor
  pretender (*see:* im·
  posture)
im·pos″ture
  fraud (*see:* impostor)

im″po·tence
im″po·tent
im·pound″
im·pov″er·ish
im″prac″ti·ca·ble
im·prac″ti·cal
im·prac′ti·cal″i·ty
im″pre·cate′
im″pre·cat′ing
im′pre·ca″tion
im″pre·ca·to′ry
im′pre·cise″
im·pre·ci″sion
im·preg″na·ble
im·preg″nate
im·preg″nat·ing
im′preg·na″tion
im·pre·sa″ri·o
im′pre·scrip″ti·ble
im·press″, *v.*
  command; print
im″press, *n.*
  mark
im·press″i·ble
im·pres″sion
im·pres″sion·a·ble
im·prcs″sion·ism′
im·pres″sion·ist
im·pres″sive·ly
im·press″ment
im·pres″sor
im·prim″i·tive
im′pri·ma″tur
im·print″, *v.*
  affix
im″print, *n.*
  mark
im·pris″on
im·pris″on·ment
im·prob′a·bil″i·ty
  (*pl.* im·prob′a·bil″i·
  ties)
im·prob″a·ble
im·prompt″
im·promp″tu
im·prop″er

im·pro·pri''e·ty
  (*pl.* im'pro·pri''e·
   ties)
im·prov''a·ble
im·prove''
im·prove''ment
im·prov''i·dence
im·prov''i·dent'ial
im·prov''ing
im·prov'i·sa''tion
im''pro·vise'
im''pro·vis''ing
im·pru''dence
im·pru''dent
im·pu''ber·ty
im''pu·dence
im''pu·dent
im·pugn''
im·puis''sance
im''pulse
im·pul''sive
im·pu''ni·ty
im·pun''i·tive
im·pure''
im·pu''ri·ty
  (*pl.* im·pu''ri·ties)
im''pu·ta''tion
im·pute''
in·a·bil''i·ty
in'ab·sen''tia
in'ac·ces''si·ble
in'ac''cu·ra·cy
  (*pl.* in·ac''cu·ra·
   cies)
in·ac''cu·rate
in·ac''tion
in·ac''ti·vate'
in·ac''ti·vat'ing
in·ac'ti·va''tion
in·ac''tive
in·ac·tiv''i·ty
in'a·dept''ness
in·ad''e·qua·cy
in·ad''e·quate
in'ad·ven''tur·ous
in'ad·ver''tence

in'ad·ver''tent
in'ad·vis'a·bil''i·ty
in'ad·vis''a·ble
in·af·fec·ta''tion
in·al''ien·a·ble
in·al'ter·a·bil''i·ty
in·al''ter·a·ble
in·am'o·ra''ta
in·ane''
in·an''i·mate
in·an''i·ty
  (*pl.* in·an''i·ties)
in'ap·pell''a·ble
in·ap''pli·ca·ble
in'ap·pre''ci·a·ble
in'ap·pre''ci·a·tive
in'ap·pro''pri·ate
in·apt''
  unsuitable (*see:* in-
   ept)
in·ap''ti·tude'
in·arch''
in·ar·tic''u·late
in'as·much'' as'
in'as·sim''i·la·ble
in·at·ten''tion
in·at·ten''tive
in·au''di·ble
in·au''gu·ral
in·au''gu·rate'
in·au''gu·rat'ing
in·au'gu·ra''tion
in'aus·pi''cious
in''beam
in'-be·tween''
in''born
in''bound''
in''bred''
in''breed'
in''breed'ing
In''ca
in·cal''cu·la·ble
in·ca·les''cent
in·can·des''cence
in·can·des''cent
in'can·ta''tion

in·ca''pa·bil''i·ty
in·ca''pa·ble
in·ca·pac''i·tate'
in·ca·pac''i·tat'ing
in·ca·pac''i·ty
in·cap''su·late'
in·car''cer·ate'
in·car''cer·at'ing
in·car'cer·a''tion
in·car''nate
in·car''nat·ing
in·car·na''tion
in·cav''ern
in·cau''tious
in·cen''di·a·rism
in·cen''di·ar'y
  (*pl.* in·cen''di·ar'
   ies)
in·cense'', *v.*
  enrage
in''cense, *n.*
  odorous smoke
in·cens''ing
in·cen''tive
in·cep''tion
in·cep''tive
in·cer''ti·tude'
in·ces''sant
in''cest
in·ces''tu·ous
inch''meal'
in·cho''ate
in·cho·a''tion
inch''worm'
in''ci·dence
in''ci·dent
in·ci·den''tal·ly
in·cin''er·ate'
in·cin''er·at'ing
in·cin'er·a''tion
in·cip''i·ence
in·cip''i·ent
in·cise''
in·cis''ing
in·ci''sion
in·ci''sive·ness

in·ci″sor
in·ci·ta″tion
in·cite″
  urge to act (*see:* in-
  sight)
in·cit″ing
in·ci·vil″i·ty
  (*pl.* in·ci·vil″i·ties)
in·clem″ent
in·clin″a·ble
in·cli·na″tion
in·cline″, *v.*
  slant
in″cline, *n.*
  slope
in·clin″ing
in·cli·nom″e·ter
in·clo″sure
in·clud″a·ble
in·clude″
in·clud″ing
in·clu″sion
in·clu″sive
in·clu″sor·y
in·cog·ni″to′
in·cog″ni·zant
in·co′her″ence
in·co′her″ent
in·co·he″sion
in·com·bus″ti·ble
in″come
in″com·ing
in·com·men″sur·a·ble
in·com·men″su·rate
in″com·mode″
in″com·mod″ing
in″com·mo″di·ous
in″com·mo″di·ty
in″com·mu″ni·ca·ble
in″com·mu″ni·ca″do
in″com·mu″ni·ca′tive
in·com″pa·ra·ble
in·com·pat′i·bil″i·ty
in·com·pat″i·ble
in·com″pe·tence
in·com″pe·ten·cy

in·com″pe·tent
in·com·plete″
in·com″pli″an·cy
in·com·pre·hen″si·ble
in·com·press″i·ble
in·con·ceiv″a·bil″i·ty
in·con·ceiv″a·ble
in·con″cin·nate′
in·con·clu″sive
in·con·dens″i·ble
in·con·gen″er·ous
in·con″gru·ent
in·con·gru″i·ty
  (*pl.* in·con·gru″i·
  ties)
in·con″gru·ous
in·con·se·quen″tial
in·con·sid″er·a·ble
in·con·sid″er·ate
in·con·sis″ten·cy
  (*pl.* in·con·sis″ten·
  cies)
in·con·sis″tent
in·con·sol′a·bil″i·ty
in·con·sol″a·ble
in·con″so·nant
in·con·spic″u·ous
in·con″stan·cy
in·con″stant
in·con·sul″ta·ble
in·con·test′a·bil″i·ty
in·con·test″a·ble
in·con″ti·nent
in·con·tin″u·ous
in·con·tro·vert i·bil″i·
  ty
in·con·tro·vert″i·ble
in·con·ven″ience
in·con·ven″ienc·ing
in·con·ven″ient
in·co′or·di·na″tion
in·cor″po·rate′
  in·cor″po·rat″ed
  in·cor″po·rat″ing
in·cor·po·ra″tion
in·cor·po″re·al

in′cor·po″re·al·ly
in′cor·rect″
in·cor′ri·gi·bil″i·ty
in·cor″ri·gi·ble
in·cor·rupt″
in·cor·rupt′i·bil″i·ty
in·cor·rupt″i·ble
in·crease″, *v.*
  add to
in″crease, *n.*
  a growth
in·creas″ing
in·cred′i·bil″i·ty
in·cred″i·ble
in·cre·du″li·ty
in·cred″u·lous
in·cre″ment
in·cre·men″tal
in·crim″i·nate′
in·crim″i·nat′ing
in·crim″i·na″tion
in·crim″i·na·to′ry
in·crust″
in·crus·ta″tion
in·cu″bate
in·cu″bat′ing
in·cu·ba″tion
in·cu″ba·tor
in·cu″bus
in·cul″cate
in·cul″cat·ing
in·cul·ca″tion
in·cul″pa·ble
in·cul″pate
in·cul″pat·ing
in·cul·pa″tion
in·cum″ben·cy
  (*pl.* in·cum″ben·
  cies)
in·cum″bent
in·cu·nab″u·la
in·cu″ne·a″tion
in·cur″
in·cur′a·bil″i·ty
in·cur″a·ble
in·cu″ri·ous

in·cur″ring
in·cur″sion
in·cuse″
in·debt″ed
in·de″cen·cy
  (*pl.* in·de″cen·cies)
in·de″cent
in′de·ci″pher·a·ble
in′de·ci″sion
in′de·ci″sive
in·dec″o·rous
in·deed″
in′de·fat″i·ga·ble
in′de·fen″si·ble
in′de·fin″a·ble
in·def″i·nite
in·del″i·ble
in·del″i·ca·cy
  (*pl.* in·del″i·ca·cies)
in·del″i·cate
in·dem″ni·fi·ca″tion
in·dem″ni·fied′
in·dem″ni·fy′
in·dem″ni·fy′ing
in·dem″ni·ty
  (*pl.* in·dem″ni·ties)
in·dent″
in·den·ta″tion
in·den″tion
in·den″ture
in′de·pend″ence
in′de·pend″en·cy
in′de·pend″ent
in″-depth″
in′de·scrib″a·ble
in′de·struct″i·ble
in′de·ter″min·a·ble
in′de·ter″mi·na·cy
in′de·ter″mi·nate
in′de·ter″mi·na″tion
in″dex
  (*pl.* in″dex·es *or*
  in″di·ces)
in″dex·er
in′dex·ter″i·ty
In″di·a

In′di·an″a
In′di·an·ap″o·lis
In′di·a pa′per
in′di·cate′
in′di·cat″ing
in′di·ca″tion
in·dic″a·tive
in′di·ca″tor
in·dict″
  charge (*see:* indite)
in·dict″a·ble
in·dict″ment
in″dif″fer·ence
in·dif″fer·ent
in″di·gence
in·dig″e·nous
in″di·gent
in′di·gest″i·ble
in′di·ges″tion
in·dig″nant
in′dig·na″tion
in·dig″ni·ty
  (*pl.* in·dig″ni·ties)
in·dign″ly
in″di·go′
in′di·men″sion·al
in′di·rect″
in′di·rec″tion
in′dis·cern″i·ble
in′dis·cerp″ti·ble
in′dis·creet″
  unwise (*see:* indis-
  crete)
in′dis·crete″
  not separate (*see:* in-
  discreet)
in′dis·cre″tion
in·dis·crim″i·nate
in′dis·pen″sa·ble
in′dis·pose″
in′dis·posed″
in′dis·pos″ing
in′dis·po·si″tion
in′dis·put″a·ble
in′dis·sol″u·ble
in′dis·sol″va·ble

in′dis·tinct″
in′dis·tin″guish·a·ble
in·dite″
  write (*see:* indict)
in′di·vid″u·al
in′di·vid″u·al·ism′
in′di·vid″u·al·is″tic
in′di·vid″u·al″i·ty
  (*pl.* in′di·vid″u·al″i·
  ties)
in′di·vid″u·al·ize′
in′di·vid″u·al·iz′ing
in′di·vid″u·al·ly
in′di·vis′i·bil″i·ty
in′di·vis″i·ble
in″doc″trine
in·doc″tri·nate′
in·doc″tri·nat′ing
in·doc′tri·na″tion
in″do·lence
in″do·lent
in·dom″i·ta·ble
In′do·ne″sia
in·doors″
in·dorse″
in·dorse″ment
in·dors″ing
in′du·bi·ta·ble
in·duce″
in·duce″ment
in·duc″ing
in·duct″
in·duct″ance
in·duc·tee″
in·duc″tile
in·duc″tion
in·duc″tor
in·dulge″
in·dul″gence
in·dul″gent
in·dulg″ing
in′du·men″tum
in″du·rate′
in″du·rat′ing
in′du·ra″tion
in·dus″tri·al

in·dus"tri·al·ism'
in·dus"tri·al·ist'
in·dus"tri·al·i·za"tion
in·dus"tri·al·ize'
in·dus"tri·al·iz'ing
in·dus"tri·ous
in"dus·try
  (*pl.* in"dus·tries)
in·e"bri·ate'
in·e"bri·at'ing
in·ed"i·ble
in·ed"u·ca·ble
in·ef"fa·ble
in·ef·face"a·ble
in'ef·fec"tive
in'ef·fec"tu·al
in'ef·fi·ca"cious
in'ef·fi"cien·cy
  (*pl.* in'ef·fi"cien·
  cies)
in'ef·fi"cient
in'e·las"tic
in'e·las·tic"i·ty
in·el"e·gant
in·el"i·gi·ble
in'e·luc"ta·ble
in·ept"
  unfit (*see:* inapt)
in·ept"i·tude'
in'e·qual"i·ty
  (*pl.* in'e·qual"i·
  ties)
in'e·qua"tion
in·eq"ui·ta·ble
in·eq"ui·ty
  injustice (*pl.* in·eq"
  ui·ties) (*see:* iniq-
  uity)
in'e·qui"va·lent
in'e·rad"i·ca·ble
in·er"tia
in·er"tial
in·ert"ly
in'es·cap"a·ble
in'es·sen"tial
in·es"ti·ma·ble

in·ev"i·dence'
in·ev'i·ta·bil"i·ty
in·ev'i·ta·ble
in·ex"act"
in'ex·clu"sive
in'ex·cus"a·ble
in'ex·haus"tive·ly
in'ex·haust"i·ble
in·ex"o·ra·ble
in'ex·pec"ted·ly
in'ex·pe"di·ent
in'ex·pen"sive
in'ex·pe"ri·ence
in·ex"pert
in·ex"pi·a·ble
in·ex"pi·ate'
in·ex'pli·ca·bil"i·ty
in·ex"pli·ca·ble
in'ex·press"i·ble
in'ex·ten"si·ble
in'ex·ten"sile
in'ex·tin"guish·a·ble
in ex·tre"mis
in'ex·tri"ca·ble
in·fal'li·bil"i·ty
in·fal"li·ble
in"fa·mil"iar
in"fa·mous
in"fa·my
  (*pl.* in"fa·mies)
in"fan·cy
  (*pl.* in"fan·cies)
in"fant
in·fan"ti·cide'
in"fan·tile'
in"fan'til·ism'
in"fan·try
  (*pl.* in"fan·tries)
in"fan·try·man
in·farct"
in·farc"tion
in·fat"u·ate'
in·fat"u·at'ing
in·fat"u·a"tion
in·faus"ting
in·fect"

in·fec"tion
in·fec"tious
in·fec"tive
in·fe·lic"i·tous
in·fe·lic"i·ty
  (*pl.* in·fe·lic"i·ties)
in·fer"
in"fer·ence
in·fer·en"tial
in·fe"ri·or
in·fe·ri·or"i·ty
in·fer"nal
in·fer"no
  (*pl.* in·fer"nos)
in·fer"ring
in·fer"tile
in·fer·til"i·ty
in·fest"
in·fes·ta"tion
in"fi·del
in·fi·del"i·ty
  (*pl.* in"fi·del"i·ties)
in"field"
in"fight'ing
in·fil"trate
in·fil"trat·ing
in"fil·tra"tion
in"fil·tra'tor
in"fi·nite
in"fi·nite·ly
in·fin·i·tes"i·mal
in·fin"i·tive
in·fin"i·tude'
in·fin"i·ty
  (*pl.* in·fin"i·ties)
in·firm"
in·fir"ma·ry
  (*pl.* in·fir"ma·ries)
in·fir"mi·ty
  (*pl.* in·fir"mi·ties)
in fla·gran"te de·lic"
  to
in·flame"
in·flam"ing
in·flam"ma·ble
in flam·ma"tion

in·flam″ma·to′ry
in·flat″a·ble
in·flate″
in·flat″ing
in·fla″tion
in·fla″tion·ar′y
in·flect″
in·flec″tion
in·flexed″
in·flex′i·bil″i·ty
in·flex″i·ble
in·flict″
in·flic″tion
in″-flight′
in·flo·res″cence
in″flow′
in·flu·ence
in·flu·enc·ing
in·flu·en″tial
in·flu·en″za
in″flux′
in·flux″ion
in″fo·bit′
in·form″
in·for″mal
in for·mal″i·ty
in·form″ant
in·for·ma″tion
in·form″a·tive
in·form″er
in·form″id·a·ble
in·fra″can·thal
in·frac″tion
in·fran″gi·ble
in′fra·no″dal
in·fra·red″
in′fra·son″ic
in″fra·struc′ture
in·fre″quent
in·fre″quent·cy
in·fringe″
in·fringe″ment
in·fring″ing
in·fru″gal
in·fur″i·ate′
  in·fur″i·at′ed

in·fur″i·at′ing
in·fuse″
in·fu″si·ble
in·fu″sile
in·fus″ing
in·fu″sion
in″gath·er
in·gen″er·ate
in·gen″ious
  clever (*see:* ingenu-
  ous)
in″ge·nue′
in′ge·nu″i·ty
in·gen″u·ous
  naive (*see:* ingen-
  ious)
in·gest″
in·gest″i·ble
in·ges″tion
in·globe″
in·glo″ri·ous
in″got
in·grained″
in′gram·mat″i·cism
in″grate
in·gra″ti·ate′
in·gra″ti·at′ing
in·grat″i·tude
in′gra·ves″cent
in·gre″di·ent
in″gress
in″group′
in″grown′
in″gui·nal
in·hab″it
in·hab″it·a·ble
in·hab″i·tant
in·hal″ant
in·ha·la″tion
in·ha·la″tor
in·hale″
in·hal″er
in·hal″ing
in·har·mon″ic
in·har·mo″ni·ous
in·haul″er

in·here″
in·her″ence
in·her″ent
in·her″ing
in·her″it
in·her″it·a·ble
in·her″i·tance
in·hib″it
in·hib″it·a·ble
in′hi·bi″tion
in·hib″i·tor
in·hom′o·gen″e·ous
in·hos″pi·ta·ble
in″-house″
in·hu″man
in′hu·mane″
in′hu·man″i·ty
  (*pl.* in′hu·man″i·
  ties)
in·im″i·cal
in·im″i·ta·ble
in·iq″ui·tous
in·iq″ui·ty
  wickedness (*pl.* in·
  iq″ui·ties) (*see:* in·
  equity)
in·i″tial
in·i″tialed
in·i″tial·ing
in·i″tial·i·za′tion
in·i″tial·ly
in·i″ti·ate′
in·i″ti·at′ing
in·i″ti·a″tion
in·i″ti·a·tive
in·i″ti·a·tor
in·i″ti·a·to′ry
in·ject″
in·jec″tion
in·ju·di″cious
in·junc″tion
in″jure
in″jur·ing
in·ju″ri·ous
in″jury
  (*pl.* in″ju·ries)

in·jus″tice
ink″ber′ry
ink″blot′
ink″ling
ink″stand′
ink″well′
in″laid′
in″land
in″-law
in″lay′
in″lay′ing
in·leagued″
in″let
in lo′co pa·ren″tis
in″mate′
in′ me·mo″ri·um
in″most′
in″nards
in·nate″
in″nel·ite
in″ner cit′y
in″ner-di·rect″ed
in″ner·most
in·ner″vate
in·ner″vat·ing
in·ner·va″tion
in″ning
inn″keep′er
in″no·cence
in″no·cent
in·noc″u·ous
in″no·date′
in″no·vate′
in″no·vat′ing
in″no·va″tion
in″no·va″tive
in″no·va′tor
in′nu·en″do
in·nu″mer·a·ble
in·nu″mer·ous
in·ob·ser″vant
in·oc″u·late′
in·oc″u·lat′ing
in·oc·u·la″tion
in·of·fend″ing
in·of·fen″sive

in·op″er·a·ble
in·op″er·a·tive
in·op′por·tune″
in·or″di·nate
in·or·gan″ic
in·os″cu·late′
in·ox″i·dize′
in″pa′tient
in″put′
in″put′ting
in″quest
in·qui″e·tude′
in·qui·lin″i·ty
in·quire″
in·quir″ing
in·quir″y
  (*pl.* in·quir″ies)
in′qui·si″tion
in·quis″i·tive
in·quis″i·tor
in″road′
in″rush′
in·sa·lu″bri·ous
in·sane″
in·san″i·tar′y
in·san″i·ty
in·sa″tia·ble
in·sa″ti·ate
in·scribe″
in·scrib″ing
in·scrip″tion
in″scroll′
in·scru·ta·bil″i·ty
in·scru″ta·ble
in″seam″
in″sect
in·sec″tar″y
in·sec″ti·cide′
in·sec·tiv″o·rous
in·se·cure″
in·se·cu″ri·ty
  (*pl.* in·se·cu″ri·
  ties)
in·seer″
in·sem″i·nate′
in·sem″i·nat′ing

in·sem′i·na″tion
in·sen″sate
in·sen′si·bil″i·ty
  (*pl.* in·sen′si·bil″i·
  ties)
in·sen″si·ble
in·sen″si·tive
in·sen″si·tiv″i·ty
in·sen″ti·ence
in·sen″ti·ent
in·sep′a·ra·bil″i·ty
in·sep″a·ra·ble
in·sert″, *v.*
  place into
in″sert, *n.*
  thing inserted
in·ser″tion
in·ser″vi·ent
in·set″, *v.*
  set in
in″set, *n.*
  thing set in
in·set″ting
in·shin″ing
in″shore″
in″side″
in·sid″i·ous
in″sight
  understanding (*see:*
  incite)
in·sig″ni·a
in·sig·nif″i·cance
in·sig·nif″i·cant
in·sin·cere″
in·sin·cer″i·ty
  (*pl.* in′sin·cer″i·
  ties)
in·sin″u·ate′
in·sin″u·at′ing
in·sin″u·a″tion
in·sip″id
in·sist″
in·sist″ence
in·sist″en·cy
in·sist″ent
in·soc″i·a·ble

in'so·far"
in"sole'
in"so·lence
in"so·lent
in·sol"u·ble
in·solv"a·ble
in·sol"ven·cy
in·sol"vent
in·som"ni·a
in"so·much"
in·sou"ci·ance
in·sou"ci·ant
in·spect"
in·spec"tion
in·spec"tor
in·spi·ra"tion
in·spire"
in·spir"ing
in·spir"it
in'sta·bil"i·ty
in·stall"
in·stal·la"tion
in·stall"ment
in"stance
in"stant
in"stan·ta"ne·ous
in"stan"ter
in·state"
 in·stat"ed
 in·stat"ing
in·stead'
in"step'
in"sti·gate'
in"sti·gat'ing
in"sti·ga"tion
in"sti·ga'tor
in·still"
in·stil·la"tion
in·stilled"
in"stinct
in·stinc"tive
in"sti·tute·
in"sti·tut'ing
in"sti·tu"tion
in'sti·tu"tion·al·ize'
in'sti·tu"tion·al·iz'ing

in·struct"
in·struc"tion
in·struc"tive
in·struc"tor
in"stru·ment
in'stru·men"tal
in'stru·men·tal"i·ty
in'stru·men·ta"tion
in·sub·or"di·nate
in·sub·or'di·na"tion
in·sub·stan"tial
in'sub·stan'ti·al"i·ty
in·suf"fer·a·ble
in·suf·fi"cien·cy
 (*pl.* in'suf·fi"cien·
 cies)
in·suf·fi"cient
in"su·lar
in'su·lar"i·ty
in"su·late'
in"su·lat'ing
in"su·la"tion
in"su·lin
in·sul"si·ty
in·sult", *v.*
 treat badly
in"sult, *n.*
 epithet
in·su"per·a·ble
in'sup·port"a·ble
in'sup·press"i·ble
in'sur·a·bil"i·ty
in·sur"a·ble
in·sur"ance
in·sure"
in·sur"er
in·sur"gence
in·sur"gen·cy
in·sur"gent
in·sur"ing
in'sur·mount"a·ble
in'sur·rec"tion
in'sur·rec"tion·ist
in'sus·cep"ti·ble
in·tact"
in·ta"glio

 (*pl.* in·ta"glios)
in"take'
in·tan'gi·bil"i·ty
in·tan"gi·ble
in·tar"si·a
in"te·ger
in"te·gral
in"te·grate'
in"te·grat'ed
in"te·grat'ing
in"te·gra"tion
in"te·gra"tion·ist
in"te·gra'tive
in·teg"ri·ty
in·teg"u·ment
in"tel·lect"
in·tel"lec"tu·al
in·tel·lec"tu·al·ize'
in·tel·lec"tu·al·iz'ing
in·tel·lec"tu·al·ly
in·tel"li·gent
in·tel'li·gent"si·a
in·tel'li·gi·bil"i·ty
 (*pl.* in·tel'li·gi·bil"
 i·ties)
in·tel"li·gi·ble
in·tem"e·rate'
in·tem"per·ance
in·tem"per·ate
in"tem·por·al
in·tend"ed
in·ten"den·cy
in·ten·sa"tive
in·tense"
in·tense"ly
in·ten'si·fi·ca"tion
in·ten"si·fied'
in·ten"si·fy'
in·ten"si·fy'ing
in·ten"si·ty
in·ten"sive
in·tent"ness
in·ten"tion
in·ten"tion·al
in·ten"tion·al·ly
in·ter"

in″ter·act″
in′ter·ac″tion
in′ter·ag·glu″ti·nate
in″ter a″li·a′
in·ter-A·mer″i·can
in′ter·an″gu·lar
in′ter·a·ryt″e·noid
in′ter·bred″
in·ter·breed″
in·ter·breed″ing
in′ter·ca″dent
in′ter·ca·ro″tid
in′ter·cede″
in′ter·ced″ing
in′ter·cen″trum
in′ter·cept″
in′ter·cep″tion
in′ter·cep″tor
in·ter·ces″sion
  mediating (*see:* in-
  tersession)
in′ter·ces″so·ry
in·ter·change″, *v.*
  exchange
in″ter·change′, *n.*
  highway access
in′ter·change″a·ble
in′ter·chang″ing
in′ter·charge″
in′ter·cir″cle
in·ter·col·le″giate
in″ter·com
in′ter·com·mu″ni·
  cate′
in′ter·com·mu″nion·al
in′ter·con·ti·nen″tal
in′ter·cos″tal
in′ter·cos·to·hu·mer″
  al
in″ter·course′
in′ter·cul″tur·al
in′ter·cur·sa″tion
in′ter·de·nom·i·na″
  tion·al
in′ter·de·part·men″tal
in′ter·de·pend″en·cy

in′ter·de·pend″ent
in′ter·de·ter″min·ing
in′ter·dict″, *v.*
  prohibit
in″ter·dict′, *n.*
  prohibition
in″ter·dic″tion
in′ter·dis″ci·pli·nar′y
in′ter·dif·fu″sion
in′ter·dor″sal
in″ter·est
in″ter·est·ed
in″ter·est·ing
in′ter·face′
in′ter·fac″ing
in′ter·faith″
in·ter·fere″
in·ter·fer″ence
in·ter·fer″ing
in′ter·fer″on
in′ter·fib″ril·lar·y
in′ter·fret″
in′ter·gra″di·ent
in″ter·fuse″
in′ter·fus″ing
in′ter·ga·lac″tic
in″ter·im
in′ter·in″di·cate
in·te″ri·or
in′ter·jac″u·la·tor·y
in′ter·ject″
in′ter·jec″tion
in′ter·knit″ting
in′ter·lace″
in′ter·lac″ing
in′ter·laid
in″ter·leaf′
  (*pl.* in″ter·leaves′)
in″ter·leave″
in′ter·leav″ing
in′ter·li″brar·y
in″ter·lin″e·ar
in′ter·lin″ing
in″ter·link″
in′ter·lock″, *v.*
  lock together

in′ter·lock′, *n.*
  being interlocked;
  device
in″ter·lo·cu″tion
in′ter·loc″u·tor
in′ter·loc″u·to′ry
in′ter·lope″
in″ter·lop′er
in′tor·lop″ing
in″ter·lude″
in′ter·mar″gi·nal
in′ter·mar″riage
in′ter·mar″ried
in′ter·mar″ry
in′ter·me″di·ar′y
  (*pl.* in′ter·me″di·ar′
  ies)
in′ter·me″di·ate
in·ter″ment
  burial (*see:* intern-
  ment)
in′ter·mez″zo
  (*pl.* in′ter·mez″zos)
in·ter″mi·na·ble
in′ter″min·gle
in′ter·min″gling
in′ter·mis″sion
in′ter·mit″
in′ter·mit″tent
in·ter·mit″ting
in′ter·mix″
in′ter·moun″tain
in′ter·mu″ral
in·tern″, *v.*
  serve; detain
in″tern, *n.*
  apprentice
in·ter″nal
in·ter″nal·ize
in·ter″nal·iz′ing
in′ter·na″tion·al
in′ter·na″tion·al·ly
in′ter·na″tion·al·ism′
in′ter·na″tion·al·ist
in′ter·na″tion·al·ize′

in·ter·na″tion·al·iz′ing

in′ter·ne″cine

in tern·ee″

in″tern·ist

in·tern″ment
  confinement (*see:*
   interment)

in′ter·no″dal

in·ter·nun″ci·o′

in′ter·nup″tial

in·ter·of″fice

in′ter·par″en·the′tic

in·ter·pel″late
  question (*see:* inter-
   polate)

in′ter·pen″e·trate′

in·ter·pen′e·tra″tion

in·ter·per″son·al

in·ter·per″son·al·ly

in″ter·phase

in″ter·phone

in″ter·plan″e·tar′y

in·ter·play″, *v.*
  influence recipro-
   cally

in″ter·play′, *n.*
  action; effect

In″ter·pol′

in·ter″po·late′
  alter (*see:* interpel-
   late)

in·ter″po·lat′ing

in·ter′po·la″tion

in′ter·pose″

in·ter·pos″ing

in·ter·po·si″tion

in·ter′pre·ta″tion

in·ter″pret·er

in·ter″pre·tive

in·ter·ra″cial

in·ter·rad″i·ate

in·terred″

in′ter·reg″num

in·ter·re·late″

in·ter·re·lat″ing

in″ter″ring

in·ter″ro·gate′

in·ter″ro·gat′ing

in·ter·ro·ga″tion

in·ter·rog″a·tive

in·ter″ro·ga′tor

in·ter·rog″a·to′ry

in·ter·rupt″

in·ter·rup″tion

in″ter·scho·las″tic

in″ter·scrip″tion

in·ter·sect″

in·ter·sec″tion

in″ter·ses′sion
  short session (*see:*
   intercession)

in′ter·shock″

in·ter·sol″u·ble

in″ter·sperse″

in′ter·spers″ing

in′ter·sper″sion

in·ter·state″
  between states (*see:*
   intrastate)

in·ter·stel″lar

in·ter″stice

in·ter·tar″sal

in″ter·twine″

in′ter·twin″ing

in′ter·twist″

in·ter·ur″ban

in″ter·val

in·ter·vas″cu·lar

in·ter·vene″

in·ter·ven″ing

in·ter·ven″tion

in·ter·ven″tion·ist

in″ter·view′

in″ter·view″er

in″ter·weave″

in″ter·weav″ing

in″ter·wove″

in′ter·wo″ven

in·tes″tate

in·tes″ti·nal

in·tes″tine

in·tex″ture

in″ti·ma·cy
  (*pl.* in″ti·ma·cies)

in″ti·mate

in″ti·mat′ing

in′ti·ma″tion

in·tim″i·date′

in·tim″i·dat′ing

in·tim′i·da″tion

in·tol″er·a·bil″i·ty

in·tol″er·a·ble

in·tol″er·ance

in·tol″er·ant

in·to·na″tion

in·tone″

in·ton″ing

in to″to

in·tox″i·cant

in·tox″i·cate′

in·tox″i·cat′ing

in·tox′i·ca″tion

in′tra·cell″u·lar

in′tra·com″pa·ny

in·trac′ta·bil″i·ty

in·trac″ta·ble

in′tra·mu″ral

in′tra·mus″cu·lar

in′tra·per″i·ton′e·al

in·tran″si·gent

in·tran″si·tive

in′tra·state″
  within a state (*see:*
   interstate)

in′tra·u″ter·ine

in′tra·ve″nous

in·trep″id

in·tre·pid″i·ty

in″tri·ca·cy
  (*pl.* in″tri·ca·cies)

in″tri·cate

in·trigue″

in·trigu″ing

in·trin″sic

in′tro·duce″

in′tro·duc″ing

in′tro·duc″tion

in'tro·duc"to·ry
in"tro·ject'
in"tro·spec"tion
in'tro·spec"tive
in"tro·ver"sion
in"tro·vert", *v.*
  bend inward
in"tro·vert', *n.*
  withdrawn person
in·trude"
in·trud"ing
in·tru"sion
in·tru"sive
in·tu·i"tion
in·tu"i·tive
in·tu·mesce"
in"tus·sus·cept"
in"un·date
in"un·dat'ing
in"un·da"tion
in·ure"
in·ur"ing
in·vade"
in·vad"er
in·vad"ing
in"va·lid, *n.*
  sick person
in·val"id, *adj.*
  not valid
in·val"i·date'
in·val"i·dat'ing
in·val'i·da"tion
in·val"u·a·ble
in·var'i·a·bil"i·ty
in·var"i·a·ble
in·var"i·ant
in·va"sion
in·va"sive
in·vec"tive
in·veigh"
in·vei"gle
in·vei"gling
in·ven"ient
in·vent"
in·ven"tion
in·ven"tive

in·ven"tor
in"ven·to·ried
in"ven·to·ry
  (*pl.* in"ven·to·ries)
in"ven·to·ry·ing
in·ver'i·si·mil"i·tude
in·verse"
in·ver"sion
in·vert"
in·ver"te·brate
in·ves"ti·gate'
in·ves"ti·gat'ing
in·ves"ti·ga"tion
in·ves"ti·ga'tor
in·ves"ti·ture
in·vest"ment
in·vet"er·ate
in·vid"i·ous
in·vig"or·ate'
in·vig"or·at'ing
in·vig'or·a"tion
in·vin'ci·bil"i·ty
in·vin"ci·ble
in·vi"o·la·ble
in·vi"o·late
in·vis'i·bil"i·ty
in·vis"i·ble
in·vi·ta"tion
in·vite"
in·vit"ing
in'vi"tro
in"vo·ca"tion
in"voice
in"voic·ing
in·voke"
in·vok"ing
in·vol"un·tar'i·ly
in·vol"un·tar'y
in"vo·lute'
in"vo·lut'ing
in"vo·lu"tion
in·volve'
in·volve"ment
in·volv"ing
in·vul"ner·a·ble
in"ward·ly

in"wards
i"o·dide'
i"o·dine'
i"o·dize'
i"o·diz'ing
i"on
i·on"ic
i·on"i·um
i'on·i·za"tion
i"on·ize'
i"on·iz'ing
i·on"o·sphere'
i·o"ta
I'O'U"
I"o·wa
ip'e·cac'
ip"se·i·ty
ip"so fac"to
I·ran"
I·raq"
i·ras'ci·bil"i·ty
i·ras"ci·ble
  easily angered (*see:*
  erasable)
i·rate"
ire"ful
Ire"land
i·ren"ic
ir'i·des"cence
ir'i·des"cent
i·rid"i·um
i"ris
  (*pl.* i"ris·es)
irk"some
i"ron·bound'
i"ron·clad'
i"ron·hand"ed
i·ron"ic
i·ron"i·cal·ly
i"ron lung"
i"ron·shod'
i"ron·stone'
i"ron·ware'
i"ron·wood'
i"ron·work'
i"ron·wort'

i″ro·ny
  (*pl*. i″ro·nies)
Ir″o·quois′
  (*pl*. Ir″o·quois′)
ir·ra″di·ate′
ir·ra″di·at′ing
ir·ra·di·a″tion
ir·ra″tion·al
ir·ra″tion·al″i·ty
ir·ra″tion·al·ly
ir·re·claim″a·ble
ir·rec·on·cil″a·ble
ir·re·cov″er·a·ble
ir·re·deem″a·ble
ir·re·den″tism
ir·re·den″tist
ir·re·duc″i·ble
ir·re·form″a·ble
ir·ref′u·ta·bil″i·ty
ir·ref″u·ta·ble
ir·re·gen″er·ate
ir·reg″u·lar
ir·reg·u·lar″i·ty
  (*see*: ir·reg′u·lar″i·ties)
ir·re·la″tion
ir·rel″e·vant
ir·re·li″gious
ir·re·me″di·a·ble
ir·re·mov″a·ble
ir·rep′a·ra·bil″i·ty
ir·rep″a·ra·ble
ir·re·place″a·ble
ir·re·press″i·ble
ir·re·proach″a·ble
ir·re·sil″ien·cy
ir·re·sist′i·bil″i·ty
ir·re·sist″i·ble
ir·res″o·lute′
ir·re·solv″a·ble
ir·re·spec″tive
ir·re·spon′si·bil″i·ty
ir·re·spon″si·ble
ir·re·triev″a·ble
ir·rev″er·ence
ir·rev″er·ent

ir·re·vers″i·ble
ir·re·vert″i·ble
ir·rev″o·ca·ble
ir″ri·gate′
ir″ri·gat′ing
ir″ri·ga″tion
ir·ri·ta·bil″i·ty
  (*pl*. ir′ri·ta·bil″i·ties)
ir″ri·ta·ble
ir″ri·tant
ir″ri·tate′
ir″ri·tat′ing
ir′ri·ta″tion
ir·rupt″
  burst into (*see*:
    erupt)
ir·rup″tion
  bursting into (*see*:
    eruption)
is·ab·nor″mal
is·ap′o·stol″ic
is·au·xet″ic
is·che″mi·a
is·chi·o·cav″er·nous
is·chi·o·ver″te·bral
is″chi·um
  (*pl*. is″chi·a)
i″sin·glass′
Is″lam
Is·lam″a·bad′
is″land
isle
  island (*see*: aisle)
is″let
  small island (*see*:
    eyelet)
isl″ing
i″so·bar′
i′so·bront″
i′so·car″pous
i′so·chi″mal
i′so·chron″ism
i′so·co·deine
i′so·gen′o·typ″ic
i′so·hep″tane

i′so·ker·aun″ic
i″so·late′
i″so·lat′ing
i′so·la″tion
i′so·la″tion·ist
i″so·mer
i′so·mer″ic
i′so·met″ric
i′so·met″ri·cal·ly
i′so·pro″pyl
i·sos″ce·les
i′so·seis″mic
i′so·ther″mal
i″so·tope′
i′so·top″ic
Is″ra·el
is″su·ance
is″sue
is″su·ing
Is·tan·bul″
isth″mus
  (*pl*. isth″mus·es)
i′ta·con″ic
i·tal″ic
i·tal″i·cize′
i·tal″i·ciz′ing
It″a·ly
itch
  (*pl*. itch″es)
itch″i·er
itch″i·ness
itch″y
i″tem·ize′
i″tem·iz′ing
it″er·ate′
it″er·at′ing
it′er·a″tion
it″er·a′tive
i·tin″er·ant
i·tin″er·ar′y
  (*pl*. i·tin″er·ar′ies)
its
  possessive of it (*see*:
    it's)
it's
  it is (*see*: its)

it·self''
I'U'D''
i''vo·ry
  (*pl.* i''vo·ries)
I''vo·ry Coast''
i''vy
  (*pl.* i''vies)

J

jab
jab''ber
jab''ber·cr
Jab''ber·wock'y
jab''bing
ja·bot''
ja''ca·na'
ja''ca·too'
jack''al
jack''a·napes'
jack''ass'
jack''boot'
jack''daw'
jack''et
jack''ham'mer
jack''-in-the-box
  (*pl.* jack''-in-the-
  box'es)
jack''-in-the-pul''pit
jack''knife'
  (*pl.* jack''knives')
jack''light·er
jack''-of-all-trades''
  (*pl.* jacks''-of-all'-
  trades'')
jack''-o'-lan'tern
jack''pile
jack''pot'
jack'' rab'bit
jack''screw
jack''shaft'
jack''snipe'
Jack''son
Jack''son·ville
jack''stay

jack''straw'
jack''wood
Jac''o·be'an
jac''quard
jac''ti·ta''tion
jac''u·late'
Ja·cuz''zi™
jade
  jad''ed
  jad''ing
jag''ged
jag''uar
jai'' a·lai''
jail''bird'
jail''er
jail''house'
Ja·kar''ta
jak''fruit
ja·la·peñ''o
ja·lop''y
  (*pl.* ja·lop''ies)
jal''ou·sie'
  blind (*see:* jealous)
jam
  crowd; fruit (*see:*
  jamb)
Ja·mai''ca
ja'mais vu''
jamb
  doorway (*see:* jam)
jam'ba·lay''a
jam'bo·ree''
jam·dan''i
James''town
jam''like
jammed
jam''ming
jam''-packed''
jam''pan·ee
jam'' ses'sion
jan''gle
jan''gling
jan''is·sar'y
jan''i·tor
jan·i·to''ri·al
jan''ty

Jan''u·ar'y
  (*pl.* Jan''u·ar'ies)
Ja·pan''
  ja·panned''
  ja·pan''ning
Ja·pan''o·phile'
jap''er·y
ja·pon''i·ca
jar
  jarred
  jar''ring
jar'di·niere''
jar''gon
jar''gon·al
jar''goon'
jar''rah
jas''mine
jas·pé''
jas''per
jas''pi·lyte'
jas''soid
ja''to
jaun''dice
  jaun''diced
  jaun''dic·ing
jaun''ti·er
jaun''ti·ly
jaun''ti·ness
jaun''ty
jaup
ja''va
jave''lin
jaw''bone'
jaw''break'er
jaw''fish
jay
jay''hawk'er
jay''walk'er
Jayne
jay''vee
jazz
jazz''i·er
jazz''i·ness
jazz''y
jeal''ous
jeal''ous·y

envy (*pl.* jeal″ous·
ies) (*see:* jalousie)
jeaned
jeans
Jed′e·di″ah
jeep
jeer″ing
jeer″proof′
Je″ho″vah
je·june″
je·jun′o·du·o·den″al
je·ju″num
Jek″yll
jell
    harden (*see:* gel)
jel″lied
Jell″-O™
jel″ly
    (*pl.* jel″lies)
jel″ly·bean′
jel″ly·fish′
jel″ly·ing
jel″ly roll′
jem″i·dar′
jen″ny
    (*pl.* jen″nies)
jen·net″ing
jeop″ard·ize′
jeop″ard·iz′ing
jeop″ard·y
je·quir″i·ty
jer′e·mi″ad
je·rib″
Jer″i·cho′
jerk″i·er
jerk″i·ly
jer″kin
jerk″i·ness
jerk″y
jer″ry·built′
jer″ry·can′
jer″sey
    (*pl.* jer″seys)
Je·ru″sa·lem
jes″sing
jes″sa·mine

jest
    joke (*see:* gist)
jest″er
Jes″u·it
jet
    jet″ted
    jet″ting
jet″-black″
je·té′
jet″ en″gine
jet″ lag′
jet″lin′er
jet″port′
jet pro·pelled″
jet″sam
jet″ set′
jet″ stream′
jet″tied
jet″ti·son
jet″ty
    (*pl.* jet″ties)
jet″ty·ing
jew″el
jew″el·er
jew″el·ing
jew″el·ry
jew″el·weed′
Jew″ish
Jew″ry
Jew′s″-harp′
jhow
jib
    boom; sail; balk
    (*see:* jibe and gibe)
jibbed
    balked (*see:* jibed)
jib″bing
    balking (*see:* jibing
    and gibing)
jibe
    shift; agreement
    (*see:* jib and gibe)
jibed
    shifted (*see:* jibbed)
jib″ing

shifting (*see:* gibing
    and jibbing)
jif″fy
    (*pl.* jif″fies)
jig
jig″ger
jig″ger·mast′
jig″ging
jig″gle
jig″saw′
jig″saw puz′zle
Ji·had″
jilt
Jim″ Crow″
jim″mied
jim″my
    (*pl.* jim″mies)
jim″my·ing
Jim″son weed′
jin″gle
jin″gle·bob′
jin″gling
jin″go
    (*pl.* jin″goes)
jin″go·ism′
jinn
    (*sing.* jin″ni)
jin·rik″i·sha
jinx
    (*pl.* jinx″es)
jit″ney
jit″ter·bug′
jit″ter·bug′ging
jit″ter·y
job″ber
job″bing
job″hold′er
job″less
job″ lot′
jock″ey
jock″eyed
jock″ey·ing
jock″strap′
jo·cose″
joc′o·ser″i·ous
jo·cos″i·ty

joc″u·lar
joc u·lar″i·ty
joc″und
jo·cun″di·ty
  (*pl.* jo·cun″di·ties)
jo″del
jodh″purs
jog
jog″ger
jog″ging
jog″gle
jog″gling
Jo·han″nes·burg′
john″ny·cake′
john″ny-come′-late″ly
john″ny-jump″-up′
joie de vi″vre
join″er
joint″ed
joint″wood
joist
joke
joke″ster
jok″ing
Jo″liet
jol″li·er
jol″li·ty
  (*pl.* jol″li·ties)
jol″ly
  (jol″lies)
Jol″ly Rog″er
jolt
jon″quil
Jor″dan
josh
jos″tle
jos″tling
jot
jot″ting
jounce
jour″nal
jour″nal·ism′
jour″nal·ist
jour′nal·is″tic
jour″ney
  (*pl.* jour″neys)

jour″neyed
jour″ney·ing
jour″ney·man
joust
jo″vi·al
jo′vi·al″i·ty
jo″vi·al·ly
jow″er
jowl
joy″ful
joy″ful·ly
joy″hop′
joy″ous
joy″ride′
joy″stick′
ju″bi·lance
ju″bi·lant
ju′bi·la″tion
ju″bi·lee′
Ju″dah
Ju″da·i·ca
Ju″da·ism′
Ju·de″a
judge
judge″ ad″vo·cate
judg″ing
judg″ment
ju″di·ca·ble
ju″di·ca′tor
ju″di·ca′ture
ju·di″cial
ju·di″ci·ar″y
  (*pl.* ju·di″ci·ar″ies)
ju·di″cious
ju″do
jug
ju″gate′
jug″ger·naut′
jug″ging
jug″gle
jug″gling
jug″u·lar
juice
juic″er
juic″i·er
juic″y

ju·jit″su
ju″ju′
ju″ju·be′
juke″box′
ju″lep
ju·li·enne″
Ju·ly″
  (*pl.* Ju·lies″)
jum″ble
jum″bling
jum″bo
jump″er
jump″i·er
jump″i·ness
jump″ing bean′
jump″ing jack′
jump″y
junc″tion
junc″ture
jun″cus
June
Ju″neau
Jung
jung″i·an
jun″gle
jun″ior
ju″ni·per
jun″ket
junk″ food′
junk″ie
junk″ mail′
junk″man
junk″yard′
jun″ta
Ju″pi·ter
ju·ra″ment
ju·rid″i·cal
ju·rid″i·cal·ly
ju·ris·dic″tion
ju·ris·pru″dence
ju″rist
ju·ris″tic
ju″ror
ju″ry
  (*pl.* ju″ries)
ju″ry·man

ju″ry rigged
ju″ry·wom′an
jus″tice
jus″ti·fi′a·ble
jus″ti·fi·ca″tion
jus″ti·fied
jus″ti·fy′
jus″ti·fy′ing
just″ler
just″ly
jut
  stick out (*see:* jute)
jute
  fiber; plant (*see:* jut)
jut″ted
jut″ting
ju″ve·nal
ju″ve·nile
ju′ve·nil″i·a
ju′ve·nil″i·try
jux′ta·pose″
jux′ta·pos″ing
jux′ta·po·si″tion

K

Kaa″ba
ka·bob″
ka·bu″ki
Ka″bul
ka·chi″na
Kad″dish
Ka″du
kaf″fee·klatsch
ka·fir″in
ka″go
ka·hi″li
kai
kail
kai″ser
kal″a·da′na
kale
ka·lei″do·scope′
ka·lei′do·scop″ic
ka·li″gen·ous

ka″li·nite′
ka′ma·ru″pic
ka′mi·ka″ze
Kam·pa″la
kamp″to·morph
Kam′pu·che″a
ka·nar″i
kan′ga·roo″
kan″ke·dort′
Kan″sas
ka″o·lin
ka″o·lin·ized′
ka″pok
kap″pa
ka·put″
ka·ra″chi
kar″a·kul
ka·ra″te
kar″ma
kar″mic
kar″ri
kar·y′o·lymph″
kar′y′o·type″
kas″be·ke
ka″sha
Kash″mir
ka′ta·kan″a
kath
Kat′man·du″
kat″mon
ka″ty·did
kat″zen·jamm′er
ka″vass
Ka′wa·sa″ki
kay″ak
kay″o
ka·zoo″
ke·bab″
keb″yar
ked″gy
keel″boat′
keel″haul′
keel″son
keen″ing
keen″ly
keep″ing

keep″sake′
ke″fir
keg″ler
kele
kell
kell·up″weed
kelp
kelp″fish
kel″vin
kemp″y
ken
kenned
ken″nel
ke″no
ke·nog″e·ny
ken″spec·kle
Ken·tuck″y
Ken″ya
Ke″pone™
kept
ker″a·tin
ker′a·ti″tis
ker′a·to·gen″ic
ker′a·tol″y·sis
kerb″stone
ker″chief
ker″nel
  seed; nut (*see:* colo-nel)
ker″o·gen
ker″o·sene′
ker·plunk″
kes″trel
ke″tal
ketch″up
ke′to·gen″e·sis
ke″tone
ke″to·side′
ket″tle
ket″tle·drum′
kex″y
key
  metal object; music (*pl.* keys) (*see:* cay and quay)
key″board′

key''club'
key''hole'
key''note'
key''not'er
key''not'ing
key''punch'
key''stone'
key''stroke'
khak''i
Khar·toum''
khat
khe''da
Khy''ber Pass''
ki·al''kee
kib·butz''
 (*pl.* kib·but·zim')
kib''itz·er
ki''bosh
kick''back'
kick''off'
kick''stand'
kick''xi·a
kid
 kid''ded
 kid''ding
kiddie
 (*pl.* kid''dies)
kid''nap
 kid''napped
 kid''nap·ping
kid''nap·per
kid''ney bean'
kid''ney stone'
kiel·ba''sa
Ki''ev
Ki·ga''li
kill''buck
kill''deer'
kill''er
kil''li·fish'
kill''-joy'
kil''low
kiln
kiln''-dry'
 kiln''-dried'
 kiln''-dry'ing

kil''o·cal'o·rie
kil''o·cy'cle
kil''o·gram'
kil''o·hertz'
kil''o·li'ter
kil·om''e·ter
kil''o·volt'
kil''o·watt'
kil''o·watt'-hour''
kil''ter
ki·mo''no
 (*pl.* ki·mo''nos)
kin''ase
kin''der·gar'ten
kind''heart''ed
kin''dle
kind''li·ness
kin''dling
kind''ness
kin''dred
kin'e·mat''ics
kin'e·mom''e·ter
kin'e·scope'
kin'e·sim''e·ter
kin'es·thet''ic
ki·net''ics
ki·net''o·plast'
kin''folk'
king''dom
king''fish'
 (*pl.* king''fish')
king''fish'er
king''let
king''ly
king''mak'er
king''pin''
king's Eng''lish'
king''-size'
Kings''port
Kings''ton
kink
kin''ka·jou'
kink''i·er
kink''y
kins''folk
kin''ship

kin·sha''sa
kins''man
kins''wom'an
ki'o·nec''to·my
ki''osk
Ki''o·wa
 (*pl.* Ki''o·wa)
kip''per
kirsch
kis''met
kiss''a·ble
kiss''age
kiss''er
kitch''en
kitch'en·ette''
kitch''en·ware
kite
kith'' and kin''
kitsch
kit''ten·ish
kit''ty
 (*pl.* kit''ties)
kit''ty-cor''nered
ki''wi
 (*pl.* ki''wis)
klan
Klans''man
 (*pl.* Klans''men)
Kleen''ex™
klep'to·ma''ni·a
klip''fish
Klon''dike
kludge
kludg''ing
klutz
klutz''y
knab''ble
knack
knack''wurst
knappe
knap''sack'
knap''scull'
knave
 rascal; jack (*see:* nave)
knav''er·y

knav''ish

knead
  press (*see:* need and
    kneed)

knee''cap'

kneed
  hit with knee (*see:*
    knead and need)

knee''-deep''

knee''-high''

knee''ing

knee'' jerk'

kneel

kneel''ing

knee''pad'

knell

knelt

knew
  did know (*see:* gnu
    and new)

knick''er·bock'ers

knick''ers

knick''knack'

knife
  (*pl.* knives)

knif''ing

knight
  soldier (*see:* night)

knight''-er''rant
  (*pl.* knights''-er''
    rant)

knight''hood

knish

knit

knit''ted

knit''ter

knit''ting

knitch

knit''work'

knob

knob''bi·er

knob''bing

knob''by

knock''a·bout'

knock''down'

knock''er

knock''-knee'

knock''-kneed'

knock''out'

knock''wurst

knoll

knol''ler

Knos''sos

knot
  fastening; nautical
    measure (*see:* not)

knot''hole'

knot''ti·er

knot''ting

knot''ty

knot''weed

know''a·ble

know''-how'

know''ing

know''-it-all'

knowl''edge

knowl''edge·a·ble

known

know''-noth'ing

knuck''le

knuck''le·ball'

knuck''le·head'

knuck''ling

knurl''y

ko·a''la

kohl·ra''bi
  (*pl.* kohl·ra''bies)

koi

Koi'' Ni''dre

ko'i·non''i·a

ko''la

ko''ni·scope'

kook

kook''a·bur'ra

kook''i·er

kook''y
  silly (*see:* cookie)

ko''peck

ko'po·phob''i·a

Ko·ran''

Ko·re''a

ko·sher

kow''tow''

K''-point'

kraal

krait

kraut

Krem''lin

krep''lach

krill
  (*pl.* krill)

Krish''na

kro''by·los'

kro''nos

kryp''ton

Kua''la Lum''pur

ku''chen

ku''dos

kud''zu

Ku'' Klux'' Klan''

ku·lak''

ku·mi''te

kum''mel

kum''quat

kung'' fu''

Ku·wait''

kvetch

kwash'i·or''kor

kyat

ky''lie

kym''ba·lon'

ky'nu·rine''

Kyo''to

Kyr''i·e' e·le''i·son'

L

la''bel

la''beled

la''bel·ing

la''bi·a

la''bi·al

la''bi·ate'

la''bile

la''bi·um
  (*pl.* la''bi·a)

la''bor

lab''o·ra·to''ry
  (*pl.* lab''o·ra·to'
  ries)
la''bor·er
la·bo''ri·ous
la''bor·sav'ing
la''bor·some'
Lab''ra·dor'
lab''y·rinth
lab'y·rin''thine
lac''co·lite'
lace
lace''like'
lac''er·ate'
lac''er·at'ing
lac'er·a''tion
lace''wing'
lace''wood'
lace''work'
lach''ry·mose'
lac''i·er
lac''ing
lack
lack'a·dai''si·cal
lack'a·dai''si·cal·ly
lack''ey
  (*pl.* lack''eys)
lack''land
lack''lus'ter
la·con''ic
la·con''i·cal·ly
lac''quer
la·crosse''
lac''tase
lac''tate
lac''tat·ing
lac·ta''tion
lac''te·al
lac''tic
lac''tid
lac''ti·gen'ic
lac''to·chrome'
lac''tose
la·cu''na
lac''y
lad''der

lad''der·back'
lad''der·man
lade
  load; dip (*see:* laid)
lad''en
la''dies' room'
la''dle
la''dle·wood
la''dling
la''dy
  (*pl.* la''dies)
la''dy·bug'
la''dy·fin'ger
la''dy-in-wait''ing
la''dy·like'
la''dy·love'
la''dy·ship'
la''dy's maid''
la''dy's-slip'per
la''e·trile'
lag
la''gan
la''ger
lag''gard
lag''ging
la·gniappe''
la·goon''
La''gos
La·hore''
laich
laid
  put down (*see:* lade)
laid''-back''
lain
  was lying (see: lane)
lair
  den (*see:* layer)
laird
lais'sez faire''
la''i·ty
lake''front'
lak''er
lam
  beat; escape (*see:* lamb)
la''ma

monk (*see:* llama)
La·maze''
lamb
  sheep (*see:* lam)
lam·baste''
lam·bast''ing
lam''ben·cy
lam''bent
lamb''kin
lamb''skin'
lame
  cripple (*see:* lamé)
la·mé''
  fabric (*see:* lame)
lame''brain'
lame'' duck''
la·mel''la
la·ment''
lam''en·ta·ble
lam·en·ta''tion
lam''i·nate'
lam''i·nat'ing
lam'i·na''tion
lam''i·na'tor
lam''mer
lam·pa'de·phor''i·a
lamp''black'
lamp''light'
lamp''light'er
lam·poon''
lam·poon''er
lam·poon''ist
lamp''post'
lam''prel
lam''prey
lamp''shade'
lance
lan''cet
lanc''ing
lan''dau
land''fall'
land''fill'
land''folk'
land'' grant'
land''hold'er
land''ing

land"ing strip'
land"la'dy
land"locked'
land"lord'
land"lub'ber
land"mark'
land"mass
land"mine'
land"own'er
land"scape'
land"scap'ist
land"slide'
lands"man
land"wards
lane
   path (*see:* lain)
lang'syne"
lan"guage
lan"guette
lan"guid
lan"guish
lan"guor
lan"guor·ous
lan"i·form'
lank
lank"i·er
lank"i·ness
lank"y
lan"o·lin
Lan"sing
lan"tern
lan"yard
La"os
La Paz"
lap" dog'
la·pel"
lap"i·dar'y
   (*pl.* lap"i·dar'ies)
lap"i·date'
la·pid'i·fi·ca"tion
lap"ing
lap"is laz"u·li
Lap"land'
lap"ping
lap" robe'
lapse

laps"ing
lar"ce·nist
lar"ce·nous
lar"ce·ny
   (*pl.* lar"ce·nies)
larch
lar"der
large"ly
large"ness
large"-scale"
lar·gess"
larg"est
lar·ghet"to
lar"go
lar"i·at
la·rix"in
lark"spur'
lar"ri·gan
lar"va
   (*pl.* lar"vae)
lar"val
la·ryn"ge·al
lar"yn·gi"tis
la·ryn"go·scope'
lar"ynx
   (*pl.* lar"ynx·es)
la·sa"gna
las·civ"i·ous
la"ser disk'
lass
las"sie
las"si·tude'
las"so
   (*pl.* las"sos)
las"so·ing
last"ing
Las Ve"gas
latch"key'
latch"string'
late
late"com'er
la·teen"
late"ly
la"ten·cy
la·tens'i·fi·ca"tion
la"tent

lat"er
lat"er·al
lat'er·a·li·za"tion
la"tex
   (*pl.* lat"i·ces')
lath
   strip (*see:* lathe)
lathe
   machine (*see:* lath)
lathed
lath"er
lath"ing
Lat"in
La·ti"no
lat"i·tude'
lat'i·tu"di·nal
la·trine"
lat"ter
lat"ter-day"
lat"tice
lat"tice·leaf'
lat"tice·work'
lat"tic·ing
Lat"vi·a
laud
laud'a·bil"i·ty
laud"a·ble
lau"da·num
laud"a·to'ry
laugh"a·ble
laugh"ing·stock'
laugh"ter
lau"mon·tite'
launch"er
launch" pad'
laun"der
laun"der·ette"
laun"dress
   (*pl.* laun"dress·es)
Laun"dro·mat™
laun"dry
   (*pl.* laun"dries)
lau"re·ate
lau"rel
lau"re·ole'
la"va

la·va″bo
  (*pl.* la·va″boes)
lav′a·liere″
lav″ash
lav″a·to·ry
  (*pl.* lav″a·to·ries)
lave
lav″en·der
lav″ing
lav″ish
law″-a·bid′ing
law″break′er
law″ful·ly
law″full·ness
law″giv′er
law″less
law″mak′er
law″man′
lawn
law·ren″cite′
law″suit′
law″yer
lax″a·tive
lax″i·ty
lax″ly
lay
  set down; ballad
  (*see:* lei)
lay″a·way
lay″er
  thickness (*see:* lair)
lay·ette″
lay″ing
lay″man
lay″off′
lay″out′
lay″o′ver
laze
la″zi·est
la″zi·ly
la″zi·ness
laz″ing
la″zy·bones′
la″zy Su″san
L-do″pa
lea

meadow (*see:* lee)
leach
  dissolve (*see:* leech)
lead
lead″en
lead″er·less′
lead″er·ship′
lead″-in′
lead″off′
leaf
  foliage (*pl.* leaves)
  (*see:* lief)
leaf·age
leaf″hop·per
leaf″i·er
leaf″i·ness
leaf″let
leaf″stalk′
leaf″y
league
lea″guer
leagu″ing
leak
  release (*see:* leek)
leak″age
leak″i·er
leak″y
lean
  bend; thin (*see:* lien)
lean″ing
lean″ness
lean″-to′
  (*pl.* lean″-tos′)
leap″frog″
leap″frog′ging
leap″ing
leap″ year′
learn
learned
learn″ing
lease
lease″hold′
leash
leas″ing
least
least″wise′

leath″er
leath″er·flow′er
leath″er·neck′
leath″er·y
leave
leav″en
leave″-tak′ing
leav″ings
Leb″a·non
lech″er·ous
lech″er·y
lec″i·thin
lect
lec″tern
lec″tion
lec″tor
lec″ture
lec″tur·ing
le″der·ho·sen
ledge
ledg″er
ledg″er·dom′
lee
  shelter (*see:* lea)
leech
  worm (*pl.* leech″es)
  (*see:* leach)
lee″ful
leek
  vegetable (*see:* leak)
leer″i·er
leer″y
lee″ward
lee″way′
left″ field″
left″-hand″ed
left″-hand″er
left″ist
left″ments
left″o′ver
left″ wing″
left″-wing″er
left″y
  (*pl.* left″ies)
leg″a·cy
  (*pl.* leg″a·cies)

le″gal
le″gal·ism′
le gal·is″tic
le·gal″i·ty
   (*pl.* le·gal″i·ties)
le″gal·i·za″tion
le″gal·ize′
le″gal·iz′ing
le″gal·ly
leg″ate
leg′a·tee″
leg′a·tine″
le·ga″tion
le·ga″to
leg″end
le·gen″da
leg″en·dar′y
leg″er·de·main″
leg·gie·ro″
leg″ging
leg″gy
leg′i·bil″i·ty
leg″i·ble
leg″i·bly
le″gion
le″gion·ar′y
le″gion·naire″
leg″is·late′
leg″is·lat′ing
leg′is·la″tion
leg″is·la′tive
leg″is·la′tor
leg″is·la′ture
le·git″i·ma·cy
le·git″i·mate
le·git″i·mat′ing
le·git″i·mize′
le·git″i·miz′ing
leg″man′
leg″room′
leg″ume
le″gu·min′
leg work′
lei
   garland (*pl.* leis)
   (*see:* lay)

lei″sure
lei″sure·li·ness
lei″sure·ly
leit″mo·tif′
lem″ma
lem″ming
le·mog″ra
lem″on
lem′on·ade″
lem′on·like′
le″mur
lend″er
lend″ing
lend″-lease″
length″en
length″i·er
length″ways′
length″wise′
length″y
le″ni·ence
le″ni·en·cy
le″ni·ent
Len″in·grad′
len″i·tive
len″i·ty
lens
Lent
Lent″en
len·tic″u·lare
len·tig″i·nous′
len″til
le″o·nine′
leop″ard
le″o·tard′
lep″er
lep′i·din″
lep′i·dop″ter·ous
lep″re·chaun″
lep″ro·sar′·i·um
lep″ro·sy
lep″rous
lep″sar′i·a
lep′to·ceph″a·lous
lep′to·derm″ous
lep″ton
lep′to·some′

les″bi·an
les″bi·an·ism′
le″sion
Le·so″tho
les·see″
less″en
   decrease (*see:* lesson)
less″er
   smaller (*see:* lesson)
les″son
   instruction (*see:* lessen)
les″sor
   landlord (*see:* lesser)
letch
let″down′
le″thal
le″thal·ly
le·thar″gic
le·thar″gi·cal″ness
leth″ar·gy
let″ter box′
let″tered
let″ter·form′
let″ter·head′
let″ter·ing
let″ter·man′
let″ter-per″fect
let″ter·press′
let″ter-spaced′
let″ting
let″tuce
let″up′
leu·can″thous
leu′co·cy′to·gen″e·sis
leu·co″ma
leu·coph″a·nite′
leu·ke″mi·a
leu″ko·blast′
leu″ko·cyte′
leu″ko·pen′ic
lev″ee
   embankment (*see:* levy)
lev″eed

lev″ee·ing
lev″el
lev″eled
lev″el·er
lev″el·head″ed
lev″el·ing
lev″er
lev″er·age
le·vi″a·than
lev″ied
lev″i·gate′
Le″vi's™
lev″i·tate′
lev″i·tat′ing
lev′i·ta″tion
lev″i·ty
  (*pl.* lev″i·ties)
lev″y
  tax (*pl.* lev″ies)
  (*see:* levee)
lev″y·ing
lewd
lewd″ness
lex′i·cog″ra·pher
lex′i·co·graph″i·cal
lex′i·cog″ra·phy
lex″i·con
Lex″ing·ton
Lha″sa
li′a·bil″i·ty
  (*pl.* li′a·bil″i·ties)
li″a·ble
  responsible; likely
  (*see:* libel)
li′ai·son″
li′ane″
li″ar
  teller of lies (*see:* lyre)
li′ard″
li·ba″tion
lib″bard
li″bel
  defame (*see:* liable)
li″beled
li″bel·ing

li″bel·ous
lib″er·al
lib″er·al·ism′
lib′er·al″i·ty
lib′er·al·i·za″tion
lib″er·al·ize′
lib″er·al·iz′ing
lib″er·al·ly
lib″er·ate′
lib″er·at′ing
lib″er·a″tion
lib″er·a″tor
Li·be″ri·a
lib′er·tar″i·an
lib″er·ti·cide′
lib″er·tine′
lib″er·ty
  (*pl.* lib″er·ties)
li·bid″i·nal
li·bid″i·nous
li·bi″do
li·brar″i·an
li″brar·y
  (*pl.* li″brar·ies)
li·bret″tist
li·bret″to
  (*pl.* li·bret″tos)
Li·bre·ville″
Lib″y·a
li″cense
li″cen·see″
li″cens·ing
li·cen″ti·ate
li·cen″tious
li″chen
  plant (*see:* liken)
li″chen·ous
lich″wake
lic″it
lick″e·ty-split″
lic″o·rice
lid″ded
lie
  rest; deceive (*see:* lye)
Liech″ten·stein

lie″ de·tec″tor
lief
  willingly (*see:* leaf)
liege
liege″dom
lien
  claim (*see:* lean)
lien″cu·lus
lierne
lieu
lieu·ten″an·cy
lieu·ten″ant
life
  (*pl.* lives)
life″ belt′
life″blood′
life″boat′
life″ buoy′
life″guard′
life″ jack′et
life″less
life″like′
life″line′
life″long′
life″ pre·serv′er
life″ raft′
life″root′
life″sav′er
life″-sized″
life″ span′
life″style′
life″time′
life″work″
lift″off′
lig″a·ment
lig″and
lig″a·ture
lig″a·tur·ing
light″ed
light″en
light″face′
light″-fin″gered
light″-foot″ed
light″-head″ed
light″heart″ed
light″house′

light"ing
light"ly
light"mind'ed
light"ness
light"ning
light"ship'
lights"man
light"weight'
light"-year'
lig"ne·ous
lig"ni·fy'
lig"nite
lik"a·ble
liked
like"li·er
like"li·hood'
like"ly
like"-mind"ed
lik"en
   compare (*see:* li-chen)
like"ness
like"wise'
lik"ing
li"lac
li·lack"y
lil"i·a'ceous
lil"y
   (*pl.* lil"ies)
lil"y-white"
lilt
lilt"ing
Li"ma
li"ma bean'
li"mail
limb
   branch; arm (*see:* limn)
lim"bec
lim"ber
lim"bo
lim"burg·er
lime'ade"
lime"light'
lim"er·ick
lime"stone'

lim"ing
lim"it·a·ble
lim"i·tal
lim"i·ta"tion
lim"it·ed
lim"mock
limn
   portray (*see:* limb)
lim"ner
Li·moges"
lim"ou·sine'
lim"pid
limp"ly
lim"y
lin"age
   lines (*see:* lineage)
linch"pin'
lin"den
lin"e·a
lin"e·age
   ancestry (*see:* linage)
lin"e·al
lin"e·a·ment
   feature (*see:* lini-ment)
lin"e·ar
lin"e·ate
line"back'er
line" drive"
lin"e·i·form
line"man
lin"en
lin"er
lines"man
line"-up
ling"ber·ries
lin"ger
lin"ge·rie"
lin"go
   (*pl.* lin"goes)
lin"gua
lin"gua fran"ca
lin"gual
lin·gui"ni
lin"guist
lin·guis"tics

lin"gul·i·fer'ous
lin"i·ment
   medication (*see:* lin-eament)
lin"ing
link"age
link"men
links
   golf course (*see:* lynx)
link"up'
lin"net
lin"o·cut'
li·no"le·um
li·non'o·pho"bi·a
Li"no·type'™
li·nox"yn
lin"seed'
lin"sey-wool"sey
lint
lin"tel
li"on
li"on·ess
li"on·et'
li"on-heart'ed
li'on·i·za"tion
li"on·ize
li"on·iz'ing
lip"id
lip"o·ma'ta
lip"o·pod
lip"o·tro'pin
lip"-read'
lip" ser'vice
lip"stick'
liq'ue·fac"tion
liq'ue·fi'a·ble
liq'ue·fied
liq'ue·fi'er
liq'ue·fy'
liq'ue·fy'ing
li·ques"cent
li·queur"
   strong liquor (*see:* liquor)
liq"uid

liq″ui·date′
liq″ui·dat′ing
liq′ui·da″tion
liq′ui·da′tor
li·quid″i·ty
li·quid·ize′
liq′ui·fy′
liq″uor
  liquid; alchoholic
    drink (*see:* liqueur)
Lis″bon
lisle
lisp
lisp″er
lis″some
lis″ten
lis″ten·er
list″ing
list″less
list″ price′
lit″a·ny
  (*pl.* lit″a·nies)
li″tchi nut′
li″ter
lit″er·a·cy
lit″er·al
  exact (*see:* littoral)
lit″er·al·ly
lit″er·ar′y
lit″er·ate
lit′e·ra″ti
lit″er·a·ture
li·tharge″
lithe
lithe″some
lith″ite
lith″i·um
lith′o·chrom′a·tog″ra·
  phy
lith′o·did″
lith·og″e·ny
lith″o·graph′
li·thog″ra·pher
li·thog″ra·phy
lith′o·log″i·cal·ly
lith′o·pho·tog″ra·phy

lith″o·sphere′
Lith′u·a″ni·a
lit″i·ga·ble
lit″i·gant
lit″i·gate′
lit″i·gat′ing
lit′i·ga″tion
li·ti″gious
lit″mus
lit″ter·bag′
lit″ter·bug′
lit″tle
Lit″tle Rock′
lit″to·ral
  shore (*see:* literal)
li·tur″gi·cal
li·tur″gi·cal·ly
lit″ur·gist
lit″ur·gy
  (*pl.* lit″ur·gies)
litz
liv″a·ble
live″-a·board
live″bear·er
live″-in″
live″li·hood′
live″li·ness
live″long′
live″ly
liv″en
liv″er
liv″er·ied
liv″er·wurst′
liv″er·y
  (*pl.* liv″er·ies)
live″stock′
liv″id
liv″ing room′
li·xiv″i·at′ed
liz″ard
lla″ma
  animal (see: lama)
lla″no
  (*pl.* lla″nos)
load

thing carried (*see:*
  lode)
load″ed
load″ing
loaf
  (*pl.* loaves)
loaf″er
loam″y
loan
  lend (*see:* lone)
loath
  reluctant (*see:*
  loathe)
loathe
  dislike (*see:* loath)
loath″ing
loath″some
lob
  hurl (*see:* lobe)
lob″bied
lob″bing
lob″by
  (*pl.* lob″bies)
lob″by·ing
lob″by·ist
lobe
  projection (*see:* lob)
lo″bo
  (*pl.* lo″bos)
lo·bot″o·my
  (*pl.* lo·bot″o·mies)
lob″ster
lo″cal
lo·cale′
lo·cal″i·ty
  (*pl.* lo·cal″i·ties)
lo′cal·i·za″tion
lo″cal·ize′
lo″cal·iz′ing
lo″cal·ly
lo″cate
lo″cat·ing
lo·ca″tion
loc″a·tive
loch
  lake (*see:* lock)

lock
   door device; canal;
   curl (*see:* loch)
lock"a·ble
lock"er room'
lock"et
lock"fast'
lock"jaw'
lock"ma·ker
lock"out'
lock"smith'
lock"spit'
lock" step'
lock"up'
lo'co·mo"tion
lo'co·mo"tive
lo"co·weed'
loc"u·late'
lo"cus
   (*pl.* lo"ci)
lo"cust
lo·cu"tion
lode
   metallic ore (see:
   load)
lodes"men
lode"star
lode"stone
lodge
   house (*see:* loge)
lodg"er
lodg"ing
lodg"ment
lo·ess"
loft
loft"i·er
loft"i·ly
loft"i·ness
loft"y
lo"gan·ber'ry
log"a·rithm'
log'a·rith"mic
log"cock'
loge
   theater mezzanine
   (*see:* lodge)

log"ger·head'
log"gia
log"ging
log"ic
log"i·cal
log"i·cal·ly
lo·gi"cian
lo·gi"ci·ty
lo·gis"tic
lo·gis"ti·cal
lo·gis"tics
log"jam'
lo"go
lo·gol"a·try
lo·go·met"ric
log"-on
log"o·type'
log"roll'ing
log"work'
loin"cloth'
loi"ter
lol"li·pop'
lom"mock
Lon"don
lone
   single (*see:* loan)
lone"li·er
lone"li·ness
lone"ly
lone"some
long"a·cre'
Long" Beach'
long"cloth'
long"-dis"tance
long"-drawn" out"
lon·gev"i·ty
long"hair"
long"-haired'
long"hand'
long"horn'
lon"gi·tude'
lon'gi·tu"di·nal
lon'gi·tu"di·nal·ly
long"-lived"
long" play"ing
long"-range"

long"shore'man
long"-sight"ed
long" stand"ing
long"-suf"fer·ing
long"-term"
long"time'
lon"gueurs
long"-wind'ed
look"er-on'
   (*pl.* look"ers-on')
look"ing glass'
look"out'
look" see'
loom
loon
looped
loop"hole'
loop" the loop"
loose
   not tight (*see:* lose)
loosed
loose"-joint"ed
loose"-leaf'
loose"ly
loose"ness
loos"ing
loot
   things stolen (*see:*
   lute)
lop
   chop (*see:* lope)
lope
   easy stride (*see:* lop)
lop"ing
   striding (*see:* lop-
   ping)
lop"ping
   chopping (*see:* lop-
   ing)
lop"sid"ed
lo·qua"cious
lo·quac"i·ty
lord"ing
lord"ly
lor·do"sis
lor·do"tic

lord″ship
lore
lor·gnette″
lor″ry
  (*pl.* lor″ries)
Los An″ge·les
lose
  misplace (*see:* loose)
los″er
los″ing
loss
  (*pl.* loss″es)
lo·thar″i·o
lo″tion
lot″ter·y
  (*pl.* lot″ter·ies)
lot″to
lo″tus
  (*pl.* lo″tus·es)
louch
loud″mouth′
loud″mouthed′
loud″speak′er
Lou·i′si·an″a
Lou″is·ville′
lounge
loung″ing
loured
louse
  (*pl.* lice)
lous″ing
lous″y
lout″ish
lou″ver
lov″a·ble
love″ af·fair′
love″bird′
love″less
love″li·er
love″li·ness
love″lorn′
love″ly
love″mak′ing
love″ seat′
love″sick′
lov″ing

low″boy′
low″bred″
low″brow′
low″-cal″
Low″ Church″
low″-down′
low″er
low″er-case″
low″er·class″men
low″er·most′
low″-keyed″
low″land
low″-lev″el
low″lif·er
low″light′
low″li·ness
low″ly
Low″ Mass′
low″-mind″ed
low″-pres″sure
low″-priced″
low″ pro″file
low″-spir″it·ed
low″tech
low-tide″
low″wood
lox″o·drome′
lox″ot′ic
loy″al
loy″al·ist
loy″al·ly
loy″al·ty
  (pl. loy″al·ties)
loz″enge
Lu·an″da
lu·au″
lub″ber
lu″bri·cant
lu″bri·cate′
lu″bri·cat′ing
lu″bri·ca″tion
lu″bri·ca′tor
lu·bri″cious
lu″cent
lu″cid
lu·cid″i·ty

Lu″cite™
luck″i·er
luck″i·ly
luck″i·ness
luck″y
lu″cra·tive
lu″cre
lu″crum
lu″cu·bra″tion
lu″cu·lent″ly
lud″den
lu″di·crous
lug
lug″gage
lug″ging
lu·gu″bri·ous
luke″warm″
lull
lull″a·bied′
lull″a·by
  (*pl.* lull″a·bies)
lull″a·by′ing
lum″bang
lum″bar
  of loins (*see;* lumber)
lum″ber
  wood (*see:* lumbar)
lum″ber·jack′
lum″ber·man′
lum″ber·mill′
lum″ber·yard′
lu″men
  (*pl.* lu″mi·na)
lu″mi·nar′y
  (*pl.* lu″mi·nar′ies)
lu′mi·nesce″
lu′mi·nes″cence
lu′mi·nesc″ing
lum′i·nif″er·ous
lu′mi·nos″i·ty
lu″mi·nous
lum″mox
lump″i·er
lump″ish
lump″y

lu″na·cy
 (*pl.* lu″na·cies)
lu″nar
lu″nar·ist′
lu″na·tic
lunch″eon
lunch′eon·ette″
lunch″room′
lunch″time′
lung
lunge
lung″ing
lu″pine
lu″pus
lurch
lure
lu″rid
lur″ing
lurk
Lu·sa″ka
lus″cious
lus″ter
lust″ful
lust″ful·ly
lust″i·er
lust″i·ly
lust″i·ness
lus″trous
lust″y
lute
 musical instrument
 (*see:* loot)
Lu″ther·an
lut″ing
lut″ist
Lux″em·bourg′
lux·u″ri·ance
lux·u″ri·ant
lux·u″ri·ate′
lux·u″ri·at′ing
lux′u″ri·ous
lux″u·ry
 (*pl.* lux″u·ries)
ly″art
ly·can″throp′y
ly·ce″um

lye
 chemical (*see:* lie)
ly″ing-in′
lym·phat″ic
lymph′a·tol″y·sis
lym·pho″bia
lynch
lynx
 animal (*pl.* lynx″es)
 (*see:* links)
ly′on·naise″
lyre
 harp (*see:* liar)
lyr″ic
lyr″i·cal
lyr″i·cal·ly
lyr″i·cism′
lyr″i·cist′

M

ma·ca″bre
mac·ad″am
mac·a·da″mi·a nut″
mac·ad″am·ize′
mac·ad″am·iz′ing
mac·a·ro″ni
mac·a·roon″
ma·caw″
mac′chi·net″ta
mace
mac″er·a·ble′
mac″er·ate′
mac′er·a″tion
ma·chet″e
Mach′i·a·vel″li·an
mach″i·nate′
mach″i·nat′ing
mach′i·na″tion
ma·chine″
ma·chine″ gun′
ma·chine″ gun′ning
ma·chin″er·y
ma·chin″ing
ma·chin″ist

ma·chis″mo
ma″cho
mack″er·el
 (*pl.* mack″er·el)
mack″i·naw′
mack″in·tosh′
 raincoat (*see:* McIntosh)
mac″ra·me′
mac′ro·bi·ot″ics
mac″ro·cosm′
mac′ro·cos″mic
mac′ro·e′co·nom″ics
mac′ro·fos″sil
mac″ro·mere′
ma″cron
mac′ro·scop″ic
mac″u·late′
mac″u·lat′ing
mac·u·la″tion
Mad′a·gas″car
mad″am
mad″ame
 (*pl.* mes·dames″)
mad″cap′
mad″den
mad″der
ma·dei″ra
mad′e·moi·selle″
 (*pl.* mad′e·moi·selles″)
made″-to-or″der
made″-up′
mad″house′
mad″ly
mad″man′
mad″ness
Ma·don″na
Ma·drid″
mad″ri·gal
mael″strom
maes″tro
 (*pl.* maes″tros)
ma″fi·a
maf″flin′
mag′a·zine″

ma·gen"ta
mag"got
mag"got·y
ma"gi
mag"ic
mag"i·cal
mag"i·cal·ly
ma·gi"cian
mag·is·te"ri·al
mag"is·trate
mag"ma
mag"na cum lau"de
mag'na·nim"i·ty
mag·nan"i·mous
mag"nate
  wealthy man (*see:*
  magnet)
mag·ne"sia
mag·ne"si·um
mag"net
  attracting object
  (*see:* magnate)
mag·net"ic
mag"net·ism'
mag"net·i·za"tion
mag"net·ize'
mag"net·iz'ing
mag·ne"to
  (*pl.* mag·ne"tos)
mag'ne·tom"e·ter
mag'ne·to·trans"mit·
  ter
mag'ni·fi·ca"tion
mag·nif"i·cence
mag·nif"i·cent
mag"ni·fied
mag"ni·fi'er
mag"ni·fy'
mag"ni·fy'ing
mag·nil"o·quence
mag·nil"o·quent
mag"ni·tude'
mag·no"lia
mag"num
mag"pie
ma'ha·ra"jah

ma'ha·ra"ni
ma·hat"na
mah'-jongg"
ma·hog"a·ny
ma·hout"
mah"zors
maid"en·hair'
maid"en·hood'
maid"en·ly
maid"en·weed'
maid"-in-wait"ing
  (*pl.* maids"-in-wait"
  ing)
maid" of hon"or
maid"ser'vant
mail
  letters; armor (*see:*
  male)
mail"bag
mail"box'
mail"man
mail" or'der
maim
main
  principal (*see:* mane
  and Maine)
Maine
  state (*see:* main and
  mane)
main"frame'
main"land
main"line"
main"mast
main"sail
main"sheet
main"spring'
main"stay
main"stream'
mains"worn
main·tain'
main"te·nance
mai'tre d'ho·tel"
maize
  corn (*see:* maze)
ma·jes"tic
ma·jes"ti·cal·ly

maj"es·ty
  (*pl.* maj"es·ties)
ma·jol"i·ca
ma"jor
Ma·jor"ca
ma'jor·ette"
ma·jor"i·ty
  (*pl.* ma·jor"i·ties)
ma·jus"cule
make"-be·lieve
make"-read'y
make"shift'
make"up'
make"-work'
mak"ing
mal"a·chite
mal'ad·just"ed
mal'ad·just"ment
mal'ad·min"is·ter
mal'ad·min"is·tra"
  tion
mal'a·droit"
mal'a·dy
  (*pl.* mal"a·dies)
Ma"la·ga
ma·laise"
Mal'a·kai"
mal'a·prop·ism'
mal'ap·ro·pos"
ma·lar"i·a
ma·lar"i·al
ma·lar"key
mal'as·so·ci·a"tion
Ma·la"wi
Ma·lay"sia
mal·be·hav"ior
mal"con·tent
mal de mer"
male
  masculine (*see:*
  mail)
mal'e·dic"tion
mal'e·fac"tor
ma·lef"i·cence
ma·lef"i·cent
mal"e·mute'

male"ness
ma·lev"o·lence
ma·lev"o·lent
mal·fea"sance
mal·fea"sant
mal'for·ma"tion
mal·formed"
mal·for"tune
mal·func"tion
Ma"li
ma"lic
mal"ice
ma·li"cious
ma·lign"
ma·lig"nan·cy
  (*pl.* ma·lig"nan·
  cies)
ma·lig"nant
ma·lig"ni·ty
ma·lin"ger
ma·lin"ger·er
mall
  area (*see:* maul)
mal"lard
mal'le·a·bil"i·ty
mal"le·a·ble
mal"let
mal"low
malm"sey
mal'nour"ished
mal'nu·tri"tion
mal·oc·clu"sion
mal·o"dor·ous
mal·prac"tice
Mal"ta
malt"ase
malt"ed milk"
Mal·thu"si·an
malt"ose
mal·treat"
mam"ba
mam"bo
mam·mif"er·ous
mam"mal
mam·ma"li·an
mam"ma·ry

mam"mo·gram'
mam·mog"ra·phy
mam"mon
mam"moth
man"a·cle
man"a·cling
man"age
man'age·a·bil"i·ty
man"age·a·ble
man"age·ment
man"a·ger
man'a·ge"ri·al
man"ag·ing
Ma·na"gua
ma·na"na
man"-at-arms"
  (*pl.* men"-at-arms")
man"a·tee'
man·con"o
Man·chu"ri·a
man"da·la
man·da"mus
Man da·lay"
man"da·rin
man"date
man"dat·ing
man"da·to'ry
man·del"ic
man"di·ble
man"do·lin
man"drake
man"drel
  support (*see:* man-
  drill)
man"drill
  baboon (*see:* man-
  drel)
man'du·ca"ting
mane
  hair (*see:* main and
  Maine)
ma·nege"
  horsemanship (*see:*
  manage)
ma·neu"ver
ma·neu'ver·a·bil"i·ty

ma·neu"ver·a·ble
man"ful·ly
man·gan"bru·cite'
man"ga·nese
mange
man"ger
man"gi·er
man"gle
man"gling
man"go
  (*pl.* man"goes)
man"grove
man"gy
man"han'dle
man"han'dling
Man·hat"tan
man"hole'
man"hood
man"-hour'
man"hunt
ma"ni·a
ma"ni·ac
ma·ni"a·cal
ma·ni"a·cal·ly
man"ic-de·pres"sive
man"i·chord'
ma·ni·cot"ti
man"i·cure'
man"i·cur'ing
man"i·cur'ist
man"i·fest'
man'i·fes·ta"tion
man"i·fes'ting
man'i·fes"to
  (*pl.* man'i·fes"toes)
man"i·fold'
man"i·kin
Ma·nil"a
ma·nip"u·la·ble
ma·nip"u·late
ma·nip"u·lat'ing
ma·nip'u·la"tion
ma·nip"u·la'tive
Man'i·to"ba
man"kind
man"li·er

man″li·ness
man″ly
man″-made″
man″na
manned
man″ne·quin
man″ner
  way; sort (*see:* manor)
man″ner·a′ble
man″ner·ism′
man″ner·ly
man″ning
man″nish
man″-of-war″
  (*pl.* men″-of-war″)
ma·nom″e·ter
man″or
  estate (*see:* manner)
ma·no″ri·al
man″pow′er
man″sard
man″serv″ant
  (*pl.* men″serv″ant)
man″sion
man″-sized
man″slaugh″ter
man″ti·core′
man″ta ray
man″tel
  shelf (*see:* mantle)
man″tel·piece
man·til″la
man″tle
  cloak (*see:* mantel)
man″tling
man″u·al
man″u·al·ly
man″u·bri′al
man′u·fac″ture
man′u·fac″tur·er
man′u·fac″tur·ing
man″u·mis″sion
man″u·mit″
man″u·mit″ting
ma·nure″

ma·nur″ing
man″u·script
man″y sid″ed
Mao″ism
Mao″ist
ma″ple su′gar
ma″ple syrup
map″ping
mar
mar″a·bou′
ma·ra″ca
mar′a·schi″no
mar″a·thon
ma·raud″er
mar″ble
mar″ble cake
mar″bling
mar·cel″
march
  (*pl.* march″es)
March
mar″chion·ess
Mar″di Gras
mare's″-nest
mar″ga·rine
mar″gin
mar′gin·al
mar′gi·na″li·a
mar″gin·al·ly
mar″grave
ma′ri·a″chi
ma″ri·gold′
ma′ri·jua″na
ma·rim″ba
ma·ri″na
mar″i·nade
ma·ri·na″ra
mar″i·nate′
mar″i·nat′ing
mar′i·na″tion
ma·rine″
mar″i·ner
mar′i·o·nette″
mar″i·tal
mar″i·time′
mar″jo·ram

mark″down′
marked
mark″er
mar″ket
mar′ket·a·bil″i·ty
mar″ket·a·ble
mar″ket·ing
mar″ket·place′
mark″ing
marks″man
  (*pl.* marks″men)
marks″man·ship′
mark″up′
mar″lin
  fish (*see:* marline)
mar″line
  cord (*see:* marlin)
mar″line·spike
mar″ma·lade
mar″mo·set
mar″mot
ma·roon″
marque
mar·quee″
mar″que·try
mar″quis
mar·quise″
mar″qui·sette″
mar″ram
mar″riage
mar″riage·a·ble
mar″ried
mar″ring
mar″ron
mar″row·bone
mar″ry
  unite (*see:* merry)
mar″ry·ing
Mars
Mar·seilles″
mar″shal
  sheriff; order (*see:*
  martial)
mar″shal·ing
marsh″ber·ries
marsh″i·er

marsh''mal'low
marsh''y
mar·su''pi·al
mar''ten
  animal (*see:* martin)
mar''tial
  military (*see:* mar-
  shal)
mar''tin
  bird (*see:* marten)
mar'ti·net''
mar''tin·gale
mar·ti''ni
mar·tite''
mar''tyr
mar''tyr·dom
mar''vel
mar''veled
mar''vel·ing
mar''vel·ous
Marx''ism
Marx''ist
Mar''y·land
mar''zi·pan
mas·car''a
mas''cot
mas''cu·line
mas'cu·lin''i·ty
mas'cu·lin·ize'
mash''er
mash''ie
mask
  covering (*see:*
  masque)
mas''och·ism'
mas''och·ist
mas'och·is''tic
ma''son
ma·son''ic
ma''son·ry
masque
  drama (*see:* mask)
mas'quer·ade''
mas'quer·ad''er
mas'quer·ad''ing
mass

(*pl.* mass''es)
Mas''sa·chu''setts
mas''sa·cre
mas''sa·cring
mas·sage''
mas·sag''ing
mas·seur''
mas·seuse''
mas''sif
  mountain (*see:* mas-
  sive)
massive
  large (*see:* massif)
mass'' me''di·a
mass''-pro·duce''
mass''-pro·duc''ing
mass'' pro·duc''tion
mas·tec''to·my
  (*pl.* mas·tec''to·
  mies)
mas''ter-at-arms''
  (*pl.* mas''ters-at-
  arms'')
mas''ter·ful
mas''ter·ful·ly
mas''ter·hood
mas''ter·ly
mas''ter·mind
mas''ter·piece''
mas''ter stroke''
mas''ter·work'
mas''ter·y
  (*pl.* mas''ter·ies)
mast''ful
mast''head
mas''tic
mas''ti·cate'
mas''ti·cat'ing
mas''ti·ca''tion
mas''tiff
mas''to·don'
mas''to·don'ic
mas''toid
mas'to·plast''i·a
mas''tur·bate'
mas''tur·bat'ing

mas'tur·ba''tion
mat
  flat object (*see:*
  matte)
mat''a·dor
mat''a·pan
match''board'
match''book'
match''box'
match''less
match''lock'
match''mak'er
match''mak'ing
match''wood'
mate
mate''milk'
ma·te''ri·al
  matter (*see:* mate-
  riel)
ma·te''ri·al·ism'
ma·te''ri·al·is''tic
ma·te''ri·al·is''ti·cal·ly
ma·te''ri·al·i·za''tion
ma·te''ri·al·ize'
ma·te''ri·al·iz'ing
ma·te''ri·al·ly
ma·te''ri·el''
  supplies (*see:* mate-
  rial)
ma·ter''nal
ma·ter''nal·ly
ma·ter''ni·ty
math'e·mat''i·cal
math'e·mat''i·cal·ly
math'e·ma·ti''cian
math'e·mat''ics
mat'i·nee''
mat''ing''
  joining (*see:* mat-
  ting)
ma''tri·arch
ma''tri·ar''chal
ma''tri·ar'chy
  (*pl.* ma''tri·ar'
  chies)
mat'ri·cid''al

mat″ri·cide′
ma·tric″u·late′
ma·tric″u·lat′ing
ma·tric′u·la″tion
ma′tri·lin″e·al·ly
mat′ri·mo″ni·al
mat′ri·mo″ni·al·ly
mat″ri·mo′ny
ma″trix
  (*pl.* ma″tri·ces)
ma·tron
ma″tron·ly
matte
  dull (*see:* mat)
mat″ter-of-fact″
mat″ting
  fabric; finish (*see:*
  mating
mat″tock
mat″tress
  (*pl.* mat″tress·es)
mat″u·rate′
mat″u·rat′ing
mat′u·ra″tion
ma·ture″
ma·tur″ing
ma·tu″ri·ty
mat″zo
  (*pl.* mat″zoth)
maud″lin
maul
  handle severely (*see:*
  mall)
maun
maun″der
Maun″dy Thurs″day
Mau′ri·ta″ni·a
Mau·ri″ti·us
mau·so·le″um
mauve
ma″ven
mav″er·ick
maw″bound
mawk″ish
max·il″la
  (*pl.* max·il″lae)

max″il·lar′y
max″im
max″i·mal
max″i·mal·ly
max″i·mate′
max″i·mize′
max″i·miz′ing
max″i·mum
May
Ma″ya
  (*pl.* Ma″yas)
May″ Ap′ple
may″be
may″bush′
May″ Day′
  May 1
may″day′
  signal
may″fly′
  (*pl.* may″flies′)
may″hap
may″hem
may″on·naise′
may″or
may″or·al
may″or·al·ty
  (*pl.* may″or·al·ties)
may″or·ess
may″pole′
maze
  confuse (see: maize)
maz″el tov′
maz″ing
ma·zur″ka
Mc″In·tosh′
  apple (*see:* mackin-
  tosh)
me″a cul″pa
mead″ow
mead″ow·lark·
mea″ger
meal″i·er
meal″time′
meal″y
meal″y-mouthed″
mean

  intend; ill-tempered;
  average
me·an″der
me·an″drous
mean″ing·ful
mean″ing·less
mean″ly
mean″ness
meant
mean″time′
mean″while′
mea″sles
mea″sli·er
mea″sly
meas′ur·a·bil″i·ty
meas″ur·a·ble
meas″ure
meas″ure·less
meas″ure·ment
meas″ur·er
meas″ur·ing
meat
  flesh (*see:* meet and
  mete)
meat″ball′
meat″i·er
meat″less
meat″loaf′
meat″man′
me·a″tus
meat″y
Mec″ca
mech″a·nal·ize
me·chan″i·cal
me·chan″i·cal·ly
me·chan″ics
mech″a·nism′
mech′a·ni·za″tion
mech″a·nize′
mech″a·niz′ing
mech″a·tron″ics
med″al
  flat metal; award
  (*see:* meddle)
med″aled
med″al·ing

med″al·ist
me·dal″lion
med″dle
   interfere (see: medal)
med″dler
med″dle·some
med″dling
med″ e·vac′
me″di·a
   (sing: me″di·um)
me″di·al
me″di·an
me″di·ant′
me″di·ate′
me″di·at′ing
me″di·a″tion
me″di·a′tor
med″ic
med″i·ca·ble
med″i·caid′
med″i·cal
med″i·cal·ly
me·di″ca·ment
Med″i·care′
med″i·cate′
med″i·cat′ing
med″i·ca″tion
me·dic″i·nal
me·dic″i·nal·ly
med″i·cine man
med″i·co
   (pl. med″i·cos)
me′di·e″val
me′di·e″val·ist
me′di·gla″cial
me′di·o″cre
me′di·oc″ri·ty .
   (pl. me′di·oc″ri·ties)
med″i·tate′
med″i·tat′ing
med″i·ta″tion
med″i·ta′tive
med″i·ta′tor
Med′i·ter·ra″ne·an

me″di·um
med″ley
   (pl. med″leys)
me·dul″la
meech
meek″ly
meer″schaum
meet
   encounter (see: meat and mete)
meet″ing
   gathering (see: meting)
meet″ing-house
meg″a·cy″cle
meg″a·hertz′
meg″a·lith
meg′a·lith″ic
meg′a·lo·ceph″a·lous
meg′a·lo·ma″ni·a
meg′a·lo·ma·ni″a·cal
meg′a·lop″o·lis
meg″a·phone
meg″a·ther′mic
meg″a·ton′
meg″a·volt′
meg″a·watt
mei·o″sis
   (pl. mei·o″ses)
mel″a·mine
mel″an·chol″li·a
mel″an·chol″ic
mel″an·chol′y
   (pl. mel″an·chol′ies)
Mel′a·ne″sia
me·lange″
mel″a·nin
mel″a·nite′
mel′a·no″ma
Mel″bourne
me″lee
mel″io·rate′
mel″io·rat′ing
mel″io·ra″tion
mel″io·ra′tive

mel·lif″lu·ous
mel″low
me·lo″de·on
me·lo″di·a
me·lod″ic
me·lod″i·cal·ly
me·lo″di·ous
mel″o·dra′ma
mel′o·dra·mat″ic
mel′o·dra·mat″i·cal·ly
mel″o·dy
   (pl. mel″o·dies)
mel″on
mel″o·poe″ia
melt″down
melt″ing point′
mel″ton
mem″ber·ship′
mem″brane
mem″bra·nous
me·men″to
   (pl. me·men″tos)
mem″oir
mem′o·ra·bil″i·a
mem″o·ra·ble
mem′o·ran″dum
me·mo″ri·al
me·mo′ri·al·i·za″tion
me·mo″ri·al·ize′
me·mo″ri·al·iz′ing
mem′o·ri·za″tion
mem″o·rize
mem″o·riz′ing
mem″o·ry
   (pl. mem″o·ries)
Mem″phis
men″ace
men″ac·ing·ly
me·nage″
   household (see: manege)
me·nag″er·ie
men·da″cious
men·dac″i·ty
Men·de″li·an
men″di·cant

men''folks
me''ni·al
me·nin''ges
  (*sing.* me''ninx)
men''in·gi''tis
me·nis''cus
  (*pl.* me·nis''cus·es)
men''i·son'
Men''non·ite
men'o·paus''al
men''o·pause
men·o''rah
mensch
men''ses
men''stru·al
men''stru·ate'
men''stru·at'ing
men'stru·a''tion
men·sur·a·bil''i·ty
men'sur·a·ble
men'su·ra''tion
men·tal''i·ty
men''tal·ly
men''the·nol'
men''thol
men''tho·lat'ed
men''tion
men''tion·a·ble
men''tor
men''u
  (*pl.* men''us)
me·ow''
me·phit''ic
mep'ro·bam''ate
mer''can·tile'
mer''can·til·ism'
mer''ce·nar'y
  (*pl.* mer''ce·nar'ies)
mer''cer·ize'
mer''cer·iz'ing
mer''chan·dise
mer''chan·dis'er
mer''chan·dis'ing
mer''chant
mer''ci·ful
mer''ci·ful·ly

mer''ci·less
mer·cu''ri·al
mer·cu''ri·fi·ca''tion
mer·cu''ro·chrome
mer''cu·ry
mer''cy
  (*pl.* mer''cies)
mere
mere''ly
me·ren''gue
  dance (*see:* merin-
  gue)
mer''est
mer'e·tri''cious
merge
merg''er
merg''ing
me·rid''i·an
me·ringue''
  egg white (*see:* me-
  rengue)
me·ri''no
  (*pl.* me·ri''nos)
mer''it
mer'i·toc''ra·cy
mer''i·to·crat
mer'i·to''ri·ous
mer''maid'
mer'o·sto·ma''tous
mer''ri·er
mer''ri·ly
mer''ri·ment
mer''ry
  cheerful (*see:*
  marry)
mer''ry-go-round'
mer''ry·mak'er
mes'al''liance''
mes·cal''
mes''ca·line'
mes·dames''
mes'de·moi·selles''
mesh''work'
mes''mer·ism'
mes''mer·ize'
mes''mer·iz'er

mes''mer·iz'ing
mes''mer·o·man·i·a
mes'o·ceph'al'
mes''o·derm'
mes''o·morph'
mes'o·mor''phic
me''son
mes'o·nas''al
Mes'o·po·ta''mi·a
mes''quin
mes·quite''
mes''sage
mes''sen·ger
mess'' hall'
Mes·si''ah
Mes'si·an''ic
mess'i·er
mes''sieurs
mess''i·ly
mess''i·ness
mess'' kit'
mess''mate'
messy
mes·ti''zo
  (*pl.* mes·ti''zos)
met'a·bol''ic
me·tab''o·lism'
me·tab''o·lite'
me·tab''o·lize'
me·tab''o·liz'ing
met'a·car''pal
met'a·crom''i·al
met'a·ge·net''i·cal·ly
met''al
  iron, etc. (*see:* met-
  tle)
met'al·ing
me·tal''lic
met'al·lur''gic
met'al·lur''gi·cal
met''al·lur'gist
met''al·lur'gy
met''al·work'
met'a·mor''phic
met'a·mor''phism
met'a·mor''phos·ing

met'a·mor''pho·sis
  (*pl.* met'a·mor''pho·
  ses')
met'a·nil''ic
met'a·phor'
met'a·phor''ic
met'a·phor''i·cal·ly
met'a·phys''i·cal
met'a·phy·si''cian
met'a·phys''ics
me·tas''ta·sis
  (*pl.* me·tas''ta·ses')
me·tas''ta·size'
me·tas''ta·siz'ing
met'a·tar''sal
mete
  allot; limit (*see:*
  meat and meet
me''te·or
me''te·or''i·cal·ly
me''te·or·ite'
me''te·or·oid'
me''te·or·o·log''i·cal·
  ly
me''te·or·ol''o·gist
me''te·or·ol''o·gy
me''ter
me''ter maid'
meth''a·done'
meth''ane
meth''a·nol'
me·thod''ic
me·thod''i·cal·ly
Meth''od·ist
meth'od·o·log''i·cal
meth'od·ol''o·gy
  (*pl.* meth'od·ol''o·
  gies)
meth''yl
me·tic''u·lous
me''tier
met''ing
  alloting (*see:*
  meeting)
me·ton''y·my
me-too''ism

met''ric
met''ri·cal
met''ri·ca''tion
met''rics
met''ro
me·trol''o·gy
  (*pl.* me·trol''o·gies)
met''ro·nome'
met''ro·nom''ic
me·trop''o·lis
met'ro·pol''i·tan
met''tle
  courage (*see:* metal)
met''tle·some
mews
  street (*see:* muse)
Mex''i·co'
me·zu''zah
mez''za·nine'
mez''zo
mez''zo-so·pran''o
  (*pl.* mez''zo-so·
  pran''os)
mez''zo·tint'
Mi·am''i
mi·as''ma
mi·as''mal
mi·as''mat''ic
mi·as''mic
mi''ca
Mich''ael·mas
Mich''i·gan
mic''kle'
Mic''mac
  (*pl.* Mic''mac)
mic''ri·fy'
mi''cro
mi''crobe
mi·cro''bi·al
mi·cro·bi'o·log''i·cal
mi''cro·bi·ol''o·gist
mi''cro·bi·ol''o·gy
mi''cro·cam''e·ra'
mi''cro·cir''cuit
mi''cro·com·put''er
mi''cro·cop'y

mi''cro·cosm'
mi''cro·cos''mic
mi''cro·cos''mi·cal
mi''cro·dot'
mi·cro·e'co·nom''ics
mi''cro·es'ti·ma''tion
mi''cro·fiche'
mi''cro·film'
mi''cro·form'
mi''cro·gas'trine
mi''cro·gram''
mi''cro·groove'
mi''cro·li''ter
mi·crom''e·ter
  measuring device
mi''cro·met''er
  unit of measure
mi''cro·min'e·ral·o''gy
Mi''cro·ne''sia
mi''cro·or''gan·ism'
mi''cro·phone'
mi''cro·pho''to·graph'
mi''cro·print'
mi''cro·proc''es·sor
mi''cro·scope'
mi''cro·scop''ic
mi''cro·scop''i·cal·ly
mi·cros''co·pist
mi·cros''co·py
mi''cro·ton'al
mi''cro·volt'
mi''cro·watt'
mi''cro·wave'
mid·air''
mid''day''
mid''dle age''
mid''dle-aged''
Mid''dle Ag'es
mid''dle·brow'
mid''dle class''
Mid''dle East''
mid''dle·man'
mid''dle-of-the-road
mid''dle school''
mid''dle-sized'
mid''dle·weight'

Mid"dle West"
Mid"dle West"ern
mid"dling
mid"dy
  blouse (*pl.* mid"
  dies) (*see:* midi)
Mid"east"
midg"et
mid"i
  skirt (*see:* middy)
mid"i'ron
mid"night'
mid"point
mid"rib'
mid"riff'
mid"sec'tion
mid"ship'man
midst
mid"stream"
mid"sum"mer
mid"tar'sal
mid"term'
mid"-Vic·to·ri"an
mid"way'
mid"week'
Mid"west"
Mid·west"ern
mid"wife'
  (*pl.* mid"wives)
mid"wife'ry
mid"win"ter
mid"wise'
mid"year'
mien
  bearing (*see:* mean)
MIG
might
  strength (*see:* mite)
might"i·er
might"i·ly
might"i·ness
might"y
mi"graine
mi"grant
mi"grate
mi"grat·ing

mi·gra"tion
mi"gra·to'ry
mi·ka"do
  (*pl.* mi·ka"dos)
mik"ron
mil
  unit of length (*see:*
  mill)
mi·la"dy
milch
mil"dew
mild"ly
mile"age
mile"post'
mil"er
mile"stone
mi·lieu"
mil"i·tan·cy
mil"i·tant
mil"i·tar"i·ly
mil'i·ta·ris"tic
mil'i·ta·ri·za"tion
mil"i·ta·rize'
mil"i·ta·riz'ing
mil"i·tar'y
mil"i·tate
mil"i·tat'ing
mi·li"tia
mi·li"tia·man
milk"i·er
milk"i·ness
milk"maid
milk"man
milk"shake
milk"sop
milk" toast')
  food (*see:* milque-
  toast)
milk"weed'
milk"wort'
milk"y
Milk"y Way"
mill
  factory; move about
  (*see:* mil)

mill"dam'
mille"fleur'
mil·len"ni·al
mil·len"ni·um
mill"er
mill"let
mil"liard
mil"li·bar
mil"li·gram'
mil"li·li'ter
mil"li·me'ter
mil"li·ner
mil"li·ner'y
mill"ing
mil"lion
mil"lion·aire"
mil"lionth
mil"li·pede
mil"li·sec'ond
mill"pond'
mill"race'
mill"rind'
mill"stone'
mill"stream'
mill"work'
mill"wright'
mi·lord"
milque"toast"
  timid person (*see:*
  milk toast)
Mil·wau"kee
mim"bar
mime
mim"e·o·graph'
mi·me"sis
mi·met"ic
mim"ic
mim"ick·ing
mim"ic·ry
  (*pl.* mim"ic·ries)
mim"ing
mim"o·dram'a
mi·mo"sa
min"a·ret"
min"a·to'ry
mince

mince"meat'
minc"ing
mind"ed
mind"ful
mind"ful·ly
mind"less
mine"field
mine"lay'er
min"er
  one who mines (*see:*
  minor)
min"er·al
min"er·al·i·za"tion
min"er·al·ize
min"er·al·iz'ing
min"er·al·og"i·cal
min"er·al"o·gist
min"er·al"o·gy
min·e·stro"ne
mine"sweep'er
min"gle
min"gling
ming"wort
min"i·a·ture
min"i·a·tur·i·za"tion
min"i·a·tur·ize
min"i·a·tur·iz'ing
min"i·bus'
min"i·mal
min"i·mal·ly
min"i·mi·za"tion
min"i·mize'
min"i·miz'ing
min"i·mum
min"i·ing
min"ion
min"i·se'ries
min"i·skirt'
min"is·ter
min"is·te"ri·al
min"is·trant
min"is·tra"tion
min"is·try
  (*pl.* min"is·tries)
min"i·track
mink

Min'ne·ap"o·lis
min"ne·sing'er
Min'ne·so"ta
Min'ne·ton"ka
min"now
mi"nor
  lesser (*see:* miner)
mi·nor"i·ty
  (*pl.* mi·nor"i·ties)
min"strel
min"strel·sy
mint"age
mint"y
min"u·end
min"u·et"
mi"nus
mi·nus"cu·lar
mi"nus·cule'
mi·nute", *adj.*
  tiny
min"ute, *n.*
  time unit
mi·nute"ly
mi·nut"er
mi·nu"ti·ae'
  (*pl.* mi·nu"ti·a)
minx
mir"a·cle
mi·rac"u·lous
mi·rage"
mire
mir"i·er
mir"ing
mir"ror
mirth
mirth"ful
mirth"ful·ly
mir"y
mis'ac·cep"tion
mis'ad·ven"ture
mis"an·thrope'
mis'an·throp"ic
mis·an"thro·py
mis'ap·pli·ca"tion
mis'ap·ply"
  mis'ap·plied"

mis'ap·ply"ing
mis'ap·pre·hend"
mis'ap·pre·hen"sion
mis'ap·pro"pri·ate'
mis'ap·pro"pri·at'ing
mis'ap·pro·pri·a"tion
mis"arch"ist
mis·be·got"ten
mis·be·have"
mis·be·hav"ing
mis·be·hav"ior
mis·be·lief"
mis·cal"cu·late'
mis·cal"cu·lat'ing
mis·cal·cu·la"tion
mis·car"riage
mis·car"ried
mis·car"ry
mis·car"ry·ing
mis·cast"
mis·ce·ge·na"tion
mis·cel·la"ne·a
mis·cel·la"ne·ous
mis"cel·la'ny
  (*pl.* mis"cel·la'nies)
mis·chance"
mis·char"act·e·rize'
mis"chief
mis"chie·vous
mis"ci·ble
mis·com·pute"
mis·con·ceive"
mis·con·ceived"
mis·con·ceiv"ing
mis·con·cep"tion
mis·con·duct", *v.*
  manage badly
mis·con"duct, *n.*
  bad management
mis·con·struc"tion
mis·con·strue"
mis·con·strued"
mis·con·stru"ing
mis·count"
mis·cov"et
mis·cre"ant

mis·cue"
mis·deal"
mis·deal"ing
mis·dealt"
mis·deed"
mis·de·mean"or
mis'di·rect"
mis'di·rec"tion
mis·ed"u·cate'
mi"ser
mis"er·a·ble
mi"scr·ly
mis"er·y
   (*pl.* mis"er·ies)
mis·fea"sance
mis·file"
mis·fil"ing
mis·fire"
mis·fir"ing
mis"fit
mis·for"tune
mis·giv"ing
mis·gov"ern
mis·graff"
mis·guid"ance
mis·guide"
mis·guid"lng
mis·han"dle
mis·han"dling
mis"hap
mis·hear"
mis·heard"
mis·hear"ing
mish"mash
mish"nah
mis'in·form"
mis'in·for·ma"tion
mis'in·ter"pret
mis'in·ter"pre·ta"tion
mis·judge"
mis·judg"ing
mis·judg"ment
mis·laid"
mis·lay"
mis·lay"ing
mis·lead"

mis·lead"ing
mis·led"
mis·man"age
mis·man"age·ment
mis·man"ag·ing
mis·match"
mis·name"
mis·nam"ing
mis·no"mer
mi·sog"y·nist
mi·sog"y·nous
mi·sog"y·ny
mis·place"
mis·plac"ing
mis·play"
mis·print", *v.*
   print incorrectly
mis"print, *n.*
   error
mis'pro·nounce"
mis'pro·nounc"ing
mis'pro·nun·ci·a"tion
mis'quo·ta"tion
mis·quote"
mis·quot"ing
mis·read"
mis'rep·re·sen·ta"tion
mis·rule"
mis·rul"ing
miss
   (*pl.* misses)
mis"sal
   book (*see:* missile)
mis·shape"
mis·shaped"
mis·shap"en
mis·shap"ing
mis"sile
   aimed object (*see:*
   missal)
miss"ing
mis"sion
mis"sion·ar'y
   (*pl.* mis"sion·ar'
   ies)
Mis'sis·sip"pi

mis"sive
Mis·sou"ri
mis·spell"
mis·spelled"
mis·spell"ing
mis·spend"
mis·spend"ing
mis·spent"
mis·state"
mis·state"ment
mis·stat"ing
mis·step"
mis·step"ping
mist
mis·tak"a·ble
mis·take"
mis·tak"ing
mis"ter
mist"i·er
mist"i·ness
mis"tle·toe
mis·took"
mis"tral
mis·treat"
mis·treat"ment
mis"tress
mis·tri"al
mis·trust"
mist"y
mis'un·der·stand"
mis'un·der·stood"
mis·us"age
mis·use"
mis·us"ing
mite
   tiny arachnid; money
   (*see:* might)
mite·proof"
mi"ter
mit"i·ga·ble
mit"i·gate'
mit"i·gat'ing
mit'i·ga"tion
mit"i·ga'tor
mi'to·chon"dri·on

(*pl.* mi·to·chon''dri·
a)
mi·to''sis
mitt
mit''ten
mixed'-up''
mix''er
mix''ing
mix''ture
mix''-up'
mize
miz''zen·mast'
mne·mon''ic
moan
  sad sound (*see:*
  mown)
moat
  ditch (*see:* mote and
  mot)
mob
mob''bing
Mo·bile''
mo''bile home''
mo·bil''i·ty
mo'bi·li·za''tion
mo''bi·lize'
mo''bi·liz'ing
Mo''bi·us strip
mob·oc''ra·cy
  (*pl.* mob·oc''ra·
  cies)
mob''ster
moc''ca·sin
mo''cha
mock''er·y
  (*pl.* mock''er·ies)
mock''-he·ro''ic
mock''ing·bird
mock''up
mod''al
  of a mode (*see:*
  model)
mo·dal''i·ty
  (*pl.* mo·dal''i·ties)
mode
mod''el

copy (*see:* modal)
mod''el·ing
mo''dem
mod''er·ate
mod''er·at'ing
mod'er·a''tion
mod'e·ra'to
mod''er·a'tor
mod''ern
mod''ern·ism
mod'ern·is''tic
mo·der''ni·ty
  (*pl.* mo·der''ni·ties)
mod'ern·i·za''tion
mod''ern·ize'
mod''ern·iz'ing
mod''est
mod''es·ty
  (*pl.* mod''es·ties)
mod''i·cum
mod i·fi·ca''tion
mod''i·fied
mod''i·fi'er
mod''i·fy
mod''i·fy'ing
mod''ish
mo·diste''
mod''is·try'
mod''u·lar
mod''u·late
mod'u·lat'ing
mod'u·la''tion
mod''u·la'tor
mod'u·la·to'ry
mod''ule
mo''dus o'pe·ran'di
Moe''bi·us
mo''gul
mo''hair
Mo·ha''ve
  (*pl.* Mo·ha''ve)
  (*see:* Mo·ja''ve)
Mo''hawk
  (*pl.* Mo''hawk)
Mo·he''gan
  (*pl.* Mo·he''gan)

Mo·hi''can''
  (*pl.* Mo·hi''can)
moi''e·ty
  (*pl.* moi''e·ties)
moi·re''
mois''ten
mois''ture'
mois'tur·ize
mois''tur·iz'ing
Mo·ja''ve
  (*see:* Mo·ha''ve)
mo''lar
mo·las''ses
mold''a·ble
mold''er
mold''i·er
mold''i·ness
mold''ing
mold''y
mole
mo·lec''u·lar
mol''e·cule'
mole''hill''
mole''skin
mo·lest''
mo·les·ta''tion
mol'li·fi·ca''tion
mol''li·fied'
mol''li·fy
mol''li·fy'ing
mol''lusk
mol''ly·cod'dle
Mol''o·tov'
molt
mol''ten
mol''ton
mo·lyb''de·num
mo''ment
mo'men·tar''i·ly
mo''men·tar'y
mo·men''tous
mo·men''tum
mom''my
Mon''a·co
mo''nad'
mon''arch

mo·nar"chi·cal
mon"ar·chism
mon"ar·chist
mon"ar·chy
  (pl. mon"ar·chies)
mon"as·ter'y
  (pl. mon"as·ter'ies)
mo·nas"tic
mo·nas"ti·cism
mon·au"ral
Mon"day
mon"e·tar"i·ly
mon"e·tar'ism
mon"e·tar'y
mon"e·tize'
mon"e·tiz'ing
mon"ey
  (pl. mon"eys)
mon"ey·bag'
mon"ey·chang'er
mon"eyed
mon"ey·lend'er
mon"ey·mak'er
mon"ey·mak'ing
mon"ger
Mon·go"li·a
mon"gol·ism'
mon"gol·oid'
mon"goose
  (pl. mon"goos'es)
mon"grel
mon"i·ker
mon"ism
mon"ist
mo·nis"tic
mon"i·tor
mon"i·to'ry
  (pl. mon"i·to'ries)
mon"key
  (pl. mon"keys)
mon"key·shine'
mon"key wrench'
monk"ish
mon'o·bro'mi·na"tion
mon'o·cer'os
mon'o·chro·mat"ic

mon"o·chrome'
mon"o·cle
mon'o·cot'y·le"don
mo·noc"u·lar
mon'o·der"mic
mon"o·dy
mo·nog"a·mist
mo·nog"a·mous
mo·nog"a·my
mon"o·gram'
mon"o·graph'
mon"o·lay'er
mon"o·lith'
mon'o·lith"ic
mon"o·logue'
mon"o·logu'ist
mon'o·ma"ni·a
mon'o·ma"ni·ac'
mon'o·ma·ni"a·cal
mon'o·morph"ous
mon'o·nu·cle'o·sis
mon'o·phon"ic
mon"o·plane'
mon'o·plas·ma"tic
mo·nop'o·lis"tic
mo·nop'o·li·za"tion
mo·nop'o·lize'
mo·nop'o·liz'ing
mo·nop'o·ly
  (pl. mo·nop'o·lies)
mon"o·rail'
mon'o·so"di·um glu"
  ta·mate'
mon'o·syl·lab"ic
mon'o·syl"la·ble
mon'o·the·ism
mon'o·the·is"tic
mon"o·tone'
mo·not"o·nous
mo·not"o·ny
mon"o·type'
mon·ox"ide
mon·ro"vi·a
mon·sei·gneur"
  (pl. mons·sei·
  gneurs")

mon·sieur"
  (pl. mes"sieurs)
mon·si"gnor
  (pl. mon·si"gnors)
mon·soon"
mon"ster
mon·stros"i·ty
  mon·stros"i·ties)
mon"strous
mon·tage"
Mon·tan"a
Mon"te Car"lo
Mon"tes·so"ri
Mon"te·vi·de"o
Mont·gom"er·y
month
month"ly
Mon"ti·cel"lo
Mont·pel"ier
Mont"re·al"
mon"u·ment
mon"u·men"tal
mon"u·men"tal·ly
mooch
mooch"er
mood
mood"i·er
mood"i·ly
mood"i·ness
mood"y
moon"beam'
moon"calf'
moon"light'
moon"light'er
moon"light'ing
moon"like'
moon"lit'
moon"scape'
moon"shine'
moon"shin'er
moon"stone'
moon"strick'en
moon"struck'
moon"tide'
moor
moor"age

moor"ing

moose
  deer (*pl.* moose)
  (*see:* mousse and
  mouse)

moose"ber·ry

moot
  questionable (*see:*
  mute)

mop

mope

mo"ped

mop"ing
  brooding (*see:* mop-
  ping)

mop"pet

mop"ping
  cleaning (*see:* mop-
  ing)

mop"-up'

mo·raine"

mor"al
  ethical (*see:* morale)

mo·rale"
  confidence (*see:*
  moral)

mor"al·ist

mor'al·is"ti·cal·ly

mo·ral"i·ty
  (*pl.* mo·ral"i·ties)

mor·al·i·za"tion

mor"al·ize'

mor"al·iz'ine

mo·rass"

mo·ras"sic

mor·a·to"ri·um

mor"bid

mor·bid"i·ty

mor"dan·cy

mor"dant
  biting (*see:* mordent)

mor"dent
  musical term (*see:*
  mordant)

mo·rel"

more·o"ver

mo"res

mor'ga·nat"ic

mor'ga·nat"i·cal·ly

morgue

mor"i·bund'

Mor"mon

morn
  morning (*see:*
  mourn)

morn"ing
  early day (*see:*
  mourning)

morn"ing-glo'ry

morn"ing sick"ness

morn"ing star"

Mo·roc"co

mo"ron

mo·ron"ic

mo·ron"i·cal·ly

mo·rose"

mor"pheme

mor"phine

mor'pho·log"i·cal

mor'pho·log"i·cal·ly

mor·phol"o·gy

mor"ris dance"

mor"row

Morse" code"

mor"sel

mor"tal

mor·tal"i·ty

mor"tal·ly

mor"tar

mor"tar·board'

mort"gage

mort'ga·gee"

mort"gag·ing

mort'a·gor"

mor·ti"cian

mor·ti·fi·ca"tion

mor"ti·fied'

mor"ti·fy

mor"ti·fy'ing

mor"tise

mor"tis·ing

mor"tu·ar'y
  (*pl.* mor"tu·ar'ies)

mo·sa"ic
  picture

mo·sa"ic
  of Moses

Mos"cow

mo"sey

mo"sey·ing

mosque

mos·qui"to
  (*pl.* mos·qui"toes)

moss"back

moss"i·er

moss"like

moss"y

most"ly

mot
  remark (*see:* moat
  and mote)

mote
  particle (*see:* moat
  and mot)

mo·tel"

mo·tet"

moth"ball

moth"-eat'en

moth"er·hood

moth"er-in-law
  (*pl.* moth"ers-in-
  law')

moth"er·land

moth"er·li·ness

moth"er·ly

moth"er-of-pearl"

moth"proof'

moth"y

mo·tif"

mo"tile

mo·til"i·ty

mo"tion·less

mo"tion pic"ture

mo"ti·vate'

mo"ti·vat'ing

mo'ti·va"tion

mo"tive

mot″ley
mo″tor·bike′
mo″tor·boat′
mo″tor·cade′
mo″tor·car′
mo″tor·cy′cle
mo″tor·cy′cling
mo″tor·cy′clist
mo″tor·ist
mo′tor·i·za″tion
mo″tor·ize′
mo″tor·iz′ing
mo″tor lodge′
mo″tor·man′
mo″tor ship′
mo″tor truck′
mot″tle
mot″tling
mot″to
  (*pl.* mot″toes)
moul″i·nage′
mound
mount
mount″a·ble
moun′tain·eer″
moun″tain·ous
moun″tain range′
moun″tain·side′
moun″tain·top′
moun″te·bank′
mount″ed
Mount″ie
mount″ing
mourn
  lament (*see:* morn)
mourn″er
mourn″ful
mourn″ing
  lamenting (*see:*
  morning)
mouse
  rodent (*pl.* mice)
  (*see:* moose)
mous″er
mouse″trap′
mous″i·er

mousse
  dessert (*see:* moose
  and mouse)
mous·se·line″
mous″tache
mou″tan
mouth″ful′
  (*pl.* mouth″fuls′)
mouth″ or′gan
mouth″piece′
mouth″wash′
mouth″-wa′ter·ing
mou″ton
  sheepskin (*see:* mut-
  ton)
mov′a·bil″i·ty
mov′a·ble
move″ment
mov″ie
mov″ie·go′er
mov″ing pic″ture
mow
mowed
mow″er
mow″ing
mown
  cut (*see:* moan)
mow″rah
mox″ie
Mo′zam·bique′
moz′za·rel″la
much
mu″ci·lage
mu′ci·lag″i·nous
muck″rake′
muck″rak′er
muck″rak′ing
muck″y
mu″co·cele′
mu″cous, *adj.*
  slimy
mu″cus, *n.*
  secretion
mud″der
mud″died
mud″di·er

mud″di·ness
mud″dle
mud″dle-head′ed
mud″dle·some′
mud″dling
mud″dy
mud″dy·ing
mud″guard′
mud″pack
mud″sling′er
mud″sling′ing
muen″ster
mu·ez″zin
muff
muf″fin
muf″fle
muf″fler
muf″fling
muf″ti
  (*pl.* muf″tis)
mug″ger
mug″gi·er
mug″gi·ness
mug″ging
mug″gy
mug″wet
mug″wump
muk″luk
mu·la″to
  (*pl.* mu·la″toes)
mul″ber·ry
mulch
mulct
mule
mul″ish
mull
mul″lah
mul″let
mul″li·gan
mul″lion
mul′ti·cell″u·lar′
mul′ti·col″ored
mul′ti·far″i·ous
mul·tif″e·rous′
mul′ti·form′
mul′ti·lat″er·al

mul′ti·lin″gual
mul′ti·me″di·a
mul′ti·mil′lion·aire″
mul′ti·na″tion·al
mul′ti·ple-choice″
mul′ti·pli·cand″
mul′ti·pli·ca″tion
mul′ti·plic″i·ty
mul″ti·plied′
mul″ti·pli′er
mul″ti·ply
mul″ti·ply′ing
mul·ti·pol″ar
mul′ti·pur″pose
mul′ti·ra″cial
mul′ti·task″ing
mul″ti·tude
mul′ti·tu″di·nous
mul′ti·vi″ta·min
mum″ble
mum″bling
mum″bo jum″bo
mum″mer·y
mum″mi·fi·ca″tion
mum″mi·fied′
mum″mi·fy
mum″mi·fy′ing
mum″my
  (*pl.* mum″mies)
mumps
munch
munch″a·ble
mun·dane″
Mu″nich
mu·nic″i·pal
mu·nic′i·pal″i·ty
  (*pl.* mu·nic′i·pal″i·
  ties)
mu·nic″i·pal·ly
mu·nif″i·cence
mu·nif″i·cent
mu·ni″tions
mu″ral
mu″ral·ist
mur″der
mur″der·er

mur″der·ess
mur″der·ous
murk″i·er
murk″i·ly
murk″i·ness
murk″y
mur″mur
mur″mur·er
mus″ca·dine
mus′ca·tel″
mus″cle
  body tissue (*see:*
  mussel)
mus″cle-bound
mus″cling
mus″cu·lar
mus″cu·la·ture
muse
  meditate (*see:* mews)
mu·sette″
mu·se″um
mush″i·er
mush″i·ness
mush″room
mush″y
mu″si·cal
  of music (*see:* musi-
  cale)
mu si·cale″
  party (*see:* musical)
mu″si·cal·ly
mu″sic box
mu″sic hall
mu·si″cian
mu·si·col″o·gist
mu·si·col″o·gy
mus″ing
musk
mus″kel·lunge′
mus″ket
mus′ket·eer″
musk″mel′on
musk″rat′
musk″y
Mus″lim
mus″lin

mus″sel
  mollusk (*see:* mus-
  cle)
muss″i·er
muss″i·ly
muss″i·ness
muss″y
mus″tache
mus″tang
mus″tard
mus″ter
mus″ti·er
mus″ti·ness
mus″ty
mu·ta·bil″i·ty
mu″ta·ble
mu″tant
mu″tate
mu″tat·ing
mu″ta·tive
mu·ta″tion
mute
  not speaking (*see:*
  moot)
mute″ly
mute″ness
mu″ti·late′
mu″ti·lat′ing
mu″ti·la″tion
mu″ti·la″tor
mu″ti·neer″
mu″ti·nied
mu″tin·ing
mu″ti·nous
mu″ti·ny
  (*pl.* mu″ti·nies)
mu″ti·ny·ing
mut″ter
mut″ton
  meat (*see:* mouton)
mu″tu·al
mu″tu·al″i·ty
mu″tu·al·ly
muu″muu
Mu″zak′™
muz″zle-load′er

muz"zling
my'as·the"ni·a
my'cel"i·a
my'co·log"i·cal
my·col"o·gy
my·co"sis
my'ec·top"i·a
my'e·li"tis
my"lar™
my"na
my'o·car"di·al
my'o·clon"us
my·o"pi·a
my·op"ic
my·op"i·cal·ly
myr"i·ad
myr"mi·don'
myrrh
myr"tle
my·self"
mys·te"ri·ous
mys"ter·y
  (pl. mys"ter·ies)
mys"tic
mys"ti·cal
mys"ti·cal·ly
mys"ti·cism'
mys'ti·fi·ca"tion
mys"ti·fied'
mys"ti·fy'
mys"ti·fy'ing
mys·tique"
myth"i·cal
myth'o·log"i·cal
my·thol"o·gist
my·thol"o·gize'
my·thol"o·giz'ing
my·thol"o·gy
  (pl. my·thol"o·gies)

N

nab
nab"bing
Nab"buk

na"bob
na·celle"
na"cre
na"cre·ous
na"da
na"dir
nag
nag"ging
nai"ad
nail" filc'
nail" head'
nail" pol'ish
nain"sook
Nai·ro"bi
na·ive"
na·ive·te
na"ked
nam"by-pam"by
  (pl. nam"by-pam"
  bies)
name
name"a·ble
name"-drop'ping
name"less
name"ly
name"plate'
name"sake'
name"tag'
Na·mib"i·a
nam"ing
nan·keen"
nan"ny
  (pl. nan"nies)
nan"ny goat'
nan"oid
na"no·sec'ond
Nan·tuck"et
nap
na"palm
nape
na"per·y
naph"tha
naph"tha·lene'
nap"kin ring'
Na"ples
nap"ping

nap"py
narc
nar"cis·sism'
nar"cis·sist
nar'cis·sis"tic
nar·cis"sus
nar'co·lep'sy
nar'co·me·du"san
nar·co"sis
nar·cot"ic
nar"co·tism'
Nar'ra·gan"sett
  (pl. Nar'ra·gan"
  setts)
nar"rate
nar"rat·ing
nar·ra"tion
nar"ra·tive
nar"ra·tor
nar"row-gauge"
nar"row·ly
nar"row-mind'ed
nar"whal
nar"whal"i·an
na"sal
na·sal"i·ty
na"sal·ize'
na"sal·iz'ing
na"sal·ly
nas"cence
nas"cent
Nash"ville
na"so·front"al
Nas"sau
na·stur"tium
nas"ti·er
nas"ti·ness
nas"ty
na"tal
na"tal·ist'
na"tant
na'ta·to"ri·al
na'ta·to"ri·um
na"ta·to'ry
Natch"ez
na"tion·al

na"tion·al·ism'
na"tion·al·ist
na"tion·al·is"tic
na"tion·al·is"ti·cal·ly
na'tion·al"i·ty
  (*pl.* na'tion·al"i·
  ties)
na tion·al·i·za"tion
na"tion·al·ize'
na"tion·al·iz'ing
na"tion·hood'
na"tion-state"
na"tion·wide
na"tive
na"tive-born"
na·tiv"i·ty
  (*pl.* na·tiv"i·ties)
nat"ti·er
nat"ti·ly
nat"ty
nat"u·ral
nat"u·ral·ism
nat"u·ral·is"tic
nat u·ral·is"ti·cal·ly
nat"u·ral·i·za"tion
nat"u·ral·ize'
nat"u·ral·iz'ing
nat"u·ral·ly
na"ture
na'tur·op"ath·y
Nau"ga·hyde'™
naught
naugh"ti·er
naugh"ti·ly
naugh"ti·ness
naugh"ty
nau"se·a
nau"se·ate'
nau"se·at'ing
nau"seous
nau"ti·cal
nau"ti·la·ce"an
nau"ti·lus
  (*pl.* nau"ti·lus·es)
Nav"a·ho
  (*pl.* Nav"a·ho')

naval
  of a navy (*see:* na-
  vel)
nave
  church (*see:* knave)
na"vel
  umbilicus (*see:* na-
  val)
nav'i·cel"la
nav'i·ga·bil"i·ty
nav"i·ga·ble
nav"i·gate'
nav"i·gat'ing
nav'i·ga"tion
nav"i·ga'tor
na"vy
  (*pl.* na"vies)
na"vy bean'
nay
  no (*see:* neigh and
  nee)
Naz"a·reth
Ne·an"der·thal'
ne'an·throp"ic
neap" tide"
near"by"
Near" East"
near"ly
near"ness
near"sight'ed
neath
neat"ly
neat"ness
neat's"-foot' oil"
neb"bish
Ne·bras"ka
neb"u·la
  (*pl.* neb"u·lae')
neb"u·lar
neb'u·lar'i·za"tion
neb'u·los"i·ty
neb"u·lous
nec'es·sar"i·ly
nec"es·sar'y
  (*pl.* nec"es·sar'ies)
ne·ces"si·tate'

ne·ces"si·tat'ing
ne·ces"si·tous
ne·ces"si·ty
  (*pl.* ne·ces"si·ties)
neck"band'
neck"er·chief
neck"lace
neck"line'
neck"piece'
neck"tie'
neck"wear'
neck"yoke'
ne·crol"o·gy
  (*pl.* ne·crol"o·gies)
nec"ro·man'cy
nec"ro·man'cer
nec'ro·phil"i·a
nec"tar
nec'ta·re"al
nec'tar·ine"
nee
  born (*see:* neigh and
  ney)
need
  lack (*see:* kneed and
  knead)
need"ful
need"i·er
need"i·ness
nee"dle
nee"dle·bill'
nee"dle·point'
need"less
nee"dle·work'
nee"dling
need"n't
ne·far"i·ous
ne·gate"
ne·gat"ing
ne·ga"tion
neg"a·tive
neg"a·tive·ly
neg"a·tiv·ism'
neg'a·tiv·ist
neg'a·tiv·is"tic
ne·glect"

ne·glect"ful
neg'li·gee"
neg"li·gence
neg"li·gent
neg'li·gi·bil"i·ty
neg"li·gi·ble
ne·go'ti·a·bil"i·ty
ne·go'ti·a·ble
ne·go'ti·ate'
ne·go'ti·at'ing
ne·go'ti·a"tion
ne·go'ti·a"tor
Ne"gro
  (*pl.* Ne"groes)
neigh
  horse sound (*see:*
  nay and nee)
neigh"bor
neigh"bor·hood'
neigh"bor·ing
neigh"bor·li·ness
neigh"bor·ly
nei"ther
ne·lum"bi'an
nem"a·tode'
ne·mat'o·gen"ic
nem"e·sis
  (*pl.* nem"e·ses')
ne'o·bot"an·ist
ne'o·clas"sic
ne'o·clas"si·cal
ne'o·clas"si·cism'
ne'o·co·lo"ni·al·ism
ne'o·fe"tal
ne'o·im·pres"sion·
  ism'
ne'o·lith"ic
ne'o·lo"gic
ne·ol"o·gism'
ne'o·my"cin
ne"on
ne'o·phyte'
ne"o·plasm'
ne"o·prene'
Ne·pal"
ne·pen"the

neph"ew
neph"rite
ne·phri"tis
ne·phro"
ne'phro·tox"in
nep"o·tism'
nep'o·tis"tic
ne'po·tis"ti·cal
Nep"tune
nerd
nerts
nerve" cen'ter
nerve" gas'
nerve"less
nerve"-rack'ing
nerv"i·er
nerv"ous
nerv"y
ne"science
nest" egg'
nes"tle
nes"tling, *v.*
  settling down
nest"ling, *n.*
  young bird
net
net"ball'
neth"er
Neth"er·lands
neth"er·most'
neth"er world'
net"ting
net"tle
net"tle·foot'
net"tle·some
net"tling
net"work'
net"work'ing
neu"ral
neu·ral"gia
neu·ral"gic
neu·ras·the"ni·a
neu·ra·tax"i·a
neu·ri"tis
neu·ro·blast"
neu'ro·lep"tic

neu'ro·log"i·cal
neu·rol"o·gist
neu·rol"o·gy
neu·ro·psy·chi"a·try
neu·ro"sis
  (*pl.* neu·ro"ses)
neu'ro·sur"ger·y
neu'ro·ten"sion
neu·rot"ic
neu'ro·trans·mis"sion
neu"ter
neu"tral
neu"tral·ism'
neu"tral·ist
neu·tral"i·ty
neu"tral·i·za"tion
neu"tral·ize'
neu"tral·iz'er
neu"tral·iz'ing
neu·tri"no
  (neu·tri"nos)
neu"tron
Ne·va"da
ne"vel
nev'er·more"
nev'er·the·less"
ne"vus
  (*pl.* ne"vi)
new
  fresh (*see:* gnu and
  knew)
New"ark
new"born"
New' Bruns"wick
new"com'er
New' Deal"
New" Del"hi
new"el
New" En"gland
new"fan"gled
New"found·land'
New' Hamp"shire
New" Jer"sey
new"ly·wed'
New' Mex"i·co
new"ness

New' Or"le·ans
news"bill'
news"boy'
news"break'
news"cast'
news"cast'er
news"deal'er
news"let'ter
news"mak'er
news"man
news"pa'per
news"pa'per·man'
new"speak'
news"print
news"room'
news"stand'
news"wor'thy
news"y
newt
New' Years' Eve
New York"
New' Zea"land
next'-door"
nex"us
Nez" Perce
  (*pl.* Nez" Perce)
ni"a·cin
Ni·ag"a·ra
nib
nibbed
nib"bing
nib"ble
nib"bing
nib"lick
Nic'a·ra"gua
nice
  agreeable (*see:*
  gneiss)
nice"ly
Ni"cene Creed"
nic"er
ni"ce·ty
  (*pl.* ni"ce·ties)
niche
nick
nick"el

nick"el·ing
nick'el·o"de·on
nick"el plate"
nick"name'
nick"named'
Nic'o·si"a
nic"o·tine'
nic"o·tism'
niece
nif"ty
Ni"ger
Ni·ge"ri·a
nig"gard·li·ness
nig"gard·ly
nig"gling
nigh
night
  dark time (*see:*
  knight
night"-blind"
night"cap'
night" clothes'
night"club'
night"dress'
night"fall'
night"gown'
night"in·gale'
night" light'
night" long'
night"ly
night"mare'
night" owl'
night"rid'er
night" school'
night" shift'
night"shirt'
night"spot'
night" stick'
night" ta'ble
night"time'
night"wards'
night" watch"man
ni"hil·ist'
ni"hil·is"tic
nil
Nile

nim"ble
nim"bler
nim"bly
nim"bose'
nim·bo·stra"tus
nim"bus
  (*pl.* nim"bi)
nin"com·poop'
nine"bark'
nine"pins'
nine"teen"
nine"ti·eth
nine"ty
  (*pl.* nine"ties)
nin"ny
  (*pl.* nin"nies)
ni·non"
ninth
nip
nip"per
nip"pi·er
nip"ping
nip"ple
nip"py
nip"-up'
nir·va"na
nitch
nit"pick'
ni"trate
ni"trat·ing
ni·tra"tion
ni"tric
ni"tride
ni·tri·fi·ca"tion
ni"tri·fy
ni"trite
ni·tro·bac·te"ri·a
ni·tro·cel"lu·lose'
ni"tro·gen
ni·trog"e·nous
ni·tro·glyc"er·in
ni·tro·par"a·fin'
ni"trous
nit"ty-grit"ty
nit"wit'
nix

no·bil''i·ty
  (*pl.* no·bil''i·ties)
no''ble·man
no''bler
no·blesse'' o·blige''
no''ble·wom·an
no''bly
no''bod·y
  (*pl.* no''bod·ies)
noct·amb''u·lant'
noc·tur''nal
noc''turne
nod
nod''al
nod''ding
node
nod''u·lar
nod''u·la''ted
nod''ule
no·el''
no''-fault'
no''-frills
nog''gin
no''-good'
no''-growth
no''-hit''ter
noise
noise''less
noise''mak'er
nois''i·er
nois''i·ly
nois''i·ness
nois''ing
noi''some
nois''y
no''lo con·ten''de·re
no·mad''ic
no'' man's land
nom de plume''
no''men·cla''ture
nom''i·nal
nom''i·nal·ly
nom''i·nate'
nom''i·nat'ing
nom''i·na''tion
nom''i·na''tive

nom''i·na'tor
nom'i·nee''
non'a·ge·nar''i·an
non'ag·gres''sion
non·a'cid''ic
non'al·co·hol''ic
non'a·ligned''
non a·lign''ment
non'al·ler·gen''ic
non'a·tro''phic'
non·be·liev''er
non'bel·lig''er·ent
non·bru''tal·ly
nonce
non·cha·lance''
non'cha·lant''
non·cler''i·cal
non''com
non·com''bat·ant
non'com·bus''ti·ble
non'com·mis''sioned
non'com·mit''tal
non'com·pet''i·tive
non'com·pli''ance
non'con·form''ist
non'con·ta''gious
non'con·tro·ver''sial
non'co·op'er·a''tion
non·de''ist
non'de·script''
non'dex''ter·ous·ly
non'dis·crim'i·na''tion
non'dis·tinc''tive
non'dra·mat''ic
none
  not one (*see:* nun)
non'e·lec''tive'
non'en''ti·ty
  (*pl.* non'en''ti·ties)
non·er''rant·ly
non'es·sen''tial
none''such'
none'the·less''
non'e·vent''
non'ex·ist''ence
non·fa''cial

non·faul''ty
non'fer''rous
non·fic''tion
non·fis''cal
non·fla''ky
non·flam''ma·ble
non·ge·ner''ic
non·gra''cious
non'har·mon''i·ous
non·hu''man
non'hyp·not''ic
non'i·de·a·log''i·cal
non'in·fe·ren''tial
non'in·ter·fer''ence
non'in·ter·ven''tion
non'in·tox''i·cat'ing
non·jur''ant
non·ko''sher
non·le''gal
non·li''cit
non'lox·o·drom''i·cal
non·mag·net''ic
non·mem''ber
non·met''ric
non·nav''i·ga'ble
non·norm''al
no''-no'
  (*pl.* no''-nos')
non'ob·stet''ri·cal
non'o·dor·if''er·ous
non·oil''y
non·pal''pa·ble
non'pa·ral''y·sis
non·pa·reil''
non·par''tial
non'par·tic''i·pat'ing
non·par''ti·san
non·pay''ment
non'per·form''ance
non·plus''
non·plused''
non·plus''ing
non'pro·duc''tive
non·prof''it
non'pro·lif'er·a''tion
non·qual''i·ties

non·re·ac″tion·ar·y
non·res″i·dent
non′re·sid″u·al
non′re·stric″tive
non·rig″id
non·scho·las″tic
non′se·quen″tial
non′sec·tar″i·an
non″sense
non·sen″si·cal·ly
non se″qui·tur
non·skid″
non·smok″er
non·spec″u·la·tive′
non″stop″
non′sup·port″
non·sur″gi·cal
non·tech″ni·cal
non·tens″ile′
non·trac′ta·bil″i·ty
non·un″ion
non′u·nite″a·ble
non·u″til·lized′
non·ver″bal
non·vi″o·lence
non·vi″o·lent
non·vir″ile
non·vol″a·tile′
non·white″
non·zeal″ous
noo″dle
nook
noon″day′
no″ one
noon·flow″er
noon″tide′
noon″time′
noose
noos″ing
no″-par′
nope
Nor″folk
nor″mal
nor″mal·cy
nor″mal″i·ty
nor″mal·i·za″tion

nor″mal·ize
nor″mal·iz″ing
nor″mal·ly
nor″ma·tive
North″ A·mer″i·ca
north″bound′
North″ Car′o·li″na
North″ Da·ko″ta
north″east′
north″east″er·ly
north″east″wards
north″er
north″er·ly
north″ern
North″ern Ire″land
north″ern·most′
north″-north″east″
north″-north″west″
North″ Pole″
north″wards
north″west″
north″west″er·ly
north″west″ward
Nor″way
nose″bleed′
nose″ cone′
nose″ dive′
nose″-div′ing
nose″gay′
nose″piece′
no″-show″
nos″i·er
nos″i·ness
nos″ing
nos·tal″gia
nos·talg′ic
nos·tal″gi·cal·ly
nos″tril
nos″trum
nos″y
not
   negative (*see:* knot)
no′ta·bil″i·ty
no″ta·ble
no″ta·rize′
no″ta·riz′ing

no″ta·ry pub″lic
  (*pl.* no″ta·ries pub″
  lic)
no″tate
no″tat′ing
no·ta″tion
notch″back′
note″book′
not″ed
note″pap′er
note″wor′thi·ly
note″wor′thy
noth″ing·ness
no″tice
no″tice·a·ble
no″tic·ing
no″ti·fi·ca″tion
no″ti·fied′
no″ti·fi′er
no″ti·fy′
no″ti·fy′ing
not″ing
no″tion
no″to·chord′
no′to·ri″e·ty
no·to″ri·ous
no″-trump″
not′with·stand″ing
nou″gat
noun
nour″ish·ment
nou·veau riche″
  (*pl.* nou″veaux
  riches″)
no″va
No″va Sco″tia
nov′el
nov′el·ette″
nov″el·ist
nov′el·i·za″tion
nov′el·ize′
no·vel″la
nov′el·ty
  (*pl.* nov″el·ties)
No·vem″ber

no·ve''na
nov''ice
no·vi''ti·ate
No''vo·caine'™
now''a·days'
no''way'
no''where'
no''wise'
nox''ious
noz''zle
nu''ance
nub''bin
nub''ble
nub''bly
nub''by
nu''bile
nu''cle·ar
nu''cle·ate'
nu''cle·at'ing
nu·cle''ic ac''id
nu·cle''o·lar
nu·cle''o·lus
   (*pl.* nu·cle''o·li')
nu''cle·on
nu·cle·on''ics
nu·cle·o''plas·mat''ic
nu''cle·us
   (*pl.* nu''cle·i')
nude
nudge
nudg''ing
nud''ism
nud''ist
nu''di·ty
   (*pl.* nu''di·ties)
nu''ga·to'ry
nug''get
nui''sance
nuke
nul'li·fi·ca''tion
nul''li·fied'
nul''li·fy'
nul''li·fy'ing
num''ber crunch''er
num''ber·less
numb''ing

numb''ly
numb''ness
nu''mer·a·ble
nu''mer·al
nu''mer·ate'
nu''mer·at'ing
nu''mer·a''tion
nu''mer·a'tor
nu·mer''i·cal·ly
nu'mer·ol''o·gy''
nu''mer·ous
nu mis·mat''ics
nu·mis''ma·tist
num''skull
nun
   sister (*see:* none)
nun''ci·o
   (*pl.* nun''ci·os)
nup''tial
nurse''maid
nurs''er·y
   (*pl.* nurs''er·ies)
nurs''ing·home'
nur''ture
nur''tur·ing
nut''crack'er
nut''meat'
nut''meg'
nut''pick'
nu''tri·a
nu''tri·ent
nu''tri·ment
nu·tri''tion
nu·tri''tion·al
nu·tri''tion·ist
nu·tri''tious
nu''tri·tive
nut''shell'
nut''ti·er
nut''ting
nut''ty
nuz''zle
nuz''zling
nye'ta·lo''pi·a
ny''lon
nymph

nym·phet''
nym'pho·ma''ni·ac'

O

oaf
oak''en
oak''land
oa''kum
oar
   blade (*see:* or and
   ore)
oar''lock'
oars''man
o·a''sis
   (*pl.* o·a''ses)
oath
oat''meal'
ob'bli·ga''to
   (*pl.* ob'bli·ga''tos)
ob''du·ra·cy
ob''du·rate
o·be''di·ence
o·be''di·ent
o·bei''sance
o·bei''sant
ob''e·lisk
ob''e·lisk·oid
o·bese''
o·be''si·ty
o·bey''
ob·fus''cate
ob·fus''cat·ing
ob·fus·ca''tion
o'bi·ter dic''tum
   (*pl.* o'bi·ter dic''ta)
o·bit''u·ar'y
   (*pl.* o·bit''u·ar'ies)
ob·ject'', *v.*
   protest
ob''ject, *n.*
   thing
ob·jec''ti·fy'
ob·jec''ti·fy'ing
ob·jec''tion

ob·jec″tion·a·ble
ob·jec″tive
ob·jec″tive·ly
ob·jec″tive·ness
ob·jec′tiv″i·ty
ob·jec″tor
ob·jet d'art″
  (*pl.* ob·jets d'art″)
ob″jur·gate′
ob″jur·gat′ing
ob′jur·ga″tion
ob″late
ob·la″tion
ob″li·gate′
ob″li·gat′ing
ob′li·ga″tion
o·blig″a·to·ry
o·blige″
o·blig″ing
ob·lique″
ob·lique″ly
ob liq″ui·ty
ob·lit″er·ate′
ob·lit″er·at′ing
ob·lit′er·a″tion
ob·liv″i·on
ob·liv″i·ous
ob″long′
ob″lo·quy
  (*pl.* ob″lo·quies)
ob·nox″ious
ob″nounce
o″boe
o″bo·ist
ob·scene″
ob·scene″ly
ob·scen″i·ty
  (*pl.* ob·scen″i·ties)
ob″scu·ran′cy
ob·scu″ran·tist
ob·scure″
ob·scure″ly
ob·scur″ing
ob·scu″ri·ty
  (*pl.* ob·scu″ri·ties)
ob·se″qui·ous

ob·serv″a·ble
ob·serv″ance
ob·serv″ant
ob·ser·va″tion
ob·serv″a·to·ry
  (*pl.* ob·serv″a·to′ries)
ob·serve″
ob·serv″er
ob·serv″ing
ob·sess″
ob·ses″sion
ob·ses″sive
ob·sid″i·an
ob·sid″i·an·ite′
ob′so·lesce″
ob′so·les″cence
ob′so·les″cent
ob′so·lesc″ing
ob′so·lete″
ob″sta·cle
ob·stet″ri·cal
ob·stet′ri·ca″tion
ob·ste·tri″cian
ob·stet″rics
ob″sti·na·cy
  (*pl.* ob″sti·na·cies)
ob″stinate
ob″sti·nate·ly
ob·strep″er·ous
ob·struct″
ob·struc″tion
ob·struc″tion·ist
ob·struc″tive
ob·tain″
ob·tain″a·ble
ob″tent′
ob·trude″
ob·trud″ing
ob·tru″sive
ob·tuse″
ob·um·bra″ted
ob·verse″, *adj.*
  toward observer
ob″verse, *n.*
  counterpart

ob·vert″
ob″vi·ate
ob″vi·at′ing
ob′vi·a″tion
ob″vi·ous
oc′a·ri″na
oc·ca″sion·al·ly
oc·ci·den″tal
oc·cip″i·tal
oc·clude″
oc·clud″ing
oc·clu″sal
oc·clu″sion
oc·cult″
oc·cul·ta″tion
oc·cult″ist
oc″cu·pan·cy
  (*pl.* oc″cu·pan·cies)
oc″cu·pant
oc′cu·pa″tion
oc′cu·pa″tion·al·ly
oc′cu·pied″
oc″cu·pi·er
oc″cu·py
oc″cu·py′ing
oc·cur″
oc·cur″rence
oc·cur″ring
o′cean·et
o″cean·front
o″cean·go′ing
O′ce·an″i·a
o′ce·an·og″ra·pher
o′ce·an·og″ra·phy
o″cel·late′
o″ce·lot
o″cher
o·clock″
oc·ta·chor″dal
oc″ta·gon
oc·tag″o′nal·ly
oc′ta·hy″drate
oc′ta·he″dral
oc′ta·he″dron
oc″tane
oc″tant′

oc"tave
oc·ta"vo
  (*pl.* oc·ta"vos)
oc·tet"
Oc·to"ber
oc"to·fid
oc"to·ge·nar"i·an
oc"to·lat'er·al
oc"to·ped'
oc"to·pus
  (*pl.* oc"to·pus·es)
oc"u·lar
oc"u·list
odd"ball
odd"i·ty
  (*pl.* odd"i·ties)
odd"ly
odd"ment
odds"-on"
ode
  poem (*see:* owed)
o"dic
o"di·ous
o"di·um
o·dom"e·ter
o·don'to·blas"tic
o·don'to·lox"i·a
o"dor
o·dor·if"er·ous
o"dor·ous
oed"i·pal
oes'tru·a"tion
oeu"vre
of"fal
  refuse (*see:* awful)
off"beat
off" Broad"way
off"-cen"ter
off"-col"or
of·fend"
of·fense"
of·fen"sive
of"fer
of"fer·ing
of"fer·to·ry
  (*pl.* of"fer·to·ries)

off"hand
of"fice·hold'er
of"fice·mate'
of"fi·cer
of·fi"cial
of·fi"cial·dom
of·fi"cial·ese"
of·fi"cial·ism'
of·fi"cial·ly
of·fi"ci·ate'
of·fi"ci·at'ing
of·fi"ci·a"tion
of·fi"cious
off"ing
off"-key"
off"-lim"its
off"-line'
off"-load"
offed"
off print
off"scour"
off"screen"
off"-sea"son
off"set", *v.*
  balance
off"set', *n., adj.*
  offshoot
off"set"ting
off"shoot"
off"shore"
off"side"
off"spring'
off"stage"
off"-the-re"cord
off"track"
off"type"
off"-white"
of"ten·times'
o"gen·e·sis
o"gle
o"gling
o"gre
o"gre·ish
oh
  exclamation (*see:* owe)

O·hi"o
ohm
ohm"me'ter
oil" cake'
oil"can'
oil"cloth'
oil" field'
oil"i·er
oil"i·ness
oil"man'
oil"skin'
oil"stone'
oil" well'
oil"y
oink
oint"ment
O."K."
o"kay"
  all right
o·kay"
  approve
O'kla·ho"ma
o"kra
old
old"er
old"-fash"ioned
old" fo"gy
old" maid"
old"ster
old"-time"
old"-tim"er
old"-world"
o'le·o·mar"gar·ine
ol·fac"tion
ol·fac"to·ry
  (*pl.* ol·fac"to·ries)
ol"i·garch'
ol'i·gar"chic
ol'i·gar"chi·cal
ol'i·gar"chism'
ol'i·gar"chy
  (*pl.* ol"i·gar'chies)
ol"i·go·cene"
ol"i·go·chrome"
ol"i·go·pep'si·a
ol'i·gop"o·ly

ol'i·go·troph''ic
ol''ive oil'
O·lym''pi·a
O·lym''pi·ad'
O·lym''pic
O''ma·ha'
O·man''
om''buds·man'
o·me''ga
om''e·let
o''men
om''i·nous
o·mis''sion
o·mit''
o·mit''ting
om''ni·bus
om''ni·cide
om''ni·cred''u·lous
om''ni·form
om·nip''o·tence
om·nip''o·ten·cy
om·nip''o·tent
om''ni·pres''ence
om''ni·pres''ent
om·nis''cience
om·nis''cient
om''ni·ton'al
om''ni·vo·ra''ci·ty
om''ni·vore'
om''niv''o·rous
on
once
once''-o'ver
on·com''e·ter
on''com'ing
one''-lin''er
one''ness
one''-on-one''
on''er·ous
one·self''
one''-sid''ed
one''time'
one''-up''man·ship'
one''-way''
on''flow
on''go'ing

on''ion
on''ion·skin'
on''-line'
on''look'er
on''ly
on·o''mat'o·poe''ia
on''rush'
on''set'
on''shore''
on''slaught''
on''stage''
on''-stream''
On·tar''i·o
on''to
on·tol''o·gy
o''nus
on''ward
on''yx
oo''dles
oomph
ooze
ooz''i·er
ooz''ing
ooz''y
o·pac''i·ty
o''pal
o''pal·es''cent
o·paque''
o·paqu''ing
open air'', *n*.
  the outdoors
open-air'', *adj*.
  outdoor
o''pen-and-shut''
o''pen·bill'
o''pen-end''
o''pen·er
o''pen-eyed''
o''pen-face''
o''pen·hand''ed
o''pen·heart''ed
o''pen house''
o''pen·ing
o''pen-mind''ed
o''pen·mouthed''
o''pen·ness

o''pen shop''
op''er·a
op''er·a·ble
op''er·a glass''es
op''er·a house'
op''er·ate'
op''er·at''ic
op''er·at''ing
op''er·a''tion
op''er·a''tion·al
op''er·a''tive
op''er·a·tor
op''er·et''ta
oph·thal''mic
oph·thal''mo·log''i·cal
oph''thal·mol''o·gist
oph''thal·mol''o·gy
o''pi·ate
o·pine''
o·pin''ing
o·pin''ion
o·pin''ion·at'ed
o''pi·um
o·pos''sum
op·po''nent
op''por·tune''
op'por·tun''ing
op·pos''a·ble
op·pose''
op·pos''ing
op'po·site
  different from (*see*:
  apposite)
op'po·si''tion
op·press''
op·pres''sion
op·pres''sive
op·pres''sive·ly
op·pres''sor
op·pro''bri·ous
op·pro''bri·um
op''ta·tion
op''tic
op''ti·cal
op·ti''cian
op''ti·cal

op″ti·cism′
op′ti·cis″tic
op′ti·cis″ti·cal·ly
op″ti·mist
op″ti·mize
op″ti·miz′ing
op″ti·mum
op″tion
op″tion·al
op″tion·al·ly
op·tom″e·trist
op·tom″e·try
op″u·lence
op″u·lent
o″pus
  (*pl.* op″er·a)
or
  (*see:* ore and oar)
or″a·cle
o·rac″u·lar
o″ral
  spoken (*see:* aural)
o″ral·ly
or″ange
or′ange·ade″
o·rate″
o·rat″ing
o·ra″tion
or′a·tor
or′a·tor″i·cal
or′a·to″ri·o
  (*pl.* or′a·to″ri·os)
or′a·to″ry
or·bic″u·lar
or″bit
or″bit·al
or″ca
or″chard
or″ches·tra
or·ches″tral
or″ches·trate′
or″ches·trat′ing
or·ches·tra″tion
or″chid
or·dain″
or·deal″

or″der
or″der·li·ness
or″der·ly
  (*pl.* or″der·lies)
or″di·nal
or″di·nance
  law (*see:* ordnance)
or″di·nand′
or′di·nar″i·ly
or″di·nar′y
  (*pl.* or″di·nar′ies)
or″di·nate′
or′di·na″tion
ord″nance
  weapons (*see:* ordi-
  nance)
or″dure
ore
  mineral (*see:* or and
  oar)
o·reg″a·no
Or″e·gon
or″gan
or″gan·dy
or·gan″ic
or·gan″i·cal·ly
or″gan·ism′
or″gan·ist
or·gan·iz″a·ble
or′gan·i·za″tion
or″gan·ize′
or″gan·iz′er
or″gan·iz′ing
or·gan″za
or″gasm
or·gas″mic
or′gi·as″tic
or″gy
  (*pl.* or″gies)
o″ri·ent′
O′ri·en″tal
o″ri·en·tate′
o″ri·en·tat′ing
o′ri·en·ta″tion
or″i·fice
o′ri·ga″mi

or″i·gin
  (*pl.* or″i·gins)
o·rig″i·nal
o·rig′i·nal″i·ty
o·rig″i·nal·ly
o·rig″i·nate′
o·rig″i·nat′ing
o·rig′i·na″tion
o·rig″i·na′tor
o″ri·ole′
O″ri·on
or″na·ment
or′na·men″tal
or·na·men·ta″tion
or·nate″
or·nate″ly
or″ner·y
or′ni·tho·log″ic
or′ni·tho·log″i·cal
or′ni·thol″o·gist
or′ni·thol″o·gy
or′ni·tho·man″i·a
or′ni·tho·pho″bi·a
o′ro·tund′
or″phan
or″phan·age
or″thi·con′
or′tho·ceph″a·ly
or′tho·don″tics
or′tho·don″tist
or″tho·dox′
or″tho·dox′y
  (*pl.* or″tho·dox′ies)
or·tho″e·py
or·thog″o·nal
or′tho·graph″ic
or·thog″ra·phy
or′tho·pe″dics
or′tho·pe″dist
O′R′V″
  off-road vehicle
o″ryx
  (*pl.* o″ryx·es)
O·sa″ka
os″cil·late′

back and forth (*see:*
  osculate)
os″cil·lat′ing
os′cil·la″tion
os′cil·la′tor
os·cil″lo·scope′
os″cu·late′
  kiss (*see:* oscillate)
os″cu·lat′ing
os′cu·la″tion
Os″lo
os·mo″graph
os·mo″sis
os″prey
  (*pl.* os″preys)
os·si·fi·ca″tion
os″si·fied′
os″si·fy′
os·ten″si·ble
os·ten″sion
os·ten·ta″tion
os·ten·ta″tious
os″te·o·der″mi·a
os″te·o·my′e·li″tis
os″te·o·path′
os″te·o·path″ic
os″te·op″a·thy
os″te·o·scle·ro″sis
os″tra·cism′
os″tra·cize′
os″tra·ciz′ing
os″trich
os″trich·like′
oth″er·wise′
oth″er world″
oth″er·world″ly″
o′ti·ose′
o·ti″tis
o′to·plas″tic
o′to·lar″yn·gol″o·gy
Ot″ta·wa
ot″ter
ot″to·man
ought
  should (*see:* aught)
ounce

our·selves″
oust
oust″er
out″age
out″-and-out″
out″back
out″bend′
out″bid′
out″board′
out″bound″
out″break′
out″bred′
out″build′ing
out″burst′
out″cast′
out class″
out″come′
out″crop″, *v.*
out″crop′, *n.*
  rock
out″crop″ping
out″cry′
  (*pl.* out″cries′)
out″cull
out″dared′
out″date″
out″dat″ing
out″did″
out″dis″tance
out″dis″tanc·ing
out″do″
out″do″ing
out″done″
out″doors″
out″eat
out″er·most″
out″face″
out″fac″ing
out″fast
out″field″er
out″fit
out″fit′ter
out″fit′ting
out″flank″
out″flow′
out″gas

out′gen″er·al
out′gen″er·al·ing
out″gleam
out″go, *v.*
  go beyond
out″go, *n.*
  outflow
out″go″ing
out″gone″
out″grew″
out″grin
out″grow″
out″grow″ing
out″grown″
out″growth
out guess″
out″house
out″ing
out″laid″
out″land′er
out″land″ish
out″last″
out″law
out″law′ry
out″lay″, *v.*
  spend
out″lay, *n.*
  expenditure
out″lay″ing
out″let
out″line
out″lin′ing
out″live″
out″liv″ing
out″look
out″ly″ing
out″mod″ed
out″mod″ing
out″most
out″num″ber
out″-of-bounds′
out″-of-date″
out″-of-doors″
out″-of-the-way″
out″pa′tient
out″post

out'pour''
out''prac·ticed
out''put
out''race
out''rage
out''ra''geous
out''ran''
out''range
out''rank''
out''reach'', *v.*
  reach out; surpass
out''reach, *n.*
  act of reaching out
out''rid''den
out''ride''
out''rid''er
out''rid''ing
out''rig''ger
out''right'
out''rode''
out''run''
out''run''ning
out''sell''
out''sell''ing
out''set'
out''sharp·en
out''shine''
out''shin''ing
out''shone''
out''shoot'', *v.*
  protrude
out''shoot, *n.*
  thing that protrudes
out''showed
out''side''
out''sid''er
out''sized'
out''skirts'
out''smart''
out''snore''
out''sold''
out''source'
out''sourc·ing
out''spar·kle
out''spend
out''spo''ken

out''spread'', *v.*
  expand
out''spread', *n., adj.*
  extended
out''stand''ing
out''stare''
out''star''ing
out''sta''tion
out''stay''
out''stretch''
out''strip''
out''strip''ping
out''sweep
out''vote''
out''vot''ing
out''ward·ly
out''wards
out''wear''
out''wear''ing
out''weigh''
out''went''
out''wit''
out''wit''ting
out''wore''
out''work'', *v.*
  work better
out''work, *n.*
  fortification
out''worn''
ou''zel
o''val
o·var''i·an
o''va·ry
  (*pl.* o''va·ries)
o·va''tion
ov''en·ware
over·a·bun''dance
over·a·bun''dant
o'ver·a·chieve''
o'ver·a·chiev''er
o'ver·a·chiev''ing
o'ver·act''
o'ver·ac''tive
o'ver·age'', *adj.*
  too old
o''ver·age, *n.*

  surplus
o''ver·all''
o''ver·alls
o''ver·arm'
o'ver·awe''
o'ver·aw''ing
o'ver·bal''ance
o'ver·bal''anc·ing
o'ver·bear''ing
o'ver·bid'', *v.*
  outbid
o''ver·bid', *n.*
  higher bid
o'ver·bid''ding
o''ver·bite
o'ver·blown''
o''ver·board'
o''ver·book'
o'ver·break''age
o'ver·bur''den
o''ver·burn
o'ver·came''
o''ver·cast', *adj.*
  cloudy
o''ver·cast', *n.*
  sew over
over·charge'', *v.*
  charge too much
over''charge', *n.*
  high charge
o'ver·charg''ing
o''ver·clothes
o''ver·coat
o'ver·come''
o'ver·com''ing
o'ver·con''fi·dence
o'ver·con''fi·dent
o'ver·con''cen·tra''tion
o'ver·con·trolled''
o'ver·cros''sing
o'ver·crowd''
o'ver·de''tailed
o'ver·did''
o'ver·dis''traught
o'ver·do''

do too much (*see:* overdue)

o'ver·do''ing

o'ver·done''

o'ver·dose'', *v.*
dose too much

o''ver·dose', *n.*
large dose

o'ver·draft'

o'ver·draw''

o'ver·draw''ing

o'ver·drawn''

o'ver·dream''

o'ver·dress'', *v.*

o'ver·drew''

o''ver·drive'

o'ver·due''
late (*see:* overdo)

o'ver·eat''

o'ver·e·lab''o·rate

o'ver·em''pha·sis

o'ver·em''pha·size'

o'ver·em''pha·siz'ing

o'ver·en''vi·ous

o'ver·es''ti·mate', *v.*
estimate high

o'ver·es''ti·mate, *n.*
a high estimate

o'ver·ex·er''tion

o'ver·ex·pose''

o'er·ex·po·sure''

o'ver·ex·tend''

o'ver·fas·tid''i·ous

o'ver·flight''

o'ver·flow'', *v.*
flow over

o''ver·flow', *n.*
surplus

o'ver·frus·tra''tion

o'ver·glaze'', *v.*
cover

o''ver·glaze', *n., adj.*
second glaze

o'ver·graze''

o'ver·grew''

o'ver·grow''

o'ver·grow''ing

o'ver·grown''

o''ver·growth'

over·hand'

o'ver·hang'', *v.*
hang over

o''ver·hang', *n.*
projection

o'ver·hang''ing

o'ver·haul'', *v.*
inspect

o''ver·haul', *n.*
inspection

o''ver·head''

o'ver·hear''

o''ver·heard''

o'ver·hear''ing

o'ver·heat''

o'ver·hung''

o''ver·hunt''

o'ver·in·dulge''

o'ver·in·dul''gence

o'ver·in·dul''gent

o'ver·in·dulg''ing

o'ver·in·vest''

o'ver·joy''

o''ver·kill'

o'ver·lac''tate

o'ver·laid''

o'ver·lain''

o''ver·land'

o'ver·lap'', *v.*
extend

o''ver·lap', *n.*
act of overlapping

o'ver·lap''ping

o'ver·lay'', *v.*
cover over

o''ver·lay', *n.*
covering

o'ver·lay''ing

o'ver·leap''

o''ver·lie''

o'ver·load'', *v.*
put big load in

o''ver·load', *n.*

big load

over·long''

o'ver·look'', *v.*
omit; look at

o''ver·look', *n.*
a height

o''ver·lord'

o''ver·ly

o'ver·ly''ing

o'ver·match''

o'ver·mike''

o'ver·night''

o'ver·paid''

o''ver·pass'

o'ver·pay''

o'ver·pow''er

o'ver·price''

o'ver·pro·duce''

o'ver·pro·duc''ing

over·pro·duc''tion

o'ver·pro·tect''

o'ver·ran''

o'ver·rate''

o'ver·rat''ing

o'ver·reach''

over·rid''den

over·ride'', *v.*
nullify

o''ver·ride', *n.*
commission

o'ver·rid''ing

o'ver·ripe''

o'ver·rode''

o'ver·rule''

o'ver·rul''ing

o'ver·run'', *v.*
invade; overflow

o''ver·run', *n.*
excess amount

o'ver·run''ning

o''ver·saw''

o''ver·seas''

o''ver·see''

o''ver·seen''

o''ver·se'er

o'ver·sell''

o′′ver·sen′′si·tive
o′′ver·sexed′′
o′′ver·shad′′ow
o′′ver·shoe′
o′′ver·shoot′′
o′′ver·shot′
o′′ver·sight′
o′′ver·sim′′pli·fi·ca′′
tion
o′′ver·sim′′pli·fied′
o′′ver·sim′′pli·fy′
o′′ver·size′
o′′ver·sleep′′
o′′ver·slept′′
o′′ver·sold′′
o′′ver·spend′′
o′′ver·spent′′
o′′ver·spread′′
o′′ver·state′′
o′′ver·state′′ment
o′′ver·stat′′ing
o′′ver·stay′′
o′′ver·step′′
o′′ver·step′′ping
o′′ver·stock′′, *v.*
stock too much
o′′ver·stock′, *n.*
big stock
o′′ver·stuff′′
o′′ver·sub·scribe′′
o′′ver·sup·plied′′
o′′ver·sup·ply′′
o·vert′′
o′′ver·take′′
o′′ver·tak′′en
o′′ver·tak′′ing
o′′ver·tax′′
o′′ver-the-coun′′ter
o′′ver·throw′′
o′′ver·tone′′
o′′ver·took′′
o′′ver·ture′
o′′ver·turn′′
o′′ver·use′′
o′′ver·view′
o′′ver·ween′′ing

o′′ver·weigh′′
o′′ver·weight′
o′′ver·whelm′′
o′′ver·wind′′
o′′ver·work′′
o′′ver·wound′′
o′′ver·wrought′′
o·vip′′a·rous
o′′void
egg-shaped (*see:*
avoid)
o′′vu·late′
o′′vu·lat′ing
o′′vu·la′′tion
o′′vule
o′′vum
(*pl.* o′′va)
owe
obligation (*see:* ode)
owed
did owe (*see:* ode)
ow′′ing
owl′′et
owl′′ish
own′′er
own′′er·ship′
ox
(*pl.* ox′′en)
ox′′blood′
ox′′bow′
ox′′cart′
ox′′ford
ox′i·dant
ox′i·da′′tion
ox′′ide
ox′i·di·za′′tion
ox′′i·dize′
ox′′i·diz′ing
ox′′tail′
ox′y·a·cet′′y·lene′
ox′′y·gen
ox′′y·gen·ate′
ox′′y·gen·at′ing
ox′y·gen·a′′t ion
ox′y·mo′′ron
(*pl.* ox′y·mo′′ra)

o′′yez
oys′′ter bed′
oys′′ter·man
O′′zarks
o′′zone
Oz′y·man′′di·an

P

pab′′u·lum
pace′′mak′er
pace′′set′ter
pach′′y·derm′
pach′′y·glos′si·a
pach′y·san′′dra
Pa·cif′′ic
pac·i·fi·ca′′tion
pac′′i·fied
pac′′i·fi′er
pac′′i·fism′
pac′′i·fist
pac′′i·fy′
pac′′i·fy′ing
pac′′ing
pack′′age
pack′′ag·ing
pack′′et
pack′′horse′
pack′ing house
pack′′ rat′
pack′′sack′
pack′′sad′dle
pact
pac′′tion·al
pad
pad′′ding
pad′′dle-ball′
pad′′dle·fish′
pad′′dle wheel′′
pad′′dling
pad′′dock
pad′′dy
(*pl.* pad′′dies)
pad′′dy·whack′
pad′′lock′

pa″dre
pae″an
  song (*see:* peon)
pa″gan
pa″gan·ism′
page
pag″eant
pag″eant·ry
  (*pl.* pag″eant·ries)
page″boy′
pag″i·nate′
pag″i·nat′ing
pag′i·na″tion
pag″ing
pa·go″da
paid
pail
  bucket (*see:* pale)
pail″ful′
  (*pl.* pail″fuls′)
pain
  suffering (*see:* pane)
pain″ful
pain″ful·ly
pain″ kil′ler
pain″less
pains″tak′ing
paint″brush′
paint″ed
paint″er
paint″ing
pair
  two (*see:* pear and
   pare)
pais″ley
Pai′ute′
  (*pl.* Pai′utes′)
pa·ja″mas
Pa″ki·stan′
pal
pal″ace
pal″a·din
pal″an·quin″
pal′at·a·bil″i·ty
pal″at·a·ble
pal″a·tal

pal″ate
  roof of mouth (*see:*
   pallet and palette)
pa·la″tial
pa·lat″i·nate′
pal″a·tine′
pa·lav″er
pale
  whitish; limits (*see:*
   pail)
pale″face′
pa′le·o·anth′ro·pol″-
  o·gy
pa′le·o·eth·nog″-
  raph·y
pa′le·og″ra·pher
pa′le·o·graph″i·cal
pa′le·og″ra·phy
pa′le·o·lith″ic
pa′le·on·tol″o·gist
pa′le·on·tol″o·gy
pa′le·o·trop″i·cal
pa′le·o·zo″ic
pal″er
Pal″es·tine′
pal″ette
  paint board (*see:*
   palate and pallet)
pal″imp·sest′
pal″in·drome′
pal″ing
  being pale; board
   (*see:* palling)
pal″i·node′
pal′i·sade″
pall
  being bored; dark
   cloud (*see:* pawl)
pal·la″di·um
pall″bear′er
pal″let
  mattress; tool (*see:*
   palate and palette)
pal″li·ate′
pal″li·at′ing
pal′li·a″tion

pal″li·a′tive
pal″lid
pal″ling
  being pals (*see:* pal-
   ing)
pal″lor
palm
pal″mate
pal·met″to
palm″ist
palm″is·try
palm″y
pa·lo″ma
pal′o·mi″no
  (*pl.* pal′o·mi″nos)
pa·loo″ka
pal′pa·bil″i·ty
pal″pa·ble
pal″pate
  examine (*see:* palpi-
   tate)
pal″pat′ing
pal·pa″tion
pal″pi·tate′
  pulsate (*see:* palpate)
pal″pi·tat′ing
pal′pi·ta″tion
pal″sied
pal″sy
  (*pl.* pal″sies)
pal″tri·er
pal″tri·ness
pal″try
pam″pas
  (*pl.* pam″pa)
pam″per
pam″phlet
pam′phlet·eer″
pan
pan′a·ce″a
pa·nache″
Pan″a·ma′
Pan″a·ma′ hat″
Pan′-A·mer″i·can
pan″-broil″
pan″cake′

pan'chro·mat''ic
pan''cre·as
pan''cre·at''ic
pan''da
pan·dem''ic
pan·de·mo''ni·um
pan''der
pan''der·er
pan·de·struc''tion
pan·dow''dy
  (*pl.* pan·dow''dies)
pane
  glass (*see:* pain)
pan'e·gyr''ic
pan'e·gyr''i·cal
pan'e·gyr''i·con'
pan'e·gyr''ist
pan''el
pan''el·ing
pan''el·ist
pan''-fried'
pan''-fry'
pang
pan'gam·ic
pan·go''lin
pan''han''dle
pan''han''dling
pan''ic
pan''ick·ing
pan''ick·y
pan''ic-strick'en
pan·jan''drum
pan''nier
pan''ning
pan''o·ply
  (*pl.* pan''o·plies)
pan'o·ram''a
pan'o·ram''ic
pan''pipe'
pan''sy
  (*pl.* pan''sies)
pan''ta·loons''
pan''the·ism'
pan''the·ist
pan''the·is''tic
pan''the·on'

pan''ther
pant''ies
pan''to·mime
pan''to·mim''ic
pan''to·mim''ing
pan''to·morph
pan''try
  (*pl.* pan''tries)
pant''suit'
pant''y hose'
pant
pant''y·waist
pan''zer
pa''pa·cy
pa''pal
pa'pal''ist''ic
pa'pa·raz''zo
  (*pl.* pa'pa·raz''zi)
pa''paw
pa·pa''ya
pa''per·board
pa''per·bound
pa''per·boy
pa''per clip'
pa''per cut''ter
pa''per·girl
pa''per·hanger
pa''per mon'ey
pa''per·weight'
pa''per·work'
pa''per·y
pa'pier-ma·che''
pa·pil''la
pap''il·lar'y
pap'il·lo''ma
pa·poose''
pap·ri''ka
Pap'' test'
pap''ule
pa·py''rus
  (*pl.* pa·py''ri)
par
par''a·ble
pa·rab''o·la
par'a·bol''ic
par'a·bol''i·cal

par'a·chute'
par'a·chut''ing
par'a·chut''ist
pa·rade''
par''a·digm
pa·rad''ing
par'a·dise'
par'a·dox'
par'a·dox''i·cal
par'a·dox''i·cal·ly
par''af·fin
par'a·gon'
par''a·graph'
Par''a·guay'
par''a·keet'
par'a·lin·guis''tic
par''al·lax'
par''al·lel'
par'al·lel'e·pi''ped
par''al·lel'ing
par''al·lel'ism
par'al·lel''o·gram'
pa·ral''y·sis
  (*pl.* pa·ral''y·ses')
par'a·lyt''ic
par''a·lyze'
par''a·lyz'ing
par'a·me''ci·um
  (*pl.* par'a·me''ci·a)
par'a·med''ic
par'a·med''i·cal
pa·ram''e·ter
  constant; factor (*see:*
  perimeter)
par'a·mil''i·tar'y
par'a·morph''ic
par''a·mount'
par''a·mour'
par'a·noi''a
par''a·noid
par'a·phenal''ia
par'a·phrase'
par'a·phras'ing
par'a·ple''gi·a
par'a·ple''gic
par'a·pro·fes''sion·al

par''a·psy·chol''o·gy
par''a·site'
par''a·sit''ic
par''a·sit''i·cide''
par''a·sit·tol''o·gist
par''a·sit·tol''o·gy
par''a·sol
par''a·troops
par''a·vion''
par''boil'
par''buck'le
par''cel
par''cel·ing
Par·chee''si™
parch''ment
par''dieu
par''don·a·ble
pare
   trim (see: pair and
   pear)
par''e·gor''ic
par''ent·age
pa·ren''tal
pa·ren''the·sis
   (pl. pa·ren''the·
   ses')
pa·ren''the·size'
pa·ren''the·siz'ing
par'en·thet''ic
par'en·thet''i·cal
par''ent·hood'
par''ent·like'
pa·re''sis
par ex·cel·lence''
par·fait''
pa·ri''ah
par''i·fy'
par'i·mu''tu·el
par''ing
   trimming (see: par-
   ring)
Par''is
par''ish
   church district (see:
   perish)
pa·rish''ion·er

par''i·ty
par''ka
park''ing me'ter
park''land'
park''way'
par''lance
par''lay
   bet (see: parley)
par''ley
   conference (pl. par''
   leys) (see: parlay)
par''leyed
par''ley·ing
par''lia·ment
par''lia·men·tar''i·an
par''lia·men''ta·ry
par''lor
par''lor·maid'
par''lous
Par''me·san'
par''mi·gia''na
pa·ro''chi·al
pa·ro''chi·al·ism'
par''o·died
par''o·dist
par''o·dy
   (pl. par''o·dies)
pa·role''
pa·rol''ing
pa·rot''id
par''ox·ysm'
par·ox·ys''mal
par''quet'
par''quet·ry
par''ri·cide'
par''ried
par''ring
   golf score (see: par-
   ing)
par''rot
par''ry
par''ry·ing
parse
par''sec'
par'si·mo''ni·ous
par'si·mo''ny

pars''ley
pars''nip
par''son
par''son·age
par·take''
par·tak''en
par·tak''ing
par·terre''
par''the·no·gen''e·sis
par''tial
par·ti·al''i·ty
   (pl. par·ti·al''i·ties)
part''i·ble
par·tic''i·pant
par·tic''i·pate'
par·tic''i·pat'ing
par·tic'i·pa''tion
par·ti·ci·pa·to'ry
par·ti''cip''i·al
par·ti''cip''i·al·ly
par·ti''ci·ple
par''ti·cle
par''ti·col'ored
par·tic''u·lar
par·tic·u·lar''i·ty
   (pl. par·tic'u·lar''i·
   ties)
par·tic'u·lar·i·za''tion
par·tic''u·lar·ize'
par·tic''u·lar·iz'ing
par·tic''u·lar·ly
par·tic''u·late
par''tied
part''ing
par''ti·san
par''ti·san·ship'
par·ti''tion
part''ner
part''ner·ship'
par·took''
part''tridge
part''song'
part''-time''
par·tu''ri·ent
par'tu·ri''tion
par''ty

(*pl.* par"ties)
par"ve·nu
pas"chal
pas de deux"
  (*pl.* pas de deux")
pa·sha"
pass"a·ble
  good enough (*see:*
   passible)
pas'sa·ca"glia
pas"sage
pas"sage·way'
pass"book'
pas·se"
passed
  did pass (*see:* past)
pas"sel
pas"sen·ger
passe'-par·tout"
pass"er-by'
  (*pl.* pass"ers-by")
pas"si·ble
  that can feel (*see:*
   passable)
pas"sion·ate
pas"sion·ate·ly
pas"sion·flow'er
pas"sion·fruit
pas"sion·less
pas"sive
pas"sive·ly
pas·siv"i·ty
pass"key'
pass"o·ver
pass"port
pass"word'
past
  earlier time (*see:*
   passed)
pas"ta
paste
paste"board
pas·tel"
pas"tern
paste"-up
pas'teur·i·za"tion

pas"teur·ize
pas"teur·iz"ing
pas·tiche"
past"i·er
pas·tille"
pas"time'
past"i·ness
past"ing
pas"tor
pas"to·ral
pas"tor·ate
pas·tra"mi
pas"try
  (*pl.* pas"tries)
pas"ture
pas"tur·ing
past"y
  (*pl.* past"ies)
past"y-faced"
pat
patch"i·er
patch"work
patch"y
pa·te"
pa·te" de foie gras"
pa·tel"la
pat"ent
pat"ent·a·ble
pa'ter·fa·mil"i·as
  (*pl.* pa'ters·fa·mil"
   i·as)
pa·ter"nal
pa·ter"nal·ism
pa·ter"nal·is"tic
pa·ter"nal·ly
pa·ter"ni·ty
pat'er·nos"ter
pa·thet"ic
pa·thet"i·cal·ly
path"find'er
path'o·gen"ic
path'o·log"i·cal
path'o·log"i·cal·ly
pa·thol"o·gist
pa·thol"o·gy
pa"thos

path"way
pa"tience
pa"tient
pat"i·na
pa"ti·o
pa·tis·se·rie"
pa"tri·arch
pa"tri·ar"chal
pa"tri·ar'chate
pa"tri·ar'chy
pa·tri"cian
pa·tri"ci·ate'
pat"ri·cide
pat'ri·lin"e·al
pat'ri·mo"ni·al
pat"ri·mo'ny
  (*pl.* pat"ri·mo'nies)
pa'tri·ot"ic
pa'tri·ot"i·cal·ly
pa"tri·ot·ism
pa·tris"tic
pa·trol"
pa·trol"ling
pa·trol"man
pa"tron
pa"tron·age
pa"tron·ess
pa"tron·ize
pa"tron·iz"ing
pa"tron saint"
pat'ro·nym"ic
pat"sy
  (*pl.* pat"sies)
pat"ter
pat"tern
pat"ting
pat"ty
  (*pl.* pat"ties)
pau"ci·ty
paunch"i·er
paunch"i·ness
paunch"y
pau"per
pau"per·ism
pau"per·ize
pause

paus"ing
pa·vane"
pave
pave"ment
pa·vil"ion
pav"ing
paw
pawl
  mechanical tool (*see:* pall)
pawn"bro'ker
Paw·nee"
  (*pl.* Paw·nee")
pawn"shop
pay"a·ble
pay"back'
pay"check
pay"day'
pay·ee"
pay"load
pay"mas'ter
pay"ment
pay"off'
pay·o"la
pay"out
pay" phone
pay"roll
pay"sage
pea
  (*pl.* peas)
peace
  calm (*see:* piece)
peace"a·ble
peace"ful
peace"ful·ly
peace"keep'ing
peace"mak'er
peace" of 'fi·cer
peace"time'
peach
peach"y
pea"cock
pea"hen
pea" jack'et
peak

point (*see:* peek and pique)
peaked
  pointed
peak"ed
  pale
peal
  ringing (*see:* peel)
pea"nut
pear
  fruit (*see:* pair and pare)
pearl
  gem (*see:* purl)
pearl"y
pear"-shaped'"
peas"ant
peas"ant·ry
peat" moss
peat"y
peb"ble
peb"bling
peb"bly
pe·can"
pec'ca·dil"lo
  (*pl.* pec"ca·dil" loes)
pec"ca·ry
  (*pl.* pec"ca·ries)
pecht
peck
peck"er·wood'
pec"tin
pec"to·ral
pec"u·late
pec"u·lating"
pec·u·la"tion
pec"u·la'tor
pe·cu"liar
pe·cu·li·ar"i·ty
  (*pl.* pe·cu·li·ar"i·ties)
pe·cu"liar·ly
pe·cu"ni·ar·y
ped'a·gog"ic
ped'a·gog"i·cal

ped"a·gogue
ped"a·go'gy
  (*pl.* ped"a·go'gies)
ped"al
  foot lever (*see:* peddle)
ped"al·ing
ped"al
ped'o·phil"ic
push"ers
ped"ant
pe·dan"tic
pe·dan"ti·cal·ly
pe·dan"tize
ped"ant·ry
  (*pl.* ped"ant·ries)
ped"dle
  sell (*see:* pedal)
ped"dler
ped"dling
ped"er·as'ty
ped"es·tal
pe·des"tri·an
pe'di·at"ric
pe'di·a·tri"cian
pe'di·at"rics
ped"i·cure'
ped"i·gree
ped"i·greed
ped"i·ment
ped'lar
pe·dom"e·ter
peek
  glance (*see:* peak and pique)
peek"a·boo'
peel
  skin (*see:* peal)
peel"ing
peep"er
peep"hole'
peep"ing Tom"
peep" show'
peer
  look; equal (*see:* pier)

peer''age
peer''less
peeve
peev''ing
peev''ish
pee''wee'
  small one (see: pe-
  wee)
peg''board'
peg''ging
peign·oir''
pe·jo''ra·tive
Pe'king·ese''
pe''koe
pel''i·can
pel·la''gram
pel·la''grous
pel''let
pell''-mell''
pel·lu''cid
pe·lo''ta
pel''vic
pel''vis
pem''mi·can
pe''nal
pe''nal·ize'
pe''nal·iz'ing
pen''al·ty
  (pl. pen''al·ties)
pen''ance
pen''chant
pen''cil
pen''cil·ing
pen''dant
  hanging ornament
  (see: pendent)
pen''dent
  hanging (see: pen-
  dant)
pend''ing
pen''du·lous
pen''du·lum
pen'e·tra·bil''i·ty
pen''e·tra·ble
pen''e·trate
pen''e·trat'ing

pen'e·tra''tion
pen''guin
pen'i·cil''lin
pen·in''su·la
pen·in''su·lar
pe''nis
  (pl. pe''nis·es)
pen''i·tence
pen''i·tent
pen'i·ten''tial
pen'i·ten''tial·ly
pen'i·ten''tia·ry
  (pl. pen'i·ten''tia·
  ries)
pen''knife'
  (pl. pen''knives')
pen''man·ship'
pen''name'
pen''nant
pen''ni·less
pen''ning
pen''non
Penn'syl·va''ni·a
pen''ny
  (pl. pen''nies)
pen''ny an''te
pen''ny pinch'er
pen''ny-pinch'ing
pen''ny·weight'
pen''ny-wise''
Pe·nob''scot
  (pl. Pe·nob''scot)
pe·nol''o·gist
pe·nol''o·gy
pen'' pal'
pen''point'
pen''rack
pen''sion·er
pen''sive
pen''sive·ly
pen''stock'
pen'ta·car''bon
pen''ta·gon·
pen·tag''o·nal
pen''ta·gram'
pen·tam''e·rism'

pen·tam''e·ter
pen·ta·spher''ic
Pen'ta·teuch'
pen·tath''lon
Pen''te·cost'
pent''house'
pen·tom''ic
pent''-up'
pe''nult
pc·nul''ti·mate
pe·num''bra
  (pl. pe·num''brae or
  pe·num''bras)
pe·nu''ri·ous
pen''u·ry
pe''on
  worker (see: paean)
pe''on·age
pe''o·ny
  (pl. pe''o·nies)
peo''ple
peo''pling
pep
pep'er·o''ni
pep''per and salt''
pep''per·corn'
pep''per·mint
pep''per pot'
pep''per·y
pep''pi·er
pep''pi·ness
pep''ping
pep''py
pep''sin
pep''talk'
pep''tic
pep''ton·ize'
per'ad·ven''ture
per·am''bu·late'
per·am''bu·lat'ing
per·am''bu·la''tion
per·am''bu·la'tor
per an''num
per''bor·ate'
per·cale''
per cap''i·ta

per·ceiv"a·ble
per·ceive"
per·ceiv"ing
per·cent"
per·cent"age
per·cen"tile
per"cept
per·cep"ti·bil"i·ty
per·cep"ti·ble
per·cep"tion
per·cep"tive
per·cep"tu·al
perch
per·chance"
per·cip"i·ent
per"co·late'
per"co·lat'ing
per"co·la"tion
per"co·la'tor
per·cus"sion
per·cus"sive
per di"em
per·di"tion
per"e·gri·nate'
per"e·gri·na"tion
per"e·grine
per·emp"to·ri·ly
per·emp"to·ry
per·en"ni·al
per·en"ni·al·ly
pe·rei"a
per"e·stroi·ka
per·fect", *v.*
  make perfect
per"fect i·bil"i·ty
per·fect"i·ble
per·fec"tion·ism'
per·fec"tion·ist
per·fid"i·ous
per"fi·dy
  (*pl.* per"fi·dies)
per"fo·rate'
per"fo·rat'ing
per"fo·ra"tion

per"fo·ra'tor
per·force"
per·form"
  enact (*see:* preform)
per·form"a·ble
per·form"ance
per·form"er
per·fume
per·fum"ing
per·func"to·ri·ly
per·func"to·ry
per·go·la
per·haps"
per'i·act"us
per'i·bronch"i·al
per'i·car"di·um
  (*pl.* per'i·car"di·a)
per'i·cra·ni"tis
per"i·gee'
per'i·he"li·on
per"il
per"il·ous
per'i·lune'
pe·rim"e·ter
  boundary (*see:* pa-
  rameter)
per'i·ne"um
  (*pl.* per'i·ne"a)
pe"ri·od
pe'ri·od"i·cal
pe'ri·od"i·cal·ly
pe'ri·o·dic"i·ty
per'i·o·don"tal
per'i·o·don"tics
per'i·pa·tet"ic
pe·riph"er·al
pe·riph"er·al·ly
pe·riph"er·y
  (*pl.* pe·riph"er·ies)
pe·riph"ra·sis
  (*pl.* pe·riph"ra·ses)
per'i·phras"tic
per"i·scope'
per'i·scop"ic
per"ish
  die (*see:* parish)

per'ish·a·bil"i·ty
per"ish·a·ble
per'i·stal"sis
per"i·style
per'i·to·ne"um
  (*pl.* per'i·to·ne"a)
per'i·to·ni"tis
per"i·win
per"i·win'kles
per"jure
per"jur·er
per"jur·ing
per"ju·ry
  (*pl.* per"ju·ries)
perk"i·er
perk"i·ly
perk"i·ness
perk"y
per"ma·frost
per"ma·nence
per"ma·nen·cy
  (*pl.* per"ma·nen·
  cies)
per"ma·nent
per·man"ga·nate'
per"me·a·bil"i·ty
per"me·a·ble
per"me·ate'
per"me·at'ing
per"me·a"tion
per·miss"
per·mis"si·bil"i·ty
per·mis"si·ble
per·mis"sion
per·mis"sive
per·mis"sive·ly
per·mis"sive·ness
per·mit", *v.*
  allow
per"mit, *n.*
  license
per·mit"ting
per"mu·tate
per"mu·tat'ing
per"mu·ta"tion
per·mute"

per·mut″ing
per·ni″cious
per′o·rate′
per″o·rat′ing
per·o·ra″tion
per·ox″ide
per·ox″id·ing
per·ox″i·date′
per·pen·dic″u·lar
per′pe·trate′
per′pe·trat′ing
per·pe·tra″tion
per·pe·tra″tor
per·pet″u·al
per·pet″u·al·ly
per·pet″u·ate
per·pet″u·at′ing
per·pet′u·a″tion
per·pet″u·a′tor
per·pe·tu″i·ty
  (*pl.* per′pc·tu″i·
  ties)
per·plex″
per·plexed″
per·plexed″ly
per·plex″i·ty
  (*pl.* per·plex″i·ties)
per′qui·site
per se″
per″se·cute
  oppress (*see:* prose-
  cute)
per″se·cut′ing
per″se·cu″tion
per″se·cu′tor
per′se·ver″ance
per′se·vere″
per′se·ver″ing
Per″sia
per·si·flage′
per·sim″mon
per·sist″
per·sist″ence
per·sis″tent
per·snick″e·ty
per″son

per·so″na
  (*pl.* per·so″nae *or*
  per·so″na)
per″son·a·ble
per″son·age
per″son·al
  private (*see:* person-
  nel)
per′son·al″i·ty
  character (*pl.* per′
  son·al″i·ties)
per″son·al·ize
per″son·al·iz·ing
per″son·al·ly
per″son·al·ty
  property (*pl.* per″
  son·al·ties)
per·so″na non gra″ta
per·son′i·fi·ca″tion
per·son″i·fied
per·son″i·fi′er
per·son″i·fy′
per·son″i·fy′ing
per′son·nel″
  employees (*see:* per-
  sonal)
per·spec″tive
  view (*see:* prospec-
  tive)
per′spi·ca″cious
per′spi·cac″i·ty
per′spi·cu″i·ty
per′spi·ra″tion
per·spire″
per·suad″a·ble
per·suade″
per·suad″er
per·suad″ing
per·sua″sion
per·sua″sive
per·tain″
per′ti·na″cious
per′ti·nac″i·ty
per″ti·nence
per″ti·nen·cy
per″ti·nent

per·turb″
per′tur·ba″tion
Pe·ru″
pe·rus″a·ble
pe·rus″al
pe·ruse″
pe·rus″er
pe·rus″ing
per·vade″
per·vad″ing
per·va″sive
per·verse″
per·verse″ly
per·verse″ness
per·ver″sion
per·ver″si·ty
  (*pl.* per·ver″si·ties)
per·vert″, *v.*
  distort
per″vert, *n.*
  perverted person
Pe″sach
pes″ki·er
pes″ky
pe″so
  (*pl.* pe″sos)
pes″si·mist′
pes″si·mis″tic
pes″si·mis″ti·cal·ly
pes″ter
pest″hole′
pes″ti·cide′
pes·tif″er·ous
pes″ti·lence
pes″ti·lent
pes′ti·len″tial
pes″tle
pes″tling
pet
pet″aled
pe·tard″
pet″cock′
pet″i·ole′
pet″it
  petty (*see:* petite)
pe·tit″ bour·geois″

pe·tite"
  tiny (*see:* petit)
pe·tite" bour'geoi'sie"
pet"it four"
pe·ti"tion
pet"it ju"ry
pet"it point'
pe"tri dish'
pet'ri·fac"tion
pet"ri·fied
pet"ri·fy'
pet"ri·fy'ing
pet'ro·chem"i·cal
pet'ro·chem"is·try
pet'ro·dol"lar
pet'ro·gen"e·sis
pe·trog"ra·phy
pet'ro·la"tum
pe·tro"le·um
pe·trol"o·gist
pe·trol"o·gy
pet"ti·coat'
pet"ti·er
pet"ti·fog'
pet"ti·fog'ger
pet"ti·fog'ging
pet"ti·ness
pet"ting
pet"tish
pet"ty cash"
pet'u·lance
pet'u·lant
pe·tu"ni·a
pew
pe"wee
  bird (*see:* peewee)
pew"ter
pe·yo"te
pha"e·ton
phag"o·cyte'
pha"lanx
  (*pl.* pha"lanx·es *or*
   pha"lanx)
phal'a·rope'
phal"lic
phal"lus

(*pl.* phal"li)
phan"tasm
phan·tas"ma·go"ri·a
phan"tom
Pha"raoh
phar'i·sa"ic
phar"i·see'
phar'ma·ceu"ti·cal
phar'ma·ceu"tics
phar"ma·cist
phar'ma·co·log"i·cal
phar'ma·col"o·gist
phar'ma·col"o·gy
phar'ma·co·poe"ia
phar"ma·cy
  (*pl.* phar"ma·cies)
pha·ryn"ge·al
phar"ynx
  (*pl.* phar"ynx·es)
phase
  stage (*see:* faze)
phase"ing
  introducing gradu-
  ally (*see:* fazing)
phase"-out'
phas"ma
pheas"ant
phe·net"ic
phe'no·bar"bi·tal
phe"nol
phe·no"lic
phe'nol·phthal"ein
phe'nol·sul"phon·ate'
phe·nom"e·nal
phe·nom"e·non
  (*pl.* phe·nom"e·na)
phe"no·type'
phe'no·typ"ic
pher"o·mone'
phew
Phil'a·del"phi·a
phi·lan"der
phi·lan"der·er
phil'an·throp"ic
phi·lan"thro·pist
phi·lan"thro·py

(*pl.* phi·lan"thro·
  pies)
phil'a·tel"ic
phi·lat"e·list
phi·lat"e·ly
phil'har·mon"ic
Phil"ip·pines'
Phil"is·tine'
phil'o·den"dron
phil'o·log"i·cal
phi·lol"o·gist
phi·lol"o·gy
phi·los"o·pher
phil'o·soph"ic
phil'o·soph"i·cal
phil'o·soph"i·cal·ly
phi·los"o·phize'
phi·los"o·phiz'er
phi·los"o·phiz'ing
phi·los"o·phy
  (*pl.* phi·los"o·phies)
phil"ter
  potion (*see:* filter)
phle·bi"tis
phle·boi"dal
phle·bot"o·my
  (*pl.* phle·bot"o·
  mies)
phlegm
phleg·mat"ic
phleg·mat"i·cal·ly
phlo"em
phlox
Phnom" Penh"
pho"bi·a
pho"bic
phoe"be
phoe"nix
  mythical bird
Phoe"nix
  city; constellation
phone
pho"neme
pho·ne"mic
pho·ne"mi·cal·ly
pho·net"i·cal·ly

pho·net''ics
phon''i·cal·ly
phon''ics
pho''ni·er
pho''ni·ness
phon''ing
pho''no·car'di·og''ra·phy
pho''no·graph'
pho''no·graph''ic
pho''no·log''i·cal·ly
pho·nol''o·gist
pho·nol''o·gy
  (*pl.* pho·nol''o·gies)
pho''ny
  (*pl.* pho''nies)
phoo''ey
phos''gene
phos''phate
phos''phor
phos'pho·resce''
phos'pho·res''cence
phos'pho·res''cent
phos'pho·resc''ing
phos·phor''ic
phos''pho·rus
pho''to
  (*pl.* pho''tos)
pho''to·cell'
pho''to·com'
pho''to·gene''
po·si''tion
pho''to·cop'ied
pho''to·cop'i·er
pho''to·cop'y
  (*pl.* pho''to·cop'ies)
pho''to·cop'y·ing
pho''to·e·lec'tric''i·ty
pho'to·e·lec''tron
pho''to·en·grave'
pho''to·en·grav'er
pho''to·en·grav'ing
pho''to''fin''ish
pho''to·flash'
pho''to·flood'
pho''to·gen''ic

pho''to·graph'
pho·tog''ra·pher
pho'to·graph''ic
pho'to·graph''i·cal·ly
pho·tog''ra·phy
pho'to·gra·vure''
pho'to·jour''nal·ism'
pho to·li·thog''ra·phy
pho·tom''e·ter
pho'to·met''ric
pho·tom''e·try
pho'to·mon·tage''
pho''to·pho''ton
pho'to-off''set'
pho''to·play'
pho'to·sen''si·tive
pho'to·sen'si·tiv''i·ty
Pho''to·stat'™
pho''to·syn''the·sis
pho'to·syn''thet''ic
pho''to·trop''ic
pho·tot''ro·pism'
pho'to·vol·ta''ic
phras''al
phrase
phra'se·ol''o·gy
phras''ing
phren''ic
phre·nol''o·gist
phre·nol''o·gy
phy·lac''ter·y
phy''gi·um
phy·log''e·ny
phy''la
  (*pl.* phy''la)
phys''ic
  medicine (*see:* physique and psychic)
phys''i·cal
phys''i·cal·ly
phy·si''cian
phys''i·cist
phys''ics
phys'i·og''no·my
phys'i·o·graph''ic
phys'i·og''ra·phy

phys'i·o·log''i·cal
phys'i·o·log''i·cal·ly
phys'i·ol''o·gist
phys'i·ol''o·gy
phys'i·o·ther''a·pist
phys'i·o·ther''a·py
phy·sique''
  body build (*see:* physic)
phy'to·gen''e·sis
phy'to·ge·net''ic
pi''ma''tcr
pi'a·nis''si·mo'
pi·an''ist
pi·an''o
  (*pl.* pi·an''os)
pi·an'o·for''te
pi·as''ter
pi·az''za
pi''ca
pic'a·dor
  (*pl.* pic'a·dors')
pic'a·resque''
pic'a·yune''
pic''ca·lil'li
pic''co·lo'
  (*pl.* pic''co·los')
pick''ax'
  (*pl.* pick''ax'es)
pick''er·el
pick''et line'
pick''i·er
pick''ing
pick''le
pick''ling
pick''-me-up'
pick''pock'et
pick''up
pick·wick''i·an
pick''y
pic''nic
pic''nick·er
pic''nick·ing
pi''co·sec'ond
pi''cot
pic''to·graph'

pic'to·graph''ic
pic·tog''ra·phy
pic·to''ri·al
pic·to''ri·al·ly
pic''ture
pic'tur·esque''
pic''tur·ing
pid''dle
pid''dling
pidg''in
  language (*see:* pi-
  geon)
pie
pie''bald
piece
  part (*see:* peace)
piece'' de re·sis·tance''
piece''meal
piece''work'
piece''work'er
piec''ing
pied
pier
  dock (*see:* peer)
pierce
pierc''ing
Pi·erre''
pi''e·tism
pi''e·ty
  (*pl.* pi''e·ties)
pi·e'zo·e·lec''tric
pi·e zo·e·lec·tric''i·ty
pif''fle
pi''geon
  bird (*see:* pidgin)
pi''geon·hole
pi''geon·hol'ing
pi''geon-toed
pig''gish
pig''gy
  (*pl.* pig''gies)
pig''gy·back'
pig''gy bank
pig''head'ed
pig'' iron
pig'' Lat'in

pig''let
pig''ment
pig''men·ta''tion
pig''pen
pig''skin
pig''sty'
  (*pl.* pig''sties)
pig''tail'
pig''widge·on
pike
pik''er
pike''staff
  (*pl.* pike''staves)
pi·laf''
pil''a·strade'
pi·las''ter
pil''chard
pile''up
pil''fer
pil''fer·age
pil''grim
pil''grim·age
pil''ing
pil''lage
pil''lar
pill''box
pil''lion
pil''lo·ried
pil''lo·ry
  (*pl.* pil''lo·ries)
pil''lo·ry·ing
pil''low·case'
pil''low·like'
pi''lot·age
pi''lot·house'
pi''lot lamp
pi''lot light
pi''ma
  (*pl.* pi''mas)
pi·men''to
  (*pl.* pi·men''tos)
pimp
pim''per·nel
pim''ple
pim''ply
pin

  fasten (*see:* pine)
pin''a·fore
pi·na''ta
pin''ball
pin'' boy
pince''-nez
pinch''crust'
pin''check
pinch''-hit''
pinch''-hit''ting
pin'' curl
pin''cush'ion
pine
  yearn; tree (*see:* pin)
pin''e·al
pine''ap'ple
pine''cone'
pine'' nee'dle
pine'' tar'
pin''feath'er
ping
Ping''-Pong™
pin''head'
pin''hole'
pin''ing
  yearning (*see:* pin-
  ning)
pin''ion
  wine; restrain (*see:*
  Pinyin)
pink''eye'
pink''ie
  (*pl.* pink''ies)
pin'' mon'ey
pin''na·cle
pin''na·cling
pin''nate
pin''ning
  fastening (*see:* pin-
  ing)
pin'' oak'
pi''noch·le
pin''point'
pin''prick'
pin''set'ter
pin''striped'

pin"strip'er
pin"to
  (*pl.* pin"tos)
pint"-size'
pint'-sized'
pin"up'
pin"wheel'
pin"worm'
Pin"yin"
  translation system
  (*see:* pinion and
  pinyon)
pin"yon
  tree (*see:* pinion and
  Pinyin)
pi·o·neer"
pi"ous
pip
pipe" dream'
pipe"ful'
  (*pl.* pipe"fuls')
pipe"line'
pip"er
pi·pette"
pip"ing
pip"pin
pip"-squeak'
pi"quan·cy
pi"quant
pique"
  resentment (*see:*
  peek and pique)
pi·que"
  fabric
piqu"ing
pi"ra·cy
pi·ra"nha
pi"rate
pi·rat"i·cal
pi·rosh·ki"
pir'ou·ette"
pir'ou·et"ting
Pi"sa
pis'ca·to"ri·al
pis"ta"chi·o
  (*pl.* pis·ta"chi·os)

pis"tic
pis"til
  flower part (*see:* pis-
  tol)
pis"til·late
pis"tol
  firearm (*see:* pistil)
pis"tol-whipped'
pis"ton ring'
pis"ton rod'
pi"ta
pit"a·pat'
pit"a·pat'ting
pitch"-black"
pitch"blende'
pitch"-dark"
pitch"er
pitch"fork'
pitch"man
pitch"out'
pitch" pipe'
pit"e·ous
pit"fall'
pit"head'
pith"i·er
pith"i·ly
pith"y
pit"i·a·ble
pit"ied
pit"i·ful
pit"i·ful·ly
pit"i·less
pi"ton
pit"tance
pit"ter-pat'ter
pit"ting
Pitts"burgh
pi·tu"i·tar'y
  (*pl.* pi·tu"i·tar'ies)
pit"y
  (*pl.* pit"ies)
pit"y·ing
piv"ot
piv"ot·al
pix"ie
pix"i·lat'ed

pi·zazz"
piz"za
piz'ze·ri"a
piz'zi·ca"to
plac'a·bil"i·ty
plac"a·ble
plac"ard
pla"cate
pla"cat·ing
pla·ca"tion
pla·ce"bo
place" card'
place"-kick', *v.*
  to kick
place" kick', *n.*
  a kick
place" mat
place"ment
pla·cen"ta
plac"er
plac"id
pla·cid"i·ty
plac"ing
plack"et
pla"gia·rism
pla"gia·rist
pla"gia·rize
pla"gia·riz'er
pla"gia·riz'ing
plain
  evident; flat ground
  (*see:* plane)
plain"ly
plain"ness
plains"man
plain"song
plain"-spo"ken
plain"tiff
plain"tive
plain"tive·ly
plait
  braid (*see:* plate and
  plat)
plan
plan"cher
plane

airplane; tool; flat
  surface (*see:* plain)
plan″er
plan″et
plan·e·tar″i·um
  (*pl.* plan′e·tar″i·
  ums)
plan″e·tar′y
plan″et·oid′
plan″gent
plan″ing
  gliding (*see:* plan-
  ning)
plank″ing
plank″ton
plan″ner
plan″ning
  scheming (*see:* plan-
  ing)
plant
plan″tain
plan″tar
  of sole of foot (*see:*
  planter)
plan·ta″tion
plant″er
  one who plants (*see:*
  plantar)
plaque
plash
plas″ma
plas″mic
plas″ter·board′
plas″ter cast″
plas″ter·er
plas″tic
plas·tic″i·ty
plas″ti·cize′
plas″ti·ciz′ing
plat
  map; braid (*see:*
  plait and plate)
plat″ du jour″
plat″i·tude′
plate

dish; to coat (*see:*
  plait and plat)
pla·teau″
plat″ed
plate″ful
plate″ glass″
plate″let
plat″en
plat″er
plat″form
plat″ing
  coating (*see:* plat-
  ting)
plat″i·num
plat″i·tude′
plat″i·tu″di·nous
pla·ton″i·cal·ly
pla″to·nism′
pla·toon″
plat″ter
plat″ting
  braiding; mapping
  (*see:* plating)
pla″ty·pus
  (*pl.* pla″ty·pus)
plau″dit
plau′si·bil″i·ty
plau″si·ble
play″a·ble
play″act′
play″back′
play″bill′
play″boy′
play″-by-play″
play″er
play″fel′low
play″ful·ly
play″ful·ness
play″go′er
play″ground′
play″house′
play″ing card′
play″mate′
play″-off′′
play″pen′
play″room′

play″suit′
play″thing′
play″time′
play″wright′
pla″za
plea
plead
pleas″ant
pleas″ant·ry
  (*pl.* pleas″ant·ries)
please
pleas″ing
pleas″ur·a·ble
pleas″ure
pleas″ur·ing
pleat
plebe
ple·be″ian
pleb″i·scite′
pledge
pledg″ee
pledg″er
pledg″ing
Pleis″to·cene′
ple″na·ry
plen′i·po·ten″ti·ar′y
plen″i·tude′
plen″te·ous
plen″ti·ful
plen″ti·ful·ly
plen″ty
ple″num
ple″o·nasm′
ple″si·o·saur′
pleth″o·ra
pleu″ral
pleu″ri·sy
Plex″i·glas″™
plex″us
pli′a·bil″i·ty
pli″a·ble
pli″an·cy
pli″ant
plied
pli″ers
plight

Pli″o·cene′
plod
plod″der
plod″ding
plop
plop″ping
plot
plot″ter
plot″ting
plow″back′
plow″share′
ploy
pluck″i·er
pluck″i·ly
pluck″i·ness
pluck″y
plug
plug″ger
plug″ging
plug″-in′
plum
  fruit (see: plumb)
plum″age
plumb
  weight (see: plum)
plumb″er
plumb″ing
plume
plum″ing
plum″met
plump″ness
plun″der
plun″der·er
plunge
plung″er
plung″ing
plunk
plu·per″fect
plu″ral
plu″ral·ism
plu′ral·is″tic
plu·ral″i·ty
  (pl. plu·ral″i·ties)
plur′i·nom″i·nal
plus
  (pl. plus″es)

plush
plush″i·er
plush″y
plus″ sign
Plu″to
plu·toc″ra·cy
  (pl. plu·toc″ra·cies)
plu″to·crat′
plu·to″ni·um
plu″vi·al
ply
Plym″outh
ply″wood′
pneu·mat″ic
pneu′mo·coc″cus
  (pl. pneu′mo·coc″
  ci)
pneu·mol″o·gy
pneu·mo″nia
poach″er
pock″et·book′
pock″et·ful
  (pl. pock″et·fuls′)
pock″et·knife′
pock″et·size′
pock″et ve′to
pock″marked
pock″wood
pod
po·di″a·trist
po·di″a·try
po″di·um
po·do·branch″i·al
po″dunk
po″et
po″et·as′ter
po″et·ess
po·et″ic
po·et″i·cal
po·et″i·cal·ly
po″et·i·cize′
po″et·ry
po″go stick
po·grom″
poi
poign″an·cy

poign″ant
poin·ci·an″a
poin·set″ti·a
point″-blank″
point″ed
point″er
point″i·er
poin″til·list
point″less
point″y
poise
pois″ing
poi″son gas″
poi″son·ous
poke
pok″er
po″key
  jail (pl. po″keys)
  (see: poky)
pok″ing
pok″y
  slow (see: pokey)
Po″land
po″lar bear′
po·lar″i·ty
po·lar·i·za″tion
po″lar·ize′
po″lar·iz′ing
Po″lar·oid′™
pol″der
pole
  stick; end (see: poll)
pole″ax′
  (pl. pole″ax′es)
pole″cat′
poled
po·lem″ic
po·lem″i·cal
po·lem″i·cal·ly
pole″-vault′, v.
  jump
pole″ vault′, n.
  athletic event
pole″-vault′er
po·lice″ dog′
po·lice″man

(*pl.* po·lice″men)
po·lice″wom′an
  (*pl.* po·lice″wom′
  en)
po·lic″ing
pol″i·cy
  (*pl.* pol″i·cies)
pol″i·cy·hold′er
pol″ing
po″li·o
po·li·o·my′e·li′tis
pol″ish
Po″lit·bu′ro
po·lite″ly
po·lite″ness
po·lit″i·cal
po·lit″i·cal·ly
pol·i·ti″cian
pol″i·tick′ing
po·lit″i·co
  (*pl.* po·lit″i·cos)
pol″i·tics
pol″i·ty
  (*pl.* pol″i·ties)
pol″ka
pol″ka dot′
poll
  voting (*see:* pole)
pol″len
pol″li·nate′
pol″li·nat′ing
pol″li·na″tion
pol″li·na′tor
pol″li·gog′
poll″ster
pol·lu″tant
pol·lute″
pol·lut″er
pol·lut″ing
pol·lu″tion
po″lo
pol·o·naise″
po·lo″ni·um
pol″ter·geist′
pol·troon″
poly″·an″drous

pol″y·es′ter
pol′y·eth″yl·ene′
po·lyg″a·mist
po·lyg″a·mous
po·lyg″a·my
pol″y·glot′
pol″y·gon′
pol″y·graph′
pol″y·he′dron
pol″y·mer
po·lym″er·i·za″tion
po·lym″er·ize′
po·lym″er·iz′ing
Pol′y·ne″sia
pol′y·no″mi·al
pol″yp
pol″y·phon″ic
po·lyph″o·ny
pol′y·sty″rene
pol″y·syl′la·ble
pol′y·tech″nic
pol″y·the·ism′
pol′y·the·is″tic
pol′y·un·sat″u·rat′ed
pol′y·u″re·thane′
pol′y·vi″nyl
po·made″
po·mad″ing
po″man·der
pome″gran′ate
pom″mel
  knob; saddle part
  (*see:* pummel)
pom″mel·ing
pomp
pom″pa·dour
pom″pa·no′
Pom·pe′ii
pom″pon
pom·pos″i·ty
pomp″us
pon″cho
  (*pl.* pon″chos)
pon″der
pon″der·a·ble
pon′der·o″sa

pon″der·ous
pon″iard
pon″tiff
pon·tif″i·cal·ly
pon·tif″i·cate′
pon·tif″i·cat′ing
pon·toon″
po″ny
  (*pl.* po″nies)
po″ny·tail′
pooch
poo″dle
pooh′-pooh″
pool″room
poop″er·scoop″er
poor″house
poor″ly
pop″corn
pope
pop″eyed
pop″fly″
pop″gun′
pop″lar
  tree (*see:* popular)
pop″lin
pop″o′ver
pop″per
pop″ping
pop″py
  (*pl.* pop″pies)
pop″py·cock′
pop″py seed
pop″u·lace
  people (*see:* popu-
  lous)
pop″u·lar
  liked (*see:* poplar)
pop′u·lar″i·ty
pop″u·lar·ize
pop″u·lar·iz′ing
pop″u·lar·ly
pop″u·late
pop″u·lat′ing
pop′u·la″tion
pop″u·lous

crowded (*see:* popu-
  lace)
pop″-up′
por″ce·lain
porch
por″cine
por″cu·pine
pore
  meditate; opcning
  (*see:* pour)
por″gy
  (*pl.* por″gies)
por″ing
  meditating (*see:*
  pouring)
pork″er
pork″pie
por·nog″ra·pher
por′no·graph″ic
por·nog″ra·phy
po″rous
por″phy·ry
  (*pl.* por″phy·ries)
por″poise
por″ridge
port·a·bil″i·ty
port″a·ble
por″tage
por″tag·ing
por″tal-to-por″tal
Port′-au-Prince″
port·cul″lis
por·tend″
por″tent
por·ten″tous
por″ter·house
port·fo″li·o′
  (*pl.* port·fo″li·os)
port″hole
por″ti·co
  (*pl.* por″ti·coes)
por·tiere″
por″tion
port″land
port″li·ness
port·man″teau

por″trait
por″trait·ist
por″trai·ture
por·tray″
por·tray″al
Ports″mouth
Por″tu·gal
Por′tu·guese″
por′tu·lac″a
pose
pos″er
  one who poses (*see:*
  poseur)
po·seur″
  affected person (*see:*
  poser)
posh
pos″ing
pos″it
po·si″tion
pos″i·tive·ly
pos″i·tiv·ism
pos″i·tron
pos″se
pos·sess″
pos·sessed″
pos·ses″sion
pos·ses″sive
pos·ses″sor
pos′si·bil″i·ty
  (*pl.* pos′si·bil″i·
  ties)
pos″si·ble
pos″sum
post″age
post″bel″lum
post″card′
post·date″
post·dat″ing
post′di·lu″vi·an
post·doc″tor·al
post″er
pos·te″ri·or
pos·ter″i·ty
post·grad″u·ate
post″haste″

post″hole
post″hu·mous
post′hyp·not″ic
post″lude
post″man
  (*pl.* post″men)
post″mark
post″mas″ter
post″mas′ter gen″er·
  al
  (*pl.* post″mas′ters
  gen″er·al)
post me·rid″i·an
  of afternoon (*see:*
  post meridiem)
post″ me·rid″i·em
  P.M. (*see:* post me-
  ridian)
post″mis′tress
post-mor″tem
post·na″sal
post·na″tal
post″ of′fice
post·op″er·a·tive
post·or″bit·al
post·paid″
post′par″tum
post·pone″
post·pone″ment
post·pon″ing
post″script′
pos″tu·lant
pos″tu·late
pos″tu·lat′ing
pos′tu·la″tion
pos″tu·la′tor
pos″tur·al
pos″ture
pos″tur·ing
post″war″
po″sy
  (*pl.* po″sies)
po″ta·ble
pot″ash
po·tas″si·um
po·ta″tion

po·ta″to
  (*pl.* po·ta″toes)
pot″bel′lied
pot″bel′ly
pot″boil′er
po″ten·cy
  (*pl.* po″ten·cies)
po″tent
po″ten·tate
po·ten′tial
po·ten′ti·al″i·ty
  (*pl.* po·ten′ti·al′i·
  ties)
po·ten′tial·ly
po·ten′ti·om″e·ter
pot″ful
pot″head
pot″herb
pot″hold′er
pot″hole
pot″hook
po″tion
pot″latch
pot″luck
pot″pie
pot′pour·ri″
pot″ roast
pot″sherd′
pot″shot
pot″tage
pot″ted
pot″ter·y
  (*pl.* pot″ter·ies)
pot″ting
pouch
poult
poul″tice
poul″try
pounce
pounc″ing
pound″age
pound″ cake′
pound″-fool″ish
pour
  flow (*see:* pore)
pour″ing

flowing; raining
  (*see:* poring)
pout″er
pov″er·ty-strick′en
pow″der puff′
pow″der room′
pow″der·y
pow″er·boat′
pow″er brake′
pow″er·ful
pow″er·ful·ly
pow″er·less
pow″wow
pox
prac′ti·ca·bil″i·ty
prac″ti·ca·ble
prac″ti·cal
prac′ti·cal″i·ty
prac″ti·cal·ly
prac″tice
prac″tic·ing
prac·ti″tion·er
prae·to″ri·an
prag·mat″ic
prag·mat″i·cal·ly
prag″ma·tism′
prag″ma·tist
Prague
prai″rie dog′
praise″wor′thy
prais″ing
pra″line
pram
prance
pranc″er
pranc″ing
prank″ster
prate
prat″fall′
prat″ing
prat″tle
prat″tling
prawn
pray
  implore (*see:* prey)
prayer″ book′

prayer″ful
prayer″ful·ly
preach″er
preach″ment
pre′ad·o·les″cence
pre′ad·o·les″cent
pre″am′ble
pre·am″pli·fi·er
pre′ar·range′
pre′ar·range″ment
pre′ar·rang″ing
pre′as·sem″bly
pre′as·sign′
pre′as·sump″tion
pre·cam″bri·an
pre·can″cel
pre·can·cel·la″tion
pre·car″i·ous
pre·cau″tion
pre·cede″
  go before (*see:* pro-
  ceed)
prec″e·dence
prec″e·dent, *n.*
  example (*see:* presi-
  dent)
pre·ced″ent, *adj.*
  preceding
pre·ced″ing
pre″cept
pre·cep″tor
pre·ces″sion
  earth motion (*see:*
  procession)
pre″cinct
pre·ci·os″i·ty
pre″cious
prec″i·pice
pre·cip″i·tant
pre·cip″i·tate′
pre·cip″i·tat′ing
pre·cip′i·ta″tion
pre·cip″i·tous
pre·cis″
  summary (*pl.* pre·
  cis″) (*see:* precise)

pre·cise''
  specific (*see:* precis)
pre·cise''ly
pre·ci''sion
pre·clude''
pre·clud''ing
pre·clu''sive
pre·co''cious
pre·coc''i·ty
pre'cog·ni''tion
pre'con·ceive''
pre'con·ceiv''ing
pre'con·cep''tion
pre'con·di''tion
pre·cook''
pre·cur''sor
pre·date''
pre·dat''ing
pred''a·tor
pred''a·to'ri·ly
pred''a·to'ry
pre'de·cease''
pre'de·ceas''ing
pred'e·ces''sor
pre·des''ig·nate'
pre·des''ig·nat'ing
pre·des'ti·na''tion
pre·des''tine
pre·des''tin·ing
pre'de·ter'mi·na''tion
pre'de·ter''mine
pre'de·ter''min·ing
pred''i·ca·ble
pre·dic''a·ment
pred''i·cate'
pred''i·cat'ing
pre·dict''
pre·dict'a·bil''i·ty
pre·dict''a·ble
pre·dic''tion
pre·di·gest''
pre·di·lec''tion
pre·dis·pose''
pre·dis·pos''ing
pre·dis'po·si''tion
pre·dom''i·nance

pre·dom''i·nant
pre·dom''i·nate'
pre·dom''i·nat'ing
pre·em''i·nence
pre·em''i·nent
pre·emp''tion
pre·emp''tive
pre·emp''tor
preen
pre'ex·ist''
pre'ex·ist''ence
pre'ex·ist''ent
pre''fab'
pre·fab''ri·cate'
pre·fab''ri·cat'ing
pre·fab·ri·ca''tion
pref''ace
pref''ac·ing
pref''a·to'ry
pre''fect
pre''fec·ture
pre·fer''
pref'er·a·bil''i·ty
pref''er·a·ble
pref''er·ence
pref'er·en''tial
pre·fer''ment
pre·fer''ring
pre·fig'u·ra''tion
pre·fig''ur·a'tive
pre·fig''ure
pre·fig''ur·ing
pre''fix
pre·form''
  form in advance
  (*see:* perform)
preg''nan·cy
  (*pl.* preg''nan·cies)
preg''nant
pre·heat''
pre·hen''sile
pre·his·tor''ic
pre·his''to·ry
pre·judge''
pre·judg''ing
prej''u·dice

prej'u·di''cial
prej'u·di''cial·ly
prej''u·dic·ing
prel''ate
pre·lim''i·nar'y
  (*pl.* pre·lim''i·nar'
  ies)
prel''ude
prel''ud·ing
pre'ma·ture''ly
pre·med''
pre·med''i·tate'
pre·med''i·tat'ing
pre·med'i·ta''tion
pre·mier''
  chief officer (*see:*
  premiere)
pre·miere''
  first performance
  (*see:* premier)
prem''ise
prem''is·ing
pre''mi·um
pre''mix''
pre'mo·ni''tion
pre·mon''i·to'ry
pre·na''tal
pre·oc'cu·pa''tion
pre·oc''cu·pied'
pre·oc''cu·py
pre·oc''cu·py'ing
pre·or·dain''
pre·paid''
prep'a·ra''tion
pre·par''a·to'ry
pre·pare''
pre·par''ed·ness
pre·par''ing
pre·pay''
pre·pay''ment
pre·pon''der·ance
pre·pon''der·ate
pre·pon''der·at'ing
prep'o·si''tion·al
pre·pos·sess''
pre·pos·sess''ing

pre'pos·ses"sion
pre·pos"ter·ous
prep"pie
  (*pl.* prep"pies)
prep" school
pre"puce
pre're·cord"
pre·req"ui·site
pre·rog"a·tive
pre·sage", *v.*
  give warning; pre-
  dict
pres"age, *n.*
  omen
pre·sag"ing
Pres'by·te"ri·an
Pres'by·te"ri·an·ism
pre"school
pre"sci·ent
pre·scribe"
  order (*see:* pro-
  scribe)
pre·scrib"ing
pre·scrip"tion
pre·scrip"tive
pre·sell"
pres"ence
pre·sent", *v.*
  give; introduce
pres"ent, *n.*
  now; gift
pre·sent'a·bil"i·ty
pre·sent"a·ble
pres"en·ta"tion
pres"ent-day"
pre·sen"ti·ment
  premonition
  (*see:* presentment)
pres"ent·ly
pre·sent"ment
  presentation (*see:*
  presentiment)
pre·serv"a·ble
pres'er·va"tion
pre·serv"a·tive
pre·serve"

pre·serv"ing
pre-shrunk"
pre·side"
pres"i·den·cy
  (*pl.* pres"i·den·cies)
pres"i·dent
  chief officer (*see:*
  precedent)
pres"i·dent-e·lect"
pres'i·den"tial
pre·sid"ing
pre·sid"i·um
pre·sold"
pre·sort"
press"er
press"ing
press"man
  (*pl.* press"men)
press"room"
pres"sure cook'er
pres"sur·ing
pres'sur·i·za"tion
pres"sur·iz'ing
press"work'
pres'ti·dig'i·ta"tion
pres'ti·dig"i·ta·tor
pres·tige"
pres·tig"ious
pres"to
pre·stress"
pre·sum"a·ble
pre·sume"
pre·sum"ing
pre·sump"tion
pre·sump"tive
pre·sump"tu·ous
pre'sup·pose"
pre'sup·pos"ing
pre'sup·po·si"tion
pre·tend"er
pre·tense"
pre·ten"sion
pre·ten"tious
pre'ter·nat"u·ral
pre'ter·nat"u·ral·ly

pre·test", *v.*
  test in advance
pre"test, *n.*
  preliminary test
pre"text
pret"ti·er
pret"ti·fied'
pret"ti·fy'
pret"ti·ly
pret"ty
  (*pl.* pret"ties)
pret"zel
pre·vail"
pre·vail"ing
prev"a·lence
prev"a·lent
pre·var"i·cate
pre·var"i·cat'ing
pre·var'i·ca"tion
pre·vent'a·bil"i·ty
pre·vent"a·ble
pre·vent"a·tive
pre·ven"tion
pre·ven"tive
pre"view
pre"vi·ous
pre·vi"sion
pre"war"
pre·wire"
pre·wir"ing
prey
  victim (*see:* pray)
price"less
pric"i·er
pric"ing
pric"ey
price
prick
prick"le
prick"ling
prick"ly heat
pride
  self-respect (*see:*
  pried)
pride"ful
pride"ful·ly

pried
did pry (*see:* pride)
priest"ess
priest"hood
priest"ly
prig
prig"ging
prig"gish
prim
pri"ma·cy
pri"ma don"na
pri"ma fa"ci·e
pri"mal
pri·ma"ri·ly
pri"ma·ry
(*pl.* pri"ma·ries)
pri"mate
prime
prim"er
basic book; paint
(*see:* primmer)
pri·me"val
prim"ing
prim"i·tive
prim"i·tiv·ism
prim"mer
more prim (*see:*
primer)
pri"mo·gen"i·tor
pri"mo·gen"i·ture
pri·mor"di·al
primp
prim"rose
Prince Ed"ward Is"
land
prince"ly
prin"cess
prin"ci·pal
most important;
leader (*see:* princi-
ple)
prin'ci·pal"i·ty
(*pl.* prin'ci·pal"i·
ties)
prin"ci·pal·ly
prin"ci·ple

rule (*see:* principal)
prin"ci·pled
print"a·ble
print"er
print"ing press
print"out
print" shop
pri"or
pri"or·ess
pri·or"i·tize
pri·or"i·tiz·ing
pri·or"i·ty
(*pl.* pri·or"i·ties)
pri"o·ry
(*pl.* pri"o·ries)
prism
pris·mat"ic
pris"on
pris"on·er
pris"si·er
pris"si·ness
pris"sy
pris"tine
prith"ee
pri"va·cy
pri"vate·ly
pri·va·teer"
pri·va"tion
priv"et
priv"i·lege
priv"i·leged
priv"y
(*pl.* priv"ies)
prize"fight
prize"fight'er
prize"fighting
prize"win'ner
priz"ing
pro
(*pl.* pros)
prob'a·bil"i·ty
(*pl.* prob'a·bil"i·
ties)
prob"a·ble
pro"bate
pro"bat·ing

pro·ba"tion
pro·ba"tion·ar'y
pro·ba"tion·er
probe
prob"ing
pro"bi·ty
prob"lem
prob'lem·at"ic
prob'lem·at"i·cal·ly
pro·bos"cis
(*pl.* pro·bos"cis·es)
pro·ce"dur·al
pro·ce"dure
pro·ceed
go forward (*see:* pre-
cede)
pro·ces"sion
parade (*see:* preces-
sion)
pro·ces"sion·al
proc"es·sor
pro·claim"
proc'la·ma"tion
pro·cliv"i·ty
(*pl.* pro·cliv"i·ties)
pro·con"sul
pro·cras"ti·nate
pro·cras"ti·nat'ing
pro·cras'ti·na"tion
pro·cras"ti·na'tor
pro"cre·ate
pro"cre·at'ing
pro'cre·a"tion
pro"cre·a'tive
pro"cre·a'tor
pro·crus"te·an
proc·tol"o·gist
proc·tol"o·gy
proc"tor
proc"to·scope
proc·tos"co·py
pro·cur"a·ble
proc"u·ra·tor
pro·cure"
pro·cure"ment
pro·cur"er

pro·cur″ess
pro·cur″ing
prod
prod″der
prod″ding
prod″i·gal
prod″i·gal·ly
pro·di″gious
prod″i·gy
  (*pl.* prod″i·gies)
pro·duce″ *v.*
  bring into existence
pro″duce *n.*
  fresh food
pro·duc″er
pro·duc″ing
pro·duc″tion
pro·duc″tive·ly
pro·duc″tive·ness
pro·duc·tiv″i·ty
pro·fan″i·ty
prof′a·na″tion
pro·fane″
pro·fane″ly
pro·fan″ing
pro·fan″i·ty
  (*pl.* pro·fan″i·ties)
pro·fessed″
pro·fes″sion
pro·fes″sion·al·ism
pro·fes″sion·al·ly
pro·fes″sor
pro·fes″sor·ship
prof″fer
pro·fi″cien·cy
pro·fi″cient
pro″file
pro″fil·ing
prof″it
  gain (*see:* prophet)
prof″it·a·bil″i·ty
prof″it·a·ble
prof″i·teer″
prof″it shar′ing
prof″li·gate
pro for″ma

pro·found″
pro·fun″di·ty
  (*pl.* pro·fun″di·ties)
pro·fuse″ly
pro·fu″sion
pro·gen″i·tor
prog″e·ny
pro·ges″ter·one′
prog·no″sis
  (*pl.* prog·no″ses)
prog·nos″tic
prog·nos″ti·cate
prog·nos″ti·cat′ing
prog·nos″ti·ca′tor
pro″gram
pro″gram·ma·ble
pro″gram·mat″ic
pro″gram·mer
pro″gram·ming
pro·gress″, *v.*
  advance
prog″ress, *n.*
  advancement
pro·gres″sion
pro·gres″sive·ly
pro·hib″it
pro′hi·bi″tion
pro′hi·bi″tion·ist
pro·hib″i·tive
pro·ject″, *v.*
  intend; throw
proj″ect, *n.*
  plan
pro·jec″tile
pro·jec″tion·ist
pro·jec″tive
pro·jec″tor
pro·lapse″
pro·laps″ing
pro′le·gom″e·non
  (*pl.* pro′le·gom″e·
  na)
pro′le·tar″i·an
pro′le·tar″i·at
pro″-life″
pro·lif″er·ate

pro·lif″er·at′ing
pro·lif′er·a″tion
pro·lif″ic
pro·lif″i·cal·ly
pro·lix″
pro·lix″i·ty
pro″logue
pro·long″
pro·lon″gate
pro·lon″gat·ing
pro·lon·ga″tion
prom′e·nade″
prom′e·nad″ing
Pro·me″the·an
prom″i·nence
prom″i·nent
prom′is·cu″i·ty
pro·mis″cu·ous
prom″ise
prom″is·ing
prom″is·so′ry
prom″on·to′ry
  (*pl.* prom″on·to′
  ries)
pro·mote″
pro·mot″er
pro·mot″ing
pro·mo″tion
pro·mo″tion·al
prompt″er
promp″ti·tude′
prompt″ly
prompt″ness
prom″ul·gate′
prom″ul·gat′ing
prom″ul·ga″tion
prom″ul·ga′tor
prone
prone″ness
prong
prong″horn′
pro·nom″i·nal
pro″noun′
pro·nounce″
pro·nounce″a·ble
pro·nounce″ment

pro·nounc''er
pro·nounc''ing
pron''to
pro·nun'ci·a''tion
proof''read'
proof''read'er
proof''read'ing
prop
prop'a·gan''da
prop'a·gan''dist
prop'a·gan''dize
prop'a·gan''diz·ing
prop''a·gate'
prop''a·gat'ing
prop'a·ga''tion
prop''a·ga'tor
pro''pane
pro·pel''
pro·pel''lant
pro·pel''ler
pro·pel''ling
pro·pen''si·ty
  (*pl.* pro·pen''si·ties)
prop'er noun''
prop''er·tied
prop''er·ty
  (*pl.* prop''er·ties)
proph''e·cy
  prediction (*pl.*
  proph''e·cies)
proph''e·sied'
proph''e·sy'
  predict (*see:* proph-
  ecy)
proph''e·sy'ing
proph''et
  revealer (*see:* profit)
proph''et·ess
pro·phet''i·cal·ly
pro'phy·lac''tic
pro'phy·lax''is
pro·pin''qui·ty
pro·pi''ti·ate'
pro·pi''ti·at'ing
pro·pi''ti·a''tion
pro·pi''ti·a·to'ry

pro·pi''tious
prop''jet'
pro·po''nent
pro·por''tion
pro·por''tion·a·ble
pro·por''tion·al
pro·por''tion·al''i·ty
pro·por''tion·al·ly
pro·por''tion·ate
pro·por''tion·ate·ly
pro·pos''al
pro·pose''
pro·pos''ing
prop'o·si''tion
pro·pound''
prop''ping
pro·pri''e·tar'y
pro·pri''e·tor
pro·pri''e·tor·ship'
pro·pri''e·tress
pro·pri''e·ty
pro·pul''sion
pro·pul''sive
pro ra''ta
pro·rate''
pro·rat''ing
pro·ra''tion
pro·sa''ic
pro·sa''i·cal·ly
pro·sce''ni·um
pro·scribe''
  outlaw (*see:* pre-
  scribe)
pro·scrib''er
pro·scrib''ing
pro·scrip''tion
pro·scrip''tive
prose
pros''e·cut'a·ble
pros''e·cute'
  legal proceeding
  (*see:* persecute)
pros''e·cut'ing
pros'e·cu''tion
pros''e·cu'tor
pros''e·lute

pros''e·lyt·ize
pros''e·lyt·iz'er
pros''e·lyt·iz'ing
pros''ing
pro·slav''er·y
pro·sod''ic
pros''o·dy
pro·spec''tive
  likely (*see:* perspec-
  tive)
pros''pec·tor
pro·spec''tus
pros''per
pros·per''i·ty
  (*pl.* pros·per''i·ties)
pros''per·ous
pros'ta·glan''din
pros''tate
  male gland (*see:*
  prostrate)
pros·the''sis
  (*pl.* pros·the''ses)
pros·thet''ics
pros''ti·tute
pros''ti·tut'ing
pros'ti·tu''tion
pros''trate
  lay flat (*see:* pros-
  tate)
pros''trat'ing
pros·tra''tion
pros''y
pro·tag''o·nist
pro·tect''
pro·tec''tion·ism
pro·tec''tive
pro·tec''tor·ate
pro·te·ge', *mas.*
pro·te·gee', *fem.*
pro''tein
pro tem''
pro tem''po·re
pro·test'', *v.*
  declare
pro·test', *n.*
  objection

Prot''es·tant
pro·tes'ta''tion
pro·tho''no·ta'ry
  (pl. pro·tho''no·tar'
  ies)
pro''to·col
pro''ton
pro''to·plasm
pro'to·plas''mic
pro''to·type
pro''to·zo''an
  (pl. pro'to·zo''a)
pro·tract''
pro·trac''tion
pro·trude''
pro·trud''ing
pro·tru''sion
pro·tu''ber·ance
pro·tu''ber·ant
proud''ly
prov'a·bil''i·ty
prov'a·ble·ness
prove
prov''e·nance
prov''en·der
prov''erb
pro·ver''bi·al
pro·ver''bi·al·ly
pro·vide''
prov''i·dence
prov'i·den''tial
prov'i·den''tial·ly
pro·vid''er
pro·vid''ing
prov''ence
pro·vin''cial
pro·vin''cial·ism'
pro·vin''cial·ly
prov''ing
pro·vi''sion
pro·vi''sion·al
pro·vi''sion·al·ly
pro·vi''so
  (pl. pro·vi''sos)
pro·vi''so·ry
pro·vo'ca·teur''

prov'o·ca''tion
pro·voc''a·tive
pro·voke''
pro·vok''ing
pro'vo·lo''ne
pro''vost mar''shal
prow''ess
proxl''er
prox''i·mal
prox''i·mate
prox''i·mate·ly
prox·im''i·ty
prox''y
  (pl. prox''ies)
prude
pru''dence
pru''dent
pru·den''tial
prud''er·y
  (pl. prud''er·ies)
prud''ish
prune
pru''ri·ence
pru''ri·ent
pry
  (pl. pries)
pry''ing
psalm''book'
Psal''ter
pseu''do
pseu'do·fam''ous
pseu'do·nym
pseu'do·re'al·ist''ic
pseu'do·sci'en·tif''ic
pshaw
pso·ri''a·sis
psych
psy''che
psych'e·del''ic
psy'chi·at''ric
psy·chi''a·trist
psy·chi''a·try
psy''chic
  clairvoyant (see:
  physic)
psy''chi·cal

psy''chi·cal·ly
psych''ing
psycho
  (pl. psy''chos)
psy'cho·a·nal''y·sis
psy'cho·an''a·lyst
psy'cho·an'a·lyt''ic
psy'cho·an'a·lyt''i·cal
psy'cho·an''a·lyze'
psy'cho·an'a·lyz''ing
psy·cho·bi·ol''o·gy
psy'cho·dra''ma
psy'cho·dy·nam''ic
psy'cho·dy·nam''ics
psy'cho·gen''e·sis
psy'cho·ge·net''ics
psy'cho·log''i·cal
psy'cho·log''i·cal·ly
psy·chol''o·gist
psy·chol''o·gize'
psy·chol''o·giz''ing
psy·chol''o·gy
  (pl. psy·chol''o·
  gies)
psy·chom''e·try
psy'cho·neu·ro''sis
psy'cho·neu·rot''ic
psy'cho·path''ic
psy'cho·path'o·log''i·
  cal
psy·cho·pa·thol''o·gy
psy·cho·sex''u·al
psy·cho''sis
  (pl. psy·cho''ses)
psy'cho·so''cial
psy'cho·so·mat''ic
psy'cho·ther''a·pist
psy'cho·ther''a·py
psy·chot''ic
pter'o·dac''tyl
ptol'e·ma''ic
pto''maine
pty''a·lin
pu''ber·ty
pu''bes
pu·bes''cent

pu″bic
pu″bis
  (*pl.* pu″bes)
pub′li·ca″tion
pub′li·cist
pub·lic″i·ty
pub″li·cize′
pub″li·ciz′ing
pub″lic·ly
pub″lic-spir″it·ed
pub″lish
pub″lish·a·ble
pub″lish·er
puce
puck
puck″er
puck″ish
pud″ding
pud″dle
pud″dling
pudg″i·ness
pudg″y
pueb″lo
  (*pl.* pueb″los)
pu″er·ile
pu′er·il″i·ty
pu·er″per·al
Puer″to Ri″co
puff″ball
puff″er
puff″er·y
puff″i·er
puf″fin
puff″y
pug
pug″ging
pu″gil·ism
pu″gil·ist
pu′gil·is″tic
pug·na″cious
pug·nac″i·ty
puke
puk″ing
puk″ka
pul″chri·tude′
pul′chri·tu″di·nous

pull″back′
pul″let
pul″ley
  (*pl.* pul″leys)
pull″ian™
pull″out′
pull″o′ver
pul″mo·nar′y
pulp″i·er
pulp″i·ness
pul″pit
pulp″wood′
pulp″y
pul″sar
pul″sate
pul″sat·ing
pul·sa″tion
pulse
puls″ing
pul″ver·ize′
pul″ver·iz′ing
pu″ma
pum″ice
pum″ic·ing
pum″mel
  thrash (*see:* pommel)
pum″mel·ing
pump
pum″per·nick′el
pump″kin·seed′
pun
punch″board′
punch″-drunk′
pun″cheon
punch″er
punch″i·er
punch″line′
punch″y
punc·til″i·o′
punc·til″i·ous
punc″tu·al
punc′tu·al″i·ty
punc″tu·al·ly
punc″tu·ate′
punc″tu·at′ing
punc′tu·a″tion

punc″ture
punc″tur·ing
pun″dit
pun″gen·cy
pun″gent
pu″ni·ness
pun″ish
pun″ish·a·ble
pun″ish·ment
pu″ni·tive
punk
pun″ning
pun″ster
punt″er
pu″ny
pu″pa
  (*pl.* pu″pae)
pu″pal
  of a pupa (*see:* pu-
  pil)
pu″pil
  student (*see:* pupal)
pup″pet
pup′pet·eer″
pup″pet·ry
pup″py
  (*pl.* pup″pies)
pup″tent′
pur″blind
pur″chas·a·ble
pur″chase
pur″chas·er
pur″chas·ing
pur″dah
pure″bred
pu·ree″
pu·ree″ing
pure″ly
pur″est
pur·ga″tion
pur″ga·tive
pur″ga·to′ry
purge
purg″ing
pu′ri·fi·ca″tion
pu″ri·fied′

pu''ri·fi'er
pu''ri·fy
pu''rim
pu''ri·tan''i·cal
pu''ri·ty
purl
  knit (*see:* pearl)
pur·loin''
pur''ple
pur''pling
pur''plish
pur·port'', *v.*
  claim
pur'port, *n.*
  significance
pur''pose
pur''pose·ful
pur''pose·ful·ly
pur''pose·less
pur''pose·ly
pur''pos·ing
purr
purs''er
purse'' strings
purs''ing
pur·su''ance
pur·su''ant
pur·sue''
pur·su''er
pur·su''ing
pur·suit''
pu''ru·lence
pu''ru·lent
pur·vey''
pur·vey''ance
pur·vey''or
pur''view
pus
  fluid (*see:* puss)
push'' but'ton
push''cart'
push''er
push''i·er
push''o'ver
push''up

push''y
pu'sil·lan''i·mous
puss
  cat (*see:* pus)
puss''y
  cat (*pl.* puss''ies)
pus''sy
  containing pus
puss''y·cat
puss''y·foot
pus''tu·lant
pus''tule
put
  place (*see:* putt)
pu''ta·tive
put''-down
put''in
put''-out
pu'tre·fac''tion
pu''tre·fied
pu''tre·fy
pu·tres''cent
pu''trid
pu·trid''i·ty
putt
  golf hit (*see:* put)
put·tee
put''ter
put''tied
put''ting
  to put
putt''ing
  to putt
put''ty
put''-up'
puz''zle
puz''zle·ment
puz''zle
puz''zling
Pyg''my
  (*pl.* Pyg''mies)
py''lon
py·lo''rus
  (*pl.* py·lo''ri)
py'or·rhe''a
pyr''a·mid

py·ram''i·dal
pyre
Pyr''e·nees'
py·re''thrum
Py''rex™
py·ri''tes
py·rol''y·sis
py'ro·ma''ni·a
py'ro·ma''ni·ac
py·rom''e·ter
py'ro·tech''nics
py·rox''y·lin
py·thag'o·re''an
py''thon
pyx

Q

Qa''tar
Quaa''lude™
quack''er·y
  (*pl.* quack''er·ies)
quad''ran·gle
quad·ran''gu·lar
quad''rant
quad'ra·phon''ic
quad·rat''ics
quad·ren''ni·al
quad·ren''ni·al·ly
quad·ren''ni·um
quad''ri·ceps'
quad'ri·lat''er·al
qua·drille''
quad·ril''lion
quad'ri·par''tite
quad'ri·ple''gi·a
quad'ri·ple''gic
quad''ru·ped'
quad·ru''ple
quad·ru''plet
quad·ru''pli·cate
quad·ru'pli·ca''tion
quad·ru''pling
quaff
quag''mire'

qua″hog
quail
quaint″ly
quake
Quak″er
quak″ing
qual′i·fi·ca″tion
qual″i·fied′
qual″i·fy′
qual″i·fy′ing
qual″i·ta′tive
qual″i·ty
  (*pl.* qual″i·ties)
qualm
quan″da·ry
  (*pl.* quan″da·ries)
quan″ti·fi′a·ble
quan′ti·fi·ca″tion
quan″ti·fied′
quan″ti·fy′
quan″ti·ta′tive
quan″ti·ty
  (*pl.* quan″ti·ties)
quan″tum′
  (*pl.* quan″ta)
quar″an·tine
quar″an·tin′ing
quark
quar″rel
quar″rel·ing
quar″ried
quar″ry
  (*pl.* quar″ries)
quart
quar″ter·back′
quar′ter·fi″nal
quar″ter horse
quar″ter·ly
quar″ter·mas′ter
quar″ter note′
quar″ter rest′
quar·tet″
quar″to
quartz
qua″sar
quash

qua″si·ju·di″ci·al
qua″ter·nar′y
  (qua·ter·nar′ies)
quat″rain
qua″ver
quay
  pier (*see:* cay and
  key)
quea″si·er
quea″si·ness
quea″sy
Que·bec″
queen″ly
queen″ moth′er
queen″-size
queer
queer″ly
quell
quench
quench″a·ble
que·nelle″
que″ried
quer″u·lous
que″ry
  (*pl.* que″ries)
quest
ques″tion
ques″tion·a·ble
ques′tion·naire″
queue
  line (*see:* cue)
queued
queu″ing
quib″ble
quib″bling
quiche
quick″en
quick″-freeze′
quick″-freez′ing
quick″-fro′zen
quick″ie
quick″sand′
quick″sil′ver
quick″-tem″pered
quick″-wit″ted
quid′ pro quo″

qui·es″cence
qui·es″cent
qui″et
  silent (*see:* quit and
  quite)
qui″e·tude′
qui·e″tus
quill
quilt
quilt″ing
quince
qui·nil″la
qui″nine
quin·quen″ni·al
quin·quen″ni·al·ly
quin·tes″sence
quin′tes·sen″tial
quin·tet″
quin·til″lion
quin·tu″ple
quin·tu″plet
quin·tu″pli·cate
quin·tu″pling
quip
quipped
quip″ster
quire
  paper (*see:* choir)
quirk
quirt
quis″ling
quit
  discontinue (*see:*
  quiet and quite)
quite
  completely (*see:*
  quiet and quit)
Qui″to
quit″tance
quit″ter
quit″ting
quiv″er
qui·vive″
quix·ot″ic
quix·ot″i·cal·ly
quiz

quiz"mas'ter
quiz"zer
quiz"zi·cal
quiz"zi·cal·ly
quiz"zing
quoin
  corner (*see:* coin)
quoit
quon"dam
quo"rum
quo"ta
quot'a·bil"i·ty
quot"a·ble
quo·ta"tion
quote
quo·tid"i·an
quo"tient
quot"ing

R

rab"bet
  notch (*see:* rabbit)
rab"bet·ing
rab"bi
  (*pl.* rab"bis)
rab·bin'i·cal
rab"bit·e·ite'
rab"bit
  animal (*see:* rabbet)
rab"ble-rous'er
rab"bling
rab'id
ra·bid"i·ty'
ra"bies
rac·coon"
rac·coon"ber·ry
race"course'
race"horse'
rac"er
race"track'
race"walk'
ra"cial
ra"cial·ism'
ra"cial·ly

rac"i·er
rac"i·ly
rac"i·ness
rac"ing
rac"ism
rac"ist
rack
  framework; gear;
  torture (*see:* wrack)
rack"board'
rack"et
rack'et·eer"
rac'on·teur'
rac"y
ra"dar·scope'
ra"di·al
ra"di·al·ly
ra"di·ance
ra"di·ant
ra"di·ate'
ra"di·at'ing
ra"di·a"tion
ra"di·a'tive
rad"i·cal
rad"i·cal·ism'
rad"i·cal·ize'
rad"i·cal·ly
ra"di·o'
  (*pl.* ra"di·os')
ra"di·o·ac"tive
ra"di·o·ac·tiv"i·ty
ra"di·o·bi'o·log"ic
ra"di·o·broad"cast'
ra"di·o·car"bon
ra"di·oed'
ra"di·o·de·tec"tor
ra"di·o·gen"ic
ra"di·o·gram'
ra"di·o·graph'
ra"di·o·graph"ic
ra"di·og"ra·phy
ra"di·o·i"so·tope'
ra"di·o·log"i·cal
ra"di·ol"o·gist
ra"di·ol"o·gy
ra"di·o·man'

ra"di·om"e·ter
ra"di·o·pho"to·graph'
ra"di·os"co·py
ra"di·o·sonde'
ra"di·o·tel"e·graph'
ra"di·o·te·leg"ra·phy
ra"di·o·tel"e·phone'
ra"di·o·ther"a·py
rad"ish
ra"di·um
ra"di·us
  (*pl.* ra"di·i')
ra"dix
  (*pl.* rad"i·ces')
ra"don
rad"waste
raf"fi·a
raf"fle
raf"fling
raf"ter
rag"a·muf'fin
rage
rag"ged
rag"ing
rag"lan
ra·gout"
rag"pick'er
rag"time'
rag"weed'
raid"er
rail"ing
rail"ler·y
  (*pl.* rail"ler·ies)
rail"road'
rail"ment
rain
  water (*see:* reign and
  rein)
rain"bow'
rain"check'
rain"coat'
rain"dance'
rain"drop'
rain"fall'
rain"for"est
rain"i·er

rain"mak'er
rain"proof
rain"spout
rain"storm
rain"wa'ter
rain"y
raise
   lift (*see:* raze)
rai"sin
rais"ing
rai"son d'e"tre
rake
rake"-off'
rak"ing
rak"ish
Ra"leigh
ral"lied
ral"ly
   (*pl.* ral"lies)
RAM
   random-access mem-
   ory
ram"ble
ram"bler
ram"bling
ram·bunc"tious
ram"e·kin
ram'i·fi·ca"tion
ram"i·fied
ram"i·fy
ra·mig"er·ous
ram"jet
ram"ming
ramp
ram·page", *v.*
   rush about
ram"page, *n.*
   violent behavior
ram·pa"geous
ram·pag"ing
ramp"ant
ram"part
ram"pier
ram"rod'
ram"rod'ding
ram"shack'le

ranch"er
ran·che"ro
   (*pl.* ran·che"ros)
ranch" house'
ran"cid
ran"cor
ran"cor·ous
ran"dom
rang
range
rang"er
rang"i·er
rang"ing
rang"y
rank"ing
ran"kle
ran"kling
rank"wise
ran"sack
ran"som
rant
ran"u·lar
rap
   strike (*see:* wrap)
ra·pa"cious
ra·pac"i·ty
rape
rape"seed'
rap·id-fire"
ra·pid"i·ty
rap"id·ly
rap"id trans"it
ra"pi·er
rap"ine
rap"ing
   forcing (*see:* rap-
   ping)
rap"ist
rap" mu"sic
rapped
   struck (*see:* rapt and
   wrapped)
rap·pel"
rap·pel"ling
rap"ping
   striking (*see:* raping)

rap·port"
rap·proche·ment"
rap·scal"lion
rapt
   engrossed (*see:*
   rapped and
   wrapped)
rap"ture
rap"tur·ous
ra'ra a"vis
rare
rare"bit
rar'e·fac"tion
rar"e·fied'
rar"e·fy
rare"ly
rar"er
ra·ri'con"stant
rar"i·ty
   (*see:* rar"i·ties)
ras"cal
ras"cal·ly
rash"er
ras"o·phore'
rasp"ber'ry
rasp"i·er
rasp"y
rat"a·ble
ratch"et wheel
rate
rath"er
rat"hole
raths"kel'ler
rat'i·fi·ca"tion
rat"i·fied
rat"i·fy
rat"ing
ra"tio
   (*pl.* ra"tios)
ra'ti·oc"i·nate'
ra'ti·oc'i·na"tion
ra"tion·al
   reasonable (*see:*
   rationale)
ra'tion·ale"

logical basis (*see:* rational)
ra"tion·al·ism
ra'tion·al·is"tic
ra'tion·al"i·ty
ra'tion·al·i·za"tion
ra"tion·al·ize
ra"tion·al·iz"ing
ra"tion·al·ly
rat"race'
rat·tan"
rat"ti·er
rat"ting
rat"tle·brained
rat"tle·pate'
rat"tler
rat"tle·snake
rat"tle·trap'
rat"tling
rat"trap
rat"ty
rau"cous
rav"age
rav"ag·ing
rave
rav"el
ra'vel·ing
ra"ven
rav"en·ous
ra·vine"
rav"ing
ra·vi·o"li
rav"ish
rav"ish·ing
raw"boned"
raw"hide
raw"hid'ing
ray
ray"on
raze
  demolish (*see:* raise)
raz"ing
ra"zor
ra"zor·back
raz"zle-daz"zle
razz"ma·tazz"

re·a·ban"don
re·ac·cum"u·late'
reach
re·ac"knowl"edge
re·act
  respond (*see:* re-act)
re-act"
  act again (*see:* react)
re·ac"tion
re·ac"tion·ar'y
  (*pl.* re·ac"tion·ar'
  ies)
re·ac"ti·vate'
re·ac"ti·vat'ing
re·ac"ti·va"tion
re·ac"tor
read
  interpret writing
  (*see:* reed)
read'a·bil"i·ty
read"a·ble
read"er·ship
read"ied
read"i·ly
read"i·ness
  preparedness (*see:*
  reediness)
read"ing room'
re'ad·just"
read"out
read"y·made"
read"y-to-wear"
re·af·firm"
Rea'gan·om"ics
re·a"gent
re"al
  genuine (*see:* reel)
re"al·ism
re'al·is"tic
re'al·is"ti·cal·ly
re·al"i·ty
  truth (*pl.* re·al"i·
  ties)
re'al·iz'a·ble
re·al·i·za"tion
re"al·ize

re"al·iz'ing
re"al·ly
realm
re·al"po·li·tik"
re"al·tor
re"al·ty
  property (*see:* reality)
ream"er
reap"er
re·ap·pear"
re'ap·por"tion
re'ap·por"tion·ment
re·ap·prais"al
re'ap·praise"
re'ap·prais"ing
rear" guard"
re·arm"
re·ar"ma·ment
rear"most'
re'ar·range"
re'ar·rang"ing
rear"ward
rea'son·a·bil"i·ty
rea"son·a·ble
rea"son·ing
re·as·sign"
re'as·sur"ance
re·as·sure"
re'as·sur"ing
re'at·tach"a·ble
re·au'then"ti·ca'ted
re·a·wak"en
re·bal"lot'ing
re·base"
re"bate
re"bat·ing
re·bel", *v.*
  arise against
reb"el, *n.*
  rebelling person
rebel"ling
re·bel"lion
re·bel"lious
re·birth"
re·blot"

re·born″
re·bor″row
re·bound″, *v.*
  bounce back
re″bound, *n.*
  act of rebounding
re·broad″cast′
re·buff″
re·buff″a·ble
re·build″
re·built″
re·buke″
re·buk″ing
re·bunch
re″bus
  (*pl.* re″bus·es)
re·but″
re·but″ta·ble
re·but″tal
re·but″ting
re·cal″ci·trance
re·cal″ci·trant
re·cal″ci·trat′ing
re·cal″cu·late′
re·cal″cu·lat′ing
re·call″
re·call″a·ble
rc·cam″paign
re·cant″
re″cap′
re·ca·pit″u·late′
re·ca·pit″u·lat′ing′
re·ca·pit″u·la″tion
re″cap′ping
re·cap″ture
re·cap″tur·ing
re·car″bon·i·za″tion
re·cast″
re·cede″
re·ced″ing
re·ceipt″
re·ceipt″er
re·ceiv″a·ble
re·ceive″
re·ceiv″er·ship
re·ceiv″ing

re·cen″sion
re″cent
re·cep″ta·cle
re·cep″tion
re·cep″tive
re·cep·tiv″i·ty
re·cep″tor
re·cer·ti·fi·ca″tion
re″cess″
re·ces″sion
re·ces″sive
re·cher″che
re·cid″i·vism′
re·ci·div″i·ty
rec″i·pe′
re·cip″i·ent
re·cip″ro·cal
re·cip″ro·cal·ly
re·cip″ro·cate′
re·cip″ro·cat′ing
re·cip′ro·ca″tion
rec′i·proc″i·ty
re·ci″sion
re·cit″al
rec′i·ta″tion
rec′i·ta·tive″
re·cite″
re·cit″ing
reck″less
reck″on·ing
re·claim″
  make usable (*see:* re-
  claim)
re-claim
  claim again (*see:* re-
  claim)
re·claim″a·ble
rec′la·ma″tion
re·cline″
re·clin″ing
rec″luse, *v.*
  shut away
rec″luse, *n.*
  secluded person
rec′og·ni″tion
rec″og·niz′a·ble

re·cog″ni·zance
re·cog″ni·zant′
rec″og·nize
rec″og·niz′ing
re·coil″
re·coil′ess
re′-col·lect″
  collect again (*see:*
  recollect)
rec′ol·lect″
  remember (*see:* re-
  collect)
rec′ol·lec″tion
re′com·bi·na″tion
rec′om·mend″
rec′om·men·da″tion
re′com·mit″
re′com·mit″tal
re′com·mit″ting
rec″om·pense
re′com·pose″
re′com·pos″ing
re′con·ces″sion
rec″on·cil″a·ble
rec″on·cilc
rec″on·cil′i·a″tion
rec″on·cil′ing
rec″on·dite
re′con·di″tion
re′con·dir
re′con·firm″
re′con·nais·sance
re′con·noi″ter
re′con·sid″er
re′con·sid′er·a″tion
re′con·sti·tute″
re′con·sti·tut′ing
re′con·struc″tion
re′con·ver″sion
re′con·vert″
re·cord″, *v.*
  make account
re″cord, *n.*
  account; disc; best
re·cord″er
re·count″

count again; narrate
re"count
  second count
re·coup"
re·cours"
re"course
re-cov"er
  cover again (*see:* re-
  cover)
re·cov"er
  get back (*see:* re-
  cover)
re·cov"er·y
  (*pl.* re·cov"er·ies)
rec"re·ance
rec"re·ant
re'-cre·ate"
  create again (*see:*
  recreate)
rec"re·ate
  refresh (*see:* re-
  create)
re'-cre·at"ing
rec"re·at'ing
re'-cre·a"tion
rec're·a"tion
re·crim"i·nate'
re·crim"i·nat'ing
re·crim"i·na"tion
rc·crim"i·na·tive
re·crim"i·na·to'ry
re'cru·des"cence
re·cruit"
rec"tal
rec"tan'gle
rec·tan"gu·lar
rec"ti·fi'a·ble
rec'ti·fi·ca"tion
rec"ti·fied'
rec"ti·fi'er
rec"ti·fy'
rec'ti·lin"e·ar
rec"ti·tude'
rec"tor
rec"to·ry
  (*pl.* rec"to·ries)

rec"tum
re·cum"ben·cy
re·cum"bent
re·cu"per·ate
re·cu"per·at'ing
re·cu'per·a"tion
re·cu'per·a'tive
re·cur"
re·cur"rence
re·cur"rent
re·cur"ring
re·curse
re·cy"cle
re·cy"cling
re·dact"
re·dac"tion
re·dac"tor
red"bay
red"-blood"ed
red"breast
red car"pet
Red" Cross"
red"den
red"dish
re·dec"o·rate
re·dec"o·rat'ing
re·dec·o·ra"tion
re·ded"i·cate'
re·ded"i·cat'ing
re·deem"a·ble
re·deem"er
re·de·fault"
re'de·liv"er
re·demp"tion
re·demp"tive
re·demp"to·ry
re'de·ploy"
re'der·i·va"tion
re'de·sign"
re'de·term"ine
re'de·vel"op·ment
re'di·min"ish
red"-hand"ed
red"head'
red"-head"ed
red" her"ring

red"-hot"
re'di·rect"
re'dis·trib"ute
re'dis·trib"ut·ing
re·dis"trict
red"-let"ter
red" light"
red"lin"ing
red" man"
red"mouth
re·do"
re·do"ing
re·done"
red"o·lence
red"o·len·cy'
red"o·lent
re·dou"ble
re·dou"bling
re·doubt"
re·doubt"a·ble
re·dound"
red"-pen"cil
re·dress", *v.*
  right a wrong
re"dress, *n.*
  act of righting
red" snap'per
red" tape"
re·duce"
re·duc"i·ble
re·duc"ing
re·duc"ti·o' ad ab·
  sur"dum
re·duc"tion
re·dun"dan·cy
  (*pl.* re·dun"dan·
  cies)
re·dun"dant
re·du"pli·cate'
re·du"pli·cat'ing
re·du'pli·ca"tion
red"wood'
re·ech"oed
re·ech"o'
re·ech"o·ing
reed

grass (*see:* read)
re·ed'u·cate'''
re·ed'u·ca''tion
reed''i·ness
  full of reeds (*see:* readiness)
reef''er
reek
  smell (*see:* wreak)
reel
  spool; dance (*see:* real)
re'e·lect''
re'e·merge''
re'e·mer''ging
re'em·ploy''
re'en·act''
re·en''ter
re·en''try
re'es·tab''lish
re'ex·am'i·na''tion
re'ex·am''ine
re'ex·am''in·ing
re·fash''ion
re·fec''to·ry
  (*pl.* re·fec''to·ries)
re·fec''to·ra'ry
re·fer''
ref''er·a·ble
ref'er·ee''
ref'er·ence
ref'er·enc·ing
ref'er·en''dum
ref''er·ent
re·fer''ral
re·fer''ring
re·fill''a·ble
re·fi''nance
re·fi''nanc·ing
re·fine''
re·fine''ment
re·fin''er
re·fin''er·y
  (*pl.* re·fin''er·ies)
re·fin''ing
re·fin''ish

re·fit''
re·fit''ting
re·flec''tion
re·flec''tive
re·flec''tor
re''flex
re·flex''ive
re·fo''cused
re·for''est
re'for·est·a''tion
re·form''
  correct (*see:* reform)
re-form''
  form again (*see:* reform)
re·for''mat
ref'or·ma''tion
re·form''a·tive
re·form''a·to·ry
  (*see:* re·form''a·to·ries)
re·form''er
re·for''ti·fy
re·fract''
re·frac''tion
re·frac·tiv''i·ty
re·frac''tor
re·frac''to·ry
  (*see:* re·frac''to·ries)
re·frain''
re·fran''gi·ble
re·fresh''
re·fresh''ment
re·frig''er·ant
re·frig''er·ate
re·frig''er·at'ing
re·frig'er·a''tion
re·frig'er·a'tor
re·fu''el
ref''uge
ref'u·gee''
re·ful''gent
re·fund'', *v.*
  repay

re''fund, *n.*
  repayment
re·fund''a·ble
re·fur''bish
re·fus''al
re·fuse''
  decline
ref''use
  rubbish
re·fus''ing
re·fu''ta·ble
ref'u·ta''tion
re·fute''
re·fut''ing
re·gain''
re''gal
  royal (*see:* regal)
re·gale''
  entertain (*see:* regal)
re·gal''ing
re·ga''li·a
re·gard''ing
re·gard''less
re·gat''ta
re·gen'cy
  (*pl.* re''gen·cies)
re·gen''er·ate'
re·gen''er·at'ing
re·gen'er·a''tion
re·gen''er·a·tive
re·gen''er·a·tor
re''gent
reg''i·cide
re·gime''
reg''i·men'
reg''i·ment'
reg'i·men''tal
reg'i·men·ta''tion
re''gion
re''gion·al·ism'
re''gion·al·ly
reg''is·ter
reg''is·trant
reg''is·trar'
reg''is·tra''tion
reg''is·try

(*pl.* reg"is·tries)
re·gress"
re·gres"sion
re·gres"sive
re·gret"
re·gret"a·ble
re·gret"ful
re·gret"ful·ly
re·gret"ting
re·group"
reg"u·lar
reg"u·lar"i·ty
reg"u·lar·ize
reg"u·lar·iz"ing
reg"u·lar·ly
reg"u·late
reg"u·lat"ing
reg"u·la"tion
reg"u·la"tor
reg"u·la·to'ry
re·gur"gi·tate
re·gur"gi·tat"ing
re·gur·gi·ta"tion
re·ha·bil"i·tate
re·ha·bil"i·tat"ing
re·ha·bil"i·ta"tion
re·ha·bil"i·ta'tive
re·hash"
re·hear"ing
re·hears"al
re·hearse"
re·hears"ing
reign
  rule (*see:* rain and rein)
re'im·burse"
re'im·burs"ing
rein
  strap (*see:* rain and reign)
re'in·car"nate
re'in·car"nat·ing
re'in·car·na"tion
rein"deer
re'in·doc"tri·nate'
re'in·fect"

re'in·fla"tion
re'in·force"
re'in·force"ment
re'in·forc"ing
re'in·sert"
re'in·state"
re'in·state"ment
re'in·stat"ing
re'in·sur"ance
re'in·sure"
re'in·sur"ing
re'in·ter"pret
re'in·vest"
re'in·vig"or·ate'
re'in·vig"or·at'ing
re·is"sue
re·is"su·ing
re·it"er·ate'
re·it"er·at'ing
re·it"er·a"tion
re·it"er·a"tive
re·ject", *v.*
  refuse
re"ject, *n.*
  rejected thing
re·jec"tion
re·joice"
re·joic"ing
re·join"der
re·ju"ve·nate'
re·ju"ve·nat'ing
re·ju"ve·na"tion
re·kin"dle
re·lade
re·lapse"
re·laps"ing
re·lat"a·ble
re·late"
re·lat"ing
re·la"tion·ship
rel"a·tive
rel"a·tive·ly
rel"a·tiv·ism
rel'a·tiv·is"tic
rel'a·tiv"i·ty
re·la"tor

re·lax"ant
re·lax·a"tion
re"lay
re"lay·ing
re·lease"
  free (*see:* re-lease)
re-lease"
  lease again (*see:* release)
re·leas"or
re·leas"ing
rel"e·gate
rel"e·gat"ing
re·lent"less
rel"e·vance
rel"e·vant
re·li·a·bil"i·ty
re·li"a·ble
re·li"ance
re·li"ant
rel"ic
re·lied"
re·lief"
re·liev"a·ble
re·lieve
re·liev"er
re·liev"ing
re·li"gion
re·lig'i·os"i·ty
re·li"gious
re·line"
re·lin"ing
re·lin"quish
rel"i·quar'y
  (*pl.* rel"i·quar'ies)
rel"ish
re·live"
re·liv"ing
re·lo"cate
re·lo"cat"ing
re'lo·ca"tion
re·luc"tance
re·luc"tant
re·ly"
rem
  radiation (*see:* REM)

REM
 eye movement (*see:*
  rem)
re·main″der
re·make″, *v.*
 make again
re″make′, *n.*
 thing remade
re·mak″ing
re·mand″
re·mark″a·ble
re·mas″ti·cate′
re·me″di·a·ble
re·me″di·al
rem″e·died
rem″e·dy
 (*pl.* rem″e·dies)
re·mem″ber
re·mem″brance
re·mim″ic
re·mind″er
rem″i·nisce″
rem″i·nis″cence
rem″i·nis″cent
rem″i·nisc″ing
re·miss″
re·mis″si·ble
re·mis″sion
re·mit″
re·mit″tance
re·mit″ting
rem″nant
re·mod″el
re·mon″strance
re·mon″strant
re·mon″strate
re·mon″strat·ing
re′mon·stra″tion
re·mon″stra·tor
re·morse″ful
re·morse″ful·ly
re·morse″less
re·mote″
re·mote″ness
re·mot″est
re·mount″

re·mov″a·ble
re·mov″al
re·move″
re·mov″ing
re·mu″ner·ate
re·mu″ner·at′ing
re·mu″ner·a″tion
re·mu″ner·a·tive
re·mu″ner·a·tor
ren′ais·sance″
re″nal
re·nas″cent
ren″der
ren″dez·vous″
 (*pl.* ren″dez·vous)
ren·di″tion
ren″e·gade′
re·nege″
re·neg″ing
re′ne·go″ti·a·ble
re′ne·go″ti·ate
re′ne·go″ti·at′ing
re′ne·go′ti·a″tion
re·new″a·ble
re·new″al
ren″net
ren″nin
re·nom″i·nate′
re·nom″i·nat′ing
re·nom·i·na″tion
re·nounce″
re·nounc″ing
ren″o·vate
ren″o·vat′ing
ren′o·va″tion
ren″o·va′tor
re·nowned″
rent″al
re·num″ber
re·nun′ci·a″tion
re·oc″cu·pied
re·oc″cu·py′
re·o″pen
re·or″der
re·or·gan·i·za″tion
re·or″gan·ize′

re·or″gan·iz′ing
re·pack″age
re·pack″ag·ing
re·pair″a·ble
re·pair″man
rep′a·ra″tion
rep′ar·tee″
re·past″
re·pa″tri·ate
re·pa″tri·at′ing
re·pa·tri·a″tion
re·pay″a·ble
re·pay″ment
re·peal″
re·peat″ed
re·pel″
re·pel″lent
re·pel″ling
re·pent″
re·pent″ance
re·pent″ant
re′per·cus″sion
rep″er·toire
rep″er·to·ry
 (*pl.* rep″er·to′ries)
rep′e·ti″tion
rep′e·ti″tious
re·pet″i·tive
re·pet″i·tive·ly
re·phrase″
re·phras″ing
re·place″
re·place″a·ble
re·place″ment
re·plac″ing
re·play″, *v.*
 play again
re″play, *n.*
 act of replaying
re·plen″ish
re·plete″
re·ple″tion
rep″li·ca
rep′li·ca″tion
re·plied″
re·ply″

re·port″a·ble
re·port″age
re·port″ed·ly
re·port″er
rep′or·to″ri·al
re·pose″
re·pos″ing
re·pos″i·tor′y
re·pos′sess″
re·pos·ses″sion
rep′re·hend″
rep′re·hen·si·bil″i·ty
rep′re·hen″si·ble
rep′re·hen″sion
rep′re·sent″
rep′re·sen·ta″tion
rep′re·sent″a·tive
re·press″
re·pres″sion
re·pres″sive
re·prieve″
re·priev″ing
rep″ri·mand
re·print″, v.
  print again
re″print, n.
  thing reprinted
re·pris″al
re·prise″
re·pris″ing
re·proach″a·ble
re·proach″ful
rep″ro·bate
rep′ro·ba″tion
re′pro·duce″
re′pro·duc″i·ble
re′pro·duc″tion
re′pro·duc″tive
re·proof″
re·prove″
re·prov″ing
rep″tile
rep·til″i·an
re·pub″lic
re·pub″li·can
re·pub·li·ca″tion

re·pub″lish
re·pu″di·ate
re·pu″di·at″ing
re·pu′di·a″tion
re·pug″nance
re·pug″nant
re·pulse″
re·puls″ing
re·pul″sion
re·pul″sive
re·pul″sive·ness
rep′u·ta·bil″i·ty
rep″u·ta·ble
rep′u·ta″tion
re·pute″
re·put″ing
re·quest″
re″qui·em
re·quire″
re·quire″ment
re·quir″ing
req″ui·site
req′ui·si″tion
re·quit″al
re·quite″
re·quit″ing
re·run″, v.
  run again
re″run′, n.
  rebroadcast
re·run″ning
re·sal″a·ble
re″sale
re·scind″
re·scis″sion
res″cue
res″cu·er
res″cu·ing
re·search″
re·sec″tion
re·sem″blance
re·sem″ble
re·sem″bling
re·send″
re·sent″
re·sent″ful

re·sent″ful·ly
re·sent″ment
res′er·va″tion
re·serve″
re·serv″ing
re·serv″ist
res″er·voir′
re·set″
re·set″ting
re·shape″
re·shap″ing
re·ship″
re·ship″ping
re·shuf″fle
re·shuf″fling
re·side″
res″i·dence
res″i·den·cy
  (pl. res″i·den·cies)
res″i·dent
res″i·den″tial
re·sid″ing
re·sid″u·al
re·sid″u·ar′y
res″i·due
re·sign″
  give up (see: re-sign)
re-sign″
  sign again (see: re-sign)
res′ig·na″tion
re·sil″ience
re·sil″ient
res″in
res″in·ous
re·sist″
re·sist″ance
re·sist″ant
re·sist″er
  one who resists (see: resistor)
re·sist″i·ble
re·sis″tor
  electrical device (see: resister)
res″o·lute

res'o·lu''tion
re·solv''a·ble
re·solve''
re·solv''ing
res''o·nance
res''o·nant
res''o·nate
res''o·nat'ing
res''o·na'tor
re·sorp''tion
re·sort''
re·sound''
re''source
re·source''ful
re·source''ful·ly
re·spect'a·bil''i·ty
  (*pl.* re·spect'a·bil''i·
  ties)
re·spect''a·ble
re·spect''ful
re·spect''ful·ly
re·spect''ing
re·spec''tive·ly
res'pi·ra''tion
res''pi·ra'tor
res''pi·ra·to'ry
re·spire''
re·spir''ing
res''pite
res''pit·ing
re·splend''ence
re·splend''ent
re·sponse''
re·spon'si·bil''i·ty
  (*pl.* re·spon'si·bil''i·
  ties)
re·spon''si·ble
re·spon''sive
rest
  repose; remainder
  (*see:* wrest)
re·state''
re·state''ment
re·stat''ing

res''tau·rant
res'tau·ra·teur''
rest''ful
rest'' home
res''ti·tu''tion
res''tive
rest''less
re·stock''
res'to·ra''tion
re·stor''a·tive
re·store''
re·stor''er
re·stor''ing
re·strain''
re·strain''a·ble
re·straint''
re·strict''
re·stric''tion
re·stric''tive
rest''room
re·sult''
re·sult''ant
re·sume''
  continue (*see:* re-
  sume)
re''su·me
  summary (*see:* re-
  sume)
re·sum''ing
re·sump''tion
re·sur''gence
res'ur·rect''
res'ur·rec''tion
res'ur·rec''tion·al
re·sus''ci·tate
re·sus''ci·tat'ing
re·sus''ci·ta''tion
re·sus''ci·ta·tor
re·swage
re·syn''the·tize'
re''tail·er
re·tain''er
re·take''
re·tal''i·ate'
re·tal''i·at'ing
re·tal'i·a''tion

re·tal''i·a·to'ry
re·tard''
re·tard''ate
re·tar·da''tion
retch
  vomit (*see:* wretch)
re·tell''
re·ten''tion
re·ten''tive
ret''i·cent
re·tic''u·lar
re·tic''u·late'
re·tic''u·lat'ing
ret''i·na
ret''i·nal
ret''i·nue'
re·tire''ment
re·tir''ing
re·told''
re·took''
re·tool''
re·tort''
re·touch''
re·trace''
re·trace''a·ble
re·trac''ing
re·tract''
re·tract''a·ble
re·trac''tile
re·trac''tion
re·trac''tor
re·tread'', *v.*
  put new tread on
  (*see:* re-tread)
re''tread', *n.*
  new tread (*see:* re-
  tread)
re-tread''
  tread again (*see:* re-
  tread)
re·treat''
re·trench''
re·tri''al
ret'ri·bu''tion
re·trib''u·to·ry
re·triev''a·ble

re·triev″al
re·trieve″
re·triev″er
re·triev″ing
ret′ro·ac″tive
ret″ro·fire′
ret″ro·fir′ing
ret″ro·fit
ret″ro·fit′ting
ret″ro·grade
ret″ro·grad′ing
ret″ro·gress
ret″ro·gres″sion
ret″ro·rock′et
ret″ro·spect
ret′ro·spec″tion
ret′ro·spec″tive
re·turn″a·ble
re·turn″ee′
re·u′ni·fi·ca″tion
re·u′ni·fied
re·u′ni·fy′
re·un″ion
re′u·nite″
re′u·nit″ing
re·us″a·ble
re·use″
re·us″ing
rev
re′va·cate′
re·val″u·ate′
re·val″u·at′ing
re·val·u·a″tion
re·vamp″
re·veal″
rev″eil·le
rev″el
rev′e·la″tion
rev″el·er
rev″el·ing
rev″el·ry
   (*pl.* rev″el·ries)
re·venge″
re·venge″ful
re·veng″er
re·veng″ing

rev″e·nu′er
rev″e·nue shar′ing
re·ver″ber·ate′
re·ver″ber·at′ing
re·ver′ber·a″tion
re·vere″
rev″er·ence
rev″er·enc·ing
rev″er·end
rev″er·ent
rev′er·en″tial
rev″er·ie
re·ver″ing
re·ver″sal
re·verse″
re·vers″i·ble
re·vers″ing
re·ver″sion
re·ver″sion·ar′y
re·vert″
re·view″
   reexamination (*see:*
   revue)
re·view″er
re·vile″
re·vil″ing
re·vise″
re·vis″er
re·vis″ing
re·vi″sion
re·vi″sion·ist
re·vis″it
re·vi·tal·i·za″tion
re·vi″tal·ize′
re·vi″tal·iz′ing
re·viv″al
re·vive″
re·viv″i·fied′
re·viv″i·fy
re·viv″ing
rev″o·ca·ble
rev′o·ca″tion
re·voke″
re·vok″ing
re·volt″
re·volt″ing

rev′o·lu″tion
rev′o·lu″tion·ar′y
   (*pl.* rev′o·lu″tion·
   ar′ies)
rev′o·lu″tion·ist
rev′o·lu″tion·ize′
rev′o·lu″tion·iz′ing
re·volv″a·ble
re·volve″
re·volv″er
re·volv″ing
re·vue″
   musical show (*see:*
   review)
re·vul″sion
rev″ving
re·wak″en
re·ward″
re·wind″
re·wire″
re·word″
re·work″
re·write″, *v.*
   write again
re″write′, *n.*
   rewritten article
re·writ″ing
re·writ″ten
re·wrote″
Rey″kya·vik′
re·zone″
re·zon″ing
rhap·sod″ic
rhap″so·dist
rhap″so·dize′
rhap″so·diz′ing
rhap″so·dy
   (*pl.* rhap″so·dies)
rhe″da
rhe″o·stat
rhe″sus
rhet″o·ric
rhe·tor″i·cal
rhe·tor″i·cal·ly
rhet′o·ri″cian
rheum

discharge (*see:* room)
rheu·mat"ic
rheu"ma·tism'
rheu"ma·toid'
R"h" fac"tor
rhi·nar"i·a
rhine"stone
rhi·noc"er·os
rhi"no·plas'ty
rhi"nor·rhe'a
rhi"zome
rhi"zo·tax'is
Rhode Is"land
Rho·de"sia
rho"do·den"dron
rhom"boid
rhom"bus
   (*pl.* rhom"bus·es)
rhu"barb
rhyme
   similar sounds (*see:* rime)
rhym"ing
rhythm
rhyth"mic
rhyth"mi·cal
rhyth"mi·cal·ly
rib
rib"ald
rib"ald·ry
rib"bing
rib"bon
ri"bo·fla"vin
ri'bo·nu·cle"ic
ri'bo·some"
rice
rich"es
rich"ly
Rich"mond
Rich"ter scale"
rich"weed
ric"ing
rick"ets
rick·ett"si·a
   (*pl.* rick·ett"si·ae')

rick"et·y
rick"rack
rick"shaw
ric'o·chet"
ric'o·chet"ing
ri·cot"ta
rid
rid"a·ble
rid"dance
rid"den
rid"ding
   freeing (*see:* riding)
rid"dle
rid"dling
ride
rid"er·ship
rid"ing
   being carried (*see:* ridding)
ridge"pole
ridg"ing
rid"i·cule
rid"i·cul'ing
ri·dic"u·lous
rife
rif"fle
   shoal; shuffle (*see:* rifle)
rif"fling
   shuffling (*see:* ri-fling)
riff"raff'
ri"fle
   gun; ransack (*see:* riffle)
ri"fle·man
ri"fling
   ransacking (*see:* rif-fling)
rift
rig
Ri"ga
rig'a·to"ni
rig"ger
   one that rigs (*see:* rigor)

rig"ging
right
   correct; not left (*see:* rite)
right"-an"gle
righ"teous
right" field
right"ful·ly
right"-hand"ed
right"ist
right"-mind"ed
right" of way"
right"-on'
right"-to-life"
right" wing"
right"-wing"er
rig"id
ri·gid"i·ty
rig"ma·role
rig"or
   strictness (*see:* rig-ger)
rig"or mor"tis
rig"or·ous
rile
ril"ing
rim
rime
   frost (*see:* rhyme)
rim"fire
rim"ing
   coating with frost
rim"ming
   roll around rim (*see:* riming)
rind
ring
   circle; sound (*see:* wring)
ring"er
ring"lead'er
ring"let
ring"master
ring"side
ring"-tailed"
ring"worm

rink
rink"y·dink
rinse
rins"ing
Ri"o de Ja·nei"ro
Ri"o Grande"
ri"ot·er
ri"ot·ous
rip
ri·par"i·an
rip" cord'
ripe
rip"en
ripe"ness
rip"er
rip"off
ri·poste"
ri·post"ing
rip"per
rip"ping
rip"ple
rip"pling
rip"-roar'ing
rip"tide'
rise
ris"er
ris'i·bil"i·ty
  (*pl.* ris'i·bil"i·ties)
ris"i·ble
ris"ing
risk"i·er
risk"i·ness
risk"y
ris·que"
rite
  ceremony (*see:* right
  and write)
rit"u·al
rit'u·al·is"tic
rit"u·al·ly
ritz"i·er
ritz"y
ri"val
ri"val·ing
ri"val·ry
  (*pl.* ri"val·ries)

rive
riv"er·bank'
riv"er·bed'
riv"er·boat'
riv"er·damp'
riv"er·side'
riv"er·wash'
riv"et
riv"et·er
riv"et·ing
riv"ing
riv"u·let
roach
road
  way (*see:* rode and
  rowed)
road"bed'
road"block'
road" hog
road" map'
road"run'ner
road"side'
road" test'
road"way'
road"work'
roam
roan
roar"ing
roast"er
rob
rob"ber
rob"ber·y
  (*pl.* rob"ber·ies)
rob"bing
  stealing (*see:* robing)
robe
rob"ing
  clothing (*see:* rob-
  bing)
rob"in
ro"bot
ro·bust"
Roch"es·ter
rock"-bot"tom
rock"-bound'
rock"er

rock"et
rock"et·teer"
rock"et·ry
rock" gar'den
rock" hound'
rock"i·er
rock"ing chair
rock" 'n' roll"
rock"-ribbed
rock"y
Rock"y Moun"tains
ro·co"co
rode
  did ride (*see:* road
  and rowed)
ro"dent
ro"de·o
  (*pl.* ro"de·os)
roe
  deer; fish eggs (*see:*
  row)
roe"buck'
roent"gen
rogue
ro"guer·y
  (*pl.* ro"guer·ies)
ro"guing
ro"guish
roil
  stir up (*see:* royal)
roist"er
role
  character (*see:* roll)
role" mod"el
role"play'ing
roll
  bread; revolve; list
  (*see:* role)
roll"a·way'
roll"back'
roll" call'
roll"er coast'er
roll"er-skate', *v.*
  gliding
roll"er skate', *n.*
  shoe

roll″er-skat′ing
rol″lick·ing
roll″ing pin′
roll″mops
roll″-on
roll″o′ver
roll″-top
ROM
　read-only memory
ro·maine″
ro″man″
ro·mance″
ro·manc″ing
Ro·ma″ni″a″
ro·man″tic
ro·man″ti·cal·ly
ro·man″ti·cism′
ro·man″ti·cist
ro·man″ti·cize
ro·man″ti·ciz′ing
rom″per
ron″do
　(pl. ron″dos)
rood
　cross (see: rude and
　　rued)
roof″er
roof″ing
roof″top
rook″er·y
　(pl. rook″er·ies)
rook″ie
room
　space (see: rheum)
room″er
　lodger (see: rumor)
room·ette″
room″ful
　(pl. room″fuls)
room″ie
room″i·er
room″mate′
room″y
roost″er
root
　plant part; cheer; dig

(see: route and
　rout)
root″ beer
root″ ca·nal′
root″er
root″less
root″stock
rope
rop″ing
Roque″fort
Ror″schach
ro″sa·ry
　(pl. ro″sa·ries)
ro·se″
ro″se·ate
rose″bud
rose″bush
rose″-col′ored
rose″mar′y
Rose″ of Shar″on
ro·se·o″la
ro·sette″
rose″ wa′ter
rose″wood
Rosh Ha·sha″nah
ros″i·er
ros″i·ly
ros″in
ros″ter
ros″trum
ros″y
rot
ro″ta·ry
　(pl. ro″ta·ries)
ro″tat·a·ble
ro″tate
ro″tat·ing
ro·ta″tion
ro″ta·tor
rote
　memorization (see:
　　wrote)
ro·tis″ser·ie
ro′to·craft″
ro′to·gra·vure″
ro″tor

rot″ten
Rot″ter·dam
rot″ting
ro·tund″
ro·tun″da
ro·tun″di·ty
rou·e″
rouge
rough
　uneven; violent (see:
　　ruff)
rough″age
rough″-and-read″y
rough″-and-tum″ble
rough″cast
rough″-dried″
rough″-dry″
rough″en
rough″-hew″
rough″-hewn″
rough″house
rough″hous′ing
rough″neck
rough″rid′er
rough″shod″
roug″ing
rou·lade″
rou·lette″
round″a·bout
roun″de·lay
round″house
round″ly
round″ rob″in
round″ ta′ble
round′-the-clock″
round″ trip″
round″ up
round″worm
rouse
rous″ing
roust″a·bout
rout
　retreat; gouge (see:
　　route and root)
route

course (*see:* rout and
  root)
rou·tine''
rout''ing
rove
rov''er
rov''ing
row
  line; fight; move
  boat (*see:* roe)
row''boat
row''di·ly
row''di·ness
row''dy
  (*pl.* row''dies)
row''dy·ist'
rowed
  did row (*see:* road
  and rode)
row''el
row''el·ing
row'' house
roy''al
  regal (*see:* roil)
roy''al·ist
roy''al·ly
roy''al·ty
  (*pl.* roy''al·ties)
rub
rub''ber band''
rub''ber ce·ment''
rub''ber·ize'
rub''ber·iz'ing
rub''ber·neck
rub''ber plant'
rub''ber stamp''
rub''ber·y
rub''bing
rub''bish
rub''ble
rub''down
ru·bel''la
ru·be''o''la
ru''bi·cund
ru''bric
ru''by

(*pl.* ru''bies)
ruck''sack
ruck''us
rud''der
rud''di·er
rud''di·ness
rud''dy
rude
  offensive (*see:* rood
  and rue)
rude''ly
rude''ness
ru''di·ment
ru'di·men''ta·ry
rue
rued
  did rue (*see:* rood
  and rude)
rue''ful
rue''ful·ly
rue''some
ruff
  collar (*see:* rough)
ruf''fi·an
ruf''fle
ruf''fling
rug''ged
ru''in
  destroy (*see:* rune)
ru'in·a''tion
ru''in·ous
rule
rul''er
rul''ing
Ru·ma''ni·a
rum''ba
rum''ble
rum''bling
ru''mi·nant
ru''mi·nate
ru''mi·nat'ing
ru'mi·na''tion
rum''mage
rum''mag·ing
rum''my
ru''mor

gossip (*see:* roomer)
rum''ple
rum''pling
rum''pus room
rum''run''ner
run
run''a·bout
run''a·round
run''a·way
run''-down''
  disrepair (*see:* run-
  down)
run''down'
  summary (*see:* run-
  down)
rune
  alphabetic character
  (*see:* ruin)
rung
  rod; did ring (*see:*
  wrung)
run''-in
run''ner-up''
  (*pl.* run''ners-up'')
run''ni·er
run''ning boar''
run''ning light
run''ny
run''off
run''-of-the-mill'
run''-through
run''way
rup''ture
rup''tur·ing
ru''ral
ruse
rush'' hour
rus''set
Rus''sia
rus''tic
rus''ti·cal·ly
rus''ti·cate'
rus''ti·cat'ing
rust''i·er
rust''i·ness
rus''tle

rus″tler
rus″tling
rust″proof
rust″y
rut
ru'ta·ba″ga
ruth″ful·ly
ruth″less
rut″ting
rut″ty
Rwan″da
rye
  grain (*see:* wry)
rye″ bread″
rye″grass

S

Sab″bath
sab·bat″i·cal
sa″ber
sa″bine
sa″ble
sa″bot
sab″o·tage'
sab″o·tag'ing
sab'o·teur″
sa″bra
sac
  pouch (*see:* sack)
sac″cha·rin, *n.*
  sugar substitute
sac″cha·rine, *adj.*
  too sweet
sac'cha·ro·ly″tic
sac'er·do″tal
sa·chet″
  scented powder (*see:* sashay)
sack
  bag; plunder (*see:* sac)
sack″cloth
sack″ful
  (*pl.* sack″fuls)

sack″ing
sac″ra·ment
sac'ra·men″tal
Sac'ra·men″to
sa″cred
sac″ri·fice
sac'ri·fi″cial
sac″ri·fic'ing
sac″ri·lege
sac″ris·tan
sac″ris·ty
  (*pl.* sac″ris·ties)
sac'ro·il″i·ac
sac″ro·sanct
sa″crum
  (*pl.* sa″cra)
sad″den
sad″dest
  most sad (*see:* sad-ist)
sad″dle-backed
sad″dle·bag'
sad″dle block
sad″dle·cloth'
sad″dler
sad″dle shoes'
sad″dle soap'
sad″dle sore'
sad″dling
sad″ism
sad″ist
  cruel person (*see:* saddest)
sa·dis″ti·cal·ly
sad'o·mas″o·chism'
sa·fa″ri
  (*pl.* sa·fa″ris)
safe″-con″duct
safe″-de·pos″it
safe″guard
safe″keep″ing
saf″er
safe″ty pin'
safe″ty valve'
saf″flow'er
saf″fron

sag
sa″ga
sa·ga″cious
sa·gac″i·ty
sage″brush
sage″ly
sag″ging
sag″gy
sa″go
Sa·ha″ra
said
sail
  boat cloth (*see:* sale)
sail″boat
sail″cloth
sail″er
  ship (*see:* sailor)
sail″fish
sail″ing
sail″or
  ship's crew (*see:* sailer)
sail″or·proof'
saint″ed
saint″hood
saint″li·er
saint″li·ness
saint″ly
sa·ith″
sake
  purpose
sa″ke
  wine
sal″a·ble
sa·la″cious
sal″ad
sal″a·man'der
sa·la″mi
sal″a·ried
sal″a·ry
sale
  act of selling (*see:* sail)
sale″a·ble
Sa″lem
sales″clerk

sales″man·ship′
sales″peo′ple
sales″tax′
sales″wom′an
sal″i·ant
sa″li·ence
sa″li·ent
sa″line
sa·lin″i·ty
Salis″bur′y
sa·li″va
sal″i·var′y
sal″i·vate′
sal″i·vat′ing
sal′i·va″tion
  secrete saliva (*see:*
   salvation)
sal″lied
sal″low
sal″ly
  (*pl.* sal″lies)
salm″on
sal′mo·nel″la
  (*pl.* sal′mo·nel″lae)
sa·lon″
  room; shop (*see:* sa-
   loon)
sa·loon″
  (*see:* salon)
sal″sa
salt″box′
salt″cel′lar
salt″i·er
sal·tine″
salt″i·ness
Salt″ Lake′ Cit′y
salt″pe′ter
salt″shak″er
salt″wa″ter
salt″y
sa·lu″bri·ous
sal″u·tar′y
sal′u·ta″tion
sa·lu″ta·to″ri·an
sa·lu″ta·to′ry

  (*pl.* sa·lu″ta·to′
   ries)
sa·lute″
sal″va·ble
Sal″va·dor′
sal″vage
  gather (*see:* selvage)
sal″vage·a·ble
sal″vag·ing
sal·va″tion
  being saved (*see:*
   salivation)
salve
sal″ver
salv″ing
sal″vo
  (*pl.* sal″vos)
sam″ba
same″ness
Sa·mo″a
sam″o·var′
sam″pan
sam″ple
sam″pler
sam″pling
sam″u·rai
  (*pl.* sam″u·rai)
San An·to″ni·o
san·a·to″ri·um
sanc′ti·fi·ca″tion
sanc″ti·fied′
sanc″ti·fy
sanc′ti·mo″ni·ous
sanc″ti·mo′ny
sanc″tion
sanc″ti·ty
sanc″tu·ar′y
  (*pl.* sanc″tu·ar′ies)
sanc″tum
san″dal·wood
sand″bag
sand″bag′ging
sand″bank
sand″bar′
sand″blast
sand″box

sand″er
sand″hog
San Di·e″go
sand″i·er
sand″i·ness
sand″lot
sand″man
sand″pa′per
sand″stone
sand″storm
sand″trap
sand″wich
sand″wiched
sand″y
sane
  mentally sound (*see:*
   seine)
sane″ly
sane″ness
San″for·ized′™
San Fran·cis″co
sang
sang-froid″
san″gri·a
san″gui·nar′y
san″guine
san′i·tar″i·um
san″i·tar′y
san′i·ta″tion
san″i·tize′
san′i·tiz′ing
san″i·ty
San Jo·se″
  California
San Jo·se″
  Costa Rica
San Juan″
sank
San Sal″va·dor
San″skrit
San″ta Claus′
San″ta Fe″
San′ti·a″go
San″to Do·min″go
sa″pi·ent
sap″ling

sap"phire
sap"pi·er
sap"ping
sap"py
sap"skull
sap"suck·er
sa·ran"
sar"casm
sar·cas"tic
sar·cas"ti·cal·ly
sar·co·lac"tic
sar·co"ma
sar·coph"a·gus
  (*pl.* sar·coph"a·gi)
sar·dine"
Sar·din"i·a
sar·don"ic
sa"ri
  (*pl.* sa"ris)
sa·rong"
sar'sa·pa·ril"la
sar·to"ri·al
sa·shay"
  move casually (*see:*
  sachet)
Sas·katch"e·wan
Sas'ka·toon"
sas"sa·fras
sas"si·er
sas"sy
Sa"tan
sa·tan"ic
sa·tan"i·cal
satch"el
sate
sa·teen"
sat"el·lite'
sa"ti·a·ble
sa"ti·ate
sa"ti·at'ing
sa"ti·a"tion
sa·ti"e·ty
sat"ing
sat"in·wood'
sat"in·y
sat"ire

sa·tir"i·cal
sat"i·rist
sat"i·rize'
sat"i·riz'ing
sat'is·fac"tion
sat'is·fac"to·ri·ly
sat'is·fac"to·ry
sat'is·fi"a·ble
sat"is·fied'
sat"is·fy
sa"trap
sat"u·rate
sat"u·rat'ing
sat'u·ra"tion
Sat"ur·day
Sat"urn
sat"ur·nine
sat"yr
sauce"pan
sau"cer
sau"ci·ness
sauc"ing
sau"cy
Sau"di A·ra"bi·a
sau"er·bra'ten
sauer"kraut'
Sauk
  (*pl.* Sauks)
sau"na
saun"ter
sau"sage
sau·te"
sau·te"ing
Sau·terne"
sav"a·ble
sav"age
sav"age·ry
  (*pl.* sav"age·ries)
sa·van"na
Sa·van"nah
sa·vant"
save
sav"er
  one who saves (*see:*
  savor)
sav"ing

sav"ior
sa"voir-faire"
sa"vor
sa"vor·y
  taste (*pl.* sa"vor·ies)
  (*see:* saver)
sav"vy
saw"dust
sawed"-off"
saw"horse
saw"mill
saw"-toothed"
saw"yer
sax"o·phone
say"a·ble
say"ing
sa·yo·na"ra
say"-so'
  (*pl.* say"-sos')
scab
scab"bard
scab"bing
sca"bies
scab"rous
scads
scaf"fold
scal"a·ble
scal"a·wag
scald
scale
scal"i·er
scal"i·ness
scal"ing
scal"lion
scal"lop
sca·lop·pi"ne
scalp
scal"peen
scal"pel
scal"y
scam
scamp
scamp"er
scam"pi
scan
scan"dal·ize'

scan''dal·iz'ing
scan''dal·mon'ger
scan''dal·ous
Scan'di·na''vi·a
scan''ner
scan''ning
scan''sion
scan''ter
scant''i·er
scant''i·ly
scant''i·ness
scant''ling
scant''y
scape''goat
scape''grace
scap''ose
scap''u·la
  (*pl.* scap''u·lae)
scap''u·lar
scar
scar''ab
scarce
scarce''ly
scar''ci·ty
  (*pl.* scar''ci·ties)
scare''crow
scarf
  (*pl.* scarfs *or*
   scarves)
scar''i·er
scar''i·fied
scar''i·fy
scar''ing
scar''let fe''ver
scarp
scar''ring
scar''y
scat
scathe
scath''ing
sca·tol''o·gy
scat''ter·brained
scat''ting
scav''enge
scav''en·ger
scav''eng·ing

sce·nar''i·o
  (*pl.* sce·nar''i·os)
sce·nar''ist
scene
  setting (*see:* seen)
scen''er·y
  (*see:* scen''er·ies)
sce''nic
scent
  smell (*see:* cent and
   sent)
scep''ter
scep''tic
scep''ti·cal
scep''ti·cism
sched''ule
sched''ul·ing
sche''ma
  (*pl.* sche''ma·ta)
sche·mat''ic
sche''ma·tize'
scheme
schem''er
schem''ing
Sche·nec''ta·dy
scher''zo
  (*pl.* scher''zos)
schism
schis·mat''ic
schist
schiz''oid
schiz'o·phre''ni·a
schiz'o·phren''ic
schiz'o·pod
schle·miel''
schlep''
schlock
schmaltz
schmo
  (*pl.* schmoes)
schnapps
schnau''zer
schnit''zel
schol''ar·ly
schol''ar·ship'
scho·las''tic

scho·las''ti·cal·ly
scho·las''ti·cism'
schone
school''board'
school''book'
school''boy'
school''bus'
school''child'
school''dis''trict
school''girl'
school''house'
school''ing
school''mate'
school''room'
school''teach'er
school''work'
school''yard'
school''year'
schoon''er
schwa
sci·a·ly''tic
sci·at''i·ca
sci''ence
sci'en·tif''ic
sci''en·tist
scil''lain
scim''i·tar
scin·til''la
scin'til·late'
scin''til·lat'ing
sci''on
scis''sors
scis''sors·bird'
scle·ro''sis
  (*pl.* scle·ro''ses)
scoff
scoff''er
scoff''law'
scold
sconce
scone
scoop''ful'
  (*pl.* scoop''fuls)
scoot''er
scope
scorch''er

score"board'
score"card'
score"keep'er
score"less
scor"ing
scorn"ful
scorn"ful·ly
scor"pi·on
scotch
Scotch"gard™
scot"-free"
Scot"land
scoun"drel
scour"
scourge
scourg"ing
scout"ing
scout"mas·ter
scow
scowl
scrab"ble
scrab"bling
scrag"gly
scrag"gy
scram
scram"ble
scram"bling
scram"ming
scrap
scrap"book
scrape
scrap"er
scrap"ing
  rubbing (*see:* scrap-
  ping)
scrap"per
scrap"ping
  discarding (*see:*
  scraping)
scrap"ple
scrap"py
scratch"i·er
scratch"i·ness
scratch"test
scratch"y
scrawl

scrawn"i·er
scrawn"y
scream"er
screech"owl'
screen
screen'door"
screen"play·
screen"test
screen"writ'er
screw"ball
screw"driv'er
screw"y
scrib"ble
scrib"bler
scribe
scrim
scrim"mage
scrim"mag·er
scrimp
scrim"shaw'
scrip
  certificate (*see:*
  script)
script
  writing (*see:* scrip)
scrip"tur·al
scrip"tur·al·ly
script"writ'er
scriv"en·er
scrof"u·lous
scroll"work
scro"tum
  (*pl.* scro"ta)
scrounge
scroung"ing
scrub
scrub"bing
scrub"by
scrub"nurse'
scrub"wom'an
scruff"i·er
scruff"y
scrump"tious
scrunch
scru"ple
scru"pling

scru"pu·lous
scru"ti·nize'
scru"ti·niz'ing
scru"ti·ny
scu"ba
  self-contained under-
  water breathing ap-
  paratus
scud
scud"ding
scuff
scuf"fle
scuf"fling
scull
  boat (*see:* skull)
scul"ler·y
  (*pl.* scul"ler·ies)
sculpt
sculp"tor
sculp"tress
sculp"tur·al
sculp"ture
sculp"tur·ing
scum
scum"mi·er
scum"my
scup"per
scurf
scur"ried
scur·ril"i·ty
  (*pl.* scur·ril"i·ties)
scur"ril·ous
scur"ry
scur"vy
scut"tle·butt'
scut"tling
scythe
S'D'I'
  Strategic Defense
  Initiative
sea
  ocean (*see:* see)
sea"bed'
sea"bird'
sea"board'
sea"borne'

sea"coast'
sea"dog'
sea"far'er
sea"far'ing
sea"food'
sea"go'ing
sea"gull'
sea"horse'
seal"ant
seal"er
seal"ing wax'
seal"skin'
seam
  juncture (*see:* seem)
.sea"man
  sailor (*pl.* sea"men)
  (*see:* semen)
seam"i·er
seam"stress
seam"y
se"ance
sea"port'
sea"pow'er
sear
  burn (*see:* seer and
  sere)
search"light'
search"war'rant
sea"scape'
sea"shell'
sea"shore'
sea"sick'
sea"side'
sea"son
sea"son·a·ble
sea"son·al
sea"son·ing
seat"belt'
seat"stone
Se·at"tle
sea"wall'
sea"wards
sea"way'
sea"weed'
sea"wor'thy
se·ba"ceous

se"cant
se·cede"
se·ced"ing
se·ces"sion
se·clude"
se·clud"ing
se·clu"sion
se·clu"sion·ist
Sec"o·nal™
sec"on·dar'i·ly
sec"ond·ar'y
sec"ond base"
sec"ond-class"
sec"ond-guess"
sec"ond hand', *n.*
  clock hand
sec"ond-hand", *adj.*
  not original
sec"ond-rate"
sec"ond-string"
se"cre·cy
se"cret
sec're·tar"i·al
sec're·tar"i·at
sec're·tar"y
se·crete"
se·cret"ing
se·cre"tion
se"cre·tive
se·cre"to·ry
sec·tar"i·an
sec"tion·al
sec"tor
sec"u·lar
sec"u·lar·ism'
sec"u·lar·ize'
sec"u·lar·iz'ing
se·cure"
se·cur"ing
se·cu"ri·ty
  (*pl.* se·cu"ri·ties)
se·dan"
se·date"
se·date"ly
se·dat"ing
se·da"tion

sed"a·tive
sed"en·tar'y
se"der
sed"i·ment
sed'i·men"ta·ry
sed'i·men·ta"tion
se·di"tion
se·di"tious
se·duce"
se·duc"ing
se·duc"tion
se·duc"tive
se·du"li·ty
sed"u·lous
see
  sense; bishopric
  (*see:* sea)
seed
  plant ovule (*see:*
  cede)
seed"i·er
seed"i·ly
seed"i·ness
seed"ling
seed"time
seed"y
see·ing
seem
  appear (*see:* seam)
seem"li·er
seem"li·ness
seem"ly
seen
  did *see* (*see:* scene)
seep"age
seer
  foreteller (*see:* sear
  and sere)
seer"suck'er
see"saw
seethe
seeth"ing
seg·ment", *v.*
  divide
seg"ment, *n.*
  portion

seg"men·tar'y
seg'men·ta"tion
seg"re·gate'
seg"re·gat'ing
seg're·ga"tion
seg're·ga"tion·ist
seine
   net (*see:* sane)
sein"ing
seis"mic
seis"mi·cal·ly
seis"mo·graph
seis·mog"ra·pher
seis·mog"ra·phy
seis·mol"o·gist
seis·mol"o·gy
seize
seiz"ing
sei"zure
sel"dom
se·lect"
se·lect·ee"
se·lec"tion
se·lec"tive·ly
se·lec·tiv"i·ty
se·lect"man
   (*pl.* se·lect"men)
self
   (*pl.* selves)
self"-a·bas"ing
self"-ad·dressed"
self"-ap·point"ed
self"-as·ser"tion
self"-as·sur"ance
self"-as·sured"
self"-cen"tered
self"-com·posed"
self"-con"cept
self"-con·fi·dence
self"-con"scious
self"-con·tained"
self"-con·trol"
self"-con·trolled"
self"-cor·rect"ing
self"-crit"i·cism'
self"-de·feat"ing

self"-de·fense"
self"-de·ni"al
self"-de·struct"
self"-de·ter'mi·na"tion
self"-dis"ci·pline
self"-ed"u·cat·ed
self"-em·ployed"
self"-es·teem"
self'-ev"i·dent
self"-ex·plan"a·to'ry
self"-ex·pres"sion
self"-ful·fill"ment
self'-gov"ern·ment
self"-ha"tred
self"-help"
self"-im"age
self"-im·por"tant
self"-im·posed"
self"-im·prove"ment
self"-in·crim"i·nat·ing
self"-in·dul"gence
self"-in·dul"gent
self"-in·flict"ed
self'-in"ter·est·ed
self"ish
self'-knowl"edge
self"less
self"-made"
self"-per·pet"u·at·ing
self'-pit"y
self'-por"trait
self"-pos·sessed"
self"-pres'er·va"tion
self"-pro·claimed"
self"-pro·pelled"
self"-pro·tec"tion
self"-reg"u·lat·ing
self"-re·li"ance
self"-re·li"ant
self"-re·spect"
self"-re·straint"
self"-righ"teous
self"-sac"ri·fice
self"same

self"-sat'is·fac"tion
self"-seal"ing
self"-seek"ing
self"-serv"ice
self"-start"er
self"-styled"
self"-suf·fi"cient
self"-sup·port"
self"-sus·tain"ing
self"-taught"
self"-wind"ing
self"-worth"
sell
   exchange for money
   (*see:* cell)
sell"ing
sell"out
sel"vage
   edge (*see:* salvage)
se·man"tics
sem"a·phore
sem"blance
se"men
   sperm (*see:* seaman)
se·mes"ter
sem'i·an"nu·al
sem'i·au'to·mat"ic
sem"i·cir'cle
sem"i·co'lon
sem'i·con·duc"tor
sem'i·con"scious
sem"i·fi"nal
sem'i·for"mal
sem'i·month"ly
sem"i·nal
sem"i·nar
sem"i·nar'y
   (*pl.* sem"i·nar'ies)
sem"i·nole
   (*pl.* sem"i·noles)
sem'i·of·fi"cial
se'mi·ot"ic
sem'i·pre"cious
sem'i·pri"vate
sem'i·pro·fes"sion·al
sem'i·rig"id

sem'i·se"ri·ous
sem'i·sol"id
sem'i·sweet"
sem"i·trail'er
sem'i·trans·par"ent
sem'i·trop"i·cal
sem'i·week"ly
sem'i·year"ly
sem·o·li"na
sem"per fi·de"lis
sen"ate
sen"a·tor
send"ing
send"-off
Sen'e·ca
Sen'e·gal"
se·nes"cent
se"nile
se·nil"i·ty
sen"ior
sen·ior"i·ty
  (*pl.* sen·ior"i·ties)
sen"na
se·nor"
  (*pl.* se·no"res)
se·no"ra
se no·ri"ta
sen·sa"tion
sen·sa"tion·al·ism
sen·sa"tion·al·ly
sen·sa·tor"i·al
sense
sense"less
sen'si·bil"i·ty
  (*pl.* sen'si·bil"i·ties)
sen"si·ble
sens"ing
sen"si·tive
sen'si·tiv"i·ty
  (*pl.* sen'si·tiv"i·ties)
sen"si·tize'
sen"si·tiz'ing
sen"sor
sen"so·ry

sen"su·al
sen'su·al"i·ty
  (*pl.* sen'su·al"i·ties)
sen"su·ous
sent
  did send (*see:* cent
  and scent)
sen"tence
sen"tenc·ing
sen·ten"tious
sen"tience
sen"tient
sen"ti·ment
sen'ti·men"tal
sen'ti·men·tal"i·ty
  (*pl.* sen'ti·men·tal"
  i·ties)
sen'ti·men"tal·ize
sen'ti·men"tal·iz'ing
sen'ti·men"tal·ly
sen"ti·nel
sen"try
  (*pl.* sen"tries)
sen"vy
Se"oul
se"pal
sep"a·ra·ble
sep"a·rate'
sep"a·rat'ing
sep'a·ra"tion
sep"a·ra·tor
se·phir"ic
se"pi·a
sep"sis
Sep·tem"ber
sep·tet"
sep"tic
sep"tole
Sep"tu·a·gint
sep"tum
sep"ul·cher
se·pul"chral
se"quel
se"quence
se·quen"tial
se·ques"ter

se·ques"trate
se·ques"trat·ing
se"quin
se·quoi"a
se"rai
se·ra"pe
ser"aph
Ser"bi·a
sere
  withered (*see:* sear
  and seer)
ser'e·nade"
ser'e·nad"ing
ser·en·dip"i·ty
se·rene"
se·ren"i·ty
serf
  slave (*see:* surf)
serge
  fabric (*see:* surge)
ser"geant
se"ri·al
  series (*see:* cereal)
se"ri·al·ize'
se"ri·al·iz'ing
se"ri·al·ly
se"ries
  (*pl.* se"ries)
ser"if
se·ri·o·com"ic
se"ri·ous
ser"mon
ser"mon·ize'
se"rous
ser"pent
ser"pen·tine
ser"rate
ser"rat·ing
se"rum
ser"vant
serve
serv"ice
serv'ice·a·bil"i·ty
serv'ice·a·ble
serv"ice·man'
serv"ic·ing

ser"vile
ser·vil"i·ty
serv"ing
ser"vi·tude
ses"a·me
ses'qui·cen·ten"ni·al
ses"sion
  gathering (*see:* ces-
   sion)
set"back'
set"off
set·tec"
set"ter
set"ting
set"tle·ment
set"tler
set"tling
set"-to
  (*pl.* set"-tos)
set"up
sev"en·teen"
sev"en·teenth"
sev"enth
sev"en·ti·eth
sev"en·ty
  (*pl.* sev"en·ties)
sev"er
sev"er·al
sev"er·al·ly
sev"er·ance
se·vere"
se·vere"ly
se·ver"i·ty
Se·ville"
sew
  join with thread
  (*see:* so and sow)
sew"age
sew"er
  waste channel (*see:*
   suer)
sew"er·age
sew"ing ma·chine
sewn
  stitched (*see:* sown)
sex'a·ge·nar"i·an

sex"i·er
sex"i·ness
sex"ism
sex"ist
sex"-linked
sex"pot
sex"tant
sex·tet"
sex"ton
sex"u·al
sex·u·al"i·ty
sex"u·al·ly
sex"y
Sey·chelles"
sfor·zan"do
shab"bi·er
shab"bi·ness
shab"by
shack"le
shack"ling
shad"dock
shade
shad"i·er
shad"i·ness
shad"ing
shad"ow box
shad"ow·y
shad"y
shaft
shag
shag"gi·er
shag"gi·ness
shag"ging
shag"gy
shak"a·ble
shak"er
Shake·spear"e·an
shake"-up'
shak"i·er
shak"i·ly
shak"i·ness
shak"ing
shak"y
shale
shall
shal"lot

shal"low
sha·lom"
sham
sha"man
sham"ble
shame
shame"faced
shame"ful
shame"ful·ly
shame"lcss
sham"ing
  make ashamed (*see:*
   shamming)
sham"ming
  imitating (*see:* sham-
   ing)
sham·poo"
sham·pooed"
sham"rock
shang"hai"
  kidnap; force
Shang·hai"
  city
shank
shan"ty
  shabby dwelling (*pl.*
   shan"ties) (*see:*
   chantey)
shan"ty·town'
shape"less
shape"li·er
shape"li·ness
shape"ly
shape"-up'
shap"ing
share"crop'per
share"hold'er
shar"ing
shark"skin
sharp"bill
sharp"en
sharp"-eyed"
sharp"ie
sharp"shoot'er
sharp"-tongued"
sharp"-wit"ted

shat"ter·proof

shave

shav"ing

shawl

Shaw·nee"
  (pl. Shaw·nee")

sheaf
  (pl. sheaves)

shear
  cut (see: sheer)

sheared

sheath

sheathe

sheath"ing

shed

shed"ding

shed"like

sheen

sheep

sheep"dog

sheep"fold'

sheep"ish

sheep"skin

sheer
  thin; steep; swerve
  (see: shear)

sheet"ing

sheik
  Arab chief (see:
  chic)

shek"el

shelf
  (pl. shelves)

shelf"life

shel·lac"

shel·lack"ing

shell"fish

shell"proof'

shell"shock

shel"ter

shelve

shelv"ing

she·nan"i·gan

shep"herd

shep"herd·ess

sher"bet

sher"iff

sher"ry
  (pl. sher"ries)

shib"bo·leth

shied

shield

shift"i·er

shift"i·ly

shift"i·ness

shift"less

shift"y

Shi"ite

shil"ly-shal'ly

shim

shim"mier

shim"mer·y

shim"mied

shim"my
  (pl. shim"mies)

shin

shin"bone

shin"dig

shine

shin"ing

shin"gle

shin"gles

shin"gling

shin"i·er

shin"ing
  brightness (see: shin-
  ning)

shin"ning
  climbing (see: shin-
  ing)

Shin"to

shin"y

ship"board

ship"load

ship"mate

ship"ment

ship"pa·ble

ship"per

ship"ping

ship"shape

ship"wreck

ship"wright

ship"yard

shire

shirk

shirr

shirt"ing

shirt"sleeve

shirt"tail

shirt"waist

shish" ke·bab

shiv"er

shoal

shock" ab·sorb'er

shock"er

shock"ing

shock"proof

shod"di·er

shod"di·ly

shod"di·ness

shod"dy

shoe"horn

shoe"lace

shoe"mak'er

shoe"shine

shoe"string'

shoe"tree'

sho"far

shone
  glowed (see: shown)

shoo"fly'

shoo"-in'

shook up

shoot
  hit with gun; plant
  growth (see: chute)

shoot"-out'

shop

shop"girl'

shop"keep'er

shop"lift'er

shoppe

shop"per

shop"ping

shop"talk'

shop"work

shop"worn'

sho"ran'

shore"leave'
shore"line'
shor"ing
short"age
short"bread'
short"cake'
short"change"
short"-chang"ing
short"cir"cuit
short"com"ing
short"cut'
short"en'
short"en·ing
short"fall'
short"hand'
short"-hand"ed
short"-lived"
short"-or'der
short"-range'
short"ribs'
short"run"
short"shrift"
short"sight"ed
short"stop'
short"-tem"pered
short"-term"
short"-waist"ed
short"wave"
short"-wind"ed
Sho·sho"ne
(*pl.* Sho·sho"nes)
shot"gun'
shot"put'
shot"star
should
shoul"der blade'
should"n't
shout
shove
shov"el
shov"el·ful
(*pl.* shov"el·fuls')
shov"el·ing
shov"ing
show"bill'
show"boat'

show"case'
show"down'
show"er
show"i·er
show"i·ness
show"ing
show"man
shown
exhibited (*see:* shone)
show"off
show"piece'
show"place'
show"room'
show"y
shrank
shrap"nel
shred
shred"ding
shrew
shrewd
shrew"ish
shrew"like
shriek
shrift
shrike
shrill"ness
shril"ly
shrimp
shrine
shrink
shrink"age
shrink"ing
shrink"-wrap'
shrink"-wrap'ping
shriv"el
shroud
shrub
shrub"ber·y
(*pl.* shrub"ber·ies)
shrug
shrug"ging
shrunk
shtick
shuck
shud"der

shuf"fle·board
shuf"fling
shun
shun"ning
shunt
shush
shut"down
shut"-eye
shut"-in
shut"off
shut"out
shut"ter·bug
shut"ting
shut"tle·cock
shut"tling
shy
shy"er
shy"ing
shy"ly
shy"ster
Si·be"ri·a
sib"i·lance
sib"i·lant
sib"ling
sic
urge to attack; thus
(*see:* sick)
Sic"i·ly
sick
sick"bay
sick"bed
sicked
sick"en
sick"ing
sick"le
sick"le cell
sick"li·er
sick"ly
sick"room'
side"arm'
side"bar'
side"board'
side"burns'
side"chair'
side"dish'
side"ef·fect

side″kick′
side″light′
side″line′
side″long′
side″piece′
si·de″re·al
side″sad′dle
side″show′
side″slip′
side″split′ting
side″step
side″step′ping
side″stroke′
side″swipe′
side″track′
side″walk
side″wall
side″ways
side″wind′er
side″wise′
sid″ing
Sidhe
si″dle
si″dling
siege
si·en″na
si·er″ra
si·es″ta
sieve
sift″er
sigh
sight
  seen with eyes (*see:*
  cite and site)
sight″ing
sight″less
sight″li·er
sight″ly
sight″-read
sight″see′ing
sight″se′er
sign
  indication (*see:* sine)
sig″nal
sig″nal·ing
sig″nal·ize

sig″nal·iz′ing
sig″nal·ly
sig″nal·man
sig″na·to′ry
  (*pl.* sig″na·to ries)
sig″na·ture
sign″board′
sig″net
  seal (*see:* cygnet)
sig·nif″i·cance
sig·nif″i·cant
sig·ni·fi·ca″tion
sig″ni·fied
sig″ni·fy
si·gnor″
si·gno″ra
sign″post
Sikh
si″lage
si″lence
si″lenc·er
si″lenc·ing
si″lent
sil′hou·ette″
sil′hou·et″ting
sil″i·ca
sil″i·cate
si·li″ceous
sil″i·con
  chemical element
  (*see:* silicone)
sil″i·cone
  polymer (*see:* sili-
  con)
sil″i·co″sis
silk″en
silk″i·er
silk″screen
silk″worm
silk″y
sill
sil″li·er
sil″li·ness
sil″ly
  (*pl.* sil″lies)
si″lo

  (*pl.* si″los)
silt
sil″ver·fish′
sil″ver fox″
sil″ver·sides
sil″ver plate″
  tableware
sil″ver-plate″
  coat with silver
sil″ver·smith′
sil″ver-tongued″
sil″ver·ware′
sil″ver·y
sim″i·an
sim″i·lar
sim·i·lar″i·ty
  (*pl.* sim·i·lar″i·ties)
sim″i·le
si·mil″i·tude
sim″mer
Si″mo·nize′™
si″mon-pure″
sim·pa″ti·co
sim″per
sim·ple-mind″ed
sim″pler
sim″ple·ton
sim·plic″i·ty
  (*pl.* sim·plic″i·ties)
sim″pli·fi·ca″tion
sim″pli·fied
sim″pli·fi′er
sim″pli·fy′
sim″ply
sim″u·late′
sim″u·lat′ing
sim′u·la″tion
sim″u·la″tor
si″mul·cast′
si′mul·ta·ne″i·ty
si′mul·ta″ne·ous
sin
sin·arch″ist
since
sin·cere″
sin·cere″ly

sin·cer″er
sin·cer″i·ty
sine
  angle ratio (*see:*
   sign)
si″ne·cure′
sin″ew·y
sin·fon″i·a
sin″ful
sin″ful·ly
sing
Sin″ga·pore′
singe
singe″ing
sing″er
sin″gle-breast″ed
sin″gle file″
sin″gle-hand″ed
sin″gle-mind″ed
sin″gle·ness
sin″gle-space″
sin″gle·ton
sin″gle·tree
sin″gling
sin″gly
sing″song′
sin″gu·lar
sin″gu·lar″i·ty
sin″is·ter
sink″er
sink″hole′
sin″ner
sin″ning
sin″u·ous
si″nus
  (*pl.* si″nus·es)
si″nus·i″tis
Sioux
  (*pl.* Sioux)
sip
si″phon
sip″ping
sire
si″ren
sir″ing
sir″loin

si·roc″co
  (*pl.* si·roc″cos)
si″sal
sis″sy
  (*pl.* sis″sies)
sis″ter·hood′
sis″ter-in-law′
  (*pl.* sis″ters-in-law′)
sis″ter·ly
sis″tern
si·tar″
sit″com′
sit″-down
site
  location (*see:* cite
   and sight)
sit″ed
sit″-in
sit″ing
sit″ter
sit″ting
sit″u·ate
sit″u·at′ing
sit′u·a″tion
sit″-up
sitz″bath′
six″-pack
six″pen′ny
six″-shoot″er
six″teen″
six″teenth″
sixth
six″ti·eth
six″ty
  (*pl.* six″ties)
siz″a·ble
size
siz″ing
siz″zle
siz″zling
skate″board
skat″ing
skeet
skein
skel″e·ton
skene

skep″tic
skep″ti·cal
skep″ti·cal·ly
skep″ti·cism
sketch″book
sketch″i·er
sketch″i·ly
sketch″i·ness
sketch″y
skew
skew″er
ski
skid″ding
skid″row″
skied
ski″er
skiff
ski″ing
ski″jump′
ski″lift
skilled
skil″let
skill″ful
skim
skim″ming
skimp″i·er
skimp″i·ly
skimp″i·ness
skimp″y
skin″-deep″
skin″-dive′
skin″flint
skin″ner
skin″ni·er
skin″ning
skin″ny-dip′
skin″ny-dip′ping
skin″tight
skin″worm′
skip
ski″plane
ski″ pole′
skip″per
skip″ping
skir″mish
skirt

skirt"ing
skit
ski" tow
skit"tish
skit"tles
skul·dug"ger·y
skulk
skull
  head bone (*see:* scull)
skull"cap
skunk
sky
  (*pl.* skies)
sky"·blue"
sky"dive'
sky" div"er
sky"div'ing
sky"-high"
sky"jack
sky"lark
sky"light'
sky"line"
sky"rock'et
sky"scrap'er
sky"walk'
sky"wards
sky"ways
sky"writ'ing
slab
slack"en
slack"er
slain
slake
slak"ing
sla"lom
slam"-bang"
slam"-dunk"
slam"ming
slan"der
slan"der·ous
slang
slang"y
slant"wise
slap"dash
slap"hap'py

slap"jack'
slap"ping
slap"stick
slash
slat
slate
slat"ing
  cover with slate; put on list (*see:* slatting)
slat"tern
slat"ting
  make with slats (*see:* slating)
slaugh"ter·house'
slave
slav"er·y
slav"ing
slav"ish
slaw
slay
  kill (*see:* sleigh)
slay"ing
slea"zi·er
slea"zi·ness
slea"zy
sled
sled"ding
sledge"ham"mer
sleek
sleep"i·er
sleep"ing
sleep"i·ness
sleep"ing bag'
sleep"ing pill
sleep"less
sleep"walk'ing
sleep"y·head'
sleet
sleeve"less
sleigh
sled
slay"
sleight
  cunning (*see:* slight)
slen"der

slen"der·ize'
slen"der·iz'ing
slept
sleuth
slew
slice
slic"ing
slick"er
slide
slid"er
slid"ing
sli"er
slight
  little; snub
sleight"
slim
slime
slim"i·er
slim"mer
slim"ming
slim"ness
slim"y
sling"shot'
slink
slink"y
slip"cov'er
slip"knot
slip"-on'
slip"o'ver
slip"page
slip"per·i·er
slip"per·i·ness
slip"per·y
slip"ping
slip"shod
slip" stitch'
slip"stream'
slip"-up
slit
slith"er
slit"ting
sliv"er
slob
slob"ber
sloe
  fruit (*see:* slow)

sloe″-eyed
slog
slo″gan
slog″ging
sloop
slop
slope
slop″ing
   angling (*see:* slop-
    ping)
slop″pi·er
slop″pi·ly
slop″pi·ness
slop″ping
   spilling (*see:* slop-
    ing)
slop″py
slosh
slot
sloth″ful
slot″ma·chine′
slot″ting
slouch
slouch″y
slough
slov″en·li·ness
slov″en·ly
slow
   not fast (*see:* sloe)
slow″down′
slow″-mo″tion
slow″-mov″ing
slow″poke′
slow″-wit″ted
sludge
sludg″y
slug″a·bed′
slug″fest′
slug″gard
slug″ger
slug″ging
slug″gish
sluice″way′
sluic″ing
slum
slum″ber

slum″ber·ous
slum″lord
slum″ming
slump
slunk
slur
slur″ring
slush″fund′
slush″y
slut
sly
sly″ly
smack
small″arm″
small″ish
small″-mind″ed
small″pox′
small″-scale″
small″talk′
small″-time″
smart″al′eck
smart″card‴
smart″en
smash″ing
smash″up′
smat″ter·ing
smear
smell
smell″i·er
smell″y
smelt
smelt″er
smid″gen
smi″lax
smile
smil″ing
smirch
smirk
smite
smith″er·eens″
smit″ing
smit″ten
smock
smock″ing
smog
smog″gi·er

smog″gy
smoke″-filled
smoke″hole
smoke″less
smok′er
smoke″screen
smoke″stack
smok″i·er
smok″i·ness
smok″ing
smok″y
smol″der
smooch
smooth″bore
smooth″-shav″en
smooth″-spo″ken
smor″gas·bord
smote
smoth″er
smudge
smudg″ing
smudg″y
smug
smug″ger
smug″gle
smug″gler
smug″gling
smut
smut″ti·er
smut″ty
snack
snaf″fle
snaf″fling
sna·fu″
snag
snag″ging
snail
snake
snake″bite′
snake″skin′
snak″ing
snak″y
snap″back′
snap″bean′
snap″drag′on
snap″per

snap"ping
snap"py
snap"shot'
snare"drum'
snar"ing
snarl
snatch
snaz"zi·er
snaz"zy
sneak"er
sneak"i·er
sneak"i·ly
sneak"i·ness
sneak"thief'
sneak"y
sneer
sneeze
sneez"ing
snick"er
snide
sniff
sniff"er
snif"fle
snif"fling
snif"ter
snip
snipe
snip"er
snip"ing
  shooting (*see:* snip-
  ping)
snip"pet
snip"ping
  cutting (*see:* sniping)
snitch
sniv"el
sniv"el·ing
snob
snob"ber·y
snob"bi·er
snob"bish
snob"by
snook"er
snoop
snoop"er
snoop"i·er

snoop"y
snoot
snoot"i·er
snoot"y
snooze
snooz"ing
snore
snor"ing
snor"kel
snort
snout
snow"ball'
snow"bank'
snow"blind'
snow"bound'
snow"capped'
snow"drift'
snow"fall'
snow"fence'
snow"flake'
snow"job'
snow"man'
snow"mo·bile'
snow"plow'
snow"shoe'
snow"storm'
snow"suit'
snow"tire'
snow"-white"
snub
snub"bing
snub"-nosed'
snuff"box'
snuff"er
snuf"fle
snuf"fling
snug
snug"ger
snug"gle
snug"gling
so
  as stated (*see:* sew
  and sow)
so"-and-so'
  (*pl.* so"-and-sos')
soap"box'

soap"i·er
soap"op'er·a
soap"suds'
soap"y
soar
  fly (*see:* sore)
sob
sob"bing
so"ber
so·bri"e·ty
so"bri·quet
so"-called"
soc"cer
so·cia·bil"i·ty
so"cia·ble
so"cial·ism
so"cial·ist
so"cial·ite'
so"cial·i·za"tion
so"cial·ize'
so"cial·iz'ing
so"cial·ly
so·ci"e·tal
so·ci"e·ty
  (*pl.* so·ci"e·ties)
so·ci·o·ec'o·nom"ic
so·ci·o·log"i·cal
so·ci·o·log"i·cal·ly
so·ci·ol"o·gist
so·ci·ol"o·gy
sock"et
sock"eye'
so·crat"ic
sod
so"da crack"er
so·dal"i·ty
  (*pl.* so·dal"i·ties)
so"da wa"ter
sod"den
sod"ding
so"di·um
sod"om·ize'
sod"om·y
so"fa
soft"ball'
soft"-boiled'

soft''bound
soft''-core''
soft''drink''
sof''ten
soft''heart''ed
soft''-ped'al
soft''sell''
soft''-shell
soft''-shoe''
soft''-spo''ken
soft''ware'
soft''y
   (*pl.* soft''ies)
sog''gi·er
sog''gi·ness
sog''gy
soil
soi·ree''
so''journ
sol''ace
so''lar
so·lar''i·um
so''lar plex''us
sol''der
sol''dier
sole
   single; fish; shoe
   part (*see:* soul)
sol''e·cism'
soled
sole''ly
sol''emn
so·lem''ni·ty
   (*pl.* so·lem''ni·ties)
sol''em·nize'
sol''em·niz'ing
so''le·noid'
so·lic''it
so·lic'i·ta''tion
so·lic''i·tor
so·lic''i·tous
so·lic''i·tude'
sol'i·dar''i·ty
so·lid'i·fi·ca''tion
so·lid''i·fied'
so·lid''i·fy'

so·lid''i·ty
sol''id-state''
sol''i·dus
so·lil''o·quize'
so·lil''o·quiz'ing
so·lil''o·quy
   (*pl.* so·lil''o·quies)
sol''ing
sol''ip·sism'
sol''ip·sis''tic
sol''i·taire'
sol''i·tar'y
sol''i·tude'
so''lo
   (*pl.* so''los)
so''lo·ist
sol''stice
sol'u·bil''i·ty
sol''u·ble
so·lu''tion
solv'a·bil''i·ty
solv''a·ble
solve
sol''ven·cy
sol''vent
solv''ing
so''ma
   (*pl.* so''ma·ta)
So·ma''ll·a
so·mat''ic
som''ber
som''bre''ro
   (*pl.* som·bre''ros)
some''bod'y
some''day'
some''how
some''one
some''place'
som''er·sault
some''thing
some''times'
some''way
some''what
some''where'
som·nam''bu·late'
som·nam''bu·lat'ing

som·nam''bu·list
som''no·lence
som''no·lent
son
   child (*see:* sun)
so''nar
so·na''ta
son'a·ti''na
sonde
song''bird
song''book'
song''ster
song''stress
song''writ'er
son''ic
son''-in-law''
   (*pl.* sons''-in-law')
son''net
son''ny
   male child (*see:*
   sunny)
son''o·gram
so·nor''i·ty
so·no''rous
soon''er
soot
soothe
sooth''ing·ly
sooth''say'er
soot''i·er
soot''i·ness
soot''y
sop
soph''ism
soph''ist
so·phis''ti·cate'
so·phis''ti·cat'ing
so·phis'ti·ca''tion
soph''ist·ry
   (*pl.* soph''ist·ries)
soph''o·more'
soph'o·mor''ic
sop'o·rif''ic
sop''ping
sop''py
so·pran''o

(*pl.* so·pran''os)
sor''cer·er
sor''cer·ess
sor''cer·y
sor''did
sore
  hurt (*see:* soar)
sore''head'
sore''ly
sor''ghum
so·ror''i·ty
  (*pl.* so·ror''i·ties)
sor''rel
sor''row
sor''row·ful
sor''ri·er
sor''ry
sort''a·ble
sor''tie
so''-so
sot''to vo''ce
sou·brette''
souf·fle''
soul
  spirit (*see:* sole)
soul''ful
soul''ful·ly
soul''less
soul''mate'
soul''-search'ing
sound''box'
sound'' ef·fect'
sound''ing board'
sound''proof'
sound''track'
sound''wave'
soup·con''
soup''spoon'
soup''y
sour''ball'
source
sour''cream'
sour''dough'
sour''puss'
sour''wood'
sou''sa·phone'

souse
South' Af''ri·ca
South' A·mer''i·ca
south''bound'
South'' Car·o·li''na
South'' Da·ko''ta
south''east''
south''east''er·ly
south''east''ern
south''east''ward
south''er·ly
south''ern
south''ern·er
south''ern·most'
south''paw'
South'' Pole'
south''ward
south''west''
south''west''er
south''west''ern
south''west''ward
sou've·nir''
sov''fer·eign
sov''er·eign·ty
  (*pl.* sov''er''eign·
  ties)
So''vi·et' Un''ion
sow
  plant (*see:* so and
  sew)
sow''er
sown
  planted (*see:* sewn)
soy''bean'
soy''sauce'
space''craft'
spaced''-out''
space''flight'
space'' heat''er
space''man'
space''port'
space''ship'
space'' shut''tle
space''sta'tion
space''suit'
space''-time'

space''walk'
spac''ey
spac''ing
spa''cious
spad
spade''work
spad''ing
spa·ghet''ti
Spain
span
span''gle
span''gling
span''iel
Span''ish
spank''ing
span''ning
spar
spare
spared
spare''rib'
spar''ing
  refraining; parting
  with (*see:* sparring)
spar''ing·ly
spar''kle
spar''kler
spar''kling
spark''plug'
spar''ring
  boxing (*see:* sparing)
spar''row
sparse
sparse''ly
spasm
spas·mod''ic
spas·mod''i·cal·ly
spas''tic
spas''ti·cal·ly
spat
spathe
spa''tial
spa''tial·ly
spat''ter
spat''ting
spat''u·la
spav''ined

spawn
spay
spay''ing
speak''-eas'y
  (*pl.* speak''-eas'ies)
speak''er
spear''fish
spear''head
spear''mint
spe''cial
spe''cial·ist
spe''cial·ize'
spe''cial·iz'ing
spe''cial·ly
spe''cial·ty
  (*pl.* spe''cial·ties)
spe''cie
  coins (*see:* species)
spe''cies
  group (*pl.* spe''cies)
  (*see:* spe''cie)
spec''i·fi'a·ble
spe·cif''ic
spe·cif''i·cal·ly
spec'i·fi·ca''tion
spec''i·fied'
spec''i·fy'
spec''i·men
spe''cious
speck''le
speck''ling
spec''ta·cle
spec·tac''u·lar
spec''ta·tor
spec''ter
spec''tral
spec·trom''e·ter
spec'tro·scop''ic
spec'tro·scop''i·cal
spec·tros''co·py
spec''trum
  (*pl.* spec''tra)
spec''u·late'
spec''u·lat'ing
spec'u·la''tion
spec''u·la''tive

spec''u·la'tor
sped
speech''less
speech''mak'er
speech''mak'ing
speed''ball'
speed''boat'
speed''bump'
speed''i·er
speed''i·ness
speed·om''e·ter
speed''-read'ing
speed''trap'
speed''up'
speed''way'
speed''y
spe'le·ol''o·gy
spell''bind'
spell''bind'ing
spell''bound'
spell''er
spe·lun''ker
spend''a·ble
spend''thrift'
spent
sperm
sper'ma·ce''ti
sperm'' whale
spew
sphag''num
sphere
spher''i·cal
sphe''roid
sphinc''ter
sphinx
spice
spic''i·er
spic''i·ness
spic''ing
spick''-and-span''
spic''y
spi''der web
spied
spiel
spiff''y
spig''ot

spike
spike''nard
spik''ing
spill''o'ver
spill''way
spilt
spin''ach
spi''nal
spin''dle
spin''dli·er
spin''dling
spin''dly
spin''drift
spine''less
spin''et
spin''na·ker
spin''ner
spin''ning wheel
spin''off'
spin''ster
spin''y
spi''ral
spire
spir''ing
spir''it·less
spir''it·u·al
spir''it·u·al·ist
spir'it·u·al''i·ty
spir''it·u·al·ly
spit''ball
spite
spite''ful
spit''fire
spit''ing
  humiliating (*see:* spitting)
spit''ting
  expectorating; impaling (*see:* spiting)
spit''tle
spit·toon''
spitz
splash''down'
splash''i·er
splash''y
splat

splat"ter
splay"foot
  (*pl.* splay"feet)
spleen"ful
splen"did
splen"dor
sple·net"ic
splice
splic"ing
splint
splin"ter
splin"ter·y
split"-lev"el
split"ting
split"-up
splotch
splotch"y
splurge
splurg"ing
splut"ter
spoil"age
spoil"sport
spoilt
Spo·kane"
spoke
spo"ken
spokes"man
spokes"wom·an
spo'li·a"tion
sponge"cake'
spon"gi·er
spon"gi·ness
spong"ing
spon"gy
spon"sor
spon·ta·ne"i·ty
spon·ta"ne·ous
spoof
spook
spook"i·er
spook"y
spool
spoon"bill'
spoon"er·ism'
spoon"-fed'
spoon"-feed'

spoon"ful'
  (*pl.* spoon"fuls)
spoor
  track (*see:* spore)
spo·rad"ic
spore
  seed (*see:* spoor)
spor"ing
sport"ing
spor"tive
sports" car'
sports"cast'
sport" shirt'
sports" jack'et
sports"man
sports"wear'
sports"wom·an
sports"writ'er
sport"y
spot
spot"-check"
spot"less
spot"light
spot"ti·er
spot"ti·ness
spot"ting
spot"ty
spou"sal
spouse
spout
sprain
sprang
sprawl
spray"can'
spray"gun
spread"-ea'gled
spread"er
spread"ing
spree
sprig
sprig"ging
spright"li·er
spright"li·ness
spright"ly
spring"board
spring"-clean"ing

spring" fe"ver
Spring"field
spring"head
spring"house
spring"i·er
spring"i·ness
spring"time'
spring"y
sprin"kler
sprin"kling
sprint"er
sprite
sprock"et
sprout
spruce
spruc"ing
sprung
spry
spry"er
spry"est
spud
spume
spum"ing
spu·mo"ni
spun
spunk"i·er
spunk"i·ly
spunk"y
spur
spu"ri·ous
spurn
spur"ring
spurt
sput"nik
sput"ter
spu"tum
  (*pl.* spu"ta)
spy
  (*pl.* spies)
spy"glass
squab"ble
squab"bling
squad"ron
squal"id
squall
squal"or

squan"der
square"-dance', v.
  to dance
square" dance', n.
  dance
square"-danc'ing
square"deal"
square"-rigged"
square" root"
square" shoot"er
square"-shoul'dered
squar"ing
squash
squash"y
squat
squat"ter
squat"ting
squaw
squawk" box'
squeak
squeak"i·er
squeak"y
squeak"y-clean"
squeal"er
squeam"ish
squee"gee
squeeze
squeez"ing
squelch
squib
squib"bing
squid
squig"gle
squig"gling
squint"-eyed
squire
squir"ing
squirm
squirm"i·er
squirm"y
squir"rel
squirt
squish"i·er
squish"y
Sri Lan"ka
stab

stab"bing
sta·bil"i·ty
sta·bi·li·za"tion
sta·bi·lize'
sta"bi·liz'ing
sta"ble
sta"bling
stac·ca"to
  (pl. stac·ca"tos)
stack
sta"di·um
  (pl. sta"di·ums or
  stad"i·a)
staff
stag
stage"coach
stage"craft
stage" door"
stage" fright
stage"hand'
stage"-man'age
stage" man'ag·er
stage"-struck
stage" whis"per
stag·fla"tion
stag"ger
stag"i·er
stag"ing
stag"nan·cy
stag"nant
stag"nate'
stag"nat·ing
stag·na"tion
stag"y
staid
stain"a·ble
stain"less
stair
  steps (see: stare)
stair"case'
stair"way'
stair"well'
stake
  post; bet (see: steak)
stake"hold'er
stake"out'

stak"ing
sta·lac"tite
sta·lag"mite
stale"mate'
stalk
stalk"ing-horse
stall
stal"lion
stal"wart
sta"men
stam"i·na
stam"mer
stamp
stam·pede"
stam·ped"ing
stance
stanch
  stop (see: staunch)
stan"chion
stand
stand"ard-bear'er
stand"ard·i·za"tion
stand"ard·ize'
stand"ard·iz'ing
stand"by
  (pl. stand"bys)
stand·ee"
stand"-in
stand"ing
stand"off'
stand"off'ish
stand"out
stand"point'
stand"still'
stand"-up'
stank
stan"za
sta"pes
staph'y·lo·coc"cus
sta"ple
sta"pler
sta"pling
star"board
starch
starch"y
star"-crossed

star″dom
star″dust
stare
  gaze (*see:* stair)
star″fish
star″gaze
star″gaz′er
star″gaz′ing
star″ing
stark″-nak″ed
star″let
star″light
star″ling
star″ri·er
star″ring
star″ route″
star″ry
star″ry-eyed
star-span′gled
star″-stud″ded
start″er
star″tle
star″tling
start″-up
star·va″tion
starve
starv″ing
stash
sta″sis
state″craft
state″hood
state″house
state″li·er
state″li·ness
state″ly
state″ment
state″room′
states″man
state″wide
stat″ic
stat″ing
sta″tion·ar′y
  not moving (*see:* sta-
  tionery)
sta″tion·er
sta″tion·er′y

  paper (*see:* station-
  ary)
sta″tion house′
sta″tion·mas′ter
sta″tion-to-sta″tion
sta″tion wag′on
sta·tis″tic
sta·tis″ti·cal
sta·tis″ti·cal·ly
stat′is·ti″cian
sta·tis″tics
stat″u·ar′y
  (*pl.* stat″u·ar′ies)
stat″ue
stat′u·esque″
stat′u·ette″
stat″ure
sta″tus quo″
stat″ute
stat″u·to′ry
staunch
  stalwart (*see:* stanch)
stave
stav″ing
stay″-at-home
stay put″
stead″fast
stead″i·er
stead″i·ly
stead″i·ness
stead″y
steak
  meat (*see:* stake)
steak″ house
steak″ knife
steal
  rob; move silently
  (*see:* steel)
stealth
stealth″i·er
stealth″i·ly
stealth″y
steam″boat′
steam″i·er
steam″i·ness
steam″roll′er

steam″ship
steam″ shov′el
steam″y
steed
steel
  metal (*see:* steal)
steel″mill′
steel″ wool″
steel″work′er
steel″y
steel″yard
steep
steep″en
stee″ple·chase
stee″ple·jack′
steer″age
steers″man
steg″o·saur′
stein
stel″lar
stem″ming
stem″ware
stench
sten″cil
sten″cil·ing
ste·nog″ra·pher
sten′o·graph″ic
ste·nog″ra·phy
sten″o·type
sten″o·typ′ist,
sten″o·ty′py
sten·to″ri·an
step
  walk (*see:* steppe)
step″broth′er
step″child
  (*pl.* step″chil′dren)
step″daugh′ter
step″-down
step″fa′ther
step″lad′der
step″moth′er
step″par′ent
steppe
  plain (*see:* step)
stepped″-up′

step″ping·stone
step″sis′ter
step″son′
ster′e·o
  (*pl.* ster′e·os′)
ster′e·o·phon″ic
ster′e·o·scop″ic
ster′e·os″co·py
ster′e·o·type′
ster′e·o·typ″i·cal
ster′e·o·typ′ing
ster″ile
ste·ril″i·ty
ster′i·li·za″tion
ster′i·lize′
ster′i·liz′ing
ster″ling
stern″ness
ster″num
stern″wheel′er
ster″oid
stet
steth″o·scope
steth′o·scop″ic
Stet″son™
stet″ting
ste″ve·dore
stew
stew″ard
stew″ard·ess
stick″ball
stick″er
stick″i·er
stick″i·ness
stick″-in-the-mud′
stick″ler
stick″pin′
stick″′
shift′
stick′-to-″it·ive·ness
stick″up′
stick″y
stiff″en
stiff″-necked′
sti″fle
sti″fling

stig″ma
stig·mat″ic
stig″ma·tism′
stig″ma·tize′
stig″ma·tiz′ing
stile
  steps (*see:* style)
sti·let″to
  (*pl.* sti·let″tos)
still″birth′
still″born′
still″ life″
stilt
stilt″ed
stil″ton
stim″u·lant
stim″u·late′
stim″u·lat′ing
stim″u·la″tion
stim″u·la′tive
stim″u·la′tor
stim″u·lus
  (*pl.* stim″u·li)
sting
stin″gi·er
stin″gi·ness
sting″ray′
stin″gy
stink″weed′
stint
sti″pend
stip″ple
stip″pling
stip″u·late
stip″u·lat′ing
stip′u·la″tion
stir″-cra′zy
stir″-fried″
stir″-fry″
stir″ring
stir″rup
stitch
St. Lou″is
stoat
stock
stock·ade″

stock″ bro′ker
stock″ car
stock″hold′er
Stock″holm
stock″i·er
stock″ing
stock″man
stock″ mar′ket
stock″pile
stock″pil′ing
stock″room
stock′-still″
stock″y
stock″yard
stodg″i·er
stodg″i·ness
stodg″y
sto″gie
sto″i·cal
sto″i·cal·ly
stoke
stoke″hole
stok″er
stok″ing
stole
sto″len
stol″id
stom″ach·ache′
stomp
Stone″ Age
stone″-broke″
stone″cut′ter
stone″-deaf″
stone″mason
stone″wall′ing
stone″ware′
stone″work′
ston″i·er
ston″i·ly
ston″ing
ston″y
stood
stooge
stool
stoop

bend; porch (*see:*
stoup)
stop"gap'
stop"light'
stop"-off'
stop"o'ver
stop"page
stop"per
stop"ping
stop"watch'
stor"a·ble
stor"age
store"front'
store"house'
store"keep'er
store"room'
store"wide'
sto"ried
stor"ing
stork
storm"bound'
storm"door'
storm"i·er
storm"i·ness
storm"proof'
storm" win'dow
storm"y
sto"ry
  (*pl.* sto"ries)
sto"ry·book'
sto"ry line"
sto"ry·tell'er
stoup
  basin (*see:* stoop)
stout"heart"ed
stove"pipe'
stow"age
stow"a·way'
St.' Paul"
  city
stra·bis"mus
strad"dle
strad"dling
strafe
straf"ing
strag"gle

strag"gli·er
strag"gling
strag"gly
straight
  direct (*see:* strait)
straight"-a·head"
straight"an'gle
straight"-arm'
straight"a·way'
straight"edge
straight"en
  make straight (*see:*
  straiten)
straight"for'ward
straight"shoot"er
strain
strain"er
strait
  waterway; difficul-
  ties (*see:* straight)
strait"en
  cause distress (*see:*
  straighten)
strait"jack'et
strait"-laced"
strand
strange
strang"er
stran"gle
stran"gle·hold'
stran"gling
stran"gu·late'
stran"gu·lat'ing
stran·gu·la"tion
strap
strap"less
strap"ping
strat"a·gem
stra·te"gic
stra·te"gi·cal·ly
strat"e·gist
strat"e·gy
  (*pl.* strat"e·gies)
strat'i·fi·ca"tion
strat"i·fied'
strat"i·fy'

strat"o·sphere
strat'o·spher"ic
stra"tum
  (*pl.* stra"ta)
stra"tus
  (*pl.* stra"ti)
straw"ber'ry
  (*pl.* straw"ber'ries)
straw"hat
stray
streak
streak"i·er
streak"i·ness
streak"y
stream"er
stream"line'
stream"lined'
stream"lin'ing
street"car'
street"light
street" peo'ple
street" smarts"
street"walk'er
street"wise
strength
strength"en
stren"u·ous
strep'to·coc"cus
  (*pl.* strep'to·coc"ci)
strep'to·my"cin
stress
stretch
stretch"a·ble
stretch"er
stretch"er-bear'er
stretch"y
strew
strewn
stri"ate
stri·a"tion
strick"en
strict
stric"ture
strid"den
stride
stri"dence

stri"dent
strid"ing
strife
strike"bound
strike"break'er
strike"out'
strike"o'ver
strike"zone
strik"ing
string
strin"gen·cy
  (pl. strin"gen·cies)
strin"gent
string"er
string"y
strip
stripe
strip"ing
  marking (see: strip-
  ping)
strip"ling
strip" mine'
strip"per
strip"ping
  removing (see:
  striping)
strip"-search
strip"tease
striv·ing
striv"ing
strobe
strode
stro"gan·off'
stroke
strok"ing
stroll
stroll"er
strong"arm'
strong"box'
strong"hold'
strong"man'
strong"room'
strong"-willed"
stron"ti·um
strop
strop"ping

strove
struck
struc"tur·al
struc"ture
struc"tur·ing
stru"del
strug"gle
strug"gling
strum
strum"ming
strum"pet
strung
strut
strut"ting
strych"nine
stub
stub"bi·er
stub"bing
stub"ble
stub"born
stub"by
stuc"co
stuck"-up'
stud"book
stud"ding
stu"dent
stud"horse
stud"ied
stu"di·o
  (pl. stu"di·os)
stu"di·ous
stud"y
  (pl. stud"ies)
stud"y hall'
stuff
stuffed" shirt"
stuff"i·er
stuff"i·ly
stuff"i·ness
stuff"ing
stuff"y
stul"ti·fi·ca"tion
stul"ti·fied
stul"ti·fy
stum"ble
stum"bling

stump"i·er
stump"y
stun
stung
stunk
stun"ning
stunt
stu'pe·fac"tion
stu"pe·fied
stu"pe·fy
stu·pen"dous
stu"pid
stu·pid"i·ty
  (pl. stu·pid"i·ties)
stu"por
stur"di·er
stur"di·ness
stur"dy
stur"geon
stut"ter
sty
  (pl. sties)
style
  manner (see: stile)
style"book
styl"ing
styl"ish
styl"ist
sty·lis"tic
styl'i·za"tion
styl"ize
styl"iz·ing
sty"lus
sty"mie
sty"mied
sty"mie·ing
styp"tic
sty"rene
Sty"ro·foam'™
su"a·ble
sua"sive
suave
suave"ly
suav"i·ty
sub·al"tern
sub'as·sem"bly

sub'a·tom''ic
sub''base'ment
sub''bing
sub''cel'lar
sub''class
sub''com·mit''tee
sub''com''pact
sub''con''scious
sub·con''ti·nent
sub·con·tract'' v.
  make contract
sub·con''tract, n.
  secondary contract
sub·con''trac·tor
sub''cul'ture
sub''cu·ta''ne·ous
sub·di·vide''
sub·di·vid''ing
sub''di·vi''sion
sub·due''
sub·du''ing
sub''floor
sub''freez''ing
sub''group
sub''gum''
sub''head
sub·hu''man
sub·ject'', v.
  bring under control
sub''ject, n., adj.
  thing thought
sub·jec''tion
sub·jec''tive
sub·jec·tiv''i·ty
sub·join''
sub''ju''di·ce
sub''ju·gate''
sub''ju·gat''ing
sub''ju·ga''tion
sub·junc''tive
sub·lease'', v.
  rent
sub''lease, n.
  a lease
sub·leas''ing
sub·let''

sub·let''ting
sub''li·mate'
sub''li·mat''ing
sub''li·ma''tion
sub·lime''
sub·lim''i·nal
sub·lim''i·nal·ly
sub·lim''i·ty
sub''ma·chine'' gun'
sub''ma·rine'', adj., v.
  under water
sub''ma·rine', n.
  ship; sandwich
sub·merge''
sub·mer''gence
sub·mer''gi·ble
sub·merg''ing
sub·mers''i·ble
sub·mer''sion
sub·mis''sion
sub·mis''sive
sub·mit''
sub·mit''ting
sub·nor''mal
sub''nor·mal''i·ty
sub·or''bit·al
sub·or''di·nate'
sub·or''di·nat''ing
sub·or''di·na''tion
sub·orn''
sub''or·na''tion
sub''plot
sub·poe''na
sub·poe''naed
sub·poe''na·ing
sub ro''sa
sub·scribe''
sub·scrib''ing
sub''script
sub·scrip''tion
sub''se·quent
sub·ser''vi·ence
sub·ser''vi·ent
sub''set
sub·side''
sub·sid''ence

sub·sid''i·ar'y
  (pl. sub·sid''i·ar'
  ies)
sub·sid''ing
sub''si·di·za''tion
sub''si·dize'
sub''si·diz''ing
sub''si·dy
  (pl. sub''si·dies)
sub·sist''ence
sub''soil
sub''spe'cies
sub''stance
sub·stand''ard
sub·stan''tial
sub·stan''tial·ly
sub·stan''ti·ate'
sub·stan''ti·at''ing
sub·stan''ti·a''tion
sub''stan·tive
sub''sta'tion
sub''sti·tut'a·ble
sub''sti·tute'
sub''sti·tut''ing
sub''sti·tu''tion
sub''stra'tum
  (pl. sub''stra·ta)
sub''struc'ture
sub·sume''
sub·sum''ing
sub''ter·fuge'
sub''ter·ra''ne·an
sub''ti'tle
sub''ti'tling
sub''tle
sub''tle·ty
  (pl. sub''tle·ties)
sub''tly
sub·to''tal
sub''tract''
sub·trac''tion
sub·tra·hend''
sub·trop''i·cal
sub''urb
sub·ur''ban
sub·ur''ban·ite'

sub·ur″bi·a
sub·ver″sion
sub·ver″sive
sub·vert″
sub″way
sub·ze″ro
suc·ceed″
suc·cess″
suc·cess″ful
suc·cess″ful·ly
suc·ces″sion
suc·ces″sive
suc·ces″sor
suc·cinct″
suc″cor
  help (*see:* sucker)
suc″co·tash
suc″cu·lence
suc″cu·lent
suc·cumb″
suck″er
  one that sucks; fish;
   candy (*see:* succor)
suck″le
suck″ling
su″crose
suc″tion
Su·dan″
sud″den
su·do·rif″ic
suds″i·er
suds″y
sue
suede
su″er
  one who sues (*see:*
   sewer)
su″et
Su·ez″
suf″fer
suf″fer·a·ble
suf″fer·ance
suf·fice″
suf·fi″cien·cy
  (*pl.* suf·fi″cien·cies)
suf·fi″cient

suf·fic″ing
suf·fix″
suf″fo·cate′
suf″fo·cat′ing
suf″fo·ca″tion
suf″frage
suf″fra·gette″
suf″fra·gist
suf·fuse″
suf·fus″ing
suf·fu″sion
su″gar beet′
sug″ar cane′
sug″ar-coat′
sug″ar·plum′
sug″ar·y
sug·gest″
sug·gest″i·ble
sug·ges″tion
sug·ges″tive
su·i·cid″al
su″i·cide
su″i ge″ne·ris
su″i′ju″ris
su″ing
suit
  clothes; lawsuit;
   cards; satisfy (*see:*
   suite)
suit′a·bil″i·ty
suit″a·ble
suit″case
suite
  rooms; music (*see:*
   suit *or* sweet)
suit″ing
suit″or
su′ki·ya″ki
suk″koth
sul″fa
sul″fate
sul″fide
sul″fite
sul″fur
sul·fu″ric
sul″fur·ous

sulk
sulk″i·er
sulk″i·ness
sulk″y
sul″len
sul″lied
sul″ly
sul″tan
sul·tan″a
sul″tri·er
sul″tri·ness
sul″try
sum
su″mac
sum″ma cum lau″de
sum·mar″i·ly
sum′ma·ri·za″tion
sum″ma·rize′
sum″ma·riz′ing
sum″ma·ry
  general idea (*pl.*
   sum″ma·ries)
sum·ma″tion
sum″mer·house′
sum″mer school′
sum″mer·time′
sum″mer·y
  of summer (*see:*
   summary)
sum″ming
sum″mit
sum″mons
sump″tu·ous
sun
  star (*see:* son)
sun″baked
sun″bath′
sun″bathe′
sun″bath′er
sun″bath′ing
sun″beam′
sun″belt′
sun″burn′
sun″burst′
sun″dae

ice cream (*see:* Sunday)
Sun''day
  day of week (*see:* sundae)
Sun''day school'
sun''deck'
sun''der
sun''di'al
sun''down'
sun''dries
sun''dry
sun''fish'
sun''flow'er
sung
sun''glass'es
sunk
sunk''en
sun''lamp'
sun''light'
sun''lit'
Sun''ni
sun''ni·er
sun''ning
sun''ny
  bright (*see:* sonny)
sun''porch'
sun''rise'
sun''roof'
sun''screen'
sun''set'
sun''shade'
sun''shine'
sun''spot'
sun''stroke'
sun''suit'
sun''tan'
sun''tanned'
sun''up'
sup
su''per
su'per·a·bun''dant
su'per·an''nu·ate'
su·perb''
su'per·car''go

(*pl.* su''per·car'' goes)
su''per·charg'er
su''per·chip
su'per·cil''i·ous
su'per·con'duc·tiv''i·ty
su'per·con·duc''tor
su'per·e''go
su'per·fi''cial
su'per·fi·ci·al''i·ty
  (*pl.* su'per·fi''ci·al'' i·ties)
su'per·fi''cial·ly
su'per·flu''i·ty
  (*pl.* su'per·flu''i· ties)
su·per''flu·ous
su'per·high''way
su'per·hu''man
su'per·im·pose''
su'per·im·pos''ing
su'per·in·tend''
su'per·in·tend''ence
su'per·in·tend''ent
su·pe''ri·or
su·pe'ri·or''i·ty
su·per''la·tive
su''per·man'
su'per·mar'ket
su'per·nat''u·ral
su'per·no''va
  (*pl.* su'per·no''vae)
su'per·nu''mer·ar'y
  (*pl.* su'per·nu''mer· ar'ies)
su'per·pow'er
su''per·scribe'
su''per·scrib'ing
su''per·script'
su'per·scrip''tion
su'per·sede''
su'per·sed''ing
su'per·sen''si·tive
su'per·son''ic
su'per·sti''tion

su'per·sti''tious
su''per·struc'ture
su'per·tank'er
su'per·vene''
su'per·ven''ing
su'per·ven''tion
su''per·vise'
su''per·vis'ing
su'per·vi''sion
su''per·vi'sor
su'per·vi''so·ry
su·pine'', *adj.*
  lying down
su''pine, *n.*
  grammatical term
sup'per·time'
sup''ping
sup·plant''
sup''ple
sup''ple·ment
sup'ple·men''tal
sup'ple·men''ta·ry
sup''pli·ant
sup''pli·cant
sup''pli·cate'
sup''pli·cat'ing
sup'pli·ca''tion
sup·plied''
sup·pli''er
sup·ply''
  (*pl.* sup·plies')
sup·port''
sup·port''er
sup·port''ive
sup·pose''
sup·posed''
sup·pos''ed·ly
sup·pos''ing
sup'po·si''tion
sup·pos''i·to'ry
  (*pl.* sup·pos''i·to' ries)
sup·press''
sup·pres''sant
sup·press''i·ble
sup·pres''sion

sup·pres"sor
sup"pu·rate'
sup"pu·rat"ing
sup"pu·ra"tion
su'pra·na"tion·al
su·prem"a·cist
su·prem"a·cy
su·preme"
sur·cease"
sur·ceas"ing
sur·charge", *v.*
  overcharge
sur"charge', *n.*
  additional charge
sur"cin'gle
sure"-fire'
sure"-foot"ed
sure"ly
sur"er
sure"ty
  (*pl.* sure"ties)
surf
  waves (*see:* serf)
sur"face
sur"fac·ing
surf"board'
surf"cast'ing
sur"feit
surf"er
surf"ing
surge
  move suddenly (*see:* serge)
sur"geon
sur"ger·y
  (*pl.* sur"ger·ies)
sur"gi·cal
sur"gi·cal·ly
surg"ing
sur"li·est
sur"li·ness
sur"ly
sur·mise"
sur·mis"ing
sur·mount
sur"name'

sur·pass"
sur"plice
  robe (*see:* surplus)
sur"plus
  excess (*see:* surplice)
sur·prise"
sur·pris"ing
sur·re"al·ism
sur·re"al·is"tic
sur·ren"der
sur·rep·ti"tious
sur"rey
  (*pl.* sur"reys)
sur"ro·ga·cy
sur"ro·gate
sur"ro·gat"ing
sur·round"
sur"tax
sur"veil"lance'
sur·vey", *v.*
  measure
sur"vey, *n., adj.*
  general summary
  (*pl.* sur"veys)
sur·vey"or
sur·viv"al
sur·vive"
sur·viv"ing
sur·vi"vor
sus·cep'ti·bil"i·ty
  (*pl.* sus·cep'ti·bil"i·ties)
sus·cep"ti·ble
su"shi
sus·pect", *v.*
  guess; untrusting
sus"pect, *n.*
  suspected person
sus·pend"
sus·pend"ers
sus·pense"
sus·pen"sion
sus·pi"cion
sus·pi"cious
sus·tain"
sus·tain"a·ble

sus"te·nance
su"ture
su"tur·ing
su"ze·rain·ty
svelte
swab
swab"bing
swad"dle
swad"dling
swag
swag"ger
swag"ging
swal"low-tailed'
swam
swa"mi
  (*pl.* swam"is)
swamp"i·er
swamp"land'
swamp"y
swan"dive'
swank
swank"y
swan"'s-down'
swan"song'
swap
swap"ping
sword
  turf (*see:* sword)
swarm
swarth"i·er
swarth"y
swash"buck'ler
swas"ti·ka
swat
swatch
swath
  own area (*see:* swathe)
swathe
  wrap (*see:* swat)
swath"ing
swat"ter
swat"ting
sway"backed'
Swa"zi·land'
swear

sweat''band'
sweat''er
sweat''i·er
sweat''i·ness
sweat'' shirt'
sweat''shop'
sweat''y
Swe''den
sweep
sweep''er
sweep''stakes'
sweet
   sugary (*see:* suite)
sweet''-and-sour''
sweet''bread
sweet''corn''
sweet''heart'
sweet''meat'
sweet''pea
sweet''po·ta''to
sweet''-talk
sweet''tooth''
swell
swel''ter
swept''back
swerve
swerv''ing
swift
swig
swig''ging
swill
swim''mer
swim''ming pool'
swim''suit
swin''dle
swin''dler
swin''dling
swine
   (*pl.* swine)
swine''herd
swing
swin''ish
swipe
swip''ing
swirl
swish

Swiss''cheese
Swiss''steak
switch''back'
switch''blade'
switch''board
switch'-hit''ter
switch''man
Swit''zer·land
swiv''el chair
swiv''el·ing
swiz''zle stick'
swol''len
swoon
swoop
sword
   weapon (*see:* sward)
sword''fish
sword''play
swords''man
swore
sworn
swum
swung
syb''a·rite'
syc''a·more'
syc''o·phant
Syd''ney
syl·lab''ic
syl·lab''i·cate'
syl·lab''i·ca''tion
syl·lab''i·fi·ca''tion
syl·lab''i·fied'
syl·lab''i·fy
syl''la·ble
syl''la·bling
syl''la·bus
syl''lo·gism'
sylph
syl''van
sym'bi·o''sis
sym'bi·ot''ic
sym''bol
   representation (*see:* cymbal)
sym·bol''ic
sym·bol''i·cal·ly

sym''bol·ism
sym''bol·ize'
sym''bol·iz'ing
sym·met''ric
sym·met''ri·cal
sym''me·try
   (*pl.* sym''me·tries)
sym'pa·thet''ic
sym'pa·thize'
sym'pa·thiz'ing
sym'pa·thy
   (*pl.* sym''pa·thies)
sym·phon''ic
sym''pho·ny
   (*pl.* sym''pho·nies)
sym·po''si·um
symp''tom
symp'to·mat''ic
syn''a·gogue
syn''apse
sync
syn''chro·mesh
syn''chro·nism'
syn''chro·ni·za''tion
syn''chro·nize'
syn''chro·niz'ing
syn''chro·nous
syn''chro·tron'
syn''cline
syn''co·pate'
syn''co·pat'ing
syn''co·pa''tion
syn''co·pe
syn''cre·tism
syn''cre·tize
syn''cre·tiz'ing
syn''dic
syn''di·cal·ism'
syn''di·cate'
syn''di·cat'ing
syn''di·ca''tion
syn''drome
syn·ec''do·che
syn·e·col''o·gy
syn·er·get''ic
syn''er·gism'

syn′er·gis″tic
syn′er·gy
  (*pl*. syn″er·gies)
syn″fuel
syn″od
syn″o·nym
syn·on″y·mous
syn·op″sis
  (*pl*. syn·op″ses)
syn·op″size
syn·op″siz·ing
syn·op″tic
syn·tac″tic
syn·tac″ti·cal·ly
syn″tax
syn″the·sis
  (*pl*. syn″the·ses)
syn″the·size′
syn″the·siz′ing
syn·thet″ic
syn·thet″i·cal
syn·thet″i·cal·ly
syph″i·lis
syphi·lit″ic
sy″phon
Syr′a·cuse′
Syr″i·a
sy·ringe″
sy·ring″ing
syr″up
sys′tem·at″ic
sys′tem·at″i·cal·ly
sys″tem·a·tize
sys″tem·a·tiz′ing
sys·tem″ic
sys″tem·ize′
sys″tem·iz′ing
sys·tol″ic

T

tab
Ta·bas″co™
tab″bing
tab″by

(*pl*. tab″bies)
tab″er·nac′le
tab″leau
  (*pl*. tab″leaux)
ta″ble·cloth′
ta″ble-hop′
ta″ble-hop′ping
ta″ble·land′
ta″ble saw″
ta″ble·spoon′
ta″ble·spoon′ful′
tab″let
ta″ble·top′
ta″ble·ware′
ta″bling
tab″loid
ta·boo″
  (*pl*. ta·boos″)
ta·booed″
ta·boo″ing
ta″bor
tab·o·ret″
tab″u·lar
tab″u·late′
tab″u·lat′ing
tab″u·la″tion
tab″u·la′tor
ta″cet
  musical direction
  (*see:* tacit)
ta·chom″e·ter
tach′y·car″di·a
tac″it
  understood (*see:* ta-
  cet)
tac″i·turn′
tac′i·tur″ni·ty
tack
tack″i·er
tack″i·ness
tack″le
tack″ling
tack″y
ta″co
  (*pl*. ta″cos)
tac″o·nite′

tact
tact″ful·ly
tac″tic
tac″ti·cal
tac·ti″cian
tac″tics
tac′tile
tact″less
tad″pole′
taf″fe·ta
taff″rail′
taf″fy
tag″board′
tag″end″
tag″sale′
tag″ging
Ta·hi″ti
tai″ga
tail
  hindmost part (*see:*
  tale)
tail″back′
tail″coat′
tail″end′
tail″gate′
tail″gat′ing
tail″light′
tail″like′
tai″lored
tail″lor-made″
tail″piece′
tail″pipe′
tail″spin′
tail″wind′
taint
Tai″pei″
Tai″wan″
take″off′
tah″er
take″out
take″o′ver
take″up
tak″ing
talc
tal″cum
tale

narrative (*see:* tail)
tale″bear′er
tal″ent
tales″man
  juror (*pl.* tales″
  men) (*see:* talis-
  man)
tale″tell′er
tal″is·man
  charm (*pl.* tal″is·
  mans) (*see:*
  tailsman)
talk″a·tive
talk″er
talk″ing-to′
  (*pl.* talk″ing-tos′)
talk″ show′
Tal″la·has″see
tal″lied
tal″low
tal″ly
  (*pl.* tal″lies)
tal′ly·ho″
Tal″mud
tal″on
tam″a·ble
ta·ma″le
tam″a·rack′
tam″a·rind
tam″bour
tam′bou·rine″
tame
tam″ing
tam″-o′-shan″ter
tamp
Tam″pa
tam″per
tam″pon
tan
tan″a·ger
tan″bark′
tan″dem
tang
tan″ge·lo′
  (*pl.* tan″ge·los′)
tan″gent

tan·gen″tial
tan′ge·rine″
tan′gi·bil″i·ty
tan″gi·ble
tang″i·er
tan″gle
tan″gling
tan″go
  (*pl.* tan″gos)
tang″y
tank
tank″age
tank″ard
tank″er
tank″ful′
  (*pl.* tank″fuls′)
tank″ top′
tan″ner
tan″ner·y
  (*pl.* tan″ner·ies)
tan″nic
tan″nin
tan″ning
tan″ta·lize′
tan″ta·liz′ing
tan″ta·mount′
tan″trun
Tan″za·ni″a
Tao
Tao″ism
tap″-dance′, *v.*
  to dance
tap″ dance′, *n.*
  a dance
tap″-danc′ing
tape″ deck′
tape″ meas′ure
ta″per
  decrease; candle
  (*see:* tapir)
tape″-re·cord′
tape″ re·cord′er
tap″es·try
  (*pl.* tap″es·tries)
tape″worm′
tap″ing

recording; binding
  (*see:* tapping)
tap′i·o″ca
ta″pir
  animal (*pl.* ta″pirs)
  (*see:* taper)
tap″per
tap″pet
tap″ping
  striking (*see:* taping)
tap″room′
tap″root′
tar
tar′an·tel″la
ta·ran″tu·la
tar″di·er
tar″di·ly
tar″di·ness
tar″dy
tare
  weight; weed (*see:*
  tear)
tar″get
tar″iff
tar″la·tan
Tar″mac™
tar″nish
tar″nish·a·ble
ta″ro
  plant (*see:* tarot)
ta″rot
  cards (*see:* taro)
tar·pau″lin
tar″pon
tar″ra·gon′
tar″ried
tar″ring
tar″ry
tar″ry·ing
tar″sal
tar″ sand″
tar″sus
  (*pl.* tar″si)
tar″tan
tar·tar″ic
tar″tar sauce′

tart"ness
task" force'
task"mas'ter
Tas·ma"ni·a
tas"sel
tas"sel·ing
taste
taste"ful
taste"ful·ly
taste"less
tast"er
tast"i·er
tast"i·ness
tast"ing
tast"y
tat
tat'ter·de·mal"ion
tat"tered
tat"ter·sail'
tat"ting
tat"tle
tat"tle·tale'
tat"tling
tat·too
  (*pl* tat·toos)
taught
  instructed (*see:* taut)
taunt
taupe
taut
  tight (*see:* taught)
tau'to·log"i·cal·ly
tau·tol"o·gy
  (*pl.* tau·tol"o·gies)
tav"ern
taw
taw"dri·ly
taw"dri·ness
taw"dry
taw"ny
tax a·bil"i·ty
tax"a·ble
tax·a"tion
tax"-de·duct'i·ble
tax"-ex·empt'
tax"i

  (*pl.* tax"is)
tax"i·cab'
tax"i·der'mist
tax"i·der'my
tax"ied
tax"i·ing
tax"i·me'ter
tax'o·nom"ic
tax'o·nom"i·cal
tax·on"o·mist
tax·on"o·my
tax"pay'er
T" bill'
T"-bone'
tea
  drink (*see:* tee)
tea" bag'
tea" ball'
tea"cart'
teach
teach"a·ble
teach"er
tea"cup'
tea"house'
teak
tea"ket'tle
teak"wood'
teal
team
  group (*see:* teem)
team"mate'
team"ster
team"work'
tea"pot'
tear
  pull apart; from cry-
  ing (*see:* tier and
  tare)
tear"drop'
tear"ful'
tear"ful·ly
tear" gas'
tear"-jerk'er
tea"room'
tear"stained'
tease

tea"sel
teas"er
teas"ing
tea"spoon'
tea"spoon·ful'
  (*pl.* tea"spoon·
  fuls')
teat
tea"time'
tea" tray'
tech"ie
tech"nic
tech"ni·cal
tech·ni·cal"i·ty
  (*pl.* tech·ni·cal"i·
  ties)
tech"ni·cal·ly
tech·ni"cian
Tech"ni·col'or™
tech·nique"
tech·noc"ra·cy
  (*pl.* tech·noc"ra·
  cies)
tech"no·crat'
tech'no·log"i·cal·ly
tech·nol"o·gist
tech·nol"o·gy
tec·ton"ics
ted"dy bear'
Te De"um
te"di·ous
te"di·um
tee
  golf stand (*see:* tea)
teed
tee"ing
teem
  swarm (*see:* team)
teen"age'
teen"ag'er
tee"ni·er
tee"ny·bop'per
tee"pee
tee"ter
teethe
teeth"ing

tee″to″tal·er
Tef″lon™
Teh·ran″
tek″tite
Tel″ A·viv″
tel″e·cast′
tel″e·cast′er
tel′e·com·mu″ni·ca″
  tion
tel″e·com·mut″ing
tel″e·com·put″ing
tel″e·con″fer·ence
tel″e·con″fer·enc·ing
tel″e·course′
tel″e·gram′
tel″e·graph′
te·leg″ra·pher
tel′e·graph″ic
te·leg″ra·phy
tel′e·ki·ne″sis
tel″e·mark′
tel′e·mar″ket·ing
tel′e·mat″ics
te·lem″e·try
tel′e·o·log″i·cal
tel′e·ol″o·gy
tel′e·path″ic
te·lep″a·thy
tel″e·phone′
tel′e·phon″ic
tel′e·phon″ing
tel″e·pho′to
tel′e·pho·tog″ra·phy
tel″e·print′er
Tel″e·prompt′er™
tel′e·ran′
tel″e·scope′
tel′e·scop″ic
tel′e·scop″ing
tel″e·thon′
Tel″e·type′™
tel′e·type″writ′er
tel′e·van″gel·ist
tel″e·view′er
tel″e·vise′
tel′e·vis′ing

tel″e·vi′sion
tel″e·work′
tel″ex™
tell″er
tell″tale′
tem″blor
te·mer″i·ty
tem″per
tem″per·a
  paint (*see:* tempura)
tem″per·a·ment
tem″per·a·men″tal
tem″per·ance
tem″per·ate
tem″per·a·ture
tem″pest
tem·pes″tu·ous
tem″plate
tem″ple
tem″po
  (*pl.* tem″pos)
tem″po·ral
tem″po·rar″i·ly
tem″po·rar′y
tem″po·rize′
tem″po·riz′ing
tempt
temp·ta″tion
tempt″er
tempt″ing
tempt″ress
tem″pu·ra′
  Japanese food (*see:*
  tempera)
ten
ten″a·ble
te·na″cious
te·nac″i·ty
ten″an·cy
  (*pl.* ten″an·cies)
ten″ant
tend
ten″den·cy
  (*pl.* ten″den·cies)
ten·den″tious
ten″der·foot′

ten″der·heart″ed
ten″der·ize′
ten″der·iz′er
ten″der·iz′ing
ten″der·loin′
ten″don
ten″dril
ten″e·ment
ten″et
ten″fold′
Ten′nes·see″
ten″nis ball′
ten″on
ten″or
tense
tense″ness
tens″er
ten″sile
tens″ing
ten″sion
ten″sor
ten″ta·cle
ten″ta·tive
ten″ta·tive·ly
ten″ter·hook′
tenth
ten″u·ous
ten″ure
ten″ured
te″pee
tep″id
te·gui″la
ter·gi″ver·sate′
ter·gi″ver·sat′ing
ter′i·ya″ki
ter″ma·gant
ter″mi·na·ble
ter″mi·nal
ter″mi·nal·ly
ter″mi·nate′
ter″mi·nat′ing
ter″mi·na″tion
ter′mi·nol″o·gy
  (*pl.* ter′mi·nol″o·
  gies)
ter″mi·nus

(*pl.* ter″mi·ni′)
ter″mite
term″ pa″per
tern
  bird (*see:* turn)
ter″na·ry
ter″race
ter″rac·ing
ter″ra cot″ta
ter″ra fir″ma
ter·rain″
Ter′ra·my″cin™
ter″ra·pin
ter·rar″i·um
ter·raz″zo
ter·res″tri·al
ter″ri·ble
ter″ri·er
ter·rif″ic
ter·rif″i·cal·ly
ter″ri·fied′
ter″ri·fy′
ter·ri·to″ri·al
ter″ri·to′ry
  (*pl.* ter″ri·to′ries)
ter″ror·ism′
ter″ror·ist
ter·ror·i·za″tion
ter″ror·ize′
ter″ror·iz′ing
ter″ror-strick′en
ter″ry
terse
terse″ly
terse″ness
ters″er
ter″ti·ar′y
tes″sel·late′
tes′sel·la″tion
tes″ser·a
  (*see:* tes″ser·ae)
tes″ta·ment
tes′ta·men″ta·ry
tes″tate
tes′ta·tor
tes·ta″trix

(*pl.* tes·ta″tri·ces)
test″case′
tes″ti·cle
tes″ti·er
tes″ti·fied′
tes″ti·fy′
tes″ti·mo″ni·al
tes″ti·mo′ny
  (*pl.* tes″ti·mo′nics)
tes″ti·ness
tes″tis
  (*pl.* tes″tes)
tes·tos″ter·one′
test″ tube′
tes″ty
tet″a·nus
tete″-a-tete″
teth″er·ball
tet″ra
tet′ra·cy″cline
tet′ra·he″dral
tet′ra·he″dron
te·tram″e·ter
Tex″as
text″book′
tex″tile
tex″tu·al
tex″tu·al·ly
tex″tur·al
tex″ture
tex″tur·ing
Thai″land
thal″a·mus
  (*pl.* thal″a·mi′)
tha·lid″o·mide′
thal″lo·phyte′
Thames
thane
thank″ful
thank″ful·ness
thank″less
thanks′giv″ing
thatch
thaw
the″a·ter
the″a·ter·go′er

the·at″ri·cal
the·at′ri·cal″i·ty
the·at″ri·cal·ly
the·at″rics
theft
their
  pertaining to them
  (*see:* there)
theirs
  belonging to them
  (*see:* there's)
the″ism
the″ist
the·mat″ic
the·mat″i·cal·ly
theme″ park′
them·selves″
thence′forth″
the·oc″ra·cy
  (*pl.* the·oc″ra·cies)
the′o·crat″ic
the·od″o·lite′
the·o′lo″gian
the·o′log″i·cal
the·ol″o·gy
  (*pl.* the·ol″o·gies)
the″o·rem
the′o·ret″ic
the′o·ret″i·cal·ly
the·o·re·ti″cian
the″o·rist
the″o·rize′
the″o·riz′ing
the″o·ry
  (*pl.* the″o·ries)
the′o·soph″i·cal
the·os″o·phy
ther′a·peu″tic
ther′a·peu″ti·cal·ly
ther″a·pist
ther″a·py
  (*pl.* ther″a·pies)
there
  at that place (*see:*
  their and they′re)
there″a·bouts′

there'af"ter
there'by"
there'for"
  for this (*see:* therefore)
there"fore'
  for this reason (*see:* therefor)
there"from"
there'in"
there'of"
there'on"
there's
  there is (*see:* theirs)
there'to"
there"up·on"
there'with"
ther"mal
therm"i'on
therm'i·on"ics
ther'mo·dy·nam"i·cal·ly
ther'mo·dy·nam"ics
ther'mo·e·lec"tric
ther·mom"e·ter
ther'mo·nu"cle·ar
ther"mos
ther"mo·set'ting
ther"mo·sphere'
ther"mo·stat'
ther'mo·stat"i·cal·ly
the·sau"rus
the"sis
  (*pl.* the"ses)
thes"pi·an
they're
  they are (*see:* their and there)
thi"a·mine'
thick"en
thick"et
thick"head·ed
thick"set"
thick skinned"
thief
  (*pl.* thieves)

thieve
thiev"er·y
  (*pl.* thiev"er·ies)
thiev"ing
thiev"ish
thigh"bone'
thim"ble
thim"ble·ful
  (*pl.* thim"ble·fuls')
thing
think
think"er
think"tank'
thin"ner
thin"ness
thin"ning
thin"-skinned"
third"base'
third"-class'
third"de·gree"
third"-rate'
Third" World'
thirst
thirst"i·er
thirst"y
thir"teen"
thir"teenth"
thir"ti·eth
thir"ty
  (*pl.* thir"ties)
this"tle·down'
thith"er
Tho"mist
thong
tho·rac"ic
tho"rax
thorn
thorn"i·er
thorn"y
thor"ough·bred'
thor"ough·fare'
thor"ough·go'ing
those
though
thought
thought"ful·ly

thought"less
thou"sand
thou"sandth
thrall
thrall"dom
thrash
thread"bare'
thread"i·ness
threat"en
three"-col'or
three"-cor"nered
three"-di·men"sion·al
three"fold'
three"-piece"
three"-ply'
three"-quar"ter
three"score'
three"some
three"-way"
three"-wheel"er
thren"o·dy
  (*pl.* thren"o·dies)
thresh"er
thresh"old
threw
  hurled (*see:* through)
thrice
thrift"i·er
thrift"i·ly
thrift"i·ness
thrift"shop'
thrift'y
thrill
thrill"er
thrive
thriv"ing
throat
throat"i·ly
throat"i·ness
throat"y
throb
throb"bing
throe
  pang (*see:* throw)
throm·bo"sis
throm"bus

throne
  chair (*see:* thrown)
thron"ing
throng
throt"tle
throt"tling
through
  finished; by means
  of (*see:* threw)
through·out"
through"way'
throw
  hurl (*see:* throe)
throw"a·way'
throw"back
thrown
  hurled (*see:* throne)
thrum
thrum"ming
thrush
thrust
thud
thud"ding
thumb"hole'
thumb" in'dex
thumb"nail'
thumb"screw"
thumb"tack'
thump"ing
thun"der·bird'
thun"der·bolt'
thun"der·clap'
thun"der·cloud'
thun"der·head'
thun"der·ous
thun"der·show'er
thun"der·storm'
thun"der·struck'
Thurs"day
thwack
thwart
thyme
  plant (*see:* time)
thy"mus
thy"roid
Tian·jin"

ti·ar"a
Ti·bet"
tib"i·a
  (*pl.* tib"i·ae)
tic
  spasm (*see:* tick)
tick
  sound; insect; mark;
    mattress
tick"er
tick"et
tick" fe'ver
tick"ing
tick"le
tick"ler
tick"ling
tick"lish
tick'-tack-toe"
tid"al wave'
tid"bit'
tid"dly·winks'
tide
  changing sea (*see:*
    tied)
tide"land'
tide"mark'
tide"wa'ter
ti"di·er
ti"di·ly
ti"di·ness
ti"dings
ti"dy
tie"back'
tie"break'er
tied
  fastened; equal
    scores (*see:* tide)
tie'-dye'
tie'-in'
tier
  row (*see:* tear)
tie"tack'
tie'-up'
tiff
ti"ger·ish
ti"ger lil'y

ti"ger's-eye'
tight"en
tight"fist"ed
tight"knit"
tight"-lipped"
tight"rope'
tight"rop'ing
tights
tight"wad'
ti"gress
tile
til"ing
till"a·ble
till"age
till"er
tim"bal
  drum (*see:* timbale)
tim"bale
  food (*see:* timbal)
tim"ber
  wood (*see:* timbre)
tim"ber·land'
tim"ber·line'
tim"ber wolf'
tim"bre
  sound (*see:* timber)
tim"brel
time
  period (*see:* thyme)
time" bomb'
time"card'
time" clock'
time"-con·sum'ing
time" frame'
time"-hon'ored
time"keep'er
time"-lapse'
time"less
time"li·ness
time"out"
time"piece'
time" sheet'
time"-re·lease"
time"sav'er
time"sav'ing
time" shar'ing

time″ta′ble
time″ test·ed
time″worn′
tim″id
ti·mid″i·ty
tim″ing
tim″or·ous
tim″o·thy
tim″pa·ni
tim″pa·nist
tin
tinc″ture
tinc″tur·ing
tin″der·box′
tine
tin″foil′
tinge
tin″gle
tin″gling
tin″horn′
ti″ni·er
  smaller (*see:* tinnier)
ti″ni·ness
tink″er
tin″kle
tin″kling
tin″ni·er
  more like tin (*see:*
   tinier)
tin″ni·ly
tin″ning
tin″ni·tus
tin″ny
  like tin (*see:* tiny)
tin″-plate′
tin″-plat′ing
tin″sel
tin″smith
tin′tin·nab·u·la″tion
tin″type′
tin″ware′
ti″ny
  small (*see:* tinny)
tip″-off′
tip″pet
tip″ping

tip″ple
tip″pling
tip″si·er
tip″ster
tip″sy
tip″toe
tip″toe′ing
tip″top′
ti″rade
tire″less
tire″some
tir″ing
tis″sue
ti″tan
ti·tan″ic
ti·ta″ni·um
tithe
tith″ing
ti″tian
tit″il·late′
tit″il·lat′ing
tit′il·la″tion
ti″tle·hold′er
ti″tle page′
ti″tling
ti″tlist
tit″mouse′
  (*pl.* tit″mice′)
ti·tra″tion
tit″tle-tat′tle
tit″u·lar
tiz″zy
  (*pl.* tiz″zies)
to
  as far as; until (*see:*
   two and too)
toad″stool′
toad″y
  (*pl.* toad″ies)
to″-and-fro″
toast″er
toast″mas′ter
to·bac″co
  (*pl.* to·bac″cos)
To·ba″go′
to·bog″gan

to·bog″gan·ist
toc·ca″ta
toc″sin
  alarm (*see:* toxin)
to·day″
tod″dle
tod″dler
tod″dling
tod″dy
  (tod″dies)
to-do″
  (*pl.* to-dos″)
toe
  foot part (*see:* tow)
toe″-dance′
toe″hold′
toe″less
toe″nail′
tof″fee
to″fu′
to″ga
to·geth″er
tog″gle
tog″gling
To″go
toil
  labor (*see:* toile)
toile
  fabric (*see:* toil)
toi″let
toi″let·ry
  (*pl.* toi″let·ries)
toi·lette″
toil″some
toil″worn′
to″ken
to″ken·ism′
To″ky·o
told
tole
  metalware (*see:* toll)
To·le″do
tol″er·a·ble
tol″er·ance
tol″er·ant
tol″er·ate′

tol''er·at'ing
tol'er·a''tion
toll
  tariff; sound (*see:*
  tole)
toll'' bridge'
toll''booth'
toll''gate'
toll''house'
toll'' road'
tom''a·hawk'
to·ma''to
  (*pl.* to·ma''toes)
tomb
tom''boy'
tomb''stone'
tom''cat'
tome
tom'fool''er·y
  (*pl.* tom'fool''er·
  ies)
to·mor''row
tom''my·rot'
tom''-tom'
ton
  weight (*see:* tun)
ton''al
to·nal''i·ty
  (*pl.* to·nal''i·ties)
tone''-deaf'
tone''less
tongs
tongue''-in-cheek''
tongue''-lash'ing
tongue''-tied'
tongu''ing
ton''ic
to·night''
ton''ing
ton''nage
ton·neau''
ton''sil
ton'sil·lec''to·my
  (*pl.* ton'sil·lec''to·
  mies)
ton'sil·li''tis

ton·so''ri·al
ton''sure
ton''sur·ing
ton''tine
too
  also (*see:* to and
  two)
took
tool
  implement (*see:*
  tulle)
tool''box'
tool''mak'er
tool''shed'
toot
tooth
  (*pl.* teeth)
tooth''ache'
tooth''brush'
tooth''paste'
tooth''pick'
tooth'' pow'der
tooth''some
tooth''y
to''paz
top''coat'
To·pe''ka
top''er
top''flight'
top'' hat'
top''-heav'y
to·pi·ar'y
top''ic
top''i·cal
top'i·cal''i·ty
top''i·cal·ly
top''knot'
top''less
top''-lev''el
top''most'
top''notch''
to·pog''ra·pher
top'o·graph''ic
top'o·graph''i·cal· ly
to·pog''ra·phy

  terrain (*pl.* to·pog''
  ra·phies)
top'o·log''i·cal
to·pol''o·gy
top''ping
top''ple
top''pling
top''sail'
top''-se''cret
top''soil'
top''sy-tur''vy
toque
To''rah
torch''light'
tore
tor''e·a·dor'
tor·ment'', *v.*
  harass
tor''ment, *n.*
  tortured state
tor·men''tor
tor·na''do
  (*pl.* tor·na''does)
To·ron''to
tor·pe''do
  (*pl.* tor·pe''does)
tor''pid
tor·pid''i·ty
tor''por
torque
tor''rent
tor·ren''tial
tor''rid
tor''sion
tor''so
  (*pl.* tor''sos)
tort
  civil wrong (*see:*
  torte)
torte
  cake (*see:* tort)
tor·til''la
tor''toise shell'
tor·to''ni
tor''tu·ous

winding (*see:* tortu-
rous)
tor″ture
tor″tur·ing
tor″tu·ous
painful (*see:* tortu-
ous)
toss″up′
to″tal
to·tal′i·tar″i·an
to·tal′i·tar″i·an·ism′
to·tal″i·ty
(*pl.* to·tal″i·ties)
to″tal·ly
tote
to″tem pole′
tot″ing
tot″ter
tou″can
touch″a·ble
touch″-and-go″
touch″back′
touch″down′
tou·che″
touch″i·er
touch″i·ness
touch″stone′
touch″tone′
touch″-type′
touch″-up′
touch″y
tough″en
tough″-mind″ed
tou·pee″
tour′ de force″
(*pl.* tours′ de force″)
tour″ism
tour″ist
tour″ma·line
tour″na·ment
tour″ney
(*pl.* tour″neys)
tour″ni·quet
tou″sle
tou″sling
tout

tout de suite″
tow
pull; fiber (*see:* toe)
to·wards″
tow″-a·way′
tow″boat′
tow″el
tow″er·ing
tow″head′ed
town″ hall″
town″ house″
towns″folk
town″ship
towns″peo′ple
tow″path′
tow″rope′
tox·e″mi·a
tox″ic
tox″i·cant
tox·ic″i·ty
tox′i·col″o·gist
tox′i·col″o·gy
tox″in
poison (*see:* tocsin)
tox″in-an″ti·tox″in
trace
trace″a·ble
trac″er
trac″er·y
tra″che·a
(*pl.* tra″che·ae)
tra″che·al
tra″che·ot″o·my
(*pl.* tra che·ot″o·
mies)
tra·cho″ma
trac″ing
track
trail; flow (*see:*
tract)
track″age
track″less
track″ meet′
tract
land; leaflet (*see:*
track)

trac′ta·bil″i·ty
trac″ta·ble
trac″tile
trac″tion
trac″tor
trade
trade″-in′
trad″ing
trade″mark′
trade″ name′
trade″-off′
trad″er
trade″ school′
trades″man
trade″ un′ion
trade″ winds′
trad″ing stamp
tra·di″tion
tra·di″tion·al
tra·di″tion·al·ist
tra·di″tion·al·ly
tra·duce″
tra·duc″er
tra·duc″ing
traf″fic
traf″ficked
traf″fick·er
traf″fick·ing
traf″fic light′
tra·ge′di·an
tra·ge′di·enne″
trag″e·dy
(*pl.* trag″e·dies)
trag″ic
trag″i·cal
trag″i·cal·ly
trag′i·com″e·dy
trag′i·com″ic
trail″blaz er
trail″er
trail″ mix′
train″a·ble
train·ee″
train″er
train″load
train″man

train″mas′ter
traipse
traips″ing
trait
trai″tor
trai″tor·ous
tra·jec″to·ry
  (pl. tra·jec″to·ries)
tram
tram″mel
tram″mel·ing
tramp
tram″ple
tram″pling
tram″po·line″
tram″way′
trance
tran″quil
tran·quil″li·ty
tran″quil·ly
tran″quil·ize′
tran″quil·iz′ing
tran″quil·iz′er
trans·act″
trans·ac″tion
trans·ac″tion·al
trans·at′lan″tic
trans·ceiv″er
tran·scend
tran·scend″ence
tran·scend″ent
tran′scen·den″tal·ism
tran′scen·den″tal·ist
trans′con·ti·nen″tal
tran·scribe″
tran·scrib″ing
tran″script
tran·scrip″tion
trans·duc″er
tran″sept
trans·fer″, v.
  move
trans″fer, n.
  act of transferring
trans·fer′a·bil″i·ty
trans·fer′a·ble

trans·fer″al
trans·fer″ence
trans·fer″ring
trans′fig·u·ra″tion
trans·fig″ure
trans·fig″ur·ing
trans·fix″
trans·form″
trans·form″a·ble
trans′for·ma″tion
trans·form″er
trans·fuse″
trans·fus″ing
trans·fu″sion
trans·gress″
trans·gres″sion
trans·gres″sor
tran″sience
tran″sient
tran·sis″tor
tran·sis″tor·ize′
trans″it
tran·si″tion
tran·si″tion·al
tran″si·tive
tran″si·to·ry
trans·lat″a·ble
trans·late″
trans·lat″ing
trans·la″tion
trans·la″tor
trans·lit″er·ate′
trans·lit″er·at′ing
trans·lit′er·a″tion
trans·lu″cence
trans·lu″cen·cy
trans·lu″cent
trans·mi″grate
trans·mi″grat·ing
trans·mi·gra″tion
trans·mis″si·ble
trans·mis″sion
trans·mit″
trans·mit″ta·ble
trans·mit″tal
trans·mit″tance

trans·mit″ter
trans·mit″ting
trans·mog″ri·fy′
trans·mut″a·ble
trans′mu·ta″tion
trans·mute″
trans·mut″ing
trans′o·ce·an″ic
tran″som
trans′pa·cif″ic
trans·par″ence
trans·par″en·cy
  (pl. trans·par″en·cies)
trans·par″ent
tran′spi·ra″tion
tran·spire″
tran·spir″ing
trans′plant′
trans′plan·ta″tion
trans·po″lar
tran·spon″der
trans·port″, v.
  carry
trans″port′, n.
  transportation
trans′por·ta″tion
trans·port″er
trans·pose″
trans·pos″ing
trans′po·si″tion
trans·pu″ter
trans·sex″u·al
trans·ship″
trans·ship″ment
trans·ship″ping
tran·son″ic
tran′sub·stan·ti·a″tion
trans′val·u·a″tion
trans·ver″sal
trans·verse″
trans·verse″ly
trans·ves″tite
trap″door″
tra·peze″
trap″e·zoid′

trap"per
trap"pings
Trap"pist
trap"shoot'ing
trash
trash"i·er
trash"i·ness
trash"y
trau"ma
trau·mat"ic
trau·mat"i·cal·ly
trau·ma·ti·za"tion
trau·ma·tize'
trau·ma·tiz'ing
tra·vail"
  agony (see: travel)
trav"el
  journey (see: travail)
trav"el·er
trav"el·ing
trav"e·logue'
tra·vers"a·ble
tra·vers"al
trav·erse"
trav·ers"ing
trav"es·tied
trav"er·tine
trav"es·ty
  (pl. trav"es·ties)
trawl
trawl"er
tray
treach"er·ous
treach"er·y
  (pl. treach"er·ies)
trea"cle
tread
trea"dle
tread"mill'
trea"son
trea"son·a·ble
trea"son·ous
treas"ur·a·ble
treas"ur·er
treas"ure-trove'
treas"ur·ing

treas"ur·y
  (pl. treas"ur·ies)
treat"a·ble
trea"tise
treat"ment
trea"ty
  (pl. trea"ties)
tre"ble
tre"bling
treed
tree" house'
tree"ing
tree"lined'
tree"top'
tre"foil
trek
trek"king
trel"lis
trem"ble
trem"bling
trem"bly
tre·men"dous
trem"o·lo
  (pl. trem"o·los')
trem"or
trem"u·lous
trench"ant
trench" mouth'
trend
trend"y
Tren"ton
trep'i·da"tion
tres"pass
tres"pass·er
tress
tres"tle·work'
tri"a·ble
tri"ad
tri"age
tri"al
tri"an'gle
tri·an'gu·lar
tri·an'gu·late'
tri·an'gu·lat'ing
tri·an'gu·la"tion
tri·ath"lon

trib"al
trib"al·ism'
tribe
tribes"man
trib·u·la"tion
tri·bu"nal
trib"une
trib"u·tar'y
  (pl. trib"u·tar'ies)
trib"ute
tri·cen·ten"ni·al
tri"ceps
  (pl. tri"ceps·es)
tri·chi"na
  (pl. tri·chi"nae)
trich'i·no"sis
tri·chot"o·my
  (pl. tri·chot"o·mies)
tri"chro·mat"ic
trick"er·y
trick"i·er
trick"i·ness
trick"le
trick"ling
trick"ster
trick"y
tri"col'or
tri"cot
tri"cy·cle
tri"dent
tri'di·men"sion·al
tried
tri·en"ni·al
tri"er
tri"fle
tri"fling
tri·fo"cal
trig"ger-hap'py
tri·glyc"er·ide'
trig'o·no·met"ric
trig'o·nom"e·try
tri·lat"er·al
tri·lin"gual
trill
tril"lion
tril"li·um

tril"o·gy
(*pl.* tril"o·gies)
trim
tri·mes"ter
trim"mer
trim"ming
tri·month"ly
Trin"i·dad'
trin"i·ty
(*pl.* trin"i·ties)
trin"ket
tri·no"mi·al
tri"o
(*pl.* tri"os)
trip
tri·par"tite
tripe
trip"ham·mer
tri"ple play"
tri"plet
tri"plex
trip"li·cate
tri"pling
tri"ply
tri"pod
Trip"o·ll
trip"per
trip"ping
trip"tych
tri·sect"
tri·state'
trite
trite"ly
trit"u·rate'
trit"u·rat'ing
tri"umph
tri·um"phal
tri·um"phant
tri·um"vi·rate
tri"une
tri·va"lent
triv"et
triv"i·a
triv"i·al
triv'i·al"i·ty
(*pl.* triv'i·al"i·ties)

tri·week"ly
(*pl.* tri·week"lies)
tro·cha"ic
tro"che
lozenge (*see:* tro-
chee)
tro"chee
poetic meter (*see:*
troche)
trod"den
trog"lo·dyte'
troi"ka
troll
trol"ley
(*pl.* trol"leys)
trol"ley car'
trol"lop
trom·bone"
trom·bon"ist
troop
soldiers (*see:* troup)
troop"ship'
tro"phy
(*pl.* tro"phies)
trop"ic
trop"i·cal
tro"pism
trop"o·sphere'
trot
trot"ter
trot"ting
trou"ba·dour'
trou"ble·mak'er
trou"ble·shoot'er
trou"ble·some
trou"bling
trough
trounce
trounc"ing
troupe
performers (*see:*
troop)
troup"ing
trou"sers
trous"seau
trout

(*pl.* trout)
trove
trow"el
trow"el·ing
tru"an·cy
(*pl.* tru"an·cies)
tru"ant
truce
truck"age
truck"driv'er
truck" farm'
truck"le
truck"ling
truck"load'
truc"u·lence
truc"u·lent
trudge
trudg"ing
true"-blue"
true"-life"
true"love'
tru"er
truf"fle
tru"ism
tru"ly
trump
trumped"-up"
trump"er·y
(*pl.* trump"er·ies)
trum"pet
trum"pet·er
trun"cate
trun"cat·ing
trun·ca"tion
trun"cheon
trun"dle bed'
trun"dling
trunk" line'
truss
trus·tee"
guardian (*see:*
trusty)
trus·tee"ship
trust"ful·ly
trust"i·er
trust"wor'thi·ness

trust"worthy
trust"y
  trustworthy (*see:*
  trustee)
truth"ful
truth"ful·ly
truth"ful·ness
try
  (*pl.* tries)
try"out'
tryst
tset"se fly"
T-shirt'
T square'
tsu·na"mi
tub
tu"ba
tub"bi·er
tub"by
tube
tu"ber
tu"ber·cle
tu·ber"cu·lar
tu·ber"cu·lin
tu·ber"cu·lo"sis
tu·ber"cu·lous
tube"rose'
tu"ber·ous
tub"ing
tu"bu·lar
tu"bule
tuck
tuck"er
Tuc"son
Tues"day
tuft
tuft"ed
tug"boat'
tug" of war"
tug"ging
tu·i"tion
tu"lip tree'
tulle
  netting (*see:* tool)
Tul"sa
tum"ble-down'

tum"bler
tum"ble·weed'
tum"bling
tum"brel
tu·mes"cence
tu·mes"cent
tu"mid
tum"my
  (*pl.* tum"mies)
tu"mor
tu"mor·ous
tu"mult
tu·mul"tu·ous
tun
  cask (*see:* ton)
tu"na
tun"a·ble
tun"dra
tune
tune"a·ble
tune"ful·ly
tune"less
tun"er
tune"-up'
tung"sten
tu"nic
tun"ing
  adjusting (*see:* tun-
  ning)
Tu"nis
Tu·ni"sia
tun"nel
tun"nel·ing
tun"ning
  storing in tuns (*see:*
  tuning)
tu"pe·lo"
  (*pl.* tu"pe·los')
tur"ban
  headdress (*see:* tur-
  bine)
tur"bid
tur"bine
  engine (*see:* turban)
tur"bo·charg"er
tur"bo·fan'

tur"bo·jet'
tur"bo·prop'
tur"bot
tur"bu·lence
tur"bu·lent
tu·reen"
turf
tur"gid
tur·gid"i·ty
tur"key
  fowl
Tur"key
  country
tur"mer·ic
tur"moil
turn
  change direction
  (*see:* tern)
turn"a·bout'
turn"a·round'
turn"buck'le
turn"coat'
turn"down'
tur"nip
turn"key'
  (*pl.* turn"keys)
turn"off'
turn"-on'
turn"out'
turn"o'ver
turn"pike'
turn"stile'
turn"ta'ble
tur"pen·tine'
tur"pi·tude'
tur"quoise
tur"ret
tur"tle·dove'
tur"tle·neck'
tusk
tus"sle
tus"sling
tus"sock
tu"te·lage
tu"te·lar'y
tu"tor

tu·to″ri·al
tut″ti frut″ti
tux·e″do
   (*pl.* tux·e″dos)
twad″dle
twad″dling
twain
twang
tweak
tweed
tweed″ɪ·er
tweed″i·ness
tweed″y
tweet
tweet″er
tweeze
tweez″ers
twelfth
twelve
twen″ti·eth
twen″ty
   (*pl.* twen″ties)
twice″-told″
twid″dle
twid″dling
twig
twi″light′
twill
twin
twine
twinge
twing″ing
twi″night′
twin″ing
   twisting (*see:* twin-
   ning)
twin″kle
twin″kling
twin″ning
   having twins (*see:*
   twining)
twin″-screw″
twirl″er
twist
twist″a·ble
twist″er

twit
twitch
twit″ter
twit″ting
two
   number (*see:* to and
   too)
two″-bit′
two″-by-four′
two″-di·men′sion·al
two″-edged″
two″-faced′
two″fist′ed
two″fold′
two″-hand″ed
two″-piece″
two″-ply″
two″-sid″ed
two″some
two″-tier′
two″-time′
two″-tim′ing
two″-way″
ty·coon″
ty″ing
tyke
tym·pan″i
tym·pan″ic
tym″pa·nist
type″-cast′
   cast type (*see:* type-
   cast)
type″cast′
   cast actor (*see:* type-
   cast)
type″face′
type″script′
type″set′
type″set′ter
type″set′ting
type″writ′ten
type″writ′er
type″writ′ing
ty″phoid
ty·phoon″
ty″phus

typ″i·cal
typ″i·cal·ly
typ″i·fied′
typ″i·fy′
typ″ing
typ″ist
ty″po
   (*pl.* ty″pos)
ty·pog″ra·pher
ty·po·graph″i·cal
ty·po·graph″i·cal·ly
ty·pog″ra·phy
   printing (*see:* topog-
   raphy)
ty·po·log″i·cal
ty·ran″nic
ty·ran″ni·cal
ty·ran″ni·cal·ly
tyr″an·nize′
tyr″an·niz′ing
ty·ran″no·saur′
ty·ran″no·saur″us
tyr″an·nous
tyr″an·ny
   (*pl.* tyr″an·nies)
ty″rant
ty″ro
   (*pl.* ty″ros)

U

u·biq″ui·tous
u·biq″ui·ty
U-boat′
ud″der
ud′o·met″ric
U·gan″da
ug″li
   fruit (*see:* ugly)
ug″li·er
ug″li·ness
ug″ly
   unattractive (*see:*
   ugli)
u″kase

U·kraine″
u′ku·le″le
ul″cer
ul″cer·ate
ul″cer·at′ing
ul′cer·a″tion
ul′cer·a′tive
ul″cer·ous
u″le·ma′
ul″na
   (*pl.* ul″nae)
Ul″ster
ul·te″ri·or
ul″ti·mate
ul″ti·mate·ly
ul′ti·ma″tum
ul′tra·con·ser″va·tive
ul″tra·fiche′
ul″tra·fid′i·an
ul′tra·high fre″quen·
   cy
ul′tra·la·bor′i·ous
ul″tra·light
ul′tra·ma·rine″
ul′tra·mi″cro·scope′
ul′tra·mod″ern
ul′tra·mon·tane′
ul′tra·plan′e·tar·y
ul′tra·short″
ul′tra·son″ics
ul″tra·sound′
ul′tra·vi″o·let
ul′tra·vi″res
ul″u·late′
ul″u·lat′ing
ul′u·la″tion
um″ber
um·bil″i·cal
um·bil″i·cus
   (*pl.* um·bil″i·ci′)
um″bles
um″bra
um″brage
um·bra″geous
um·brel″la
um″laut

um″pire
ump″teen″
un′a·bashed′
un′a·bat″ed
un′a·bet″ted
un·a″ble
un′a·bridged″
un′ac·com″pa·nied
un′ac·cord″ed
un′ac·count″a·ble
un′ac·count″ed-for′
un′ac·cus″ing
un′ac·cus″tomed
un′a·dor″a·ble
un′a·dorned″
un′a·dul″ter·at·ed
un′af·fect″ed
un′a·lert″ed
un′a·ligned″
un′al·lev″i·at′ed
un·al″lied″
un′al·loyed″
un′-A·mer″i·can
u·nan″i·mous
un·an″swer·a·ble
un·armed″
un′as·sail″a·ble
un′as·signed″
un′as·sum″ing
un′at·tached″
un·au″thor·ized′
un′a·vail″ing
un′a·void″a·ble
un′a·wares″
un·bal″anced
un·bane″
un·bear″a·ble
un·beat″a·ble
un′be·com″ing
un′be·hold″en
un′be·knownst″
un′be·lief″
un′be·liev″a·ble
un′be·liev″er
un′be·liev″ing
un·bend″

un·bi″ased
un·bid″den
un·bil″let
un·bind″
un·bolt″
un·born″
un·bos″om
un·bound″ed
un·bowed″
un·breach″a·ble
un·bri″dled
un·bro″ken
un·bur″den
un·but″ton
un·called″-for′
un·can″ny
un·capped″
un·cared″-for′
un·caste″
un·ceas″ing
un′cer·e·mo″ni·ous
un·cer″tain·ty
   (*pl.* un·cer″tain·
   ties)
un·cer″ti·fied′
un·chain″
un·change″a·ble
un·char″i·ta·ble
un·chart″ed
un·chaste″
un·chew″a·ble
un·chris″tian
un″ci·al
un·civ″il
un·civ″i·lized′
un·clad″
un·clas″si·fied′
un″cle
un·clean″li·ness
un·clear″
Un″cle Sam″
un·clogged″
un·clothed″
un·com″fort·a·ble
un·com·mit″ted
un·com″mon

un'com·mu''ni·ca'tive
un'com''pro·mis''ing
un'con·cerned''
un'con·di''tion·al
un'con·di''tion·al·ly
un'con·ju''gal
un·con''quer·a·ble
un·con''scion·a·ble
un·con''scious
un'con·sti·tu''tion·al
un'con·trol''la·ble
un'con·ven''tion·al
un'con·ven''tion·al·ly
un'con·ver''ted
un·cooked''
un·count''ed
un·cou''ple
un·couth''
un·cov''er
un·crit''i·cal
un·cross''
unc''tion
unc''tu·ous
un·curl''
un·daunt''ed
un'de·bil''i·ta'ting
un'de·cid''ed
un'de·clar''a·ble
un'de·fi''ant
un'dem·o·crat''ic
un'de·mon''stra·tive
un'de·nom'i·na''tion·al
un'de·ni''a·ble
un'der·a·chieve''
un'der·a·chiev''er
un'der·a·chiev''ing
un'der·age''
un''der·arm'
un'der·bid''
un'der·bid''ding
un''der·brush'
un''der·car'riage
un''der·charge'', v.
  charge too low
un''der·charge', n.

insufficient charge
un''der·class''man
un''der·clothes'
un''der·cloth'ing
un''der·coat'
un''der·coat'ing
un'der·cook''
un''der·count'
un'der·cov''er
un''der·cut'
un'der·de·vel''oped
un''der·dog'
un'der·es''ti·mate'
un'der·es'ti·ma''tion
un'der·ex·pose'
un'der·ex·pos''ing
un'der·ex·po''sure
un'der·fed''
un'der·foot''
un'der·gar'ment
un'der·gird''
un'der·go''
un'der·gone''
un'der·grad''u·ate
un''der·ground'
un''der·growth'
un'der·hand''ed
un'der·hung''
un'der·laid''
un'der·lay'', v.
  lay something under
un''der·lay', n.
  thing laid underneath
un'der·lay''ing
un'der·lie''
un'der·line'
un'der·ling'
un'der·lin'ing
un'der·ly''ing
un'der·mine''
un'der·min''ing
un'der·neath''
un'der·nour''ish
un'der·paid''
un''der·pants'
un''der·pass'

un'der·pay''
un'der·pin'ing
un'der·play''
un'der·priced''
un'der·priv''i·leged
un'der·pro·duc''ing
un'der·rate''
un'der·rep're·sen·ta''tion
un'der·scorc''
un''der·sea'
un'der·sec''re·tar'y
  (pl. un'der·sec''re·tar'ies)
un'der·sell''
un''der·shirt'
un'der·shoot''
un''der·shot'
un''der·side'
un'der·size''
un'der·sized''
un''der·skirt'
un'der·slung''
un'der·staffed''
un'der·stand''
un'der·stand''a·ble
un'der·stand''ing
un'der·state''
un'der·state''ment
un'der·stood''
un'der·stud'ied
un'der·stud'y
  (pl. un'der·stud'ies)
un'der·take''
un'der·tak''er
un'der·tak''ing
un'der-the-coun'ter
un''der·tone'
un'der·took''
un''der·tow'
un'der·val''ue
un'der·val''u·ing
un'der·wa''ter
un''der·way''
un''der·wear'
un''der·weight'

un"der·went"
un"der·world"
un'der·write"
un'der·writ"ing
un'der·writ"ten
un'der·wrote"
un"der·writ"er
un'de·served"
un'de·sir"a·ble
un'de·ter"mined
un'de·vel"oped
un·do"
  nullify; unfasten
  (*see:* undue)
un·do"ing
un·done"
un·doubt"ed
un'dra·mat"ic
un·dress"
un·due
  excessive (*see:* undo)
un"du·late'
un·du"ly
un·dy"ing
un·earned"
un·earn"est
un·earth"
un·eas"i·ly
un·eas"i·ness
un·eas"y
un·ed"i·fied'
un·ed"u·cat'ed
un'em·ploy"a·ble
un'em·ployed"
un'em·ploy"ment
un'en·cour"age
un·end"ing
un·en"vi·a·ble
un·e"qual
un·e"qualed
un·e"qual·ly
un'e·quiv"o·cal
un·err"ing
un'es·sen"tial
un·eth"i·cal
un·e"ven

un'e·vent"ful
un'ex·cep"tion·a·ble
un'ex·cep"tion·al
un'ex·chang"a·ble
un'ex·pect"ed
un'fac"tious
un·fail"ing
un·fair"
un·faith"ful
un'fa·mil"iar
un'fa·mil'i·ar"i·ty
un·fas"ten
un·fa"vor·a·ble
un·fear"ing
un·fed"
un·feel"ing
un·feigned"
un·fe·lon"i·ous
un·fet"tered
un·fin"ished
un·fit"
un·flag"ging
un·flap"pa·ble
un·flinch"ing
un·fold"
un'fore·seen"
un'for·get"ta·ble
un'for·giv"a·ble
un·formed"
un'for"tu·nate
un·found"ed
un·framed"
un·friend"ly
un·fre"quent·ed
un·frock"
un·fruit"ful
un·furl"
un·gain"ly
un'gan·gren"ous
un·gen"er·ous
un·giv"ing
un·god"ly
un·gov"ern·a·ble
un·grace"ful
un·gra"cious
un'gram·mat"i·cal

un·grate"ful
un·guard"ed
un"guent
un·guid"ed
un·hab"it·a·ble
un·hand"
un·hap"py
un·harm"ful
un·health"y
un·heard"-of'
un·hinged"
un·hitch"
un·ho"ly'
un·hoped"-for
un·horse"
un·hur"ried
un·hy·gi·en"ic
u'ni·cam"er·al
u'ni·cel"lu·lar
u"ni·corn
u"ni·cy'cle
u'ni·fi·ca"tion
u"ni·fied'
u"ni·fi'er
u"ni·form
u'ni·form"i·ty
  (*pl.* u'ni·form"i·
  ties)
u"ni·fy'
u'ni·lat"er·al
u'ni·ling"ual
un'i·mag"i·na'ble
un'im·peach"a·ble
un'in·hab"it·a·ble
un'in·hib"it·ed
un·in"jured
un·in'tel"li·gent
un·in'tel"li·gi·ble
un'in·ten"tion·al
un'in·ten"tion·al·ly
un'in·tim"i·dat'ed
un·in·vit"ed
un"ion
un'ion·i·za"tion
un"ion·ize'
un"ion·iz'ing

u·nique''
u''ni·sex'
u''ni·son
u''ni·son·ance'
u''ni·tar''i·an
u''ni·tar'y
u·nite''
U·nit''ed Ar''ab E·mir''ates
U·nit''ed King''dom
U·nit''ed Na''tions
U·nit''ed States''
u·nit''ing
u''ni·ty
(*pl.* u''ni·ties)
u''ni·ver''sal
u''ni·ver·sal''i·ty
(*pl.* u''ni·ver·sal''i·ties)
u''ni·ver''sal·ly
u''ni·verse
u''ni·ver''si·ty
(*pl.* u''ni·ver''si·ties)
u·niv''o·cal'
un·kempt''
un·knot''
un·know''ing
un·known''
un·lab''ored
un·lace''
un·land''ed
un·latch''
un·law''ful
un·lead''ed
un·learn''ed
un·leash''
un·leav''ened
un·less''
un·let''tered
un·li''censed
un·like''
un·like''li·hood
un·like''ly
un·lim''it·ed
un·linked''
un·list''ed

un·load''
un·lock''
un·looked''-for
un·loose''
un·loosed''
un·loos''en
un·loos''ing
un·luck''y
un·made''
un·make''
un·mal''le·a'ble
un·man''
un·man''ly
un·manned''
un·man''ner·ly
un·marked''
un·mask''
un·men''tion·a·ble
un·mer''ci·ful
un·mind''ful
un·mis·tak''a·ble
un·mit''i·gat'ed
un·mould''y
un·moved''
un·mud''dled
un·muz''zle
un·nat''u·ral
un·nec'es·sar''i·ly
un·nec''es·sar'y
un·need''ed
un·nerve''
un·nerv''ing
un·no''ticed
un·num''bered
un·ob·tru''sive
un·oc''cu·pied
un·of·fi''cial
un·or''gan·ized
un·or''tho·dox
un·pack''
un·par''al·leled
un·pay''a·ble
un·pen''e·tra·ble
un·phil'o·soph''i·cal
un·picked''
un·pleas''ant

un·pli''ant
un·plug''
un·pol''ar·ized'
un·pon''dered
un·pop''u·lar
un·pop·u·lar''i·ty
un·prac''ticed
un·prec''e·dent'ed
un·prej''u·diced
un·pre·med''i·tat'ed
un·pre·pared''
un·pre·vent''a·ble
un·prin''ci·pled
un·pro·fes''sion·al
un·prof''it·a·ble
un·pry''ing
un·qual''i·fied
un·ques''tion·a·ble
un·ques''tion·ing
un·quote''
un·rav''el
un·read''
un·read''a·ble
un·re''al
un·re·al·is''tic
un·re·al·is''ti·cal·ly
un·rea''son·a·ble
un·rea''son·ing
un·re·con·cil''a'ble
un·re·con·struct''ed
un·reel''
un·re·gen''er·ate
un·re·lent''ing
un·re·li''a·ble
un·re·mit''ting
un·re·mote''
un·re·pent''ant
un·rest''
un·re·strained''
un·re·ward''ing
un·righ''teous
un·ri''valed
un·ruf''fled
un·ru''li·ness
un·ru''ly
un·sad''dle

un·sad"dled
un·sad"dling
un·sat·is·fac"to·ry
un·sat"u·rat·ed
un·sa"vor·y
un·scathed"
un·schooled"
un·sci·en·tif"ic
un·scram"ble
un·scram"bling
un·screw"
un·scru"pu·lous
un·search"a·ble
un·sea"son·a·ble
un·sea"soned
un·seat"
un·seem"ly
un·seg"re·gat'ed
un·self"ish
un·set"tled
un·set"tling
un·sev"ered
un·shack"le
un·shak"a·ble
un·shav"en
un·sheathe"
un·sight"ly
un·skilled"
un·snarl"
un·so"cial
un·so·phis"ti·cat·ed
un·sought"
un·sound"
un·spar"ing
un·speak"a·ble
un·spec"i·fied'
un·squeez"a·ble
un·sta"ble
un·starched"
un·staunch"
un·stead"y
un·stopped"
un·stra·te"gic
un·stressed"
un·strung"
un·stud"ied

un·styl"ish
un·sub·stan"tial
un·sub"tle
un·suc·cess"ful
un·suit"a·ble
un·sul"lied
un·sung"
un·sure"
un·sus·pect"ed
un·sur·pris"ing
un·sym·pa·thet"ic
un·tan"gle
un·taw"dry
un·ten"a·ble
un·think"a·ble
un·think"ing
un·thread"a·ble
un·ti"dy
un·tie"
un·tied"
un·til"
un·time"ly
un·tir"ing
un·ti"tled
un·told"
un·touch"a·ble
un·to·ward"
un·tried"
un·true"
un·truth"ful
un·tu"tored
un·ty"ing
un·used"
un·u"su·al
un·ut"ter·a·ble
un·var"nished
un·veil"
un·voiced"
un·want"ed
    not wanted (*see:* un-
    wonted)
un·war"rant·ed
un·war"y
un·wed"
un·whole"some
un·wield"y

un·will"ing
un·will"ful
un·wind"
un·wise"
un·wished"-for'
un·wit"ting
un·wont"ed
    not common (*see:*
    unwanted)
un·world"ly
un·wor"ried
un·wor"thi·ness
un·wor"thy
un·wound"
un·yield"ing
un·yoked"
un·zip"
un·zipped"
up"-and-com"ing
up"-and-down"
up·beat'
up·braid"
up"bring'ing
up"chuck"
up"com'ing
up"coun'try
up"cry'
up·date"
up·dat"ing
up"draft"
up·end"
up" front"
up'grade"
up·heav"al
up·held"
up"hill"
up"hold"
up·hol"ster·er
up·hol"ster·y
up"keep'
up"land
up·lift", *v.*
    elevate
up"lift, *n.*
    raised land
up·on"

up″per·case″
up″per·cas″ing
up·per″-class″
upper·class″man
up″per·cut′
up″per·most′
up″pi·ty
up″right″
up″ris′ing
up″roar′
up·roar″i·ous
up″root″
up″scale′
up·set″,v.,adj.
  overturn; distressed
up″set′, n.
  actofupsetting
up·set″ting
up″shot″
up″side down″
up″si·lon′
up″stage″
up″stairs″
up·stand″ing
up″start′
up″state″
up″stream″
up·surge″, v.
  surge up
up″surge′, n.
  a surge upward
up″swept′
Pup″swing′
up″take′
up″thrust′
up″tick′
up″tight″
up″-to-date″
up·tow″er
up″town″
up·turn″, v.
  turn up
up″turn′, n.
  upward turn
up″wards
up″wind″

u·ra″ni·um
U″ra·nus
ur″ban
  of a city (see: ur-
  bane)
ur·bane″
  sophisticated (see:
  urban)
ur″ban·ite′
ur·ban″i·ty
  (pl. ur·ban″i·ties)
ur″ban·i·za″tion
ur″ban·ize′
ur″ban·ol″o·gy
ur″chin
u·re″mi·a
u·re″ter
u·re″thra
  (pl. u·re″thrae)
u·ret″ic
urge
ur″gen·cy
ur″gent
urg″ing
u″ri·nal
u′ri·nal″y·sis
  (pl. u′ri·nal″y·ses)
u″ri·nar′y
u″ri·nate′
u″ri·nat′ing
u″ri·na″tion
u″rine
urn
  vase (see: earn)
u′ro·log″ic
u·rol″o·gy
ur″sine
U″ru·guay
us′a·bil″i·ty
us″a·ble
us″age
use
use″ful
use″less
us″er-friend′ly
ush″er

us″ing
u″su·al
u″su·al·ly
u″su·fruct′
u″su·rer
u·su″ri·ous
u·surp″
u·sur″pa″tion
u·surp″er
u″su·ry
  (pl. u″su·ries)
U″tah
u·ten″sil
u″ter·ine
u″ter·us
  (pl. u″ter· i)
u·til′i·tar″i·an
u·til″i·ty
  (pl. u·til″i·ties)
u″ti·liz′a·ble
u″ti·li·za″tion
u″ti·lize′
u″ti·liz′ing
ut″most
u·to″pi·a
u·to″pi·an′
ut″ter·ance
ut″ter·most′
U″-turn′
ux·o″ri·cide′
ux·o″ri·ous

V

va″can·cy
  (pl. va″can·cies)
va″cant
va″cate
va″cat·ing
va·ca″tion
va·ca″tion·er
vac″ci·nate′
vac″ci·nat′ing
vac′ci·na″tion
vac·cine″

vac″il·late′
vac″il·lat′ing
vac′il·la″tion
vac″il·la·to′ry
va·cu″i·ty
  (*pl.* va·cu″i·ties)
vac″u·ate′
vac″u·ole′
vac″u·ous
vac″u·um-packed″
vag″a·bond′
va·gar″y
  (*pl.* va·gar″ies)
va·gi″na
vag″i·nal
vag″i·na′ted
vag″i·no·pex′y
va″gran·cy
  (*pl.* va″gran·cies)
va″grant
vague
vague″ly
va·hine″
vain
  futile; arrogant (*see:*
   vein and vane)
vain·glo″ri·ous
vain″glo′ry
vaire
val″ance
  drapery (*see:* va-
   lence)
vale
  valley (*see:* veil)
val′e·bant″
val′e·dic·to″ri·an
val′e·dic″to·ry
  (*pl.* val′e·dic″to·
   ries)
va″lence
  chemical term (*see:*
   valance)
val″en·tine′
va·le″ra·mid′
va·le″ri·an
val″et

val′e·tu′di·nar″i·an
val″gus
val″iant
val″id
val″i·date′
val″i·dat′ing
val′i·da″tion
va·lid″i·ty
va·lise″
Val″i·um™
Val″ky·rie
val″ley
  (*pl.* val″leys)
va·lon″i·a
val″or
val″u·a·ble
val″u·a″tion
val″ue-add″ed tax″
val″ue-less
val″u·ing
valve
val″vi·form
val″vu·lar
va·moose″
vam″pire
van·cou″ver
van″dal·ism′
van″dal·ize′
van″dal·iz′ing
vane
  rotating blade (*see:*
   vain and vein)
van″guard′
va·nil″la
van″ish
van″i·ty
  (*pl.* van″i·ties)
van″quish
van″tage
vap″id
va·pid″i·ty
va″por
va·por″i·um
va·por·i·za″tion
va″por·ize′
va″por·iz′er

va″por·iz′ing
va″por·ous
va″por·tight′
va·que″ro
  (*pl.* va·que″ros)
var′i·a·bil″i·ty
var″i·a·ble
var″i·ance
var″i·ant
var′i·a″tion
var″i·col″ored
var″i·cose′
var′i·cos″i·ty
  (*pl.* var′i·cos″i·ties)
var″ied
var″i·e·gate′
var″i·e·gat′ing
var′i·e·ga″tion
va·ri″e·tal
va·ri″e·ty
  (*pl.* va·ri″e·ties)
var″i·o·late′
var′i·o″rum
var″i·o·tint′
var″i·ous
var″mint
var″nish
var″si·ty
  (*pl.* var″si·ties)
var″y
  change (*see:* very)
var″y·ing′
vas″cu·lar
vas″cu·late′
vas de fe·rens′
  (*pl.* va″sa de fe·
   ren″ti·a)
vase
vas·ec″to·my
  (*pl.* vas·ec″to·mies)
Vas″e·line′™
va″so·den′tine
va″so·sec″tion
vas″sal
vas″sal·age
vat

Vat''i·can
vaude''ville
vaude·vil''lian
vault
vault''ing
vaunt
V'C'R''
  videocassette re-
  corder
V''-Day'
V'D'T''
  video display termi-
  nal
vec''tor
vec''tor·car'di·o·gram
vec·to''ri·al
ve·dal''i·a
V''-E'' Day'
vee''jay
veep
veer
ve''ga
veg''e·ta·ble
veg'i·tar''i·an
veg'e·tar''i·an·ism'
veg''e·tate'
veg''e·tat'ing
veg'e·ta''tion
veg''e·ta'tive
ve''he·mence
ve''he·ment
ve''hi·cle
ve·hic''u·lar
veil
  covering (see: vale)
vein
  blood vessel (see:
  vain and vane)
veld
vel''lum
ve·loc''ious
ve·loc''i·ty
  (pl. ve·loc''i·ties)
ve·lo''drome
ve·lour''
vel''vet

vel'vet·een''
vel''vet·leaf
vel''vet·y
ve''na ca''va
ve''nal
  mercenary (see: ve-
  nial)
ve·nal''i·ty
ve·nal'i·za''tion
vend·ee''
ven·det''ta
vend''ing ma·chine'
ven''dor
ven''due
ve·neer''
ven'er·a·bil''i·ty
ven''er·a·ble
ven''er·ate'
ven''er·at'ing
ven'er·a''tion
ve·ne''re·al
ve'ne·rance'
ve''ne·sec'tion
Ven'e·zue''la
venge''ance
venge''ful
ve''ni·al
  forgivable (see: ve-
  nal)
ve''ni·al'i·ty
Ven''ice
ven''i·son
ven'o·au·ri''cu·lar
ven''om
ven''om·ous
ve''nous
ven''ta·na
ven''ti·late'
ven''ti·lat'ing
ven''ti·la''tion
ven''ti·la'tor
ven''tral·ly
ven''tri·cle
ven·tric''u·lar
ven·tril''o·quism'
ven·tril''o·quist

ven''trose
ven''ture
ven''ture·some
ven''tur·ing
ven''tur·ous
ven''ue
Ve''nus
ve·ra''cious
  truthful (see: vora-
  cious)
ve·rac''i·ty
  truthfulness (see: vo-
  racity)
ve·ran''da
verb
ver''bal
ver''bal·ize'
ver''bal·iz''ing
ver'bal·i·za''tion
ver''bal·ly
ver·ba''tim
ver·be''na
ver''bi·age
ver''bid
ver''bile
ver·bose''
ver·bos''i·ty
ver·bo''ten
ver''dant
ver''dict
ver''di·gris'
ver''dure
verge
verg''ing
ver'i·fi·a·ble
ver'i·fi·ca''tion
ver''i·fied'
ver''i·fy''
ver''i·ly
ver'i·si·mil''i·tude'
ver''i·ta·ble
ver''i·ty
  (pl. ver''i·ties)
ver''mi·cel''li
ver·mi''cu·lar
ver·mil''ion

ver″min
  (*pl.* ver″min)
Ver·mont″
ver·mouth″
ver·nac″u·lar
ver″nal
ver″ni·er
ver″sal
Ver·sailles″
ver·sa·tile
ver′sa·til″i·ty
verse
verse″craft′
ver″si·cle
ver′si·fi·ca″tion
ver″si·fied′
ver″si·form′
ver″si·fy′
ver″sion
ver″so
  (*pl.* ver″sos)
ver″sus
ver″te·bra
  (*pl.* ver″te·brae′)
ver″te·bral
ver″te·brate′
ver″tex
ver″ti·cal
ver″ti·cal·ly
ver·tig″i·nous
ver″ti·go′
  (*pl.* ver″ti·goes)
verve
ver″y
  extremely (*see:* vary)
ves″i·cant
ves″i·cle
ve·sic″u·lar
ves″pers
ves″pid
ves″sel
ves″tal
vest″ed
ves″ti·ar′y
ves″til·gule′
ves″tige

ves·tig″i·al
vest″ment
vest″-pock′et
ves″try
  (*pl.* ves″tries)
vet
vetch
vet″er·an
vet′er·i·nar″i·an
vet″er·i·nar′y
ve″to
  (*pl.* ve″toes)
vex·a″tion
vex·a″tious
vi′a·bil″i·ty
vi″a·ble
vi″a·duct′
vi″al
  bottle (vile and viol)
vi″al·mak′ing
vi″and
vi·as″ma
vi′a·tor″i·al
vibes
vi″bran·cy
vi″brant
vi″bra·phone′
vi″brate
vi″brat·ing
vi·bra″tion
vi·bra″to
  (*pl.* vi·bra″tos)
vi″bra·tor
vic″ar
vic″ar·age
vi·car″i·ous
vice
  shortcoming (*see:* vise)
vice″-chair″man
vice″-chan″cel·lor
vice″-con″sul
vice″-pres″i·dent
vice″-pres′i·den″tial
vice″roy
vice″ squad′

vi″ce ver″sa
Vi″chy
vi″chy·ssoise″
vi·cin″i·ty
  (*pl.* vi·cin″i·ties)
vi″cious
vi·cis″si·tude″
vic″tim
vic″tim·i·za″tion
vic″tim·ize′
vic″tim·iz′ing
vic″tim·less
vic″tor
vic·to″ri·an
vic·to″ri·ous
vic″to·ry
  (*pl.* vic″to·ries)
vict″ual
vi·cu″na
vid″e·o′cas·sette″
vid″e·o·con″fer·ence
vid″e·o·disc
vid″e·o dis·play″ ter″
  mi·nal
vid″e·o game′
Vid″e·o·phone′™
vid″e·o·tape′
vid″e·o·tap′ing
vie
vied
Vi·en″na
Vi′et·nam″
view″er·ship′
view″point′
view″port′
vig″il
vig″i·lance
vig″i·lant
vig′i·lan″te
vig″i·lan·tism′
vi·gnette″
vig″or
vig″or·ous
vile
  nasty (*see:* vial and
  viol)

vile″ly

vil″er

vil″i·cate′

vil′i·fi·ca″tion

vil″i·fied′

vil″i·fi′er

vil″i·fy′

vil″la

vil″lage

vil″lag·er

vil″lain

vil″lain·ous

vil″lain·y

  (pl. vil″lain·ies)

vim

vin′ai·grette″

vin′ai·grous″

vin″ci·ble

vin·cu·la″tion

vin·di·ca·ble

vin″di·cate′

vin″di·cat′ing

vin·di·ca″tion

vin″di·ca″tor

vin·di·ca″tive

vine

vin″e·al

vin″e·gar

vin″e·gar·y

vine″yard

vin·i·cul″ture

vin·if″er·ous′

vin″tage

vint″ner

vi″nyl

vi″ol

  musical instrument

  (see: vial and vile)

vi·o″la

vi″o·la·ble

vi″o·late′

vi″o·lat′ing

vi″o·la″tion

vi″o·la″tor

vi″o·lence

vi″o·lent

vi″o·let

vi′o·lin″er

vi o·lin″ist

vi·o″list

vi″o·lon·cel″list

V I P″

vi″per

vi·per″i·form

vi″per·ous

vi″ral

vir″gin

Vir″gin Is″lands

vir″gin·al

Vir·gin″ia

vir·gin″i·ty

Vir″go

  zodiac sign

vir″gule

vir″i·al

vir″ile

vi·ril″i·ty

vi·rol″o·gy

vir·tu″

  artistic taste (see:

  virtuc)

vir″tu·al·ly

vir″tue

  morality (see: virtu)

vir·tu·os″i·ty

vir″tu·o″so

  (pl. vir′tu·o″sos)

vir″tu·ous

vir″u·lence

vir″u·lent

vi″rus

vi″sa

vis″age

vis′-a-vis″

  (pl. vis′-a-vis″)

vis″cer·a

  (pl. vis″cus)

vis″cer·ate′

vis·cid″i·ty

vis″coi·dal′

vis″cose

solution (see: vis-

  cous)

vis·cos″i·ty

  (pl. vis·cos″i·ties)

vis″count

vis″count′ess

vis″cous

  thick (see: viscose)

vise

  clamp (see: vice)

vised

vis″ing

vis·i·bil″i·ty

vis″i·ble

vi″sion

vi″sion·ar′y

  (pl. vi″sion·ar′ies)

vis″it

vis″i′tant

vis·it·a″tion

vis″i·tor

vi″sor

vis″ta

vis″u·al

vis·u·al·i·za″tion

vis″u·al·ize′

vis″u·al·iz′ing

vi″ta

  (pl. vi″tae)

vi″tal

vi·tal″i·ty

  (pl. vi·tal″i·ties)

vi″tal·ize′

vi″tal·iz′ing

vi″tal·ly

vi″tals

vi″ta·min

vi″ti·ate′

vi″ti·at′ing

vi″ti·a″tion

vit″re·ous

vit″re·os″i·ty

vit″ri·fi·ca″tion

vit″ri·fied′

vit″ri·form′

vit″ri·fy′

vit″ri·ol
vit′ri·ol″ic
vit″tles
vi·tu″per·ate′
vi·tu″per·at′ing
vi·tu″per·a″tion′
vi·va″ce
vi·va″cious
vi·vac″i·ty
vive″ly
vi″veur
viv″id
viv′i·fi·ca″tion
viv″i·fied′
viv″i·fy′
vi·vip″a·ous
viv″i·sect″
viv″i·sec″tion
vix″en
V″-J Day
V″-neck′
vo″ca·bly
vo·cab″u·lar·y
  (*pl.* vo·cab″u·lar·
  ies)
vo″cal
vo″cal·ist
vo″cal·ize′
vo″cal·iz′ing
vo″cal·ly
vo·ca″tion
vo·cif″er·ate′
vo·cif″er·at′ing
vo·cif″er·a″tion
vo·cif″er·ous
vod″ka
vogue
voice″less
voice″-o′ver
voice″print′
voic″ing
void
void″a·ble
voi·la″
voile
vol″a·tile

vol′a·til″i·ty
vol·can″ic
vol·ca″no
  (*pl.* vol·ca″noes)
vo·li″tion
vol″ley
  (*pl.* vol″leys)
vol″ley·ball′
vol″leyed
volt″age
vol·ta″ic
vol·tam″e·ter
volt″-am″pere
vol″ti
volt″me″ter
vol″u·bil″i·ty
vol″u·ble
vol″ume
vol′u·met″ric
vo·lu″mi·nous
vol″un·tar′i·ly
vol″un·tar′y
  (*pl.* vol″un·tar′ies)
vol″un·teer″
vo·lup″tu·ar·y
  (*pl.* vo·lup″tu·ar′
  ies)
vo·lup″tu·ous
vo·lute″
vol″vox
vom″it
voo″doo
  (*pl.* voo″doos′)
voo″doo·ism′
vo·ra″cious
  ravenous (*see:* vera-
  cious)
vo·rac″i·ty
  being ravenous (*see:*
  veracity)
vor″age
vor″tex
vo″ta·ry
  (*pl.* vo″ta·ries)
vo·ta″tion
vote

vot″er
vot″ing ma·chine′
vo″tive
vouch
vouch″er
vouch·safe″
vouch·saf″ing
vow
vow″el
vox″ po″pu·li′
voy″age
voy″ag·er
voy″ag·ing
vo·yeur″
vo·yeur″ism
vul′can·i·za″tion
vul″can·ize′
vul″can·iz′ing
vul″gar
vul·gar″i·an
vul″gar·ism
vul″gar·i·ty
  (*pl.* vul·gar″i·ties)
vul″gar·ize′
vul″gar·iz′ing
vul″gate
vul″ner·a·bil″i·ty
vul″ner·a·ble
vul·pin″ic
vul″ture
vul″tur·ous
vul″va
  (*pl.* vul″vae)
vul″vate′
vy″ing

W

wab″bler
wack″i·er
wack″o
wack″y
wad
wad″ding
  soft material; com-

pressing (*see:* wad-
ing)
wad"dle
wad"dling
wade .
wa"di
  (*pl.* wa"dis)
wad"ing
  walking through wa-
  ter (*see:* wadding)
wa"fer
wa"fer·work'
waf"fle
waft
wag
wage
wa"ger
wa"ger·er
wage" scale'
wag"ging
  moving rapidly (*see:*
  waging)
wag"gish
wag"gle
wag"gling
wag"ing
  carrying on (*see:*
  wagging)
wag"on
wag"tail'
waif
wail
  cry (*see:* wale and
  whale)
wail"ing
  crying (*see:* waling
  and whaling)
wain"age
wain"scot
wain"scot·ing
wain"wright'
waist
  middle of body (*see:*
  waste)
waist"band
waist"coat'

waist"-deep"
waist"-high"
waist"line'
wait
  pause (*see:* weight)
wait"er
wait"ing room'
wait"ress
waive
  give up (*see:* wave)
waiv"er
  relinquishment (*see:*
  waver)
waiv"ing
  relinquishing (*see:*
  waving)
wake
wake"ful
wak"ing
wale
  welt (*see:* wail and
  whale)
wales
wal"ing
  marking (*see:* wail-
  ing and whaling)
walk"a·thon'
walk"a·way'
walk"er
walk"ie-talk'ie
walk"-in'
Walk"man™
walk"-on'
walk"out'
walk"o'ver
walk"-through'
walk"-up'
walk"way'
wal"la·by
  (*pl.* wal"la·bies)
wall"board'
wall"cov'er·ing
wal"let
wall"eye'
wall"eyed'
wall"flow'er

wal"lop·ing
wal"low
wall"pa'per
wall"-to-wall"
wal"ly·ball'
wal"nut
wal"rus
waltz
wam"pus
wan
wan"der·lust'
wane
wan"gle
wan"gling
wan"ing
Wan"kel
wan"ner
want
  desire; need (*see:*
  wont)
want" ad'
wan"ton
  undisciplined;
  squander (*see:* won
  ton)
wan"ton·ness
war"ble
war"bler
war"bling
war"bon'net
war" cry'
ward
war" dance'
war"den
ward"er
ward" heel'er
ward"robe'
ward"room'
ward"wo'man
ware
  goods (*see:* wear
  and where)
ware"house'
ware"ma·ker
war"fare'
war" game'

war″head′
war″i·er
war″i·ly
war″like′
war″lock′
war″lord′
warm″blood″ed
warmed″-o″ver
warm″heart″ed
war″mong′er
warmth
warm″-up′
warn″ing
warp
war″path′
war″plane′
war″pow·er
war″rant
war″ran·ty
  (*pl.* war″ran·ties)
war″ren
war″ring
war″ri·or
war″saw
war″ship′
wart
war″time′
war″y
wash″a·ble
wash″-and-wear″
wash″ba′sin
wash″board′
wash″bowl′
wash″cloth′
wash″dish′
washed″-out″
washed″-up″
wash″er·wom′an
Wash″ing·ton
wash″out′
wash″room′
wash″stand′
wash″tub′
wasp″ish
wasp″y
was″sail

wast″age
waste
  use up needlessly
  (*see:* waist)
waste bas′ket
waste″ful
waste″land′
waste″pa′per
wast″ing
wast″rel
watch″band′
watch″boat′
watch″case′
watch″dog′
watch″ful
watch″ful·ly
watch″mak′er
watch″mak″ing
watch″man
watch″tow′er
watch″word′
wa″ter
wa″ter·bed′
wa″ter blis″ter
wa″ter·borne′
wa″ter buf′fa·lo
wa″ter·bush′
wa″ter·col′or
wa″ter-cool″ed′
wa″ter″cool′er
wa″ter·course′
wa″ter·craft′
wa″ter·cress′
wa″ter·fall′
wa″ter·fowl′
wa″ter·front′
wa″ter glass′
wa″ter hole′
wa″ter·i·ness
wa″ter·less
wa″ter·lil′y
  (*see:* wa″ter·lil′ies)
wa″ter·line′
wa″ter·logged′
Wa″ter·loo′
wa″ter main″

wa″ter·mark′
wa″ter·mel′on
wa″ter mill′
wa″ter·pow′er
wa″ter·proof′
wa″ter-re·pel′lent
wa″ter-re·sist″ant
wa″ter·shed′
wa″ter-ski′, *v.*
  sport
wa″ter ski, *n.*
  board
wa″ter-ski′er
wa″ter-ski″ing
wa″ter-sol′u·ble
wa″ter·spout′
wa″ter ta′ble
wa″ter·tight′
wa″ter·way′
wa″ter wheel′
wa″ter·works′
wa″ter·y
watt″age
watt″-hour′
wat″tle
watt″tling
watt″me″ter
wauch
waup
wave
  undulation (*see:*
  waive)
wave″length′
wa″ver
  sway; hesitate (*see:*
  waiver)
wav″i·er
wav″i·ness
wav″ing
  signaling (*see:* waiv-
  ing)
wav″y
wax″ bean′
wax″en
wax″i·er
wax″ pa′per

wax″work′
wax″y
way
  manner; plan; route
    (*see:* wey)
way″bill′
way″far′er
way″far′ing
way″laid′
way″lay′
way ″side′
way″ sta′tion
way″ward
weak
  not strong (*see:*
    week)
weak″en
weak″hand·ed
weak′-kneed″
weak″ling
weak″ly
  sickly (*see:* weakly)
weak″-mind′ed
weak″ness
wealth
wealth″i·er
wealth″i·ness
wealth″y
wean
wean″a·ble
weap″on
weap″on·ry
wear
  have on; deteriorate
    (*see:* ware and
    where)
wear″a·ble
wear″ and tear″
wea″ried
wea″ri·er
wea″ri·ly
wea″ri·some
wea″ry
wea″sel
weath″er

sky condition (*see:*
    whether)
weath″er-beat′en
weath″er·board′
weath″er-bound′
weath″er·cock′
weath″er eye′
weath″er·glass′
weath″er·li·ness′
weath″er·man′
weath″er map′
weath″er·proof′
weath″er·strip′
weath″er·strip′ping
weath″er·tight
weath″er vane′
weath″er·worn′
weave
weav″er·bird′
weav″ing
web
web″bing
web″-foot′ed
web″mak·ing
wed
wed″ding
wed″ding cake′
wedge
wedg″ing
wed″lock
Wednes″day
weed
weed″i·er
weed″kill′er
weed″y
week
  seven days (*see:*
    weak)
week″day′
week″end′
week″ly
  once a week (*see:*
    weakly)
week″night′ly
wee″nie
weep

weep″y
wee″vil
weft
weft″age
weigh
  measure heaviness;
    consider (*see:* way
    and whey)
weigh″-in
weight
  heaviness (*see:* wait)
weight″i·er
weight″i·ness
weight″less
weight″ lift′ing
weight″y
weir
weird
weird″o
  (*pl.* weird″os)
welch
wel″come
wel″com·ing
weld″er
wel″fare′
we'll
  we will (*see:*
    weal, wheel, and
    wheal)
well″-ad·just″ed
well″-ad·vised″
well″-ap·point″ed
well″-at·tend″ed
well″-bal″anced
well″-be·haved″
well″-be″ing
well″-be·loved″
well″-born″
well″-bred″
well″-cho″sen
well″-con·di″tioned
well″-de·fined″
well″-dis·posed″
well″-done″
well″-dressed″
well″-earned″

well″-es·tab″lished
well″-fa″vored
well″-fed″
well″-found″ed
well″-groomed″
well″-ground″ed
well″-heeled″
well″hole′
well″-in·formed″
well″-in·ten″tioned
well″-knit″
well″-known″
well″-liked″
well″-man″nered
well″-mean″ing
well″ness
well″-nigh″
well″-off″
well″-or″dered
well″-read″
well″-round″ed
well″-spo″ken
well″-spring
well″-thought″-of
well″-timed″
well″-to-do″
well″-turned″
well″-wish″er
well″-worn″
Welsh
Welsh″ rab″bit
wel″ter·weight
wench
wend
wept
were″wolf′
west″bound′
west″er·ly
west″ern
west″ern·er
west″ern·i·za″tion
west″ern·ize′
west″ern·iz′ing
west″ern·most
West″ In″dies
West″min′ster

West″ Vir·gin″ia
west″ward
wet
  moistened (*see:*
   whet)
wet″back′
wet″ bar″
wet″ blan″ket
wet″-nurse, *v.*
  act as wet nurse
wet″ nurse′, *n.*
  woman
wet″-nurs′ing
wet″ pack′
wet″ta·ble
wet″ter
wet″ting a″gent
whack
whale
  animal (*see:* wail
   and wale)
whale″boat
whale″bone
whal″er
whal″ing
  hunting (*see:* wailing
   and waling)
wham
wham″ble
wham″ming
whank
wharf
  (*pl.* wharves)
wharf″age
wharf″land′
what·ev″er
what″not′
what′so·ev″er
wheal
  swelling (*see:* we'll,
   wheel)
wheat″ cake′
wheat″ germ′
whee″dle
whee″dling
wheel

  disk (*see:* we'll,
   wheal, and weal)
wheel″bar′row
wheel″base′
wheel″chair′
wheel″er-deal″er
wheel″er·y
wheel″horse′
wheel″house′
wheel″wright′
wheels″warf
wheeze
wheez″ing
wheez″i·er
wheez″y
whelk
whelp
whence
when·ev″er″
when″so·ev″er″
where
  at what place (*see:*
   ware and wear)
where″a·bouts′
where·as″
where·by″
where″fore
where·in″
where·of″
where·on′
where″so·ev″er
where″up·on″
wher·ev″er
where″with
where″with·al″
wher″ry
  (*pl.* wher″ries)
whet
  sharpen (*see:* wet)
wheth″er
  if (*see:* weather)
whet″stone
whet″ting
whey
  part of milk (*see:*
   way and weigh)

which
what one (*see:* witch)
which·ev"er
whiff
whif"fen·poof'
whif"fle·tree'
while
time (*see:* wile)
whil"ing
whim
whim"per
whim"si·cal
whim si·cal"i·ty
(*pl.* whim'si·cal"i·ties)
whim"si·cal·ly
whim"sy
(*pl.* whim"sies)
whine
complain (*see:* wine)
whin"er
whin"ing
whin"nied
whin"ny
neigh (*see:* whiny)
whin"y
complaining (*see:* whinny)
whip"cord'
whip"lash'
whip"per·snap'per
whip"pet
whip"ping boy'
whip"poor·will'
whip"saw'
whip"stitch'
whip"stock'
whir
whirl
whirl"a·bout'
whirl"i·gig'
whirl"pool'
whirl"wind'
whir"rick'
whir"ring

whisk" broom'
whisk"er
whis"key
(*pl.* whis"keys)
whis"per
whis'per·a"tion
whis"per·er
whis"tle
whis"tle·blow'er
whis"tler
whis"tle·stop'
whis"tling
whit
small bit (*see:* wit)
white"blaze'
white"cap'
white"-col"lar
white"fish'
white" heat"
white" hope"
white"-hot"
whit"en·er
white"ness
whit"en·ing
white" pa'per
white" sale'
white" sauce'
white" tie'
white"wall'
white"ware'
white"wash
white"-wa'ter, *v.*
of rafting
white" wa'ter, *n.*
foaming water
whith"er
to what place (*see:* wither)
whith"er·wards'
whit"ing
whit"tle
whit"tling
whiz-bang"
who·dun"it
who·ev"er
whole

entire (*see:* hole)
whole"heart"ed
whole"-hog"
whole"ness
whole" note'
whole"sale'
whole"sal'er
whole"sal'ing
whole"some
whole" step'
whole"-wheat"
whol"ly
entirely (*see:* holy and holey)
whom·ev"er
whom'so·ev"er
whoop"-de-do
whoop"ee
whoop"ing cough'
whoop"ing crane"
whoops
whoosh
whop"per
whop"ping
whore
prostitute (*see:* hoar)
whore"house'
whore"like'
whor"ing
whorl
whose
who'so·ev"er
why
wick
wick"ed
wick"er·work'
wick"et
wick"i·up'
wide"-an"gle
wide"-a·wake"
wide"-eyed'
wide"ly
wide"mouthed
wid"en
wide"-o"pen
wid"er

wide″-rang″ing
wide″spread″
wid″get
wid″ow
wid″owed
wid″ow·er
wid″ow's mite″
wid″ow's walk″
width
wield
wield″i·er
wield″y
wie″ner
Wie″ner schnit″zel
wife
  (*pl.* wives)
wife″ly
wig
wigged′ out″
wig″gle
wig″gli·er
wig″gling
wig″gly
wig″let
wig″tail′
wig″wag′
wig″wam′
wild″cat′
wil″de·beest′
wil″der·ness
wild″-eyed′
wild″fire′
wild″flow′er
wild″fowl′
wild″-goose″ chase′
wild″life′
wild″ oats″
Wild″west″
wild″wood′
wile
  sly trick; beguile
  (*see:* while)
wil″i·er
wil″i·ness
wil″ing

beguiling; passing
  time (*see:* willing)
will″ful
will″ful·ly
will″ful·ness
Wil″liams·burg′
wil″lies
will″ing
  wanting; favorably
  inclined (*see:* wil-
  ing)
wil″li·waw′
will″-less
will″-o′-the-wisp
wil″low·ware′
wil″low·wort′
wil″low·y
will″pow′er
wil″ly-nil″ly
wi″ly
Wim″ble·don
wim″ple
wim″pling
win
wince
winch
winc″ing
wind″bag′
wind″blown′
wind″-borne′
wind″break′
wind″break′er
wind″burn′
wind″ chill′
wind″chill′ fac″tor
wind″ chimes″
wind″fall′
wind″flaw′
wind″flow′er
wind″i·er
wind″i·ness
wind″ing sheet′
wind″jam′mer
wind″jam′ming
wind″lass

winch (*see:* wind-
  less)
wind″less
  without wind (*see:*
  windlass)
wind″mill′
win″dow
win″dow box″
win″dow dress′ing
win″dow·pane′
win″dow shade′
win″dow-shop′
win″dow-shop′per
win″dow·sill′
wind″pipe′
wind″proof′
wind″row′
wind″shake′
wind″shield′
wind″sock′
Wind″sor
wind″storm′
wind″surf′ing
wind″-swept′
wind″up′
wind″ward
wind″way·ward
wind″y
wine
  beverage (*see:*
  whine)
wine″ cel″lar
wine″glass′
wine″grow′er
wine″press′
win″er·y
  (*pl.* win″er·ies)
Wine″sap′
wine″sop
wing″back′
wing″ chair′
wing″ding′
wing″-foot′ed
wing″ nut′
wing″seed
wing″span′

wing"spread'
wing"tip'
win"ner
win"ning
Win"ni·peg'
win"now
win"some
win"ter·green'
win"ter·ing
win"ter·i·za"tion
win"ter·ize'
win"ter·iz'ing
win"ter·kill'
win"ter·time'
win"tri·er
win"try
wipe
wip"er
wip"ing
wird
wire" cut'ter
wire"hair'
wire"-haired'
wire"less
Wire"pho'to™
wire" pull'er
wire" serv'ice
wire"tap'
wire"tap'ping
wir"i·er
wir"i·ness
wir"ing
wir"y
Wis·con"sin
wis"dom
wise
wise"a·cre
wise"crack'
wise"ly
wis"er
wish"bone'
wish"ful
wish"ful·ly
wish"y-wash'y
wisp
wisp"y

wis"sle
wis·te"ri·a
wist"ful
wit
   cleverness (*see:*
   whit)
witch
   sorceress (*see:*
   which)
witch"craft'
witch" doc'tor
witch" ha"zel
witch" hunt'
with·al"
with·draw"
with·draw"al
with·draw"ing
with·drawn"
with·drew"
with"er
   shrivel (*see:* whither)
with·held"
with·hold"
with·in"
with·out"
with·stand"
with·stand"ing
with·stood"
wit"less
wit"ness stand'
wit"tal
wit"ti·cism
wit"ti·er
wit"ti·ness
wit"ting·ly
wit"ty
wiz"ard
wiz"ard·ry
wiz"ened
wob"ble
wob"bler
wob"bling
wob"bly
woe"be·gone'
woe"ful
woe"ful·ly

wok
woke
wok"en
wolf
   (*pl.* wolves)
wolf"fish
   fish (*see:* wolfish)
wolf"hound'
wolf"ish
   wolflike (*see:* wolf-
   fish)
wolf" pack'
wol'ver·ine"
wom"an
   (*pl.* wom"en)
wom"an·hood'
wom"an·kind'
wom"an·li·ness
wom"an·ly
womb
wom"en·folk'
won"der
won"der·craft'
won"der·ful
won"der·ful·ly
won"der·land'
won"der·ment
won"der-work'er
won"drous
wont
   habit (*see:* want and
   won't)
won't
   will not (*see:* wont)
won" ton
   Chinese dish (*see:*
   wanton)
woo
wood
   lumber (*see:* would)
wood"bin'
wood"bine'
wood" block
wood"carv'er
wood"carv'ing
wood"chuck'

wood"craft'
wood"cut'
wood"cut'ter
wood"ed
wood"en·ware
wood"i·er
wood"land'
wood"lot'
wood"mote'
wood"peck'er
wood"pile'
wood"screw"
wood"shed'
woods"i·er
woods"man'
wood"sy
wood"wind'
wood"work'
wood"y
woof"er
wool"en
wool"gath'er·ing
wool"li·er
wool"li·ness
wool"ly
wool"pack
wooz"i·er
wooz"y
Worces"ter·shire
word"age
word"book'
word"-for-word"
word"game'
word"i·er
word"i·ness
word"less
word"-of-mouth"
word"play'
word"pro'cess·ing
word"pro'ces·or
word"y
wore
work"a·ble
work"a·day'
work'a·hol"ic
work"bench'

work"book'
work"day'
work"fare'
work"force'
work"horse'
work"house'
work"ing·man'
work"ing·wom'an
work"load'
work"man
work"man·like'
work"man·ship'
work"mas'ter
work"out'
work"place'
work"-re·lease'
work"room'
work"shop'
work"sta'tion
work"-stud'y
work"ta'ble
work"-up'
work"week'
world"-class"
World"Court"
world"li·er
world"li·ness
world"ly
world"ly-wise'
World"Se"ries
world"-shak'ing
world"-view
world"-wea'ry
world"wide"
worm"-eat'en
worm"gear'
worm"hole'
worm"i·er
worm"y
worn"-out"
wor"ried
wor"ri·er
wor"ri·ment
wor"ri·some
wor"ry
  (*pl.* wor"ries)

wor"ry·wart'
worse
wors"en
wor"ship
wor"ship·er
wor"ship·ful·ly
wor"ship·ing
worst
  most bad (*see:*
  wurst)
wor"sted
wor"thi·er
wor"thi·ly
wor"thi·ness
worth"less
worth"while"
wor"thy
  (*pl.* wor"thies)
would
  expressing condition
  (*see:* wood)
would"-be
wound
wove
wo"ven
wrack
  ruin (*see:* rack)
wraith
wraith"like'
wran"gle
wran"gler
wran"gling
wrap
  enclose (*see:* rap)
wrap"a·round'
wra"ple
wrapped
  did wrap (*see:*
  rapped and rapt)
wrap"per
wrap"ping pa'per
wrap"-up
wrath
wrath"ful
wreak

inflict (*see:* reek and
wreck)
wreath
circular form (*see:*
wreathe)
wreathe
encircle (*see:*
wreath)
wreath"work
wreck
destroy (*see:* wreak)
wreck"age
wreck"er
wren
wrench
wrest
pull violently (*see:*
rest)
wres"tle
wres"tler
wres"tling
wretch
unhappy person (*see:*
retch)
wretch"ed
wri"er
wrig"gle
wrig"gling
wring
twist (*see:* ring)
wring"staves
wrin"kle
wrin"kling
wrin"kly
wrist"band'
wrist"watch'
writ
write
compose (*see:* right
and rite)
write"-down'
write"-in'
write"-off'
writ"er
write"-up'
writhe

writh"ing
writ"ing pa'per
writ"proof'
writ"ten
wrong"do'er
wrong"do'ing
wrong"ful
wrong"ful·ly
wrong"head"ed
wrong"ly
wrote
did write (*see:* rote)
wrought
wrung
did wring (*see:* rung)
wry
distorted (*see:* rye)
wry"bill
wug"gish
wun"der·kind
(*pl.* wun"der·kin'
der)
wurst
sausage (*see:* worst)
Wy·o"ming
wyte

X

xan"thic
xan'tho·car"pous
xan'tho·derm
xan'tho·pter'in
xan"thous
x"-ax'is
(*pl.* x"-ax'es)
X" chrom"o·some'
xe"bec
xe"no·graft'
xe"non
xen'o·phobe'
xen'o·pho"bi·a
xen'o·pho"bic
xer"a·phin'
xe'ro·graph"ic

xe·rog"ra·phy
xe'ro·men"i·a
xe·roph"i·lous
xe'roph·thal"mi·a
xe"ro·phyte'
Xer"ox™
Xerx"es
X"mas
X"-rat"ed
x"-ray'
xy"lem
xy"loid
xy·loph"a·gous
xy"lo·phone'
xyst

Y

ya"bu
yacht
yacht"ing
yachts"man
yachts"wom·an
ya"hoo
Yah"weh
yak
ya'ki·to"ri
yak"king
yam
yam"mer
yang
yang"go·na
yank
pull
Yank
Yankee
Yan"kee'
Ya·cun·de"
yap
yap"ping
yard"age'
yard"arm'
yard"bird'
yard"mas'ter
yard" sale'

yard″stick

yard″wand′

yard″work′

yar″mul·ke

yarn″-dyed′

yash″mak′

yaw

yawl

yawn

yawp

y″-ax′is

  (*pl.* y″-ax′es)

Y″ chro″mo·some′

yea

yeah

year″book′

year″-end″

year″ling

year″long″

year″ly

yearn

yearn″ing

year″-round″

yeast

yeast″i·er

yeast″y

yell

yel″low fe″ver

yel″low·ish

yel″low·jack″et

yel″low pag″es

yel″low rain″

Yel″low·stone′

yel″low·throat′

yelp

Yem″en

yen

  Japanese money (*pl.* yen)

yen

  desire

yeo″man

  (*pl.* yeo″men)

ye·shi″va

yes″ man′

  (*pl.* yes″ men)

yes″ter·day′

yes″ter·morn′

yes″ter·year′

yet″i

yew

  tree (*see:* you and ewe)

Yid″dish

yield

yield″ing

yip

yip″pee

yip″ping

yo″del

yo″del·er

yo″del·ing

yo″gi

  (*pl.* yo″gis)

yo″gurt

yoke

  join (*see:* yolk)

yo″kel

yok″ing

Yo·ko·ha″ma

yolk

  part of egg (*see:* yoke)

Yom Kip″pur

yon″der

yoo″-hoo

yore

Yo·sem″i·te

you

  person addressed (*see:* yew and ewe)

you-all″

you″ll

  you will (*see:* yule)

young

young″ blood″

young″ster

Young″ Turk′

your

  pertaining to you (*see:* you′re)

you′re

you are (*see:* your)

yours

your·self″

  (*pl.* your·selves″)

youth

youth″ful

youth″ful·ness

yowl

yo″-yo

  (*pl.* yo″-yos)

yu·an″

yuc″ca

Yu″go·sla″vi·a

Yu″kon

yule

  Christmas (*see:* you′ll)

yule″ log′

yule″tide′

yum″mi·er

yum″my

yup″pie

Z

zai″ba·tsu″

Za·ire″

Zam″bi·a

za″ni·er

za″ni·ly

za″ni·ness

za″ny

  (*pl.* za″nies)

Zan″zi·bar′

zap

zap″ping

z″ax′is

  (*pl.* z″-ax′es)

zeal

zeal″ot

zeal″ous

ze″bra

ze″bu

ze″donk

Zeit″geist′

Zen
ze''nith
zeph''yr
zep''pe·lin
ze''ro
   (*pl.* ze''ros)
ze''ro-base budg'et·
   ing
ze''roed
ze''ro hour'
zest''ful
zest''ful·ly
zig''zag'
zig''zag'ging
zilch
zil''lion
Zim·ba''bwe
zinc
zincked
zinck''ing
zin''fan·del'
zing
zin''ni·a
zi''on
zi''on·ism'
zi''on·ist
ZIP'' code'

zip'' gun'
Zip''loc'™
zip''per
zip''pered'
zip''pi·er
zip''ping
zip''py
zir''con
zir''con·ate'
zir·co''ni·um
zit
zith''er
zo''di·ac
zom''bie
zon''al
zone
zon''ic
zon''ing
zonked
zoo
zo·og''a·mous
zo'o·ge·og''ra·phy
zo'o·graph''ic
zo·og''ra·phy
zo'o·log''ic
zo'o·log''i·cal
zo'o·log''i·cal·ly

zo·ol''o·gist
zo·ol''o·gy
zoom
zo'o·morph''ic
zo'o·phil''i·a
zo'o·scop''ic
zo·ot''o·my
zoot'' suit
Zou·ave''
zoy''sia
zuc·chet''to
   (*pl.* zuc·chet''tos)
zuc·chi''ni
zud''da
Zu''lu
   (*pl.* Zu''lus)
Zu''ni
   (*pl.* Zu''nis)
zwie''back
zy''gote
zy''mase
zy·mol''o·gy
zy·mol''o·gist
zy·mo''sis
zy'mo·tech''ni·cal
zy·mot''ic
zy''mur·gy